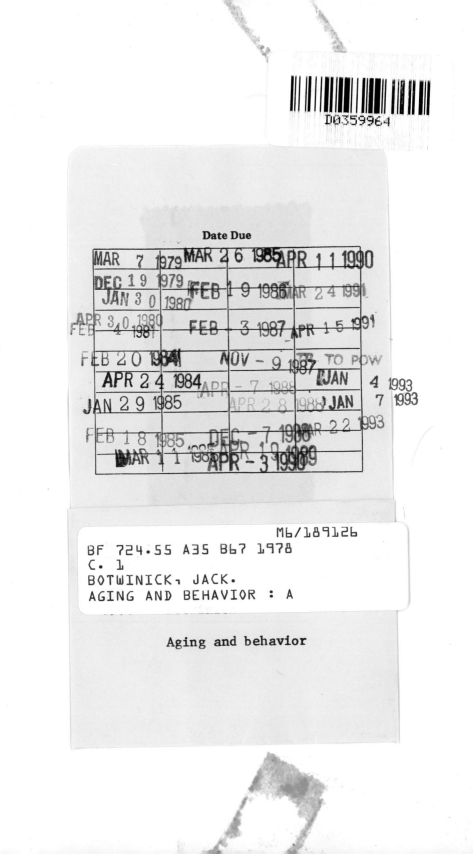

Aging and behavior

Aging and Behavior

JACK BOTWINICK, Professor of Psychology at Washington University in St. Louis, is also Director of the Aging and Development Program of the university's Department of Psychology. Previously, he was Professor of Medical Psychology at Duke University Medical School and Research Psychologist with the Laboratory of Psychology of the National Institute of Mental Health in Bethesda. A past president of the Division of Adult Development and Aging, American Psychological Association, and a former vice president of the Gerontological Society, Professor Botwinick has served on national advisory boards and been guest lecturer at many colloquia and workshops. Among these is the prestigious "Master Lecture" series conducted by the American Psychological Association. In addition to *Aging and Behavior*, he has published extensively in professional journals, contributed chapters to many edited volumes, and written two other books, one coauthored: *Memory, Related Functions and Age* (Charles C Thomas, 1974) and *Cognitive Processes in Maturity and Old Age* (Springer, 1967).

AGING
AND BEHAVIOR

A Comprehensive Integration
of Research Findings

SECOND EDITION
UPDATED AND EXPANDED

Jack Botwinick

SPRINGER PUBLISHING COMPANY / NEW YORK

Springer Publishing Company, Inc.
200 Park Avenue South
New York, N.Y. 10003

78 79 80 81 82 / 10 9 8 7 6 5 4 3 2 1

First edition, 1973

Design: Patrick Vitacco

Library of Congress Cataloging in Publication Data

Botwinick, Jack.
    Aging and behavior.

    Includes bibliographies and index.
    1. Aged—Psychology.   2. Aging—Psychological
aspects.   I.   Title.
BF724.55.A35B67   1978   155.6   78-8535
ISBN 0-8261-1441-5
ISBN 0-8261-1442-3 pbk.

Printed in the United States of America

Contents

Preface   *vii*
Preface to the First Edition   *ix*
Acknowledgments   *xi*

1
Who Are the Aged?
1

2
Biological and Environmental Factors in Longevity and Survival
9

3
Psychological and Social Factors in Longevity and Survival
25

4
Sexuality and Sexual Relations
42

5
Turning Inward
59

6
Simple Rigidity
87

7
Multidimensional Rigidity
100

8
Personality and Cognition in Cautious Behavior
113

9
Cautiousness in Decision
128

10
Contact with the Physical Environment
142

11
Processing Sense Information
156

12
Slow Response to Environmental Stimulation
185

13
Intelligence
208

14
Problem Solving
234

15
Learning and Performance
261

16
Aids and Types of Learning
282

17
Memory Theory
311

18
Retrieving Memories
337

19
Research Methods
364

20
Operational and Conceptual Issues in Research
381

Index   399

Preface

The study of adult aging is now mainstream; it is an important and accepted study area, clearly among the fastest growing in colleges and universities in the United States today. It wasn't always so. In fact, it wasn't so a short time ago, as recently as when the first edition of this book was published in 1973.

Thus, as an accepted college discipline, Adult Aging is new. In the early 1970s, few college courses included the end part of life as a part of what was studied and even fewer courses were devoted to the end part of life as the main concern. The situation is otherwise now and we can expect an increasing number of courses on aging very soon.

Between the 1973 edition and the present one, there was an explosion in the aging literature, which necessitated this update. So many studies were reported that decisions about what to include and what to leave out were often difficult to make. The intent was to review and integrate the new literature, delete the old when no longer relevant, and keep the format and organization of the book intact. The organization was kept and new literature was integrated with the old, but most of the old was retained because reanalysis showed it to still be very relevant.

Each and every chapter includes new material or involves some change, although some changes are minor. Major revisions include chapter 5 on social and personality aspects of aging. This chapter was expanded appreciably, with older literature brought in as well as new. Chapter 11, on perception, reflects new research efforts confirming a hypothesis that was little more than an idea in the first edition—stimulus persistence. Chapter 13, on intelligence, presents a totally new view. The study of learning and memory has so grown and so changed that chapters 15 through 18 also present a totally different view, with the mass of published data necessitating a change in format and considerable expansion in length for these four chapters. Chapter 19 reflects

vii

newer developments in methodology and new views of the limitations of what can be done, and chapter 20 continues with new methodological considerations.

Effort was made to keep the reading level as simple as possible throughout, while remaining true to the basic data and providing scholars comprehensive and specific bibliographic details. Unfortunately, the effort is not always visible in the results; some of the revision and update makes for more difficult reading—the complex nature of the ideas and technical advances are responsible for this. In the main, however, the reading level is no more difficult than in the first edition and, in parts, the level is simpler.

Thus, once again, while this book is intended for everyone who is interested in behavior and aging, selections will have to be made as to interests, purposes, and technical background. This book is comprehensive, if not in detail, then certainly in conceptions that are essential to the behavioral study of aging.

Preface to the First Edition

In writing this book I have attempted to fill a void which exists at the present time: that is, to provide an up-to-date, in-depth, and comprehensive study of the literature on the psychology of aging.

The book addresses itself first to those teachers presently offering courses on the psychology of aging. Since it is most probable that the near future will see more and more teachers offering courses in the psychology of aging, or integrating this special area of study into existing courses, this book will, hopefully, provide them with a secondary source book as well as offering a wide array of concepts and information on the subject.

Second, it offers investigators carrying out research projects in the psychological study of aging a comprehensive reference source.

But most important, my goal has been to write a book for students, whether or not enrolled at colleges or universities, and for all those interested in the study of the processes of aging. While certain material covered has required a highly technical approach and is, therefore, directed more to the teacher or researcher, the main body of information is not of this type and effort has been made to keep the presentation at a level suitable for the undergraduate. It is hoped that, on all levels, *Aging and Behavior* can be a help and a guide in this very important, and to some extent neglected, area of study.

Acknowledgments

In writing the first edition of this book I was helped in no minor way by Mrs. Isabel Gerber, who did everything possible to assist me, from typing many drafts of the manuscript to organizing the many details of references and other source information. For her reliability, patience, and support, I am grateful. In revising the book for this second edition several people aided me, notably Ms. Donna Cohen, and I am grateful to them.

My thanks also go to the National Institute on Aging (NIA) and its precursor, the Aging Program of the National Institute of Child Health and Human Development (NICHD), of the U.S. Public Health Service. Their training and research grants enabled me to develop the information contained in this book—information that forms the basis of our research and our courses in the psychology of aging here at Washington University.

Lastly, I would like to acknowledge and thank the copyright holders, indicated in the legends of the appropriate figures, who granted me permission to reproduce figures and quotations.

To them, to the NIA, to all those who helped me, I express my thanks.

1
Who Are the Aged?

Without formal definition, and without intent, the law makers have defined old age for us. It is 65 years of age. Most people in this country become eligible for retirement with social security benefits at this age, and this legal decision has great import in our lives. Attitudes and expectations are formed on this basis, and it would not be unreasonable to believe that many people become old because they and the world around them have accepted such definition.

Havighurst (1957) raised an interesting point of definition of old age as it involves work. Society is evolving in such a way that the role of work is becoming less important; as the work week decreases, as automation increases, as other pursuits become more important, the time marking the beginning of old age changes. The work role becomes less important and the social role more important. Havighurst suggested that old age is defined more and more by a broad social competence, and less and less by a narrow work competence. Havighurst's studies lead him to the conclusion that there is little reduction in social competence between the ages of 40 and 70. It is only in work roles due to retirement and in marital states due to death of spouse that there is a reduction in what he called role-performances. Social competence is seen as relatively independent of biological functioning, which does decline with age. Social competence is not to be understood as synonymous with cognitive and perceptual abilities which do undergo changes with age. Social competence reflects man's daily interactions and typical responsibilities.

What are the facts and figures on older Americans? The United States Department of Health, Education and Welfare has printed five booklets with just this title. The fifth booklet of the series was an overview of the first four booklets, and designed specifically for the delegates of the White House Conference on Aging held November 28 to December 2, 1971.

THE NUMBER OF OLD PEOPLE

The 1970 census disclosed that older Americans, i.e., people over 65 years of age, constitute approximately 10 percent of the total population. There are more than 200 million people in this country and more than 20 million of them are called "old." In 1900 only 4 percent of the nation was over 65; in 1930 about 5½ percent was over 65 and as recently as 1950, only 8 percent. It is expected that by the year 2025, the over-65-year group may make up almost 15 percent of the population (see U.S. Census Report, 1972).

All this is not to say that the life-span of man has been extended appreciably—it has not. It is to say, however, that the percentage of people living all their years closer to their life potential is greater. Medical advance is credited for part of this.

The Bureau of the Census reports that, while 10 percent are over 65, 21 percent are between 45 and 64 years of age. Thus, if the middle years start at 45, aging from this time involves over 30 percent of the nation. Worldwide, the number of aging people is increasing too. A United Nations periodical (1971) reports that the world's people over 65 years number about 200 million, with 24 million more people in 1971 than were living just five years prior to that time. Most of the increase, as might be expected on the basis of medical advance, took place in the "developed countries."

LIFE EXPECTANCY

People who are 45 years old have already lived as long as the average person born in 1900 could have expected to live. In the United States, men age 45 have an average life expectancy of an additional 27 years, i.e., 72 years' life-span. For women the life expectancy is nearly 5 years longer.

Women, living longer than men, constitute a larger segment of the older population. This trend appears to be increasing. Perhaps the "natural life-span" of woman relative to man is even longer than commonly recognized. Figure 1.1 shows that, while in the population of people aged under 25 years men outnumber women slightly, the reverse is true after this age and the trend becomes progressive. Figure 1.2 shows that the ratio of women to men has been increasing through the years.

Men marry later in life than do women, and they die earlier. Women are thus more often widowed than are men. Most old men are married; most old women are not.

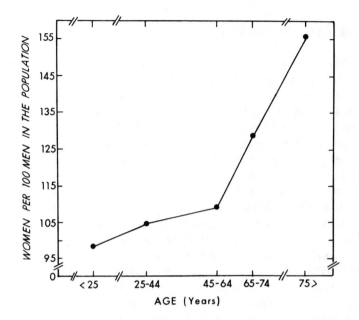

FIGURE 1.1: The ratio of American women to men in 1970 as a function of age. (Data from the table on page 4 of AOA publication No. 5, 1971.)

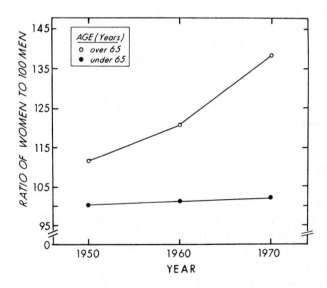

FIGURE 1.2: The ratio of American women to men during three periods of time. (Data from the table on page 7 of AOA publication No. 2, 1971.)

WHERE OLD PEOPLE LIVE

Older Americans live in geographic patterns similar to those of younger ones. They live mostly in the larger states, particularly California, New York, and Pennsylvania. A quarter of all older Americans live in these three states. This is not to say that these states have the largest percentage of older people within them—they don't. Over the years many older people have moved to Florida, making this state the largest in terms of percentage of aged residents. Other states such as Iowa, Nebraska, and Arkansas experienced an emigration of younger adults, leaving many older ones there. Florida's over-65 group comprises almost 15 percent of its population while the percentage is about 12½ in the three other states (see U.S. Census report, 1973).

Most older people live in a family setting, usually in their own households. There is a continuing and growing trend, however, of living away from their children. Of every 100 older people, 28 live alone or with nonrelatives. It comes as a surprise to many that only 4 percent of old people live in institutions. While this is so, however, it is also true that the percentage of old people who will have to be institutionalized eventually is much greater. Kastenbaum and Candy (1973) found that 4 percent of those aged 65 and older were in institutions (mostly nursing homes), but among those aged 85 and above, 17 percent were institutionalized. The percentage of adults who are institutionalized thus increases with age past 65.

While most young people live in the suburbs, most old people live in the central city. An appreciable percentage, however, live outside of metropolitan areas altogether; approximately 35 percent of old people live in small towns and 5 percent live on farms.

Overall, then, the typical over-65-year-old is found in the inner city of a populous state, living in his own home.

INCOME

There are many old rich people but, by and large, the old are poor. Older workers find it hard to get jobs once they have become unemployed. In 1900 almost two-thirds of older men were still in the work force; now it is only slightly more than a quarter. Women show a different pattern. Of those over 65, the proportion of those working rose from about 8 percent in 1900 to about 10 percent in 1970.

Most old people (90 percent) have some income from retirement payments; others work, but, in the main, the aged constitute a large segment of the poor. In 1975, half of the families with heads of household 65 or over earned about $8,000 per year or less. This is in contrast to the median income of younger families of approximately $15,000. Almost a quarter of the older families had 1975 incomes of less than $5,000. There are nearly seven million older people who either live alone or live with nonrelatives. Half of these had incomes less than $2,000 per year, and almost a third had incomes less than $2,500. These data may best be understood against an "official poverty level threshold." The 1975 poverty level for a couple was $3,232 and for an individual $2,572. By whatever index, a summary statement is clearly that many of the old are poor (Brotman, 1977).

HEALTH

The old tend to have more chronic diseases than do the young. Those over 65 have medical expenditures three-and-a-half times those of people under 65. Much of this expenditure comes about at the very time when income is most limited. Governmental programs provide help; whereas 10 percent of the population is over 65, 52 percent of the amount paid for health care by these programs is spent on older people.

Diseases of Later Life

The diseases of old age that are the major causes of death are, first, the diseases of the heart, then cancer, and next, cerebrovascular problems, mainly stroke (see U.S.P.H.S. publication, *Health in the Later Years of Life, 1971*). Together these three conditions account for 70 percent of the deaths of people aged 45 and over; heart diseases alone account for over 40 percent. Among those dying of diseases of the heart, approximately five times as many men over 65 are represented as those between 45 and 64 years; more than ten times as many women over 65 are represented as those younger. Cancers and strokes are similarly seen as diseases mainly of later life.

Theories or Models

This chapter started out with a discussion of definitions of aging. Havighurst's thinking relates to what is frequently called a sociological definition of aging. There are others, as, for example, biological aging— the combined decline in function of various organ and tissue processes, including gross behavioral changes.

There are health or medical concepts that bear on definitions of aging. There are several theoretical positions or models that have been used, most often only implicitly. Two will be discussed here: the medical model and the dependence model. These models are important because they point to different strategies of research and of training scientists in specialty areas. These models can be described very simply and briefly.

Medical Model.   Most physicians are trained to think in terms of disease and organ malfunction. In old age, cardiovascular problems and other degenerative diseases are characteristic, and they are brought to the physician's attention. It is not surprising, therefore, that the physician seems to suggest that if diseases of the heart were completely understood, if cancer and cerebrovascular diseases were understood, much of aging would be understood. Just as biostatisticians might define aging in terms of the probability of survival or of succumbing to the major diseases, and as sociologists might define aging in terms of social competence, physicians tend to see aging as accumulating disease processes.

Dependence Model.   The shortcoming of the medical model and each of the other models is that they are not sufficiently encompassing. Thus, sociological aging is unrelated to biological aging, and the medical model cannot reconcile the old man who is without apparent disease. There are such people: one study reported on them (Birren, Butler, Greenhouse, Sokoloff, and Yarrow, 1963). The men who served as subjects for this study were old by years, by appearance, by behavioral and other test functioning, but there were no recognizable disease processes. The medical definition of aging would be inadequate in dealing with these men.

The fact is, even if cures for the major killers were found, aging would go on. For example, if the major cardiovascular and renal diseases were eliminated, there would be a gain in life expectancy of about 10 years. If cancer was eliminated, life expectancy would increase less—only about 2 years. There is much more to aging than the associated disease processes (see Hayflick, 1974).

A broader model is needed, one that emphasizes the dependencies among functions. A theory is needed that would not only point to simultaneous age changes of various processes but would provide integrating concepts of these changes. Something central to aging triggers or releases organ and behavioral changes; aging cannot be defined simply by a few of these changes. That something central to aging is the needed theory. Until we have it, much of the research in aging will have to remain either in descriptive terms or in terms of very limiting models.

THE PERSON

The very first two sentences of this chapter defined old age as 65 years. Of course, this is arbitrary and even misleading. There really is no marking line; indices of old age, retirement, for example, are of no necessary value and, what is more, they change. There is now effort to make retirement mandatory at age 70. In the future, say in the year 2000, there may be a pattern of several retirements, with the first retirement coming at age 55. This is the prediction of Neugarten (1975) who suggests that the old are best thought of in at least two groupings—the "young-old," beginning at this retirement age of 55 and ranging to 75, and the "old-old," comprising those people aged over 75 years. The "young-old" tend to be healthier than the "old-old," and their sex ratios are more equal. There are other important differences, but the point is that the aged do not constitute a single homogeneous group. They constitute several groups and there is reason to think of the aging in terms of groupings other than age—groupings based on health status, for example. Much more important, however, is to think of the aged as a large number of individuals having much in common.

Who are the aged? They are people as various and as individual as any younger group. In fact, they are more so: Group trends are typically based upon greater individual differences among the old than among the young. We can best understand the aging individual with knowledge of how he compares to those younger than himself, to his age peers, and to those older. It is for this reason that group trends, from early life to old age, are important.

This book is about the psychology of aging—the behavioral changes. These are seen as consequences both of changes going on in the body and of pressures of people and circumstances in the social world. When we see the older person who has responded well to these internal and social stimulations, we might think to ourselves, "There *with* the grace of God go I."

SUMMARY

For better or for worse, Congress, in setting age 65 as the time of retirement with social security benefits, established one definition of old age. This definition is important because attitudes and expectations are developed as a result of this—becoming old may be seen, in part, as living up to these expectations. Social competence is largely independent of biological decline; it is related to daily activities other than paid employment.

Old age defined by 65 calendar years has been attained by 10 percent of America's 200 millions. There are more women than men because they live longer, and, it seems, as time goes on this becomes more and more the case. At present, women aged 45 have a life expectancy of about 77, men have an expectancy of 72. Old women tend to be without husbands, while most old men are married.

The old may be characterized as being poor, living in the inner city, but, in the main, contrary to common belief, living at home. Only 4 percent of the aged live in institutions.

The aged have great medical expenses but, fortunately, they are helped greatly by government programs. Heart diseases, cancer, and stroke are the three major medical problems leading to death. Whatever else may be said about the elderly, they are not a homogeneous entity. Old people are even more varied than are younger people.

REFERENCES

Administration on Aging (Social and Rehabilitation Service, DHEW). *Facts and figures on older Americans.*
    Number 1. Measuring Adequacy of Income, March 1971
    Number 2. The Older Population Revisited—1970 Census, 1971
    Number 3. Income & Poverty in 1970—Advance Report, June 1971
    Number 4. Federal Outlays in Aging—1967-72, June 1971
    Number 5. An Overview for the Delegates, 1971.
Birren, J.E., Butler, R.N., Greenhouse, S.W., Sokoloff, L., and Yarrow, M. *Human aging.* Washington, D.C.: Public Health Service Publication No. 986, 1963.
Brotman, H.B. Income and poverty in the older population in 1975. *The Gerontologist,* 1977, *17,* 23–26.
Havighurst, R.J. *The sociological meaning of aging.* Address given at the General Session of the International Gerontological Congress in Merano, Italy, July 15, 1957.
Hayflick, L. The strategy of senescence. *The Gerontologist,* 1974, *14,* 37–45.
Kastenbaum, R.J., and Candy, S.E. The 4% fallacy: a methodological and empirical critique of extended care facility population statistics. *International Journal of Aging,* 1973, *4,* 15–21.
National Center for Health Statistics (U.S.P.H.S.) *Health in the later years of life.* Stock No. 1722–0178, October, 1971.
Neugarten, B.L. The future and the young-old. *The Gerontologist,* 1975, *15* (No. 1, Part 2), 4–9.
United Nations General Assembly. *Question of the elderly and the aged.* A/8364, August 31, 1971.
United States Bureau of the Census. *Current population reports. Illustrative population projection for the United States: the demographic effects of alternative paths to zero growth.* Series P–25, No. 476, April, 1972.
United States Bureau of the Census. *Census of the population: characteristics of the population.* Part 1, Section 1, 1973.

2

Biological and Environmental Factors in Longevity and Survival

Biologists have long sought to discover why some people live long and some die early in life. Psychologists have only recently directed their attention to such basic matters. While most of the important answers—and perhaps most of the important questions—are not known, a body of information is developing which permits some control over our own longevities.

There are four sets of interdependent factors that are crucial for an understanding of longevity. Two sets are considered in this chapter, biological and environmental factors. The others, psychological and social factors, are discussed in the next chapter.

BIOLOGICAL FACTORS
Cellular Aging: Time Clocks

A most interesting discovery was made: Certain kinds of animal cells have what might be thought of as built-in "time clocks." These clocks function as if they count off the amount of life already lived and program the time still left. Hayflick (1974) summarized some details of his discovery in a nontechnical address, speculating how much of our future lives relate to such cell groups.

Hayflick started with the simple goal of developing human cell cultures free from disease. He chose to do this with embryonic tissue because such tissue is most likely to be free of disease. "The major surprise . . . was the finding that the normal cell populations grew and divided perfectly for many months, then slowed down, stopped dividing, and ultimately died" (Hayflick, 1974, pp. 37–38). He focused on some strains of human fibroblasts derived from embryos (cells giving rise to connective tissue—a tissue that deteriorates with age). Hayflick noted that the fibroblasts undergo 50 population doublings and then die. How-

9

ever, strains derived from young adults rather than embryos undergo only about 30 population doublings before dying. And, strains from old adults undergo even fewer doublings, about 20. This finite lifetime of cultured normal cells may well be "a manifestation of biological aging at the cellular level. . . . Cultured normal cells are mortal just as are the animals from which they are taken" (pp. 38–39).

There seems to be some biochemical mechanism—some clock—within the cells that counts the doublings and allows only so many more. Hayflick speculated that functional losses occur in cells prior to the loss of their capacity to double, and these functional losses produce age changes in animals.

Genetic Determination of Longevity

In the context of a review entitled, *General Biology of Senescence*, two tables were presented listing the length of life of various animals (Lansing, 1959, pp. 121–122). Normal life for man was estimated as 70–80 years, with a possible potential for living 110 years. The chimpanzee tends to live 15–20 years and may have a life potential greater than 30 years. The total range of life-span of mammals is very great: The rat lives about two to three years; it is possible that the fin whale lives several hundred years.

Rockstein (1958) examined data similar to Lansing's and concluded that they constituted the strongest evidence available supporting the concept of a genetic basis of longevity. There is other compelling evidence too, as will be seen, but it is well to keep in mind that, while man's genetic destiny may not include life beyond the age of 110, from his limited time perspective there is much life between the ages of 70–80, when he now dies, and 110, which may be achievable.*

Women Live Longer than Men. In Western culture, women outlive men by five years or more. It is tempting to give a social or cultural explanation as the basis for this—for example, the pressure men experience in the competitive, assertive world of work and career—but such explanations lose credibility when it is realized that the female outlives the male in many animal species, not just man. Rockstein (1958) evolved a table on the basis of a detailed literature search: The female

---

* Life spans much longer than 110 years were reported for two different groups of people living in relatively primitive and isolated surroundings: One group was in the Ecuadorian valley of Vilcabamba and the other in Abkhazia of the Georgian Soviet Socialist Republic (e.g., Leaf, 1973). Hayflick (1974, p. 43) contended, "In none of these reports is adequate scientific proof given to substantiate the claims for longevity that are made."

was found to outlive the male in rats, black widow spiders, mealworms, fruitflies, the common housefly, and other species. Rockstein pointed out that, with human beings, the female is not only the longer-lived but, with only a few exceptions, whatever the specific disease causing death, the female fares better at every adult age level.

Long-Lived Parents Make for Long-Lived Offspring. Biologists like to say, "If you want to live long, choose long-lived parents." There is some scientific evidence for the contention that there is relationship between parental longevity and that of the offspring, but the evidence is sparse. One major study to which reference is often made was first reported in 1918 by Alexander Graham Bell and then published more widely in 1922 by Pearl. The longevities of 4,000 descendents of one family were examined in relation to age of parents at death. Figure 2.1 is based upon these observations and suggests some correlation between age at death of parents and age at death of offspring.

These early data seem to constitute much of the basis for a belief in genetic determination of life-span, but there are other studies as well. Rockstein (1958) reported on another study: Beeton and Pearson (1899) examined data of 1,000 fathers and their sons, and 2,000 pairs of brothers. Very small correlations were seen between father-son longevities, and somewhat larger ones for brother-brother longevities. A more

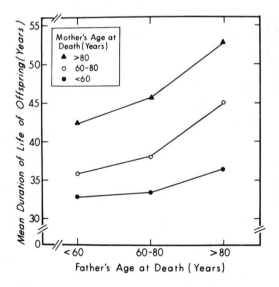

FIGURE 2.1: Longevity of offspring as a function of the longevity of mother and father. (From Table 16 of Pearl, 1922.)

recent study involved the records of American and Canadian life insurance companies. Higher death rates of the policy holders were seen when their parents died before ages 50 and 60 than when they died later in life (Dublin, Lotka, and Spiegelman, 1949). Perhaps more impressive was the study by Jalavisto (1951) who examined the longevities of nearly 13,000 Finnish and Swedish couples. These data, as discussed by Kallmann and Jarvik (1959), also indicated a positive relationship between the longevities of parent and offspring. The maternal influences were found to be greater than the paternal ones, and the life-spans of daughters were seen to be in greater relationship to parental life-spans than those of sons. Evidence in support of these latter findings was not found by Kallmann and Jarvik, although they were able to confirm clearly the parent-offspring longevity relationship.

It is a mistake to automatically attribute the apparent relationship between parental and offspring longevities to genetic factors alone. Data such as seen in Figure 2.1 could result from a variety of reasons. Long-lived parents may be healthier, wealthier, and wiser than short-lived parents in ways unrelated to a longevity gene pool but related to longevity, nevertheless. It is reasonable to expect that favorable cultural and intellectual factors alone could lengthen the life-span of both parent and child. Rockstein (1958) recognized this but maintained a respect for the genetic hypothesis on the basis of parent-offspring longevity correlations seen in the data on lower animal forms, especially those often used in laboratory experiments.

Studies of Twins. The genetic hypothesis in human studies may receive its greatest support in the study of longevities in twin pairs. The relevant data were summarized by Kallmann and Jarvik (1959), most of them being their own. Beginning in 1945, more than 2,500 twin cases were identified, and records were kept of those living to age 60 and over. Genetic control of longevity was inferred from the fact that the life-spans of twins born of one egg were more similar than those born of two eggs. Identical twins died on an average of about four years apart, and fraternal twins died an average of about five and half years apart. It was also found, however, that as late old age was approached, the similarity in life-spans of the one-egg twins decreased, and the similarity of two-egg twins increased. This latter trend was attributed, at least in part, to artifacts of the experimental problem. For example, if one of the dizygotic twin pair dies at age 97, the other cannot die very many years after this.

The evidence, overall, does seem to support the contention that "If you want to live-long, choose long-lived parents." But, again, it is obvious that within the broad limits which may be established by the germ plasm, there are many years which are vital or not, depending upon other biological factors, and certainly upon environmental and psychological factors.

Parental Age at Time of Offspring Birth

What would seem to suggest genetic control of life-span, but in fact does not, is the data of the now classic study by Lansing (1947). He demonstrated unequivocally that, in the rotifer, the length of life of the offspring is dependent in large measure on the mother's age at the time eggs are laid. The rotifer is a microscopic animal found in stagnant waters.

Lansing studied two species of rotifer, one very short-lived (*Euchlanis triquetra*) and one longer-lived (*Philodena citrina*). The short-lived rotifer reaches adolescence on day 2 and maturity on day 3; decline begins on day 5 and death on about day 7 or 8. The longer-lived rotifer reaches adolescence on the fifth day, adulthood on the sixth, with the total life-span extending about three weeks.

In the first series of experiments, Lansing examined the longer-lived species. He isolated a large number of rotifer eggs and allowed them to hatch (F_1). When the hatched rotifers laid eggs on the fourth day of their lives, Lansing gathered these (F_2). He again gathered the eggs hatched on the fourth day of the new generation, and repeated this so that all subsequent generations were always born of adolescent mothers from eggs laid on day 4 (four-day orthoclone).

Lansing also carried out this very same procedure with eggs laid on days 11 and 17; thus, he had three lines of rotifers, one of adolescent mothers, one of middle-aged mothers, and one of senescent ones. All animals of the three orthoclones were followed through their life-spans, and records were made of their ages at death. This experiment was repeated with the same species of rotifer, and it was carried out in three experiments with the short-lived species. All these experiments confirmed the same fact.

Not only were the progeny of the young parents longer lived than those of the older parents, but the effect was increased over the generations. In fact, the offspring of middle-aged and senile lines decreased in numbers and died out over the generations. Lansing (1959, pp. 127–128) wrote, "there seems no doubt but that something is transmitted through the eggs of adult or old mothers which accelerates aging in the offspring . . . the aging factor either is not operative or is lacking in eggs of adolescent females."

Lansing (1947) reversed these processes by switching the eggs laid early in life by the older orthoclones. Eggs laid in the adolescence of old lines gave rise to long-lived animals. "This observation eliminates the possibility that we are dealing with a genetic mutation. Apparently, a non-genetic factor operates here to accelerate aging" (Lansing, 1959, p. 128).

The maternal age-offspring longevity relationship was given some support and generality in a study by Rockstein (1957). His study was based upon the common housefly which reproduces bisexually. Eggs of known maternal age were collected from cages and, when hatched, the flies were kept until death. Rockstein, as did Lansing, found that the longer-lived offspring were born of young mothers. However, this held only if the offspring were female. Ninety-two percent of female flies born of very old mothers died 30 days after birth; only 50 percent of those born of young mothers died at age 30 days. The male fly showed a mortality rate of 92–97 percent irrespective of maternal age at birth, although subsequent evidence (Rockstein, 1959) indicated that even in the male fly a maternal age effect, albeit a small one, may be significant.

A review of the literature indicated that maternal age is a factor in offspring longevity for a variety of animal groups, but not all (Rockstein, 1959). Maternal age was not seen to play a role in at least one strain of fruitfly, but it was important in the longevity of the mealworm and the beetle.

It may be that the role of maternal age in longevity becomes more complicated as we go up the phylogenetic scale. For example, Sawin (1954) studied two breeds of rabbits. In one breed, the relation between maternal age and offspring longevity was similar to that reported by Lansing. In the other breed, however, the reverse pattern was seen; it was the older mother who gave birth to longer-lived progeny, but this was true only up to the age of 18 months. After this maternal age, newborn rabbits had shorter lives.

Whether or not the age of a human mother at the time of the birth of her baby is important to the longevity of the baby is not clear. Rockstein (1959) referred to data which showed that abnormalities as, for example, congenital cardiac impairment, increase in frequency in newborns as the mother's age increases after 30 years. Since the age of fathers tends to be correlated with the age of the mothers, it is possible that the father's age plays a role here. In any case, this evidence suggests that young human parents may sire more long-lived offspring than older ones, at least insofar as there may be a slight increase in the rate of abnormalities in the babies of older parents.

Disease Processes

Disease processes are clearly the main causes of death in later life. Table 2.1 shows, for example, that in 1969, of those aged 75 years and older, nearly 7,000 in each 100,000 died because of the major cardiovascular diseases alone. This statistic becomes even more impressive when it is compared to the less than 17 deaths in each 100,000 in the age group 25–34 years.

It is unclear at present whether, when a fatal disease occurs, it "hits" in a random fashion or whether with age there is a change in the "genetic program" that makes the "hit" more likely, i.e., increasing susceptibility. It is known that in mice, at least, different genetic strains are differentially susceptible to disease processes which shorten the life-span (e.g., Curtis, 1966, p. 95); in man, susceptibility to diabetes is inheritable and this too is a killer in old age (see Table 2.1). Curtis is unequivocal in his opinion about disease in later adulthood: ". . . mutations occur which predispose an individual to the development of a particular disease" (Curtis, 1966, p. 12).

Regardless of whether or not disease processes are under genetic control, they occur in increasingly greater frequency with advancing age. Table 2.1, derived from data obtained by the U.S. Public Health Service (1970), lists only some of the major age-related disease processes.

TABLE 2.1
Death Rates per 100,000 Population in the United States During 1969*

Cause of Death	Age (Years)						
	15-24	25-34	35-44	45-54	55-64	65-74	75 and over
Major cardiovascular diseases	4.4	16.8	86.3	293.5	816.9	2,155.5	6,752.7
Malignant neoplasms	7.7	16.5	62.0	180.4	420.2	770.3	1,171.2
Influenza and pneumonia	2.7	4.1	9.4	18.2	40.5	106.9	429.6
Diabetes mellitus	0.7	2.1	5.4	12.2	38.7	93.1	190.8
Bronchitis, emphysema, and asthma	0.5	0.6	2.6	9.9	38.0	89.4	138.4

* Part of Table G, Pages 6 and 7 of Monthly Vital Statistics Report of the U.S.P.H.S., 1970, *18*, No. 13.

ENVIRONMENTAL FACTORS

Just as it is presumed by many that the age-related disease processes leading to death develop as a result of genetic predisposition, so it may be presumed with other processes. For example, it will be seen later that, even in a process such as cigarette smoking, there are those who believe that biological factors predispose people both to the habit and to the ensuing diseases. Regardless of the correctness of this belief, it is only convenience which makes for a distinction between environmental and biological factors. The mode of action of the former has to be by way of the latter.

Thermal Regulation and Metabolic Rate

There is a hypothesis that relates the rate of early growth to the total length of life. The general notion is that slow growth makes for longer life and fast growth makes for shorter life. This hypothesis is enduring, but it is not always confirmed. It is possible that it is not growth rate which determines the length of life, but that both depend upon some common element. The common element may well be metabolic rate. The proposition is that animals use up about the same amount of energy per unit weight in the course of a lifetime regardless of whether the animal is long-lived or short-lived. The crucial fact is whether the energy is used up quickly or not. Since rate of energy consumption is related to factors of temperature, among others, one hypothesis is that heat makes for high metabolism and short life. Not only do species with different metabolic rates tend to have different longevities, but so do those of the same species, living in differing climatic temperatures.

This metabolic hypothesis of life duration seems to hold only within very crude limits. Despite this, it has been of interest to biologists probably because of their ability to influence metabolic rate experimentally by temperature variations. "That temperature, both environmental for cold-blooded species and central for warm-blooded animals, has something to do with the rate of aging processes seems now most probable" (Bourlière, 1958).

To test the hypothesis that colder temperatures increase longevity, the rotifer again was found to be a useful animal. Fanestil and Barrows (1965) varied the temperatures of the environmental water of the rotifer and found confirmation of the hypothesis. Rotifers kept in aqueous environments of 35, 31, and 25 degrees centigrade lived approximately 18, 30, and 34 days, respectively.

This is not to be taken as a prescription that cold environments are therapeutic or life-lengthening. The specific environmental temperatures are factors, the age at which cold is introduced is important, and, of course, so is the strain of animal under study. For example, older mice adapt less well to cold than do younger mice, and they die sooner as a result (Grad and Kral, 1957). And in the rat, lifelong exposures to cold environments (9 degrees centigrade) have resulted in shorter lives than have exposures to warmer environments of 28 degrees (Kibler, Silsby, and Johnson, 1963).

Diet

When Fanestil and Barrows (1965) varied the aqueous temperatures of their rotifers, they also varied the amount of nutriments given them. They were thus able to elucidate the factors in longevity by contrasting the effects of temperature and diet. Just as the life-span was increased with the cold, it was also increased by dietary restriction. Most important, however, was the fact that the modes of the increases were different. The dietary effect was on the earlier part of life, and the temperature effect was on the latter part of life. With food restriction, the animals took longer to develop, but, once developed, the later period of life was not extended. On the other hand, the cold did not affect the early part of life, but extended the later part. This argues for more than one mechanism of longevity: Mechanisms bearing on early phases of life are not necessarily those bearing on later phases.

It was in a much acclaimed early study on the rat that a lengthening of life due to dietary restriction was first seen. McCay, Crowell, and Maynard (1935) severely reduced the caloric intake of rats immediately after weaning in one group, two weeks later in a second group, and not at all in a third group. While the increase in longevity of the female was slight, if at all, the increase in the male was spectacular. On the average, the life-span of the male rat was extended to 820 days from 483 days in the group restricted immediately after weaning, and to 894 days in the group put on the diet two weeks later. In the female, while the average longevity was not much affected by the diet, there were some very long-lived survivors (from Rockstein, 1958).

This increase in life-span for the males was not without its cost, however. The drastic underfeeding severely stunted their growth and kept them sexually immature. Whether longevity could be lengthened with a less drastic restriction of food was investigated by Berg and Simms (1962). They kept rats, not undernourished as did McCay et al., but lean, so that they did not develop the excess body fat of ad libitum-fed animals.

When Berg and Simms compared the mortality rates of their unrestricted animals with those restricted soon after weaning, they also found that the latter lived longer. Life was extended by 200 days for male rats (from 800 to 1,000 days), and 300 days for female rats (from 1,000 to 1,300 days). On the basis of a post-mortem analysis of organ lesions, Berg and Simms attributed the increased longevity to later onset of disease in the leaner rats.

The obvious and important question—would life be lengthened in rats whose food intake was restricted in adulthood rather than after weaning?—was asked by Barrows and Roeder (1965). A severe food restriction was imposed on rats aged 12 months—an age well into adulthood. The longevities of these animals were not prolonged, in fact, "a small but significant decrement in mean life-span" was observed.

Other laboratory animals were investigated also with respect to longevity and dietary variations. Rockstein (1958) studied flies, feeding one group sugar and water only and another group sugar, water, and a milk supplement. The results were different from those with rats. There were no longevity effects with the dietary restrictions on the male; with females, the restriction shortened life! Rockstein pointed out that McCay et al.

> emphasized the *low calorie* aspect of his restricted diet, which was in reality a high protein, salt and vitamin diet. It is therefore likely that the critical factor involved in such a restricted diet may well have been the *effective* protein content of the diet (Rockstein, 1959, p. 252).

Rockstein (1959) compared the published data of animals that mature within a few hours to several days, such as his houseflies, with the data of animals where growth and maturation are not yet completed when dietary restriction is begun, such as the rat. His conclusion was that in the former cases, heavy physiological demands are made on the animal for normal functioning, and dietary enrichment provides the balance necessary for development. In the cases where growth and maturation are not yet completed when dietary restriction is begun, the diet slows growth, and in so doing delays senescence. In general, this conclusion seems reasonable; however, the data of Fanestil and Barrows (1965), which showed prolonged rotifer life with dietary restriction, may argue against the conclusion in every animal group.

In modern man, dietary restriction has become, literally, a way of life.

While few authorities, if any, recommend severe restriction of the quantity of food consumed and, certainly, while none recommend restriction to the extent that growth and sexuality are stunted, it is generally believed that obesity in adulthood is one road to heart attacks.

In later life, hardening of the arteries (arteriosclerosis) is a major problem, sometimes leading to death. It has been found that people with this problem often have large deposits of a type of fat (cholesterol) in the walls of their arteries. Certain foods—eggs and beef, for example —increase the cholesterol in the body. Although it is not certain that cholesterol causes arteriosclerosis, many physicians advise men especially against eating much of such foods.

Other fats in the body thought to be undesirable in large quantities are the triglycerides. These fats, found in the blood, are controlled by minimizing the intake of sugars, carbohydrates, and alcohol. If people reduce their consumption of eggs, meat, sugar, carbohydrates, and alcohol without reducing the overall quantity of foods consumed, it is likely they would reduce their weight. It is not a general dietary restriction that is the probable element in longevity, but the type of nutriments restricted.

Smoking

Good habits of diet and exercise, and little or no smoking of cigarettes, is the typical prescription to ward off heart attacks. Only a few sources still debate whether or not cigarette smoking is associated with longevity. "There is no longer any doubt that cigarette smokers have a higher death rate than nonsmokers. New biological studies help to explain how tobacco smoke damages the lungs, heart and other body tissues" (so stated a lead-in abstract of an article in *Scientific American* by Hammond, 1962). Newer data continue to confirm this. An article in *Science* indicated that the incidence of cardiovascular diseases "is related to several risk factors, particularly cigarette smoking" (Kolata and Marx, 1976, p. 509).

Figure 2.2 shows the percent of people in the United States during the one year between 1964 and 1965 who developed chronic health problems in relation to smoking. This figure, taken from part of a table in a PHS report (1967), shows that smoking and chronic health conditions go hand in hand. It seems that smoking is more damaging to the young than to the old; the old have a high incidence of chronic diseases independent of smoking.

Many dimensions of smoking were indicated in the magazine, *The*

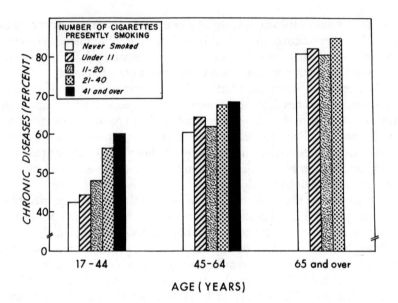

FIGURE 2.2: Percent of people with one or more chronic health problems in relation to the quantity of cigarettes smoked. Smoking has a greater effect on the health of young adults than on older people. (Data from Table 3, U.S.P.H.S. Report, 1967.)

*Lancet,** in comment on a report of the Royal College of Physicians of London, England:

> For each of the three main diseases associated with smoking [lung cancer, chronic bronchitis, and coronary heart disease] the risk is stated to be substantially less for pipe and cigar smokers than for cigarette smokers. . . . Although cancers of the mouth, larynx, and oesophagus arise more frequently in smokers of all kinds of tobacco than in nonsmokers, there is no epidemic of cancers of these types as there is of lung cancer. . . . Little prominence is given to other effects of smoking, such as the smaller size of babies, the increased risks of abortion, stillbirth, and death during the first days of life, associated with smoking during pregnancy. . . .

There are at least three lines of argument countering the research evidence of the effects of cigarette smoking. One argument is that the evidence is little other than "statistical association." This is a main argument of the Tobacco Institute, i.e., no evidence of "causal links"

* See editorial, Counterblast to Tobacco, *The Lancet,* January 9, 1971, pp. 69–70.

between smoking and disease has been elucidated. The concept of causality is discussed in chapter 20; the important point to recognize is that causality is defined by the extent of our knowledge. While a day may come when cigarette smoking will not "cause" illness because corrective measures gained from knowledge of mechanisms will be instituted, for the present at least, one way to minimize the likelihood of disease is to stop the smoking.

A second argument countering the research evidence of the effects of smoking is that genetic factors may predispose some people both to smoking and to the related illnesses; genes, not smoking, is the "cause." As reviewed by Seltzer (1967), twin studies have shown that identical twin pairs are much more alike in their smoking habits than fraternal twin pairs. And lung cancer, for example, has been found common to some families whether or not there was much smoking. Some investigators maintain that, even if there is not a genetic basis for *both* smoking and cancer, there is such a basis for cancer, and this is exacerbated by smoking.

A most adequate response to this argument may be seen in *The Lancet* article referred to earlier:

> The epidemiological and clinical evidence of reduced risk of lung cancer and chronic bronchitis after stopping smoking is especially important insofar as it counters both the genetic theory of causation of lung cancer and the argument that there is no point stopping after essential damage has been done.

A third argument is of a different kind. Smoking is pleasurable for many people, and it fulfills a need. Not only is this important, but if smoking is stopped, other, far worse forms of addiction may be developed. There is no satisfactory response to this latter point because it is unproven. Even if true, however, it may be well to indicate that many important aspects of life involve a cost, and good health and longevity are among these.

SUMMARY

Biologists and epidemiologists have contributed an interesting and important body of information bearing on problems of longevity and survival. It is quite apparent that cells age. Some cells have built-in "biological clocks" which set the limits of their mortality. It is also apparent that heredity plays a role in longevity. Perhaps the most impressive evidence for this is the extreme diversity of various animal longevities. For example, the rat lives about two to three years and the fin whale may live several hundred years.

There is evidence also that heredity plays a role in man's longevity. Long-lived parents tend to sire long-lived offspring. Other evidence is seen in the study of twins: Identical twins live to about the same age, more so at least than do fraternal twins. Very important psychosocially is the fact that women outlive men. While it might seem reasonable to attribute this sex difference to greater stress in the lives of men, a perusal of the life-spans of other animal groups such as rats, spiders, flies, and others devalues any explanation that does not involve genetic determination.

Genetics may also play a role in the disease processes known to be the main causes of death in later life. There are those who believe that such diseases occur not in random fashion but with a greater probability in some people than in others. Those more likely to be fallen by the disease may be the more genetically disposed.

A nongenetic but biological factor in longevity is the age of the mother at the time of her baby's birth. The evidence for this is excellent with the primitive organism, rotifer; it is excellent for the female housefly; and there is evidence for this with other, but not all, animal groups examined for this purpose. There is some evidence that the age of the human mother at the time her baby is born plays a role in the baby's longevity. Babies born of older mothers are more likely to have congenital defects associated with shorter life than are babies born of young mothers. The extent of this likelihood, however, is very small. Since older mothers are likely to have older husbands, it is possible that the ages of both the mother and father are important factors.

Closely associated with biological factors of longevity and survival are environmental influences. For example, there is the hypothesis which relates metabolic rate to length of life and, to an extent, metabolic rate is controlled by temperature variations. In one study, cold aqueous environments (25 degrees centigrade) increased the life-spans of rotifers almost 100-fold over warmer environments (35 degrees centigrade). However, extreme cold is a stressor. Rats and mice were seen to die in such cold, with the older mice adapting less well than younger ones and dying at a higher rate.

Life-span has also been associated with food intake; the lower the intake, the longer the life. In lower animals, whereas the cold was seen to prolong life by way of extending the later part of life (the part past reaching maturity), the dietary restriction was seen to prolong the earlier period (the period prior to reaching maturity). This argues for more than one mechanism setting the limits of life's duration.

In man, eating habits which minimize obesity are believed to increase his life potential. Diets which reduce fat intake are believed to decrease the likelihood of arteriosclerosis and heart attacks, and, in so doing, decrease the likelihood of early death.

Good food habits, exercise, and little or no smoking of cigarettes is the triumvirate typically recommended by physicians as means to ward off cardiovascular problems. There is little doubt that heavy cigarette smoking is associated with a variety of poor health conditions, not only cardiovascular problems. As with diseases in general, there are those who attribute both the smoking and ensuing illnesses to a genetic predisposition. This argument, however, is largely negated by the fact that those who stop smoking reduce their risk of illnesses, especially lung cancer and chronic bronchitis.

REFERENCES

Barrows, C.H., and Roeder, L.M. The effect of reduced dietary intake on enzymatic activities and life-span of rats. *Journal of Gerontology*, 1965, *20*, 69–71.

Beeton, M., and Pearson, K. Data for the problem of evolution in man. II. A first study of the inheritance of longevity and the selective death rate in man. *Proceedings Royal Society*, 1899, LXV, 290–305.

Bell, A.G. The duration of life and conditions associated with longevity, a study of the Hyde genealogy. Washington, privately printed, 1918.

Berg, B.N., and Simms, H.S. Relation of nutrition to longevity and onset of disease in rats. In N.W. Shock (Ed.), *Biological aspects of aging*. New York: Columbia Univ. Press, 1962.

Bourlière, F. The comparative biology of aging. *Journal of Gerontology*, 1958, Supplement No. 2, *13*, 16–24.

Curtis, H.J. Biological mechanisms of aging. Springfield, Ill.: Charles C Thomas, 1966.

Dublin, L.I., Lotka, A.J., and Spiegelman, M. *Length of life*. New York: Ronald Press, 1949.

Fanestil, D.D., and Barrows, C.H. Aging in the rotifer. *Journal of Gerontology*, 1965, *20*, 464–469.

Grad, B., and Kral, V.A. The effect of senescence on resistance to stress. *Journal of Gerontology*, 1957, *12*, 172–181.

Hammond, E.C. The effects of smoking. *Scientific American*, 1962, 207, 39–51.

Hayflick, L. The strategy of senescence. *Journal of Gerontology*, 1974, *14*, 37–45.

Jalavisto, E. Inheritance of longevity according to Finnish and Swedish genealogies. *Annals medical int. Fenniae*, 1951, 40, 263–274.

Kallmann, F.J., and Jarvik, L.F. Individual differences in constitution and genetic background. *Handbook of aging and the individual: psychological and biological aspects.* Chicago: Univ. of Chicago Press, 1959, pp. 216–263.

Kibler, H.H., Silsby, H.D., and Johnson, H.D. Metabolic trends and life-span of rats living at 9°C and 28°C. *Journal of Gerontology,* 1963, *18,* 235–239.

Kolata, G.B., and Marx, J.L. Epidemiology of heart disease: searches for causes. *Science,* 1976, *194,* 509–512.

Lansing, A.I. A transmissible, cumulative, and reversible factor in aging. *Journal of Gerontology,* 1947, *2,* 228–239.

Lansing, A.I. General biology of senescence. In J.E. Birren (Ed.), *Handbook of aging and the individual: psychological and biological aspects.* Chicago: Univ. of Chicago Press, 1959, pp. 119–135.

Leaf, A. Every day is a gift when you are over 100. *National Geographic,* 1973, *143,* 93–119.

McCay, C.M., Crowell, M.F., and Maynard, L.A. The effect of retarded growth upon the length of life span and upon the ultimate body size. *Journal of Nutrition,* 1935, *10,* 63–79.

Pearl, R. *The biology of death.* Philadelphia: J.B. Lippincott Co., 1922.

Rockstein, M. Longevity of male and female house flies. *Journal of Gerontology,* 1957, *12,* 253–256.

Rockstein, M. Heredity and longevity in the animal kingdom. *Journal of Gerontology,* 1958, Supplement No. 2, *13,* 7–12.

Rockstein, M. The biology of aging in insects. *Ciba Foundation Symposium on the Lifespan of Animals,* 1959, 247–264.

Sawin, P.B. The influence of age of mother on pattern of reproduction. *Annals of the New York Academy of Sciences,* 1954, *57,* 564–574.

Seltzer, C.C. Constitution and heredity in relation to tobacco smoking. *Annals of the New York Academy of Sciences,* 1967, *142,* 322–330.

United States Public Health Service. *Cigarette smoking and health characteristics.* National Center for Health Statistics, May 1967, Series 10, Number 34, p. 27.

United States Public Health Service. *Monthly Vital Statistic Report,* 1970, *18,* No. 13, Table G, pp. 6–7.

3

Psychological and Social Factors in Longevity and Survival

Much of the data in the previous chapter, on biological and environmental factors in longevity, was reported during the late 1940s to late 1950s. The main body of data in the present chapter, on psychological and social factors, had its origins during this period, but, because of its nature, was not reported until some ten and twenty years later.

Many studies reported in this chapter take the following form: Investigators, having collected data on elderly people for a variety of different reasons, often, but not always, without plans to carry out follow-up procedures, realized afterward that a splendid research opportunity was available to them. When, after a lapse of time, an appreciable percentage of the elderly subjects died, a comparison of the earlier test scores of those who died and those who survived presented an opportunity to investigate possible antecedent factors of survival and mortality. Further, when the research was longitudinal, i.e., when two or more measurements were available prior to death, changes in the scores over time, as well as the scores themselves, were available for post-mortem analysis.

Thus, while many of the initial data were published at the same time as were data dealing with biological and environmental factors, it was much later that the post-mortem studies appeared. They appeared in such quantity and in such close order that a special volume was necessary to describe them (*Prediction of Life Span*, edited by Palmore and Jeffers, 1971). There were subsequent studies with conflicting results among many of them, and this called for further explication (Siegler, 1975). These facts are all the more interesting when it is recognized that not so very long ago only a few short pages were all that was necessary to describe the literature (Botwinick, 1967, pp. 37–38, 42–45).

PSYCHOLOGICAL FACTORS
Cognitive Ability

While it may be quite apparent that biological factors underlie much in longevity and survival, it may not be so apparent that psychological factors are also important. For example, impending death is often preceded by a "terminal drop" in cognitive functioning. This was first observed and highlighted by Kleemeier (1961, 1962), whose studies, though perhaps lacking the precision of procedure and the elegance of statistical analysis that subsequent studies had, did point to the time of death as an anchoring date, rather than the time of birth.

Terminal Drop. Kleemeier tested 13 elderly men on four occasions during the course of 12 years. Approximately every two to three-and-a-half years during this time, an intelligence test (Wechsler-Bellevue) was given to each man, and the changes in his performances were noted. Each one of the 13 men showed decrement over the span of 12 years, but the extent of decrement varied from person to person. Shortly after the last test of the series, four men died. Kleemeier observed that these four men had declined much more rapidly in their cognitive abilities than did the surviving nine men. This decline was named "terminal drop." He also analyzed the decline in scores of 70 elderly men who had but two testings. After nearly half of them died, Kleemeier found evidence that the "drop" in scores was greater for the deceased than for the living.

These observations opened possibilities not before emphasized; they also stimulated investigations with contradictory or negative results (e.g., Berkowitz, 1965; Palmore and Cleveland, 1976). In the main, however, a new study area was begun.

Poor Performance and Prediction of Death. There were studies prior to Kleemeier's which showed that elderly people poor in cognitive abilities tend to die sooner than their more able brethren. In these studies, however, this was often a confounding artifact negating a main argument rather than an important fact in its own right. It is pointed out in chapter 20, under the heading, "Sampling Problems," that this presents special problems in longitudinal research. For example, Jarvik and Falek (1963) examined senescent twins with the Wechsler-Bellevue intelligence test and found that fewer of the initially poor performers were alive for later retest; similarly, Riegel, Riegel, and Meyer (1967), with several tests, including a verbal achievement test, found attrition rates higher for the less able; and, more recently, Baltes, Schaie, and Nardi (1971) reported similar results with a test of intelligence and of rigidity. These results complement the concept, "terminal drop"; it may well be that in these studies the "drop" had already occurred at the time of the initial testing for those subjects dying shortly afterward.

Cooperation and Retest Availability. The study by Riegel et al. was extended to a third testing and thus provides a dimensionality not yet available in many studies. In 1956 the verbal achievement and other tests were given to 380 men and women residing in northern Germany. Five years later a retest was made, and five years after this a second retest was made. Of the 380 people originally tested, 62 died by the time of the second test period, and 116 refused to be tested; at the third testing, another 100 had died. Riegel made this interesting observation: There were 116 people surviving to the time of the second testing who refused to cooperate by allowing a retest. Of these 116 people, 43 percent did not survive the next five years to the third test period. By contrast, only 25 percent of those who were tested at time 2 did not survive to time 3. "Thus," says Riegel (1971, p. 141), "cooperation in retest studies is a powerful predictor of survival."

People who were retested were compared to people who did not survive to the second testing, with respect to scores both groups made at time 1. The scores of the subsequently deceased group were lower than the group retested; but, more interesting, this was more the case for those aged less than 65 years than for those over 65. Drawing upon these and other results, Riegel concluded that, during the decade prior to 65 years, death occurs more often with less able people. At older age levels, however, "death strikes more randomly." Prediction of survival is, therefore, more reliable at the younger age levels.

Comparisons of the initial test 1 scores of those people who were tested at time 2 and survived to time 3 with those who were tested at time 2 but died by time 3, indicated a superiority in achievement scores for the former group. This again pointed to a relationship between poor initial performance and the greater likelihood of death. A comparison between these two groups with respect to the scores made at time 2 showed an even greater performance difference between them than it did with the scores made at time 1. Riegel attributed the very poor scores of those retested at time 2 and failing to survive to time 3 to "terminal drop"—"sudden deterioration, occurring during periods extending less than five years prior to the death." Riegel (1971, p. 146) concluded:

> At any time during the later periods of life, subjects who perform less well are likely to be closer to death than their more able age-mates. Differences in scores *within* age groups might thus be a function of survival probability. . . . Differences in scores *between* age groups . . . might reflect the increasing number of persons with terminal drops. . . .

Types of Loss. What potential there may be for the use of performance scores to predict ensuing death depends upon the nature of the performance under examination. Birren (1968) compared survivors and nonsurvivors five years after they were originally tested when most had been in their early 60s. The two groups were distinguished by their original performances on tests of verbal information skills, not on tests of perceptual-motor skills involving speed. The nonsurvivors had performed more poorly on the verbal tests. Eleven years later, when more of the test-takers died, Granick (1971) compared their scores again. This time poor performances on both the verbal and psychomotor tests were seen among the nonsurvivors. Thus, the type of loss together with the time period of prediction of death seem important.

Critical Loss. A similar report was seen in the context of a terminal drop notion rather than a poor performance notion. Jarvik and Falek (1963) tested 39 twin pairs (78 people) aged 60 years or older who were part of a larger sample of subjects first examined between 1946 and 1949. The 78 twins were also tested on two subsequent occasions to 1958. Each person was given four subtests of the Wechsler-Bellevue scale of adult intelligence, a vocabulary test from the Stanford Binet, and a speed of tapping test.

An "annual rate of decline" of each person was computed for each of these tests: For each individual the score made on the third test period was subtracted from the higher of the two scores made during the first two test periods, and this was divided by the product of the earlier score and the years intervening between testings. For example, if at time 1 or 2 the score was 10, and at time 3, four years later, the score was 7, the critical loss would be $10 - 7 \div 10 \times 4$. This fraction is then multiplied by 100 to provide more easily handled numbers.

Jarvik and Falek reported that an annual decrement of at least 2 percent on Digit Symbol, 10 percent on Similarities, or any decline on the Vocabulary subtest was a poor omen for survival five years following the last testing. Their subjects with two or three of these decrements showed high mortality rates: of eight people, seven died within the next five years.

More recently, Jarvik and Blum (1971, p. 204) examined these "critical loss" scores for a subsample of 26 twin pairs. Fifteen twin pairs were without "critical loss" and 11 pairs were discordant in that one twin partner showed the "loss." It is striking that in 10 of the 11 discordant pairs, "the partner with the 'critical loss' . . . succumbed earlier to death." The eleventh pair were both alive after five years, but the member with the "loss" was the more deteriorated of the pair. Of the 15 twin pairs without "critical loss," 12 pairs survived the five-year period and, of the other three pairs, one member survived in each.

All these data on terminal drop and poor performance levels portend important possibilities for prediction and, therefore, possible control of impending tragedy. A note of caution is needed here, however: "Since the given data were obtained retrospectively" (Jarvik and Falek, 1963, p. 176), it is crucial to test their validity by prospective analyses. While results of prospective studies may be expected to make for good prediction, they, in fact, may not. After all, as indicated, not all studies reported positive results (Berkowitz, 1965; Palmore and Cleveland, 1976). Retrospective analyses are but first steps to prediction of survival.

Coping Ability

Personality factors as well as cognitive ability undergo a "terminal drop." For a period of two-and-a-half years, four psychological tests were administered every three to four weeks to a group of residents of a home for the aged (Lieberman, 1965). The tests were the Bender-Gestalt, the Draw-A-Person, time reproduction, and a projective test of 12 line drawings. When the study was completed, the data of only 25 people were available for analysis, but, despite this, the data were clear in indicating that personality changes may occur many months prior to death. Lieberman reported his results in terms of a comparison between two groups of people: One group was composed of those who died less than three months after completing at least five testings, and another group was composed of people who were still living at least a year after completing ten or more testings.

Unlike Riegel, who emphasized relative standing in performance within a group, Lieberman emphasized that, in terms of survival, absolute levels did not distinguish among people; it was the level changing over time which was important, i.e., the "terminal drop" was important. Lieberman emphasized that in his study the drop did not appear to be the result of physical illness, rather it was of more psychological determination. Those residents who became seriously physically ill and recovered did not show the test performance changes shown by those who died shortly afterward.

Lieberman's data suggested to him that people close to death have lessened ability to cope with environmental demands; they have a lowered ability to organize and to integrate environmental inputs. "Individuals approaching death pull away from those around them . . . because they are preoccupied in an attempt to hold themselves together—to reduce the experience of chaos."

Relocation

In an evaluative account of the sparse literature on the effects of institutionalizing the aged, Blenkner (1967, p. 101) wrote, "Older people admitted to institutions die at excessively high rates during the first year, and particuarly during the first three months after admission."

Crisis and Stress. This conclusion is of obvious importance, but it is possible that it is a reflection of hardly more than the fact that people requiring relocation to institutions are in such poor health or are in such general crisis states as to make death imminent independently of the relocation. The crucial question then is: Does institutionalization make for a crisis and stress which often eventuates in or accelerates a process leading to death, or is the institutionalization nothing more than an event that happens to coincide in time with a person's dying?

Blenkner posed this question and a related one: Would it be better to provide service in the person's own home even if the program of care is less good than could be provided in an institution? She raised this question as a result of her disquieting observation that aged people randomly assigned to three service programs showed mortality rates proportional to the extent of the care rendered. This relationship was statistically nonsignificant, but it was alarming in its implications, nevertheless. The program of greatest care was directed toward providing better or more protected living environments, and this was associated with the highest mortality rates. The disquieting observation was not assuaged by a subsequent one, also statistically not significant. A six-month follow-up of two groups, one with extensive service and a greater institutionalization rate, and the other with less service and a lesser institutionalization rate, showed again that the better service program was associated with a higher death rate.

Depression. Efforts have been made to determine specific factors related to death in relocation. For example, Miller and Lieberman (1965) examined a group of aged women who were being transferred from one Illinois state home for the aged to another. The women were free from incapacitating mental or physical illnesses and thus were not representative of a total population of a state home. A battery of tests were given to these women two weeks prior to their move and then again six and 18 weeks after the move. The test scores were examined for their possible relation to "negative reactions," defined as death or psychological and physical health changes.

After 18 weeks in the new home, 23 of the 45 residents were judged to show the negative reactions, but, of the psychological measures made prior to the relocation, only depressive affect was significantly related to negative outcome after the move. The depressive affect was not the same as that which is normally seen in clinical depression. Interview data suggested that depressive affect involved:

(1) an extremely negative evaluation of the past life—feelings of being cheated, of having found life to be meaningless; and (2) an inability to characterize the immediate and distant future because of the feeling that, for oneself, a future does not exist—that no positive satisfaction or gratification is possible in the tomorrow (Miller and Lieberman, 1965, p. 496).

It is most important to distinguish between such affect states and severe clinical depression. Both of these can derive from loss and physical disability. Mild affect states can be tolerated, but extreme depression is, for many, so devastating as to be unbearable—so unbearable, in fact, as to make some people want to kill themselves. There is no doubt that suicide is more frequent in the aged than in the young, but the age pattern in suicide is so different for the white male in the United States than for the white female, or from nonwhites of both sexes, as to demand interpretations that go beyond explanations of loss and physical disability. Figure 3.1 shows with stark clarity how painful life must be for many aged white males. It has been suggested by Zung (1967) that feelings of inferiority and loss of self-esteem are among the major causes of depression in the elderly. If this underlies the data of Figure 3.1, then perhaps it may be speculated that this is the price many aged white men pay for opportunities achieved, never realized, or lost. It is interesting to speculate further that women and nonwhites of both sexes, having been deprived of opportunities, lose less in later life; in any event, they may not feel as personally unable and unworthy when without high social roles. A test of this may be seen in future years as nonwhites and white women are given greater opportunities. Will they too follow the suicide pattern of white men as seen in Figure 3.1?

Adjustment and Hostility. Aldrich and Mendkoff (1963) reported a follow-up study of the relocation of 182 residents in a home for the chronically disabled, a move made necessary when the home in which they had been residing was closed for administrative reasons. Since this reason and none other was responsible for the move, a natural situation experiment was available, one in which the effects of relocation could be assessed without confounding factors such as different health and dependency statuses for the different comparison groups.

Residents with satisfactory adjustments in their initial institution survived best in the move; psychotics and near psychotics fared worst of all. Residents classified as neurotics and those who denied their physical disabilities died at a rate three times that of the residents with satisfactory adjustments. Those residents characterized as hostile and demand-

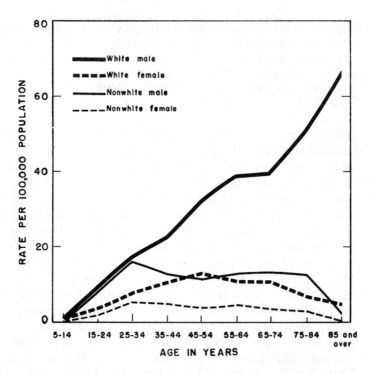

FIGURE 3.1: Suicide rates in the United States during the year 1964 in relation to age. Note that, after age 25-34 years, it is only with white males that suicide is positively related to age. (Figure from U.S.P.H.S. report, *Suicide in the United States 1950–1964*, Series 20, Number 5, 1967. Data of 1972, reported in 1976 by the U.S.P.H.S., are very similar.)

ing, while not surviving as well as those with satisfactory adjustments, died at a rate half that of the neurotic and denying residents.

Aldrich (1964) carried out a subsequent analysis in which 26 elderly residents who died within three months following relocation were compared to a like number of residents who survived the first 12 months in the new residence. Again, satisfactory adjustment in the old residence was a positive predictor of survival in the new residence, and psychosis was a negative predictor. The category "neurotic and depressed" was associated with mixed results. While nine of the 26 died within three months after relocation, an equal number survived 12 months.

A result interesting in its potential, but exceedingly limited by its small sample, is the one based upon the classification, "angry and demanding." Four times as many people so described survived one year in the new residence as died in three months; however, the specific numbers of residents were, literally, four to one. This result was strengthened by the finding that, of the five residents who made "angry" adjustments to the new location, all survived the critical three-month period and were living one year after moving in.

Evidence for the survival value of angry adjustments seems to have received support in a study by Turner, Tobin, and Lieberman (1972). Elderly persons awaiting institutionalization were tested prior to their admittance and again approximately one year after being admitted. The residents were categorized as to whether: (1) they were functioning not very differently than they had been during pre-admission, or (2) they functioned appreciably less well, or died.

> The particular trait factor found to be associated with successful institutional adaptation . . . loaded highly on activity, aggression, and narcissistic body image. This cluster of traits suggests that a vigorous, if not combative, style is facilitory for adaptation. . . . It suggests a narcissistic-hostile and controlling orientation toward the institutional environment (Turner et al., 1972, p. 67).

The notion that hostility, anger, aggressiveness, or some such dimension of personality is facilitory to survival in old age received further support in quite a different context. Gutmann (1971) studied the Navajo Indians; they live in remote Arizona deserts in such harsh conditions that Gutmann concluded that men in their 70s and over are cut from quite a different cloth than most of the men in their later 50s and 60s. He referred to the former group as "survivors," with differences between them and the younger groups most marked in the latter's "passivity." Passivity was seen as fairly typical of most Navajo men, whereas survivorship in the older group "might in some manner be related to their counter-passivity" (p. 190).

> . . . it is quite likely that passivity and disease are related in a fairly straightforward way. . . . We have found that counter-passive Navajo survivors force themselves, by sheer effort of will, to herd sheep, or to hoe corn. Their intent is to demonstrate their continued independence, but they incidentally keep their cardiovascular system in tune. . . . By the same token, the more overtly passive Navajo . . . (p. 196)

conserves his energies, drinks much alcohol, and probably develops organic disease accordingly.

Noninstitutional Moves. There is a big difference between the effects of relocation on those elderly people moving to institutions because they are too sick to continue living in the community and those elderly who are healthy and move voluntarily to other quarters—perhaps smaller apartments that are easier to maintain and where the medical and social service supervision is more readily available. Based on his studies on institutionalization, Lieberman (1974, p. 494) concluded: ". . . no matter what the condition of the individual, the nature of the environment, or the degree of sophisticated preparation, relocation entails a higher than acceptable risk. . . ." By risk, Lieberman meant negative changes in overall functioning as well as ensuing death. This is not to say that all investigators reach this conclusion. For example, Gutman and Herbert (1976, p. 357) examined death rates, but not overall functioning, and wrote: " . . . with careful planning of the move, involuntary relocation . . . need not result in increased mortality."

If there is some question regarding the effects of relocation on the institutionalized elderly, there is less question regarding moves to noninstitutional residences. Older healthy community residents relocating voluntarily to desirable residences do "not incur greater risk of dying—if anything . . . [the relocation] may decrease the risk" (Wittels and Botwinick, 1974, p. 442). Moreover, such moves do not appear to affect overall functioning negatively. Based on a study wherein healthy movers were compared to similar nonmovers, it was concluded that, "If there is indeed risk in the relocation of the institutionalized aged, there appears to be no necessary comparable risk among the noninstitutionalized old" (Storandt and Wittels, 1975, p. 608). These conclusions were comparable to those of other studies dealing with normal, healthy older adults (e.g., Carp, 1966, 1975), although Lawton and Yaffe (1970) reported that functional health may decline in moving among some elderly people but improve among others.

Medical and Attitudinal Factors

Chronic Brain Syndrome and Bodily Dysfunction. In addition to —perhaps relating to—the findings that cognitive and personality test scores are associated with survival rates, it is clear that among the institutionalized aged, those suffering from organic brain disease die soonest. Goldfarb, Fisch, and Gerber (1966) gave each of almost 1,300 institutionalized aged a series of three separate examinations: psychiatric, medical, and psychological. One year later the same people were examined again, with the finding that 24 percent had died. Severe physical incapacity, severe brain syndrome as measured by the psychiatric examinations, or brain syndrome as measured by the mental status questionnaires, indicated a death rate of from 35 to 40 percent within a year. A fourth reliable predictor was incontinence. "Persons who showed a combination of these four selected indicators had a death rate of 52 percent" (Goldfarb et al., 1966, p. 29).

A seven-year follow-up of this study indicated when any of the four indicators was present, survival potential was decreased in years 3, 4, and 5, although to a smaller extent than during the first year following the testing. When two or more indicators were present, survival rates were lower for all seven years (Goldfarb, 1969).

Attitudes and Adaptation to Illness. Attitudes toward illness and the manner in which adjustments are made seem to be very important in survival. This was seen with special vividness in a study by Garrity and Klein (1971). They investigated the attitudes of heart-attack patients during their hospitalizations, and whether or not they survived six months later.

Observations were made during the acute phase of the heart attack: During each of the first five days of hospitalization the patients were rated with respect to 21 dimensions of adaptation—dimensions such as anxiety and cheerfulness. The patients were then categorized into two groups: One group was characterized either by slight behavior disturbance, or by improvement in this disturbance over the five-day period; the other group was characterized either by great disturbance or by deteriorating behavior. Six months after hospital discharge, 12 of the original 48 patients had died: Ten of these 12 were in the behavior-disturbance group.

Garrity and Klein examined their data further and learned that the patients with negative behavior adjustments tended to be those who had experienced previous heart trouble. Thus, while it is apparent that attitudes and behavioral adaptations toward illness may be predictive of outcome, when more is learned, these may only turn out to be secondary concomitants of more direct predictors.

SOCIAL FACTORS

It was just seen how psychological factors function in relation to physiological and medical ones to affect survival. Now it will be seen how social practices affect survival, sometimes in relation to factors of personality and health.

Activity and Health

The most obvious and most persistent finding in longevity research is the importance of good health and physical functioning. In study after study, sometimes by itself, sometimes in conjunction with other factors, it is the major one affecting longevity. Thus, for example, Palmore (1969, p. 107) wrote, in describing a multi-disciplinary longitudinal study: "(a) actuarial life expectancy at initial testing, (b) physical functioning, (c) work satisfaction, and (d) performance intelligence were the four best predictors of longevity."

Three factors keep recurring as especially related to the maintenance of health and long life. Obesity and cigarette smoking are two of them; these were discussed in the previous chapter. The third is activity and exercise. In some studies, activity looms particularly important. Palmore (1971) attempted to determine from the data of the longitudinal study which of these three practices was most associated with longevity. He concluded that activity might be. One problem with such an analysis, however, is that the activity may be more a function of good health than a factor responsible for it.

Activity was seen as important to longevity in another study. Bartko, Patterson, and Butler (1971, p. 135) reported the results of an 11-year follow-up of a multi-disciplinary longitudinal study, different from most others in that, at the start, the elderly men studied were in extraordinarily good health. There were very many measurements, but two "correctly classified about 80 percent of both survivors and nonsurvivors." The activity was assessed on the basis of a five-point scale ranging from a few routine chores to many activities of a structured, planned, and self-initiated type. Here again, however, good health may have led to the activity rather than have resulted from it.

In yet another study, one designed to understand more fully the problems of coronary heart disease, the role of activity was again very clear: ". . . sedentary males were more susceptible to lethal episodes of coronary heart disease . . . than were physically active males. . . . The association between sedentary living habits and . . . mortality is also revealed using various other possible indicators of physical activity status . . . a weak hand grip, a low vital capacity, those overweight . . ." (Kannel, 1971, p. 62).

Work and Work Satisfaction

It was seen in Palmore's (1969) study that four indicators of longevity were especially important; one of these was work satisfaction. The total sample of men and women in this study ranged in age from 60 to 94, but when only men aged 60-69 were examined, work satisfaction was found to be the best predictor of longevity, "even better than life expectancy." The relationship between work satisfaction and longevity was seen also by Rose (1964). He examined the data of a very old population which ranged in age from 72 to 92, with more than half being 80-84 years. It is extraordinary that only 21 percent of these people were not working at least part time. Rose (1964, p. 35) believed that "this evidence of a refusal to 'disengage' became even more remarkable when no relationship was found between current income and age of complete cessation from work." The implication, but not the observed fact, is that aged people who are satisfied with their work and who maintain useful roles live longer than those who do not. Again, however, as with activity and exercise, it may well be that it is the healthier people who work and enjoy it. The less healthy don't work and perhaps can't enjoy it. It may be poor health, rather than dissatisfaction with the work, which makes for earlier death.

Education and Economic Status

It probably is no surprise to learn that high socioeconomic status predisposes one to longer life. Several investigators, e.g., Rose (1964) and Pfeiffer (1970), demonstrated that high education levels, high status occupations, high intelligence, all go together and make for favorable longevities. Lower status roles are associated with poor housing, poor nutrition, poor sanitation, and a host of other factors important to health and long life.

Family Relations

There are data suggesting that loss of a close, loved one can make for stress sufficient to cause the death of some older people. The notion of stress is central to what has become known as psychosomatic medicine; the thinking is that stress, such as that resulting from relocation or from bereavement due to the loss of a spouse, has organic consequences that are particularly damaging to those elderly of diminished physiological reserves.

Rowland (1977) reviewed the literature bearing on death among the elderly that may be linked to the death of spouse or some other close person. In all there were less than a dozen such studies, several of them being unclear as to whether it was bereavement that made the difference, or whether it was the poor health of the surviving member. For example, it has been speculated that the survivor who is sick and who had been cared for by the deceased spouse is particularly vulnerable when left alone without this care. This speculation suggests that it is the loss of nursing-care type of attention, not stress due to bereavement, that is associated with the death of the survivor.

The data are ambiguous but Rowland (1977, p. 356) suggested: " . . . for some people, especially males, the loss of a significant other may be detrimental. The risk of death is highest during the first year of bereavement."

Most data point to bachelorhood or spinsterhood as a negative factor in survival later in life. Not all data point to this, but many do. Rose (1964) concluded that the maintenance of a "with spouse" status provides physical and emotional support which may be crucial in survival. Pfeiffer's (1970) data indicated that only for women is the "never married" status associated negatively with longevity. However, these latter data are based on too few subjects to make reliable generalizations about men.

Another dimension of family which may relate to longevity is the number of children—fewer children make for longer life for the parents (Rose, 1964). If this be true, the mechanism, as suggested by Rose, is that fewer children limit the economic and emotional stress placed upon the parent. The smaller number of children may also be related to higher socioeconomic status, which, in turn, is related to longevity.

The Whole Man

Pfeiffer (1970, p. 273) sums it up this way:

> Persons with high intelligence, sound financial status, well maintained health, and intact marriages may be expected to live significantly longer than their less intelligent and poorer brothers and sisters whose health is also declining and whose marriages are no longer intact.

Pfeiffer is not optimistic about what may be done to improve the conditions associated with short life. Such pessimism may not be warranted —improved educational opportunities, greater financial help, better medical services, marriage counseling, and organized opportunities for remarriage may go a long way in helping to reduce the differences in life-span between long- and short-lived brothers and sisters.

SUMMARY

A body of behavioral data has been accumulating which appears useful in the prediction of physical decline and death of elderly people. The data include both cognitive and personality factors, and emphasize both the level of present functioning and the decline from prior levels. The ability to predict decline and death is of such obvious importance that it hardly needs comment; what is needed, however, is more research to develop greater precision of the predictors, and intervention procedures to minimize impending tragedies.

It was found in several studies that, when elderly people were tested for cognitive ability on two or more occasions over a period of years, decrement during this time was associated with decreased survival potential. This change for the worse in test performances has been labeled "terminal drop." Very poor performance during the initial testing has also been found to be an omen of impending death; in these studies, the "terminal drop" may have already occurred by the first test period.

While studies carried out thus far hold much promise for the prediction of death and survival, we must place only a limited faith in them at this time. To warrant confidence in the predictors, it is necessary to carry out prospective investigations, not only the retrospective ones that have been conducted so far. It is necessary to test people, then to make predictions of death and survival, and then to let time tell the correctness of the predictions. The retrospective studies have sought for the predictors after death occurred. The retrospective studies constitute but a first step; it is a most promising first step, but it is only the beginning.

Among the findings of most of these studies is the disquieting information that elderly people admitted to old people's homes and other types of institutions experience a high death rate during the first year of relocation and, particularly, during the first three months. While this is ominous in many ways, the phenomenon may simply be a reflection of the fact that many people requiring institutionalization tend to be in very poor health and die as a result of this, rather than of the stress of relocation itself. This distinction warrants further investigation; too few studies have been carried out to answer the important questions. One datum is very clear, however. Older adults in normal good health who of their own accord relocate to desirable noninstitutional residences, are not harmed by the move; in fact, they may be benefited.

Satisfactory adjustment in an institutional residence has been seen as a good omen for surviving a move to a new residence. An angry—even hostile—attitude has been seen to have survival value. Depressive affect, on the other hand, may be a poor omen for survival. When depression is severe in later life, suicide is a distinct possibility, especially for the white male; feelings of inferiority and loss of self-esteem seem to underlie this. A lessened ability to cope with environmental demands, i.e., a lowered ability to organize and integrate information in the personal and social world, also seems predictive of impending death.

When all is said and done, however, it is poor physical health and organic brain disease which are the major killers, at least of the institutionalized aged. Long life is seen associated with exercise and activity and satisfaction in work. But, just as poor health may be the basis of the death in relocation, good health may underlie the exercise and work associated with long life.

Socioeconomic factors, not surprisingly, are predisposing to long life. The prescription for long life is good health habits, intact marriage, and sound financial status with the good housing, sanitation, nutrition, and education that go with it.

REFERENCES

Aldrich, C.K. Personality factors and mortality in the relocation of the aged. *Gerontologist*, 1964, *4*, 92–93.

Aldrich, C.K., and Mendkoff, E. Relocation of the aged and disabled, a mortality study. *Journal of American Geriatrics Society*, 1963, *11*, 185–194.

Baltes, P.B., Schaie, K.W., and Nardi, A.H. Age and experimental mortality in a seven-year longitudinal study of cognitive behavior. *Developmental Psychology*, 1971, *5*, 18–26.

Bartko, J.J., Patterson, R.D., and Butler, R.N. Biomedical and behavioral predictors of survival among normal aged men: A multivariate analysis. In E. Palmore and F.C. Jeffers (Eds.), *Prediction of life span*. Lexington, Mass.: D.C. Heath Co., 1971, pp. 123–137.

Berkowitz, B. Changes in intellect with age: IV. Changes in achievement and survival in older people. *Journal of Genetic Psychology*, 1965, *107*, 3–14.

Blenkner, M. Environmental change and the aging individual. *Gerontologist*, 1967, *7*, Part 1, 101–105.

Botwinick, J. *Cognitive processes in maturity and old age*. New York: Springer Publishing Co., 1967.

Carp, F.M. *A future for the aged*. Austin, Texas: Univ. of Texas Press, 1966.

Carp, F.M. Long-range satisfaction with housing. *Gerontologist*, 1975, *15* (No. 1, Part 1), 68–72.

Garrity, T., and Klein, R.F. A behavioral predictor of survival among heart attack patients. In E. Palmore and F.C. Jeffers (Eds.), *Prediction of life span*. Lexington, Mass.: D.C. Heath Co., 1971, pp. 215–222.

Goldfarb, A.I. Predicting mortality in the institutionalized aged, a seven-year follow-up. *Archives of General Psychiatry*, 1969, *21*, 172–176.

Goldfarb, A.I., Fisch, M., and Gerber, I. Predictors of mortality in the institutionalized aged. *Diseases of the Nervous System*, 1966, *27*, 21–29.

Gutman, G.M., and Herbert, C.P. Mortality rates among relocated extended-care patients. *Journal of Gerontology*, 1976, *31*, 352–357.

Gutmann, D. Dependency, illness and survival among Navajo men. In E. Palmore and F.C. Jeffers (Eds.), *Prediction of life span*. Lexington, Mass.: D.C. Heath Co., 1971, pp. 181–198.

Jarvik, L.F., and Blum, J.E. Cognitive declines as predictors of mortality in twin pairs: A twenty-year longitudinal study of aging. In E. Palmore and F. C. Jeffers (Eds.), *Prediction of life span*. Lexington, Mass.: D.C. Heath Co., 1971, pp. 199–211.

Jarvik, L.F., and Falek, A. Intellectual stability and survival in the aged. *Journal of Gerontology*, 1963, *18*, 173–176.

Kannel, W.B. Habits and heart disease mortality. In E. Palmore and F.C. Jeffers (Eds.), *Prediction of life span*. Lexington, Mass.: D.C. Heath Co., 1971, pp. 61–69.

Kleemeier, R.W. *Intellectual change in the senium, or death and the I.Q.* Presidential Address, American Psychological Association, 1961 (Mimeograph).

Kleemeier, R.W. Intellectual change in the senium. *Proceedings of the Social Statistics Section of the American Statistical Association*, 1962, pp. 290–295.

Lawton, M.P., and Yaffe, S. Mortality, morbidity and voluntary change of residence by older people. *Journal of American Geriatrics Society*, 1970, *18*, 823–831.

Lieberman, M.A. Psychological correlates of impending death: Some preliminary observations. *Journal of Gerontology*, 1965, *20*, 181–190.

Lieberman, M.A. Symposium—Long-term care: research, policy, and practice. *Gerontologist*, 1974, *14*, 494–501.

Miller, D., and Lieberman, M.A. The relationship of affect state and adaptive capacity to reactions to stress. *Journal of Gerontology*, 1965, *20*, 492–497.

Palmore, E. Physical, mental and social factors in predicting longevity. *Gerontologist*, 1969, *9*, 103–108.

Palmore, E. Health practices, illness, and longevity. In E. Palmore and F.C. Jeffers (Eds.), *Prediction of life span*. Lexington, Mass.: D.C. Heath Co., 1971, pp. 71–77.

Palmore, E., and Cleveland, W. Aging, terminal decline, and terminal drop. *Journal of Gerontology*, 1976, *31*, 76–81.

Palmore, E., and Jeffers, F.C. (Eds.). *Prediction of life span*. Lexington, Mass.: D.C. Heath Co., 1971.

Pfeiffer, E. Survival in old age: Physical, psychological and social correlates of longevity. *Journal of the American Geriatrics Society*, 1970, *18*, 273–285.

Riegel, K.F. The prediction of death and longevity in longitudinal research. In E. Palmore and F.C. Jeffers (Eds.), *Prediction of life span*. Lexington, Mass.: D.C. Heath Co., 1971, pp. 139–152.

Riegel, K.F., Riegel, R.M., and Meyer, G. A study of the dropout rates in longitudinal research on aging and the prediction of death. *Journal of Personality and Social Psychology*, 1967, *5*, 342–348.

Rose, C.L. Social factors in longevity. *Gerontologist*, 1964, *4*, 27–37.

Rowland, K.F. Environmental events predicting death for the elderly. *Psychological Bulletin*, 1977, *84*, 349–372.

Siegler, I.C. The terminal drop hypothesis: fact or artifact? *Experimental Aging Research*, 1975, *1*, 169–185.

Storandt, M., and Wittels, I. Maintenance of function in relocation of community-dwelling older adults. *Journal of Gerontology*, 1975, *30*, 608–612.

Turner, B.F., Tobin, S.S., and Lieberman, M.A. Personality traits as predictors of institutional adaptation among the aged. *Journal of Gerontology*, 1972, *27*, 61–68.

United States Department of Health, Education and Welfare. *Suicide in the United States 1950-1964*. Washington, D.C.: National Center for Health Statistics, Series 20, Number 5, 1967.

Wittels, I., and Botwinick, J. Survival in relocation. *Journal of Gerontology*, 1974, *29*, 440–443.

Zung, W.W.K. Depression in the normal aged. *Psychosomatics*, 1967, *8*, 287–292.

4

Sexuality and
Sexual Relations

In the previous chapter it was seen that among the factors related positively to long life is intact marriage. Unfortunately, intact marriage becomes progressively less possible with increasing age, due to illness and/or death of the spouse. There are many dimensions to marriages which may not be intact, a most obvious one being sexual gratification. The present chapter deals with this dimension.

There was a time, not very many years ago, when public discussion and the written record of research on sexual relations between men and women had to be indirectly and delicately expressed. It is difficult to envision now the stir that was made in 1948 when Kinsey and his collaborators reported their findings on sexual behavior of men (Kinsey, Pomeroy, and Martin, 1948), and even as late as 1953 when findings about women were reported (Kinsey, Pomeroy, Martin, and Gebhard, 1953). The work of Masters and Johnson (1966), much more detailed with respect to sexual anatomy and physiological functioning and based much more upon laboratory participation than the earlier Kinsey reports, and the book by Rubin (1965), *Sexual Life after Sixty*, providing a much wider scope of information regarding very intimate details of sexual acts and problems, did not have nearly the social shock value of the earlier Kinsey works. College students today seem surprised to learn how revolutionary direct sexual questions in scientific investigation were so brief a period ago.

We have thus entered a period of relative freedom regarding inquiry into sexual relations, and it becomes possible to obtain new information. With regard to aged respondents, however, restriction is still the rule and difficulty in obtaining information remains. First, investigators tend to be either uninterested in the sexuality of older people, or they are uncomfortable with this concept. Accordingly, they often exclude the elderly from their focus of investigation. Second, older people, having been reared in earlier eras when open and frank discussion of sexual life was taboo often require special circumstances to be open and candid. Even when elderly people volunteer to participate as subjects in research projects on sexual behavior, their relatives often become upset and insist that they withdraw from the study (Pfeiffer, 1969, p. 152). It is not surprising, therefore, that most all the data on sexuality in later life are based on relatively small sample sizes and on low subject selection rates. For example, in the study of Masters and Johnson, 157 women of the age range 51 to 78 years were interviewed, but only 34 were selected for study, i.e., 22 percent. Of these, only eight were aged 61 to 70 years and three 71 to 78 years. In comparison, 75 percent of women aged 21 to 50 years who were interviewed were selected for study, with their total number being ten times greater than those aged 51 to 78 years. This sampling problem was not essentially different for men. It is largely for this reason, it would seem, that so much of the existing literature, especially the earlier reports, are of a clinical nature (e.g., see chapter 3 of Rubin, 1965).

There is another reason why objective and valid sexual information is difficult to obtain in regard to the elderly, especially men. Some elderly male respondents have been known to deny their disinterest or inability in sexual intercourse and have reported feats of virility instead. While this is not so frequent a factor as to negate interview methods, it is sufficiently important to warrant cross-validation by interview with spouses.

THE MYTH OF THE SEXLESS AGED

Rubin (1965, p. 3) emphasized what he calls "a dangerous myth" by highlighting it immediately in a first chapter. "All of us," he said, "have been accustomed to associate sex and love exclusively with youth. Sexual activity of any kind on the part of older persons is rarely referred to except in derogatory terms. According to our folklore, what is 'virility' at twenty-five becomes 'lechery' at sixty-five."

There are two prevailing beliefs—both wrong, both myths: One, sexuality is not typically characteristic of old people. Two, it is wrong or sinful when sexuality persists into later life. The fact is, of course, that sexuality is a characteristic of old people as well as of young people, and this is neither unusual nor immoral. What is immoral is the perpetuation of these myths and the organized restraints sometimes placed upon the aged. Perpetuation of this myth is dangerous, Rubin (1965) maintains, because the expectation that desire and ability will no longer be present at a particular age becomes "a self-fulfilling prophecy." Sex functioning is so much a matter of attitude and belief that such expectation may make the myth come true. The stereotype may make elderly men and women uncomfortable, even guilty, in their sexuality, rather than pleased that they are normal and able to enjoy this aspect of their being.

Many younger people are intolerant and uncomfortable with the idea that the aged have sexual interests and needs. Such intolerance often includes professional people who should know better. This takes a particularly inhumane form when such attitudes are held by people who have responsibilities for planning and supervision. "Many state hospitals, nursing homes, and homes for the aged practice segregation of the sexes or else permit men and women, even husbands and wives, to spend time with each other only in public dayrooms or under 'supervision'" (Pfeiffer, 1969, p. 161). These practices do more than simply ignore the sexual needs of the elderly; they negate the dignity of old people and their very existence as human beings.

SEXUAL WANING
Male Sexuality

There is no question that the human male's sexual responsiveness wanes as he ages. In fact, "In the sexual history of the male, there is no other single factor which affects frequency of outlet as much as age. . . . Age is so important that its effects are usually evident, whatever the mental status, the educational level, the religious background, or the other factors which enter the picture" (Kinsey et al., 1948, pp. 218–219).

A significant characteristic of this sexual waning, however, is its gradualness. The age of maximum sexuality, according to Kinsey et al., is in the teens and sexuality then drops almost linearly until age 60, at least. Until age 60, therefore, the drop from one age to another is of about the same magnitude as the drop between any other comparable age spans. This may be seen clearly in Figure 4.1. Kinsey et al. analyzed the sexual behavior of the human male in terms of six sources of orgasm, sources such as sexual intercourse, masturbation, and nocturnal emission. The total of these six sources was called "total sexual outlet." Figure 4.1 presents the Kinsey data in terms of the median number of orgasms per week from all sources, and from marital intercourse. In general, the aging pattern seen in Figure 4.1 was seen also for each of the six sources of outlet.

Kinsey et al. also had data on men over the age of 60, but the

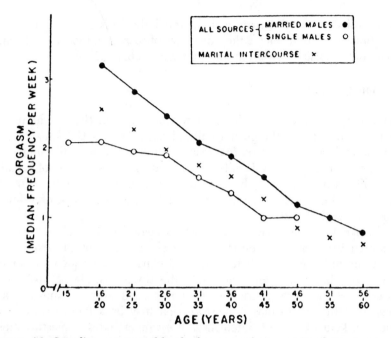

FIGURE 4.1: Sexuality, as measured by the frequency of orgasms, in relation to age of the human male. Figure from Botwinick, J. in J. E. Birren (Ed.), *Handbook of aging and the individual*. Copyright 1959 by the University of Chicago. Original data may be seen in Kinsey et al., 1948, pp. 226 and 252, Tables 45 and 46.

number of cases was judged too few to subject them to thorough analyses. The most important generalization from the data of the older men is that the pattern of gradually diminishing activity which started with 16-year-olds seems to continue. But even in the oldest age groups, many men continue to have sexual lives. At 60 years of age, 95 percent of Kinsey's male subjects were still active sexually, and at age 70, nearly 70 percent were active. The number of subjects older than 70 was too few to judge confidently, but the indication was of a continued drop.

In addition to a waning of sexual activity, there is also a change in the specific phases of the sexual cycle. According to Masters and Johnson (1966, p. 248), with age, particularly after age 60, there is a slowing of erection, of mounting, and of ejaculation. There is an increase in the time after orgasm in which the male is once again ready for ejaculation. "The psychosexual pleasure of the ejaculatory process may be impaired." In the ejaculatory process "the young male . . . is aware not only of the force of the explosive contractions but also of the localized sensation of fluid emission . . . the aging male, particularly if his erection has been long maintained, may have the experience of seepage rather than of seminal fluid expulsion" (Masters and Johnson, 1966, p. 259).

Female Sexuality

The study of female sexuality is more complex than that of the male, not only because of the greater cultural restriction on the female than on the male and, therefore, the greater inhibition of sexuality, but also because of the greater difficulty assessing it. The assessment of female sexuality is more difficult because, while the male rarely fails to reach orgasm in his sexual activities, much of the sexual activity of women does not result in orgasm.

Unlike the male, who clearly ages sexually, Kinsey et al. (1953) reported that there is little evidence of sexual aging of the female, at least, not until late life. There is an age decline in the frequency of marital coitus, but this is due mostly to the sexual waning of husbands. Because of the social restrictions on nonmarried women, Kinsey et al. suggested that frequency of masturbation may be a more appropriate index of sexuality than is intercourse. For women, rates of masturbation decline only slightly with age.

Despite Kinsey's data, there is reason to believe that there is a sexual waning in women as well as in men, but that it appears later in life. With respect to masturbation, Masters and Johnson (1966, p. 246) wrote, "As might be expected, there is a reduction in the frequency with which manipulative relief is deemed necessary beyond 60 years of age." Another bit of evidence of female sexual aging may be seen in a report by Pfeiffer (1969): In a group of women aged 60 to 94 years, only about a third acknowledged continued sexual interests. Perhaps the clearest data bearing on female sexuality during later periods of life were reported by Christenson and Gagnon (1965). These investigators culled their data from the case history files of the Kinsey laboratory.

The 1953 Kinsey report rarely involved women beyond the age of 60; Christenson and Gagnon directed their attention to the data on women aged 50 to 70, who either were married at the time of the interview or had been married. As may be seen in Table 4.1, they categorized the results of five age groups: 50, 55, 60, 65, and 70 years, keeping separate the data of married and "post-married" women. This table shows that 87.5 percent of the married women aged 50 were having sexual intercourse, but that by age 65, only 50 percent were having intercourse. Since this could be attributed to the sexual waning of their spouses, it might be more meaningful to refer to the incidence of women mastur-

TABLE 4.1
Indices of Sexuality of Married and "Post-Married" Women

	AGE (YEARS)									
	50		55		60		65		70	
	Inci-dence %	Median Frequency Per Year	Inci-dence %	Median Frequency Per Year	Inci-dence %	Median Frequency Per Year	Inci-dence %	Median Frequency Per Year	Inci-dence %	Median Frequency Per Year
Marital Activities										
Coitus	87.5	69.4	89.2	57.9	69.7	40.7	50.0	—*	—	—
Masturbation	31.2	13.3	29.7	3.7	27.3	—	25.0	—	—	—
Sex dreams	27.0	3.1	26.0	3.0	18.2	—	18.8	—	—	—
N	160		74		33		16		3	
Post-marital Activities										
Coitus	37.0	44.8	29.3	27.2	12.5	—	0.0	—	0.0	—
Masturbation	58.8	15.0	46.6	11.3	43.8	8.0	33.3	—	25.0	—
Sex dreams	34.6	8.6	27.6	4.0	18.8	—	11.1	—	16.7	—
N	81		58		32		18		12	

* Number of cases is less than ten.
This table from C.V. Christenson and J.H. Gagnon. Sexual behavior in a group of older women. *Journal of Gerontology*, 1965, 20, p. 352. Used with permission.

bating and having dreams of orgasm together with the indices of coitus. The contention that women who are deprived of coitus resort to masturbation receives support in Table 4.1. In the comparison of masturbation rates between married and "post-married" women, Table 4.1 shows that the latter masturbated at nearly twice the rate of the former.

In the married group, only a slight diminution with age in the incidence of masturbation and sex dreams was found, but when this incidence is added to the diminution in the incidence of coital activity, a sexual waning in women is indicated. The data of frequency of sexual outlet showed trends similar to those of incidence. It may be seen in the table, for example, that, of the 87.5 percent of the women engaging in coitus, their median yearly rate was 69.4—slightly more than once a week. Of the 69.7 percent of married women aged 60 years engaged in coital activity, their median yearly rate was 40.7, or less than once a week. Post-married women, often with less access to heterosexual outlet, experienced much less sexual activity than their married counterparts. However, Table 4.1 shows that they too showed signs of sexual aging.

Relative Sexual Patterns of the Two Sexes

The pattern of decline for men is gradual, with no age period marking a greater point of diminution than any other age period. The pattern for women is such that there is little, if any, decline in sexuality until age 60, but, from that point on, there are indications of decline also. In both sexes, however, the diminished sexuality is more in terms of frequency and vigor than it is of kind. For a large number of elderly men and women, sexual relations end only with death.

While the decline with age in sexuality is more apparent in men than in women, the sexual activities of men, for various reasons, are more frequent than those of women throughout most of their lives. For example, Kinsey et al. (1953, p. 173) reported that masturbation rates for unmarried women ranging in age from the teens to the fifties were approximately 0.3 to 0.4 a week. The comparative data for men were 0.4 to 1.8 a week. Similarly, a comparison of data of total sexual outlet for men (Kinsey et al., 1948, p. 226) and for women (1953, p. 549) shows a greater frequency of orgasms for men. Even among those married, the frequency is greater for men: From 3.2 per week for men aged 16 to 20 years to 0.8 for men aged 56 to 60, versus from 2.2 for women aged 16 to 20 years to 0.5 for women 56 to 60 years.

Given the double standard, it is not surprising that men are more active sexually than women; this might be expected even with an assumption that the two sexes are equal in psychobiological sexuality.

With the known age decline in men and the relatively slight decline in women, are older men also more active sexually than older women? There are few studies comparing men and women at advanced ages. The data of Kinsey et al. (1953, p. 716), which include groups only to age 60, show that the relatively rapid decline of the male brings him to a level of activity only slightly higher than that of the female. If we extrapolate the Kinsey curves, a very dubious practice, a point would be reached, at about age 70, when both sexes would seem very similar in the frequency of attaining orgasms.

Other conclusions were suggested in two later studies but these, as will be seen, also leave uncertainty. Psychiatrists interviewed many people aged 60 years and older and interviewed them again over the next decade (Verwoerdt, Pfeiffer, and Wang, 1969). So many of the people interviewed dropped out of the study for one reason or another that the results might be unique to those people remaining, rather than representative of people in general. The investigators concluded that sexuality, at least declared interest in heterosexual coitus, decreased with age past 60 but, nevertheless, men remained more sexual in this sense than women.

Similar conclusions were drawn by Cameron and Biber (1973) who did not investigate sexual performance at all but instead investigated sexuality as manifested in thought. In various situations they interrupted people of wide age range to ask them what they were thinking about during the previous five minutes. Here, any sexual thought was tabulated, not only those associated directly with orgasm or coitus. It was noted that the incidence of sex thoughts decreased with age, this being so with both sexes. In all age groups, however, including the oldest one of 65–99 years, men reported a higher frequency of sex thoughts "crossing their minds" than did women. The women may have been more inhibited in declaring sexual interests and sexual thoughts than the men, particularly the older women. More direct measures of sexuality are necessary for unequivocal conclusions regarding differences between men and women.

At all adult ages the most frequent sexual expression for most people, and certainly for elderly people, is sexual intercourse between husbands and wives. Christenson and Gagnon (1965, p. 355) hypothesized that, "Unless the wife is unusually aggressive in sexual matters in marriage, it is probably a general rule that she sets the upper limit on coital activity and that the husband probably sets the lower limit." With this hypothesis in mind, they carried out an interesting investigation.

Wives aged 50, 55, and 60 were divided into three groups—one group where the wife was older, one where she was younger, and one where she was the same age as her husband. The wives with younger husbands tended to have the most active sex lives, and those with older husbands the least active. This was true both for the incidence and frequency of sexual relations. However, of wives aged 50 and 55 engaging in sexual intercourse with their husbands, those with husbands of the same age experienced more orgasms than those with husbands either older or younger than they. "Thus, in the present data, at least, it seems that physical sexual fulfillment for the wife at these ages is either directly or indirectly related to the age of the husband" (Christenson and Gagnon, 1965, pp. 355–356).

LIMITING FACTORS IN SEXUAL FULFILLMENT

There are a variety of reasons why older people find their sex experiences less than satisfactory. It was already seen, for example, that false notions regarding sexuality in later life may be debilitating when the later years finally come. It was also seen that there is a sexual waning. While not all the limiting factors are amenable to personal and social modification, many are. Those limiting factors that can be modified should be clear to everyone. For "when so often men face the loss of their customary prestige and self-confidence and begin to feel old"; when after menopause women so often begin to question their desirability, "the continuation of sexual relations enhances the . . . feeling of being needed and of being capable of receiving love and affection . . ." (Frank, 1961, pp. 177–178, from Rubin, 1965, p. 11).

More Elderly Women than Men

Women outlive men; in the over-65 age group there are fewer men than women. As seen in chapter 2, which deals with biological and environmental factors in longevity, it does not appear reasonable to attribute this sex difference in longevity to social or cultural factors; rather, it seems to be the biological fate of women to live longer than men. In 1964, for example, the average life expectancy at birth for white males was approximately 68 years; for females the expectation of life was about 75 years—a seven-year difference (Riley and Foner, 1968, p. 28).

More often than not, men marry women who are younger than themselves. Thus, the combination of longer life and earlier marriages make widowhood a more common occurrence than widowerhood. A severe limitation to a satisfactory sex life for many women is this simple fact of widowhood. Approximately 44 percent of women between the ages of 65 and 74 are widows; only about 14 percent of men in this age bracket are widowers. Of those over 75 years of age, 72 percent are widows and 38 percent are widowers (U.S. Census, 1960).

The problem for widows is exacerbated by the fact that they find it more difficult to remarry than do men; they are more likely to remain alone. From the perspective of sexual relations, these facts become even more stark when one considers both the earlier decline in male sexuality and the greater extent of it. One study has indicated that when sexual intercourse was stopped, it was at an age nearly a decade earlier for women than for men. The frequent reason for stopping, in addition to widowhood, was a lack of interest on the part of the men (Pfeiffer, Verwoerdt, and Wang, 1968).

It is seen, then, that for many older women sexual intercourse in the context of married life is difficult or impossible. It is for this reason that Rubin (1965, p. 223) emphasized that masturbation can be an appropriate outlet. "A strategy for living in the older years must take into account . . . those who are single or widowed and who have no other opportunity for sexual release than masturbation." Counselors and physicians should make it clear to their clients and patients that there is nothing wrong and nothing to worry about in this autoerotic practice.

Psychological Factors

The Aging Male. Masters and Johnson (1966, p. 262) reported that an important factor in the sexuality of older men is the "sociosexual environment within which a male lives during his sexually formative years." When the male is stimulated to a high level of sexual expression during his early years, his middle-age and older years are usually characterized by maintained sexuality. This view that high rates of sexual activity early in life are correlated with high rates in later life was noted also in a study by Newman and Nichols (1960), who had elderly people rate themselves on the relative strength of their sexual drives during youth and during old age. The data of the Kinsey studies (1948) also support this view. From none of these studies, however, is it possible to ascertain whether the high levels of sexual expression in youth are due primarily to social learning factors, as the above quote from Masters and Johnson could suggest, or whether the same vigorous biological system serves one in old age as in youth. What can be ascertained, and what is most relevant here, is that a high rate of sexual responding in earlier life does not result in a sexual depletion, in a sexual wearing out later in life. Perhaps just the opposite is the case; Masters and Johnson (1966, p. 262) indicated that "the most important factor in the maintenance of sexuality for the aging male is consistency of active sexual expression."

In addition to the factors of infrequency and inconsistency in limiting sexual responsiveness in later life, Masters and Johnson discussed six other factors. One of these, health, will be considered in a later section; the other factors are: concern with career and economic pursuits, fatigue, overindulgence in food or drink, fear of failure, and boredom.

Most men in middle adulthood find themselves at the height of their economic needs and responsibilities. Many of these men are also in the prime of their careers with many demands on their time and energy. These economic and career pressures, particularly when adverse, tend to decrease sexual interest. According to Masters and Johnson, it is mental fatigue, more commonly than physical fatigue, that affects sexual behavior. While excessive physical fatigue from work and recreation does inhibit sexuality, it is the mental strain of work that is more accountable for reduced sexuality in marriage.

Overindulgence in food—and, more importantly, alcohol—also represses sexuality. Secondary impotence is a common result of the use of alcohol, and when an older man is traumatized by this experience, he often fails to associate the impotence with the drink. This enhances self-doubt and makes for a fear of failure.

Excessive drinking only exacerbates the fear of failure; the fear is often present without alcohol.

> There is no way to overemphasize the importance that the factor "fear of failure" plays in the aging male's withdrawal from sexual performance . . . many males withdraw voluntarily from any coital activity rather than face the ego-shattering experience of repeated episodes of sexual inadequacy (Masters and Johnson, 1966, pp. 269–270).

While some aging males withdraw in the face of their fears, others seek out new sex partners to "prove" themselves. Still others, of course, seek out new sex partners for reasons other than fear of failure. A most common reason is the excitement that often comes with novelty, an excitement which may stimulate the lagging sex drive. Kinsey et al. (1948, pp. 227–229) were clear in indicating that decline in male sexuality results partly from "a loss of interest in repetition of the same sort of experience, an exhaustion of the possibilities for exploring new techniques. . . ." Masters and Johnson (1966, pp. 264–265), in a similar view, reported that "the female partner may lose her stimulative effect as her every wish, interest and expression become too well known. . . ."

The diminution of the stimulating effects of the marriage partner is attributable to factors other than the male's boredom or monotony with the repetition of the sexual act. As wives age, their physical appearances may have a negative effect on the potency of their husbands, or they may sexually repel their husbands by slovenly habits which may develop as they grow older.

Where the wife is the basic cause of the impotence, obviously she must be involved in measures to correct it. Sometimes the husband can be induced to accept a change that has occurred as inevitable and make the best of it. In other cases, the wife must take such measures as dietary regulation, plastic surgery, or any step to correct the factor that is inhibiting her husband's potency (Rubin, 1965, p. 146).

Often it is neither the wife's appearance nor her habits that affect the potency of her husband, but simply that she has

lost herself in the demands of the children, in social activities, in an individual career. . . . By their own admission many of the women interviewed no longer showed concern for their husbands (Masters and Johnson, 1966, p. 265).

For the sexually bored, unstimulated, elderly male, philanderous behavior may restore the excitement experienced in more youthful days. However, this excitement is short-lived at best. Kinsey et al. (1948), among others, discussed the temporary rejuvenative effect of a new partner on the male. This effect, it seems, is not limited solely to the human male. It is seen also, for example, in the laboratory with rats as subjects. The "sexual adequacy of senescent rats increased with collective copulation. The number of ejaculations for 25-month-old rats was 2.1 per observation hour during isolated copulation and 3.8 during copulation of three couples in the cages" (Botwinick, 1959, p. 744). Needless to say, for the human male, the excitement of temporary rejuvenation which may come with a new partner can put such new strains on his marriage as to make his excitement of dubious worth.

The Aging Female. While it is clear that, with men, sexual interest and ability gradually diminish with age, there is little or no sexual aging in women until late in life. Even then, sexual expression seems to be diminished more by extrinsic factors than by waning psychobiological sexuality.

Despite this maintained sexuality, women do experience a very clear signal indicating the end of child-bearing potential. This "change of life," the menopause, when menstrual periods cease, means different things to different women, but, for many, it is a depressing, disturbing event. Significantly, women who have already experienced the climacterium tend to have more positive views about the recovery period which follows. These women recognize that there is no great discontinuity to life with the menopause (Neugarten, Wood, Kraines, and Loomis, 1963). "However, there is no doubt that the end of menstruation has important implications for the emotional life of the woman. For many of them, menstruation has been their badge of femininity" (Rubin, 1965, p. 126). It is with the menopause that the myth of sexlessness is most likely to come to bear: The myth that sexual desire is lost, and that sex life comes to an end. Not only is this false, but at this time, greater sexual interest and activity are often displayed. Masters and Johnson (1966, p. 243) concluded that the increase in sexuality often seen in postmenopausal women results from a release from the fear of pregnancy, on one hand, and a neurotic desire to be pregnant again, on the other. "Many a woman develops renewed interest in her husband and in the physical maintenance of her own person and has described a 'second honeymoon' during her early fifties."

The menopause does result in a loss of female hormones and it does produce a variety of physical changes, some important to appearance and, in about 40 percent of women, some changes important to health and comfort (Rubin, 1965, p. 128). Estrogen therapy is now commonplace and relieves many of the negative consequences. While in recent years a plea from some quarters has been heard to be selective and not routine in this therapy, others have emphasized that postmenopausal women, as a group, tend to be too accepting of the negative physical symptoms. These women could receive important help if they would only make their complaints known to their physicians.

Health Factors

Of the six factors emphasized by Masters and Johnson known to limit sexual fulfillment, poor health is one. This factor is increasingly important after age 40, and after age 60 it becomes especially important. "Any physical disability, acute or chronic, may and usually does lower the sexual responsiveness of the involved male" (Masters and Johnson, 1966, p. 268). While any physical disability lowers sexual responsiveness, at least in the male, cardiac problems provide a major concern. Rubin (1965, pp. 199–210) highlighted the clinical literature, some of which follows.

Many people believe that once a heart attack occurs, sexual intercourse is no longer possible. This belief is not true. After a period of recovery, usually lasting several months, most of the coronary patients resume their sexual relations. However, the attack is limiting and caution is recommended. Not only is the severity of the attack a factor in the resumption of sexual behavior, but so are the circumstances and emotional character of the patient. A man and wife who are compatible with each other, whose sexual patterns are very familiar, can achieve sexual intercourse with minimum expenditure of energy and a minimum strain on the heart. For men whose sexual outlets involve the excitement of pursuit, the stimulation of clandestine encounters, the strain on the heart can be severe.

Often an aging man is concerned about his work status; he may be fearful that he will be replaced by a younger man. Or, he is fearful about his impending retirement. If this man is also concerned with diminishing sexuality, he is a potential candidate for a heart attack. It is for this reason that failure in work or career, sexual failure or fear, and coronary problems go hand in hand. Anxiety arising out of sexual problems may precede a heart attack and it may make recovery more difficult.

The tie between cardiovascular problems and sexual activity applies to the female as well as the male. While the male is seen as the more physically active member, both the male and the female have strong pulse rate and blood pressure increases during sexual excitement. It is not just the muscular involvement, it is the emotional involvement which is taxing to the cardiovascular system. The husband may not recognize the cardiac strain a recovering wife experiences because her muscular response may appear minimal to him. It is her feelings and sexual excitement which determine the cardiovascular response, not the body movements.

For people with very severely damaged hearts, any coital behavior, however unexerting, may be contraindicated. Also, in acute phases of a heart attack, sexual intercourse should not be performed. When there are congestive problems at rest or with mild exertion, sexual intercourse should not take place. If no symptoms follow recovery from a heart attack, sexual relations may be resumed in most instances. For the heart patient, moderation, and relaxed or "sedate" coitus are the watchwords; delayed or extended periods of climax are to be avoided. The healthy spouse should cooperate in regard to posture and frequency, and should avoid as much as possible an atmosphere of emotional tension.

SEXUAL AGING IN PERSPECTIVE

Sexual waning is but an aspect of a general psychobiological decline that occurs naturally in later life. Sexual decline is unique only in its relation to psychic tensions centering around concepts of self-worth that have been built up throughout the decades by exaggerated emphases, on one hand, and by taboos, on the other. A large number of domains much more important in day-to-day functioning than sexuality—sensory-perceptual systems, or psychomotor skills, for example—decline in later life, but do not cause the doubts and self-analyses that sexual decline often does. The value and pleasure of surviving function, be it vision or sex, ought to be appreciated and used to the limit of individual prudence.

It is worth repeating: The ability to have and enjoy sexual relations is not limited to youth. In later life, the ability is simply diminished in intensity and in frequency. It is not until very advanced age that many people seem to lose their interest in and capacity for sex. Older people should not attempt heroic feats of sexuality as they should not attempt such feats on the tennis court. But sex in the older years is normal; neither the older person nor those in his social world ought to provide restrictions, be they psychological or physical.

Perhaps an ending statement of Masters and Johnson (1966, p. 270) is a good way to end this section:

> There is every reason to believe that maintained regularity of sexual expression coupled with adequate physical wellbeing and healthy mental orientation to the aging process will combine to provide a sexually stimulative climate within a marriage. . . . This climate will, in turn, improve sexual tension and provide a capacity for sexual performance that frequently may extend to and beyond the 80-year age level.

SUMMARY

There are two common beliefs, both wrong, regarding the aged: One is that sexuality is not characteristic of them, but is only characteristic of the young. The second is that, if sexuality does persist into late life, it is unusual and wrong. Actually, sexuality is common to both old and young, and the only wrong is the perpetuation of these beliefs for they can become self-fulfilling prophecies. The ability to have sexual intercourse and to enjoy it is not lost in the older years; there is, however, a diminution in the vigor and in the frequency of the sexual response. It is not until the very late years that an appreciable number of people show little interest in, and capacity for, sexual relations.

The pattern of sexual waning is different for men than for women. In men, sexuality is maximum in the teens and, from that time on, drops very gradually. For women, sexual waning does not seem to come about until late in life, and when it does, its extent is probably less than in men.

Several important psychosocial factors limit sexual fulfillment in later life. Perhaps the greatest deterrent to sexual fulfillment for women is the simple fact that they outlive men. The average life expectancy at birth is approximately seven years longer for women than for men. Also, women tend to marry men older than themselves. The combination of longer life and earlier marriages makes widowhood a common phenomenon. The problem for widows is exacerbated by the fact that, in addition to being left without marriage partners, they find it more difficult to remarry than do men. These facts become even more stark when one considers the earlier decline in the sexuality of men.

The sexual ability of men is limited by a variety of factors, including the common one of concern with career and economic responsibilities. Most men in middle adulthood find themselves with peak demands on their time and energy. These pressures, especially when adverse, tend to decrease sexual interest. The strain of mental involvement in work is more responsible for reduced sexuality than is physical fatigue.

Self-doubt and fear of failure in sexual intercourse is another limiting factor for men. It makes some men withdraw from sexual experience, but it encourages some to attempt to "prove" themselves with women other than their wives. When proof is found, however, it usually is temporary. The fear of failure often derives from secondary impotence resulting from the inhibiting effects of alcohol, from boredom with the repetitiousness of the marital coitus, and from negative changes in the physical appearance and habits of the wife. Often, the wife loses interest in the husband, immersing herself in her children, social activities, or a new career. This can have the effect of sexually inhibiting her husband.

The woman may experience emotional trauma regarding her sexuality. Despite the fact that her sexual capacities do not decline until late in her life, she does experience the menopause, which, to many women, is a disturbing event. Soon thereafter, however, most women recognize that this causes no great discontinuity to life, and tend to have less negative attitudes.

The key words in the maintenance of sexual ability seem to be: good physical and mental health, and regularity in sexuality activity. The ability to perform sexually may extend to age 80 and beyond.

REFERENCES

Botwinick, J. Drives, expectancies, and emotions. In J.E. Birren (Ed.), *Handbook of aging and the individual.* Chicago: Univ. of Chicago Press, 1959, pp. 739–768.

Cameron, P., and Biber, H. Sexual thought throughout the life-span. *The Gerontologist*, 1973, *13*, 144–147.

Christenson, C.V., and Gagnon, J.H. Sexual behavior in a group of older women. *Journal of Gerontology*, 1965, *20*, 351–356.

Frank, L.K. *The conduct of sex*. New York: William Morrow, 1961.

Kinsey, A.C., Pomeroy, W.B., and Martin, C.E. *Sexual behavior in the human male*. Philadelphia: W.B. Saunders Co., 1948.

Kinsey, A.C., Pomeroy, W.B., Martin, C.E., and Gebhard, P.H. *Sexual behavior in the human female*. Philadelphia: W. B. Saunders Co., 1953.

Masters, W.H., and Johnson, V.E. *Human sexual response*. Boston: Little, Brown and Co., 1966.

Neugarten, B.L., Wood, V., Kraines, R.J., and Loomis, B. Women's attitudes toward the menopause. *Vita Humana*, 1963, *6*, 140–151.

Newman, G., and Nichols, C.R. Sexual activities and attitudes in older persons. *Journal of the American Medical Association*, 1960, *173*, 33–35.

Pfeiffer, E. Sexual behavior in old age. In E. Pfeiffer and E. W. Busse (Eds.), *Behavior and adaptation in late life*. Boston: Little, Brown and Co., 1969.

Pfeiffer, E., Verwoerdt, A., and Wang, H. Sexual behavior in aged men and women. *Archives of General Psychiatry*, 1968, *19*, 753–758.

Riley, M.W., and Foner, A. *Aging and society*. New York: Russell Sage Foundation, 1968.

Rubin, I. *Sexual life after sixty*. New York: Basic Books, 1965.

United States Bureau of the Census, 1960 Census of the Population, Vol. 1, Part 1, pp. 424–425.

Verwoerdt, A., Pfeiffer, E., and Wang, H.S. Sexual behavior in senescence. II. Patterns of change in sexual activity and interest. *Geriatrics*, 1969, *24*, 137–154.

5

Turning Inward

Many older people, perhaps most older people, at some point in their lives direct their attention to themselves and away from others—they grow less responsive to the larger world about them; they narrow their social world. At the same time, the world of people and institutions pushes them out. Events curtail their roles and their functions, and they are often stigmatized in the process. A "swinger" becomes a "dirty old man," a man working hard during his later years of life is "hanging on." This chapter is about this interplay between turning inward and a world which isolates.

To investigate this interplay between psychological and social forces, theories are needed—to give direction for new studies and organization to the existing literature. Unfortunately, most social and personality theories of the aged are those that were developed for young people and applied to old people, providing little benefit to the investigator. Riegel, for example, in 1959, wrote a long chapter called "Personality Theory and Aging" and it included an extensive list of references. In concluding his chapter he wrote, "Up to the present, no theory exists which takes full account of the aging personality" (p. 844).

EGO DEVELOPMENT

A prominent exception to this dearth of theories encompassing old age —an exception that is very often cited—is Erikson's (1963) formulation of ego development. It is possible that these frequent references occur primarily because of the uniqueness of the work in covering the whole life-span, rather than because of its utility as a theory for understanding old age.

Erikson described eight stages of man, each focusing on a need or a crisis. If decisions are made well during one stage, then successful adaptation could be made in the subsequent stage. The first five stages cover life through adolescence. The sixth stage, early adulthood, focuses on the need to give of oneself and to take from someone else, as in marriage. Children, work, and play are part of the intensive interactions typical of this stage. The seventh stage, middle adulthood, focuses on teaching or guiding the next generation. This stage is called "generativity." There is a dependence upon the younger generation in that, without the opportunity or ability to give in this fashion, there is over self-indulgence, an over self-concern, a babying of oneself. This makes for an immature adult. The final stage of development, old age, focuses upon self-acceptance; it is called "ego-integrity." Failure in development through this stage leads to despair, a condition that many people do not escape. Erikson contended that good adjustment in this stage follows only when important matters have been arranged, and when the successes and failures of life have been seen as inevitable. Good adjustment in late life implies a type of fatalism, an acceptance of order in life, where even death is viewed without agony.

Life Review

How are important matters arranged to facilitate successful adjustment during this stage? One of the ways, it is suggested, is by a *Life Review* (Butler and Lewis, 1973, pp. 43–44; Butler, 1975, pp. 412–414). People reminisce, they dwell in the past. For Butler, this is not an idle process; it is purposive, it occurs naturally with everyone so that unresolved conflicts are brought into the focus of attention where they can be resolved. Impending death brings out and highlights the Life Review —it makes the review mandatory, for little time is left to arrange one's matters. Butler indicates that, in mild form, the Life Review is a reminiscence that makes for nostalgia and mild regret. In severe form, anxiety and depression result. This is particularly true for those people who, when young, tended to avoid the present and to emphasize the future. Depression and anxiety are also seen in the Life Review among those who had hurt others. A failure of the Life Review to resolve these conflicts, to arrange these types of important matters, makes self-acceptance difficult; it makes for failure in adjustment often seen during Erikson's eighth and final stage of "ego-integrity."

Related Studies

Not many aging studies have been carried out with Erikson's final stage in mind, but several studies can be related to it. A study by Reichard, Livson, and Peterson (1962), for example, supports at least an aspect of the theory. Reichard et al. interviewed people who were still working (55–66 years of age) and people who were retired (67–72 years), and rated them for a great number of personality traits. Of these, a sample was selected as being high in acceptance of aging and another sample was selected as being low in acceptance of aging. The high group was seen as made up largely of three subgroups, and the low group was composed mostly of two subgroups. The larger of the latter subgroups was termed aggressive; they blamed others for their miseries. The smaller of the two was very much smaller; it was made up of "self-haters." They were full of despair. These seemed to correspond to what Erikson indicated would result without proper resolution of the crises in the final stage of life. However, those who accepted aging did not seem to have the fatalistic quality Erikson implied. These people fell in three subgroups as follows: (1) they seemed to enjoy what they were doing at the moment; (2) they tended to enjoy relaxation and not having to work; or (3) they obliged themselves to keep active as a defense against getting old.

A subsequent study, in some ways similar in purpose and in procedure, was carried out by Neugarten, Crotty, and Tobin (1964). Men and women aged 50 to 90 were interviewed and tested, and rated on many dimensions. Principal-component analyses disclosed six personality types for each sex. Five tended to be similar to those reported by Reichard et al., with the sixth not seeming important, including only a few men. Neugarten et al. correlated these personality types with a rating scale of Life Satisfaction and, not unexpectedly, the better adjusted people were rated higher in life satisfaction.

There have been formulations of developmental sequences other than Erikson's, some assigning more stages to the later periods of life. In the main, however, neither these formulations nor the better-known one of Erikson provided much impetus for research, and thus new information and further theory building.

DISENGAGEMENT

An observation and theory which did provide a basis for much research is "disengagement theory." While the theory is sociological in character, with most of the research which followed the original formulation being carried out by sociologists, there is corroborating evidence from various psychological investigations.

Original Formulation: Withdrawal and Successful Aging

The heart of the theory of disengagement rests on the observation that, in later life, people tend to become withdrawn or dissociated from others and from activity. There is very little controversy regarding this observation—it has been corroborated many times. What was controversial, and what went against the grain of many social and behavioral theorists, was the original emphasis on the role played by the individual in this withdrawal rather than on the role played by the broader society in which the individual lives and works.

Cumming and Henry (1961) interviewed and tested people aged 48 to 68 living in Kansas City, and they did this on five occasions over a period of three years. In addition, they examined people in their 70s and 80s on three occasions. Cumming and Henry believed the withdrawal to have an intrinsic, almost biological, basis. They believed the person becomes more involved with himself and less with people and events in the outside world because of his inner needs, not only because society pushes him in this direction. It was believed that the outward manifestation of social disengagement is primarily a reflection of inner psychological changes.

Even more controversial, however, was the theory's statement that, as a natural or normal process, the disengaged person is the happy person. He is following his inner-directed interests and, if his disengaged behavior is compatible with the values and edicts of society, feelings of satisfaction will be high. Conversely, if he is not permitted to disengage, but is pushed into activity instead, morale and life satisfaction will suffer.

Reformulation: Different Types of Successful Aging

Many studies tested the theory of disengagement, and, as will be seen, the theory was found in need of reformulation. Indeed, the essential prescription—withdrawal for happiness—was attacked and found wanting.

Deprivation. One study in partial support of the original formulation was by Lowenthal and Boler (1965) who examined a great number of people and categorized them on the basis of voluntary disengagement versus involuntary disengagement. The former group was defined as having little social interaction, the latter as being socially deprived (i.e., by retirement, recent widowhood, or physical disabililty). There were two other groups also: not withdrawn-not deprived and not withdrawn-deprived. The involuntary disengagement group had low morale but, supporting the original Cumming and Henry thesis, the voluntarily disengaged people had high morale—nearly as high as the not withdrawn-not deprived group. Lowenthal and Boler (1965, p. 371) concluded, "It is the deprivations themselves rather than consequent changes in social interaction that are decisive."

Activity and Well-Being. As indicated, the original formulation that life satisfaction and high morale go with disengagement has not, in the main, been confirmed; in fact, just the opposite is true, but with important, often overlooked exceptions. For the most part, well-being goes with activity, not disengagement. This suggests that disengagement is neither universally natural nor normal, and it may also suggest that very often withdrawal is imposed from without.

A major contributor to the reformulation was Maddox (1965) who in a series of studies (e.g., Maddox and Eisdorfer, 1962) pointed to important dimensions of disengagement theory. Activity and morale of people aged 60 to 94 years were measured by questionnaires; the activity included physical movement, social contacts with family and friends, participation in organizations, work patterns, and leisure-time pursuits. Morale included feelings about the self, about friends, and notions of personal usefulness and happiness.

In the Maddox-Eisdorfer study, the subjects were divided into two equal groups based on their activity scores—there was thus a "high activity" group and a "low activity" group. Similarly, the subjects were divided into groups of "high morale" and "low morale." This produced four typologies: high in both activity and morale, low in both, and high in one of these and low in the other. Effort was then directed to determining the characteristics of people within the four typologies.

Since the oldest subjects tended to be those who were least high in activity, in poorest health, not working, and in least control of their living situation, an unambiguous analysis of the relationship between activity and morale was precluded. Within this limitation, however, the results were most informative in testing the disengagement theory. Seventy-three percent of the subjects were either high in both activity and morale, or low in both. The original formulation of the disengagement theory would suggest that only a small percent of the subjects, if any, would occupy these categories; from the disengagement theory one would predict that low activity, as an index of disengagement, would be associated with high morale and vice versa. If there were no relationship between activity and morale one way or the other, 25 percent of the people would be expected to fall into each of the four typologies. The actual results thus pointed to a positive relationship between activity and morale, providing evidence counter to disengagement theory. However, evidence also showed that as age increased (from 60 upward), activity may decrease without affecting the satisfaction of living (Maddox, 1965).

Those subjects typed as either "low activity" and "high morale," or vice versa, fell within the expectations of the original disengagement theory. Data were not available to permit a clear-cut differentiation between these subjects and the remaining 73 percent, but Maddox and Eisdorfer suggested that their actual or perceived inability to maintain what they thought were socially expected levels of activity may be what differentiates them from the 73 percent majority. If the activity is beyond capability, the resulting poor performance may well lead to poor morale.

Interpersonal and Non-Interpersonal Activity. Maddox made a distinction between activity which is primarily interpersonal and that which is primarily not. This distinction is crucial because inner, psychic changes must, almost by definition, restrict interpersonal investments, but not necessarily activities which are routine.

Maddox's data suggested that it is in the interpersonal realm, more than in the non-interpersonal, where the greater decline in activity with age occurred. More important, perhaps, was the finding that "the mean satisfaction score was higher among subjects who reported high non-interpersonal and low *interpersonal* activity than among those for whom the relationship between subscores (type of activity) was reversed" (Maddox, 1965, p. 123). Thus, the disengagement notion received confirmation when the data were analyzed in this way. However, Maddox also reported that the total of both types of activity was a somewhat better predictor of satisfaction than either type alone, and much better than when one was high and the other low.

Health and Social Factors. All of the foregoing notwithstanding, it seems that both physical and mental health are very much part of the disengagement picture. Maddox and Eisdorfer found that high morale, whether associated with activity or inactivity, was associated with good health. Conversely, low morale was associated with poorer health regardless of the level of activity. Physical health was defined in terms of physical disability and of self-health estimates. Mental health scores were based on assessments of clinical depression and of personal feelings of usefulness. "Satisfaction was more likely to be high when both physical and mental health states were good than when either was poor" (Maddox, 1965, p. 122).

Social factors were important in the disengagement relationships also. Those subjects who were highest in socioeconomic status and those who experienced a minimum of work-role change were the most likely to report both high activity and high satisfaction. However, neither of the social factors pointed to satisfaction when activity was low.

Personality Types. A compatible picture was developed in the course of a study of Havighurst, Neugarten, and Tobin (1968). As did Maddox, they found life satisfaction to be more related to activity than non-activity, but with many exceptions. These exceptions, they thought, were associated with "personality type, particularly by the extent to which the individual remains able to integrate emotional and rational elements of the personality" (Havighurst et al., 1968, pp. 171–172).

Those people who are satisfied in disengagement are of several types. According to Neugarten, Havighurst, and Tobin (1968), among the most successful are those who are self-directed and interested in the world, but not in personal interactions with people (in Maddox's terms, greater disengagement from interpersonal activities than non-interpersonal). These people have high self-regard, and are content and calm, but they are withdrawn nevertheless. Those who are striving, ambitious, and achievement-oriented, those to whom aging is a threat, fare less well but they may also be content in withdrawal. While they are preoccupied with losses and deficits and shrinking social involvements, they fight against this by closing themselves off. Those who also do relatively well with low activity are people who are passive and dependent. A medium level of activity and satisfaction is possible as long as there are one or two people on whom to lean. Another type of dependent person, one who is especially apathetic and passive, can be moderately satisfied with low activity, but this type was probably always this way and so differs from those who are suddenly in the midst of a late-life disengagement pattern.

The Importance of a Confidant. The theory of disengagement is subject to still another modification—one that appears crucial and one brought to light by Lowenthal and Haven (1968). While not examined in the context of disengagement theory, it matters a great deal, it seems, whether or not there is a confidant on the scene, someone in whom to confide, to talk about oneself and one's problems.

> . . . it is clear that if you have a confidant, you can decrease your social interaction and run no greater risk of becoming depressed than if you had increased it. Further, if you have no confidant, you may increase your social activities and yet be far more likely to be depressed than the individual who has a confidant but has lowered his interaction level. Finally, if you have no confidant and retrench in your social life, the odds for depression become overwhelming. The findings are simi-

lar, though not so dramatic, in regard to change in social role: if you have a confidant, roles can be decreased with no effect on morale; if you do not have a confidant, you are likely to be depressed whether your roles are increased or decreased (though slightly more so if they are decreased). In other words, the presence of an intimate relationship apparently does serve as a buffer against such decrements as loss of role or reduction of social interaction (Lowenthal and Haven, 1968, pp. 26–27).

Thus, it is seen that the disengagement theory provided much impetus for investigation and much has been found out. Even those studies not carried out with disengagement theory foremost in mind, studies such as Lowenthal and Haven's, were seen in broader perspective with the theory. In summary, the disengagement-happiness relationship is dependent upon the age of the person, the health status (both physical and mental), the personality, the social role, the type of activity in which the person engages, and whether or not there is a confidant.

PERSONALITY CHANGES

A voluntary withdrawal from activity stems largely from inner changes —changes which turn the person to himself and away from others. Psychological tests corroborate this turning inward. As Schaie and Marquette (1972) reported, the tests show that, as people become older, they perform in a way as to indicate introversion, seriousness and cautiousness, lessened responsivity, and lower needs for achievement. The tests also show lower heterosexuality and signs of psychopathology.

While many different reports have indicated this, in the main, the changes in adult personality are not marked. In fact, at least one extensive study was concluded with the statement that "personality type was independent of age" (Neugarten et al., 1964, p. 187). However, even if the patterning of personality change is not marked, it seems important, nevertheless. If the patterning could be framed in a single concept, it might be a turning inward while showing a diminished intensity of energy and affect.

Conformist and Passive Patterns

In a study by Neugarten and Gutmann (1958) a picture was presented to men and women in two age groups, a middle-aged one (40–54 years) and an older one (55–70 years). This picture, seen as Figure 5.1,

FIGURE 5.1: A family scene. Figure copyright by the Committee on Human Development, University of Chicago. Reprinted by permission of B.L. Neugarten and the Committee on Human Development.

is of four people: an elderly man and woman and a younger man and woman.

This picture was shown to each subject with the instruction to tell a story about the figures in it; to assign ages to each figure and feelings that each might have for the others. By this procedure, feelings and ideas were thought to be projected by the subjects, thus reflecting inner, psychic dimensions of their personalities.

This type of thematic apperception test (TAT) showed interesting sex-role changes with age and these will be discussed later. Here, it is simply pointed out that the older group—those mainly in their 60s—saw the young male figure as conformist and passive. The younger subjects —those mainly in their 40s—saw the figure as energetic, aggressive, and achieving.

There have been other TAT studies of aging and, as reviewed by Chown (1968), the results were compatible with those of Neugarten and Gutmann. With increasing adult age, there was found decreasing intensity and frequency of emotions, of achievement needs, and of feeling of mastery of the environment. Conformity and self-control were seen to be emphasized with increasing age, while self-indulgence was seen to be deplored. In some ways, this was also seen with the Edwards Personal Preference Schedule, an "objective" questionnaire (see Gavron, 1965; Schaie and Strother, 1968; and Spangler and Thomas, 1962). This schedule also showed the older subjects to be low on heterosexuality. Gavron's study showed this with men but not with women. This result is in accord with the actual findings of sexuality in relation to age. A special chapter is devoted to this (see chapter 4).

Introversion

Chown reviewed studies dealing with tests of introversion-extroversion. The notion of turning inward is perhaps better exemplified by this test dimension than any other. The Maudsley Personality Inventory, given to subjects aged 17–94 years (Gutman, 1966), showed that introversion increased with age, as did a test devised by Heron given to a great number of subjects aged 20–80 years (Heron and Chown, 1967). An examination of the specific correlation coefficients between age and introversion, however, disclosed them to be extremely small, even though they were statistically significant. This shows that, while the tendency for introversion increases as people become older, age alone does not account for it. Evidence for increasing introversion with age was also found with the Cattell 16 Personality Factor (PF) test (Sealy and Cattell, 1965), as it was with the Minnesota Multiphasic Personality Inventory (MMPI) (Calden and Hokanson, 1959; Slater and Scarr, 1964).

Desurgency

In the 16 PF test, there is a scale called "surgency-desurgency" (Factor F). Surgent people are thought to be heedless or happy-go-lucky; they are zestful and enthusiastic. On the other hand, desurgent individuals are sober, serious, cautious.

While these dimensions are not identical to those of introversion-extroversion, it is difficult to think of someone being desurgent and extroverted at the same time. And, in fact, introversion as measured by the 16 PF is derived from several scales, including the surgency scale. As may be anticipated from the foregoing, most 16 PF studies show increasing desurgency with age—this seems to be a frequent finding (e.g., Cattell, 1950; Sealy and Cattell, 1965; Fozard, 1972), but not an inevitable one (e.g., Botwinick and Storandt, 1974, p. 53).

Surgency-desurgency is a complex aspect of personality and it includes the concept of cautiousness. There is a growing literature on cautiousness in later life, and this literature was judged important enough to warrant separate, detailed analysis, found in chapters 8 and 9.

Depression

Psychiatric Status and Social Class. "Depression is the most frequent psychological difficulty encountered in the aged . . . at least one basic concomitant of successful aging is the ability to tolerate depression" (Zinberg and Kaufman, 1963, p. 66). There is no question that depressive affect is part of life for many older people, but it is not clear where this as a "normal" state ends and psychiatric disorder begins. Thus, Busse and Reckless (1961) wrote, "Two of the symptoms most commonly encountered in elderly patients with psychiatric problems are depressive episodes and hypochondriasis" (p. 645). "Our studies on a large group of 'normal' old persons have brought to our attention the serious problem of recurrent depressive episodes" (p. 646) .

Even with people not regarded as "patients," and even with such "objective" tests as the MMPI, depression is commonly seen (e.g., Swenson, 1961; Britton and Savage, 1966; Botwinick and Thompson, 1967). In fact, the three scales of the MMPI that are very likely to show peaks with elderly subjects support the Busse-Reckless observation. The three scales are the Depression, Hypochondriasis, and Social Inversion scales. While not all MMPI studies show elevated depression scores with age, rarely, if ever, has there been much question of the prevalence of depressive affect in later life. In fact, there is reason to believe that the extent of depression may be underestimated in later life, especially among patient populations. Goldfarb (1967) reported that physicians and other professional workers may not recognize depression in aged patients, when in fact it is there, because of their own fears and prejudices.

The study of depression in later life is not only complicated by issues of normality versus psychiatric disorder, but it is also complicated by issues of social class. For example, Hollingshead and Redlich (1958) found that "neurotic depression" was much more common in upper social classes than in lower, but "psychotic depressions" were more frequent in the lower classes.

Why Depression? There is reason to believe that much of both normal and abnormal depression arises from social and personal factors. Busse (1961, p. 280) expressed it clearly,

> . . . a normal person experiences grief when he loses someone he loves and, in effect, says to himself: "I have lost something very important. Now I have very little, but I will make up for it." The morbidly depressed person reacts somewhat differently after a loss. He experiences a loss . . . and he says: "I have lost everything. Now I have nothing."

Physical loss as well as the loss of a loved one also can make for depression. Depression and physical problems are so often related that "What comes first is very hard to determine" (Zinberg and Kaufman, 1963, p. 52).

There is another basis for depression but, as Busse indicated, this is more typical of the young than of the old. While in the old depression is most often related to the loss of loved ones, to the loss of self-esteem resulting from diminished bodily functioning, to altered social roles, to less money, in younger adults the depressions are based more on shame or guilt and on self-hate. The treatment programs for these two sources of depression are different. Busse and Pfeiffer (1969, p. 210) suggest that treatment programs for the aged who are mildly depressed be geared toward restoration of a feeling of self-worth. Their recommendation is that social engagements be encouraged so that gratification is obtained outside the doctor-patient relationship. There is another recommendation which might be worth exploring. Zacher (1971) disclosed that both middle-aged subjects (40–54 years) and those over 55 years who were classified as depressed tended to maintain their previous life goals in the face of changing life patterns. They tended to choose goals more suitable for younger people. Perhaps therapeutic recommendations should include examination of such goals with efforts to modify them when indicated. For depressions that are severe or psychotic, other recommendations are needed. Busse and Pfeiffer indicated that for such depressions, drugs, electroshock therapy, and limited psychotherapy may be indicated.

Hypochondriasis

It has already been pointed out that, in addition to depression, hypochondriasis is a frequent pattern of later life—an "anxious preoccupation with one's own body or a portion of one's own body which the patient believes to be either diseased or functioning improperly" (Busse and Pfeiffer, 1969, p. 202). Hypochondriasis as seen in patient groups, at least, is more prevalent among women than men. Not only is it noted among the elderly in psychiatric interview, but it is also disclosed by tests such as the MMPI (e.g., Calden and Hokanson, Swenson, and others).

Busse and Pfeiffer see hypochondriasis as an escape from feelings of personal failure. The sick role may be easier to tolerate than the role of failure. The older person, for example, in losing his job through retirement when work was his sole interest, in losing social and financial security, and in finding no good replacements for them, may find solace in the role of sick person, even when there is no special incapacitation. Hypochondriasis is not easily treated; it is easier to say what is not recommended than what should be done. Giving the patient an early explanation of his use of illness as a defense against his own feelings of failure is not indicated.

Rigidity

For the sake of completeness, the personality dimension of rigidity will be briefly mentioned here. The brevity is not because of its unimportance; on the contrary, it was judged so important as to also warrant two chapters for full, detailed analysis (see chapters 6 and 7). Suffice it to say here that there are several kinds of rigidity, and at least some of these seem related to intellectual status. In the most general of ways, cross-sectional studies show increasing rigidity with increasing age.

Personality Modified by Cognitive and Sensory Factors

A variety of studies based upon the Rorschach ink blot test shows deficits in later life, if not outright pathology. Ames (1960a), for example, provided Rorschach data showing increased constriction of responses in later life; some studies involve test protocols resembling those of brain-damaged patients. In the main, however, Rorschach results are characterized by individual diversity and, as Ames (1960b) reported, some of the older subjects showed patterns just in reverse of these trends. This implies that many important factors were not looked for in evaluating personality changes.

In two studies, Eisdorfer (1960a,b) looked for sensory factors in personality change. Visual and auditory tests were given to subjects aged over 60 years and categorized on the basis of their ability to see and hear. The Rorschach protocols were scored for "rigidity" in one study and "developmental level" in another study. The latter score was of perceptual organization in combination with vocabulary usage; it was meant to reflect the cognitive maturity of the subject.

Eisdorfer found in both studies that impaired hearing was associated with poor performance. Those who did not hear well were seen as both rigid and as functioning at low cognitive levels. Poor vision did not play such a role and did not add to the Rorschach deficit scores when found in combination with impaired hearing. In a later study Eisdorfer (1963) demonstrated that, without control for intellectual levels, many wrong inferences of personality might be made. He concluded that levels of intelligence, more than age itself, might account for Rorschach performance.

These studies emphasize the danger in generalizing about the personality of older people without knowing much about them other than test scores. It is important to keep generalizations in perspective. When personality changes are investigated, when therapeutic interventions are discussed, it is often difficult to keep in mind the more correct perspective that the elderly, for the most part, are not characterized by personality disorders and do not need to see psychiatrists. Most people seem to fare relatively well even in the face of physical and social losses and of severe bereavements. It is a tribute to man's hardiness that he fares as well in his old age as he does.

Longitudinal Studies

All the foregoing studies are cross-sectional age studies. As will be seen in chapter 19, age comparisons based on the cross-sectional method reflect both age or maturation differences and differences due to cultural or generational effects. Two personality studies were carried out that compared age groups both cross-sectionally and longitudinally so that cultural effects could be evaluated.

In one study, Douglas and Arenberg (1978) tested intellectually superior men ranging in age from the 20s to the 70s with the Guilford-Zimmerman Temperament Survey (GZTS). Approximately seven years later they tested them again. The GZTS has 10 scales, each representing a different personality trait. In the longitudinal phase of the study, scores on five of the 10 scales showed change between the first testing and the second one, seven years later. However, Douglas and Arenberg attributed the performances on only two of the scales to age (maturation), the others to cultural effects.

Douglas and Arenberg reported that after age 50, there is a decrease in the pace of activity. There is a decrease in liking for action that "may sometimes be impulsive." The second trait involves interests people have that can be described as "masculine." These types of interests were found to decline with age and this seems compatible with the cross-sectional questionnaire data reported earlier, which indicate a decrease in heterosexuality. It would be of interest to discover whether such traits truly change with age, or whether it is the need for men to think of themselves in "macho" terms that changes with age.

The other three scales that showed changes over the seven-year test-retest period, but which Douglas and Arenberg attributed to sociocultural reasons rather than to age or maturational reasons, were labeled Friendliness, Thoughtfulness, and Personal Relations. In general, over the seven years, there was a decline in agreeableness, tolerance and cooperativeness, and trust of others in interpersonal relations. There was a lessened tendency to indulge in analytic and evaluative thinking about behavior and about the past. It would seem that decline in this latter tendency, be it for cultural reasons or maturational ones, counteracts tendencies older people have to engage in the "Life Review."

Another study was also carried out with a seven-year test-retest interval, this one based on the 16 PF scales plus some measures of attitudes (Schaie and Parham, 1976). As did Neugarten et al. with their cross-sectional study, Schaie and Parham concluded that in regard to personality and age, stability "appears to be the rule." Nevertheless, a variety of age-related test performances were found, and depending on how the complex analyses are interpreted, many changes were observed.

Perhaps three measured changes were most clear. Men and women ranging in age from the 20s through the 70s, after seven years, were seen as more conventional and more alert to practical needs. They were seen also as less excitable and more accepting. Unlike what Douglas and Arenberg found, with age there was an increase in the trust of others.

ther, the longitudinal studies reflected what seems to be perception of aging personality. The studies showed some ith age, but not dramatic change, in the direction of less hectic, rapid, male-oriented activity, with more acceptance of people and events. This acceptance, however, does not necessarily make for agreeable and cooperative relationships.

SOCIAL FORCES

Up to now, the emphasis has been on changes with age that stem primarily from personal, inner sources and that affect social interactions and, indeed, the whole pattern of life. Now, the emphasis is on changes with age that arise primarily from social, outer sources that also affect the pattern of life. It should be clear, however, that the distinction between inner and outer sources is partly an arbitrary one, based on convenience; one does not really exist in the absence of the other. Changes from within alter the social environment and, conversely, changes in the social world alter the person.

Attitudes Toward the Aged

Life can hardly be pleasant if attitudes all around suggest negatives, especially when these are neither necessary nor even true. Withdrawal is a natural response in such an environment. People do not want to be old, it seems, at least as judged by four different surveys of persons over 60 years of age, conducted over a period of years at Cornell University (Streib, 1965). It was found that the majority of people considered themselves "middle-aged"; it was only among those over 65 that there was any noticeable tendency to identify themselves as "old" or "elderly." The cut-off age was somewhere between 65 and 70 years.

Wallach and Kogan (1961), in similar fashion, found evidence that people aged 54 to 92 years, with an average of 71, were less likely to see themselves as "elderly" than as "not elderly."

Most of the studies on attitudes toward the aged are based upon self-report type questionnaires. Among the earliest of these studies was a series by Tuckman and Lorge (e.g., 1953) in which "yes" or "no" answers were given in response to a list of attitudes thought by the investigators to be "negative stereotypes" and misconceptions of elderly people. Both young and old adults reported negative attitudes toward the elderly, with the old reporting at least as many, if not more of them (Tuckman and Lorge, 1954; 1958). An analysis of these attitudes, however, indicates that some, but probably not most, of them are based as much on reality as on myth. For example, old age was seen to be associated with economic problems—that is fact, not myth. It was also seen, on the basis of an open-ended sentence completion questionnaire, that when old and young differed, the differences centered on a concern by the old of being considered different or pushed aside (Kogan and Shelton, 1962). They were afraid of being rejected. In the main, people become increasingly negative toward others as they age. Axelrod and Eisdorfer (1961) found that opinions of young people become more negative for each age decade from 35 to 75 years.

A different view, a more heartening one, was reported more recently. Perhaps a cultural change is in process, one that is more favorable to the elderly. Borges and Dutton (1976) asked a large number of people over an extended age range to rate their own lives in terms of a continuum ranging from "very good" to "very bad." They also asked these people to rate the "average person's life," as they saw it, at different age periods. The results showed that the older respondents rated their lives as better than did the younger respondents when they projected themselves into the future as older people. Further, even though most persons over 25 chose as the "best years" those below their own age, the "best years" were seen to increase with the respondent's own age.

Age Norms and Age Constraints

Closely allied to attitudes toward the aged are expectations about what the aged should and can do. Conversely, there are expectations about what older people ought not to do and cannot do. These expectations are pervasive and affect the lives of the elderly even when the expectations are arbitrary.

These expectations are referred to as age norms, age constraints, or age grading. They all mean that older people are set in a mold, often inhibited from going out and doing publicly what younger people are permitted to do and, perhaps, even encouraged to do. As Neugarten, Moore, and Lowe (1968, pp. 22–23) put it, there exists a prescriptive time-table for ordering behavior; there are social clocks, social norms. Some of these are more arbitrary than others. Examples from Neugarten et al. are: " 'He's too old to be working so hard' or 'She's too young to wear that style of clothing' or 'That's a strange thing for a man of his age to say' . . . 'Act your age!' " Other, more graphic questions can be asked: Should a 70-year-old woman wear a bikini? Should she be topless at an appropriate beach where younger women are topless, if she so chooses? Should a 70-year-old man dance the Bump, or whatever?

y sanctions; they restrict and constrain a person; the older
d less as an individual than as an impersonal member of
The expectation of what an age group member should do
...ps uctermine what the member actually does (Riley, Johnson, and
Foner, 1972). It can keep him from activity, it can turn him inward.

Isolation and Loneliness

People tend to become isolated in late life and often become lonely.
Death of the spouse isolates, children moving away isolates, and chronic
disease and physical discomforts isolate. Figures 1.1 and 1.2 in chapter 1
suggest that it is mainly women who are left without their mates, but
men too are left alone. The social isolation resulting from the children's
moving away seems to be greater for people of the higher social classes
than the lower (Brown, 1960). For whatever reasons, the expectations of
the higher social class elderly are more often left unmet than those of
the lower class.

Physical problems beset many older people and circumscribe their
functional environment. Although the vast majority of people over 65
are neither institutionalized nor housebound, Shanas (1965) reported
that a great number have difficulty walking stairs (about 26 percent of
this majority), in washing and in bathing themselves (9 percent) and
even in dressing themselves and putting on their shoes (7 percent). In
addition, as pointed out by Busse (1961, p. 278), isolation also can come
about from a reduction in the intensity and perhaps number of perceptual stimuli resulting from decreased visual and auditory acuity. These
and other similar reductions, in making for isolation, often produce emotional stress.

Isolation and loneliness are not synonomous since "Solitude need not
be experienced as loneliness, while loneliness can be felt in the presence
of other people" (Busse and Pfeiffer, 1969, p. 188). Nevertheless, there
is a correlation of some sort between isolation and loneliness: Those
living alone tend to be more lonely than those living with others. For
those living alone, visits to and by their children help in coping with
loneliness. The most lonely are people who have recently lost their
spouses. Loss, more than isolation, may make for loneliness.

Forming Relationships

Loneliness is a problem. Friendships help. Earlier, it was said that
confidants are important for life satisfaction—for successful aging. How
do the elderly meet people to make friends? Perhaps not differently than
anyone else, but, where are they most likely to meet people? More spe-

cifically, are friends and acquaintances more likely made in places where the aged are in predominance or in places where people of all ages live? When a move is necessary or desirable, is an age-segregated community better than an age-integrated one?

Many younger people abhor the idea of segregation of any type, age-segregation included. Yet, the major study in this area suggests that, all things being equal, the choice may well be for segregation, or something close to it. Rosow (1967) examined a large number of apartment buildings in Cleveland and categorized them in terms of the density of older people living within them. He found that more friendships were developed by older people in those buildings that had higher percentages of aged residents. Moreover, the friendships were made with people of similar age. More surprising, perhaps, was that these new friends were seen as more important, closer, than old friends who were not immediately on hand.

While one important study alone should not be the basis of recommendation, the value of age-segregation—or more correctly, age-predominance—should not really be surprising. Kalish (1975, p. 87) put it succinctly: Older people "share recollections of the same ballplayers, movie actors, automobiles, and politicians; they remember dancing the same dances, using the same slang. . . ." In short, they are like most everyone else—they find those of their own generation congenial and those of other generations somewhat different. There seem to be barriers between the generations. The fewer the other bases for selecting friends, the more important is age (Hess, 1972).

There are many exceptions to this of course; many old people who might be called isolates feel worse in contexts where older adults have great opportunities for making friendships. They see how alone they really are and how bound they are to remain alone. Another exception is the fact that many older people enjoy the company of younger people and try to be with them. All these exceptions notwithstanding, however, most older people seem to fare better with regard to friendships in residential complexes where there are many older adults. This seems paradoxical next to the observation that the elderly tend not to form groups on the basis of age because they are reluctant to be identified with the negative image of old age (Binstock, 1974). This reluctance to form groups can add to loneliness.

Retirement

Loneliness can also be a result of separation from the work role and from the social relationships intrinsic to the work role, especially if the separation is involuntary. Involuntary retirement is unique in the history of man; it is seen mainly in industrial societies, not in less developed ones where people must work as long as they are able.

Retirement is an episode in the life of man, just as is birth, marriage, and death. It marks off, formally, separation from the main body of working humanity. Involuntary retirement makes room for the younger worker and it reduces payroll costs, but very often it does not relate to the ability of the older person. Under actual working conditions, the older worker has been seen to perform at least as well as the younger worker, and often better (Riley and Foner, 1968, pp. 426–434).

Meaning of Work. Retirement is difficult for many people. Work means so much more than the process itself. People, particularly men, are often described not so much as who they are, or what kind of people they are, but by what they do for a living. Who are you? I am a scientist. What kind of person is he? He is an insurance salesman. For women, this is less so but not completely different. Who are you? I am a housewife. What kind of person is she? She is a teacher. Socioeconomic status and roles played are implicit in these inquiries and answers, as may be feelings of self-worth and usefulness. The more the job or work-role provides an interest, a responsibility, an opportunity for autonomy, the less inclined the worker is to retire. More blue-collar workers than white-collar workers would prefer to retire if money were not at issue (Sheppard, 1976, p. 303).

If so much of who and what a person is becomes defined by what he does in the work-a-day world, it is only to be expected that many of the attitudes and values regarding older people derive from their retirement status. The older person is encouraged or obliged to stop work, usually at age 65. Who are you? I am retired; I am no longer working. For women, retirement takes a different form, perhaps a less severe one, but here too her role of mother-without-children makes her a different person. But the woman can still rule over her domain, her home; her husband has no domain to rule. This makes her role change easier than his except, perhaps, for the fact that with his retirement, her daily function now centers around him as never before. What strains in their relationship might have existed before his retirement will be exacerbated after it.

The Changing Role of Women. More and more women are entering the labor force; they can do this because of changing goals and values, greater work opportunities, and fewer home-care responsibilities. Women are not only entering the work force in greater numbers, they are staying in it longer.

There is evidence that work and retirement have different meaning or value to women than men. Streib and Schneider (1971) reported that only 29 percent of the women surveyed were willing to retire, compared to 37 percent of the men of the study. Further, Jacobson (1974) found that female blue-collar workers were less willing than their male counterparts to retire at the accepted age. Income does not seem to be the major issue: More female workers were inclined to continue work even if adequate income were assured. Palmore (1965) indicated that the retirement rate is increasing among men but not among women.

Successful Retirement. A desire or a reluctance to retire is one thing. Adjustment to retirement is another. As may be anticipated, successful retirement relates to three important factors: whether or not there is (1) sufficient income; (2) health; and (3) substituted satisfactions. If income is low, health is poor, and nothing satisfying replaces work, the retirement holds little promise for a happy life. A retired person who is in good health and financially secure is more likely to be happy than one still working but without these attributes (Streib, 1956). Another factor in successful retirement, perhaps less important, relates to the obvious fact that retirement involves change—it is a disruption of the pattern of life. To the extent that there are large differences between the work life and the retirement life, flexibility is needed. The rigid person is not a good candidate for successful retirement (Atchley, 1976, p. 111).

Not all people shun retirement, of course. Many find it a positive part of life. Those who never liked their jobs, those who found their work taxing, those who enjoy leisure are able to relish their retirement. To some it means that, having fulfilled their commitment to society, they can now cater to themselves. But people who like their jobs or who get other satisfactions from them tend to not want to leave (e.g., Epstein and Murray, 1968). In the main, the closer the worker is to retirement, the more the disinclination to retire (Riley and Foner, 1968, p. 445).

Mandatory versus Voluntary Retirement. Because retirement, when it is not wanted, often brings so much anguish into the lives of people, it has become accepted and fashionable to favor a policy of involuntary retirement based upon diminished ability, rather than the arbitrary standard of calendar age, i.e., 65 or 70 years. In fact, a committee of the U.S. Congress (the House Select Committee on Aging) held hearings on the proposition that mandatory retirement at any age is wrong. It is thought wrong in the same sense that discrimination against women and minorities is wrong. Many think it inevitable that we have laws making mandatory retirement based on age illegal. It is only fair, some people maintain, that retirement be based on individual desire and on individual ability to carry out work responsibilities. This assumes that people will be happier with such laws, that the economy can maintain its older workers and its younger ones too, and that it is possible to assess work ability with minimum error. Even if the latter two assumptions are accepted without further analysis, it is well to recognize that a time must come in the lives of most people, if not all, when ability will decline to a point when it is difficult to carry out job responsibilities. In higher echelon positions, even if the difficulty in carrying out specific routines is minimal, it would seem that the office, the company, would still need to refresh itself with new ideas, new vigor, new people. Would it not be more painful, more damaging to self-concept, to be retired on these bases rather than on the arbitrary one of age? From many perspectives, it seems much more desirable to train for leisure-time pursuits and for readjustment of values with respect to work and leisure than to focus on keeping people in the work force until very late in life.

CHANGES IN SEX ROLES

There is evidence that, during the later years, the years during which most people are retired from the work force, the role relationships between men and women change. The change may start in middle age, but is in full bloom in later life. Neugarten and Gutmann (1958, p. 33), in reporting the responses to the figures seen in Figure 5.1, wrote:

> Most striking was the fact that with increasing age of respondents, the Older Man and Older Woman [of Figure 5.1] reversed roles in regard to authority in the family. For younger men and women [subjects aged 40–54] the Older Man was seen as the authority figure. For older men and women [aged 55–70] the Older Woman was in the dominant role, and the Older Man, no matter what other qualities were ascribed to him, was seen as submissive. [Moreover] women, as they age, seem to become more tolerant of their own aggressive, egocentric impulses; while men, as they age, of their own nurturant and affiliative impulses.

This is just the opposite pattern of sex roles typically seen in early adulthood.

The reason for the sex reversal in social roles is not clear. Perhaps it has to do with the fact that man's usual role of breadwinner is reduced because of retirement, and his authority in the family suffers both because of this and because of increased infirmity. Women, to a greater extent than men, continue their usual ways in running the home. These sex role reversals may also relate to the restructuring of life patterns that begins in middle age. At this time, "Life is restructured in terms of time-left-to-live, rather than time-since-birth" (Neugarten, 1968, p. 97). The young say, "I am 20 years old." The old say, "I may have 10 good years left." There is a beginning awareness in middle age that time is finite; it is an "important turning point with the restructuring of time and the formulation of new perceptions of self, time and death" (Neugarten, 1968, p. 140). Perhaps woman, in seeing herself with a life-long history of dependence and submissiveness, resents this and becomes assertive before her time runs out.

It should be emphasized in closing that the reasons suggested for the sex role reversals are speculative and conjectural. The projective test material, however, is not. The test responses indicate late life sex role changes. These seem clear but their generality would benefit from further investigation.

SUMMARY

A theory which stimulated much research is "disengagement theory." The heart of this theory rests on the observation that, in later life, people tend to become withdrawn or dissociated from others and from activity. There never was much controversy regarding this observation, but there was controversy regarding the original emphasis on the role played by the individual in this withdrawal. It was believed that the person becomes more involved with himself and less with people and events, not mainly because society pushes him in this direction but because of inner, psychological changes. Even more controversial, however, was the notion that these changes are natural and normal and, as such, the disengaged person is the happy person.

Many studies were made to test this theory, and the essential prescription—withdrawal for happiness—was attacked and found wanting. For the most part, just the opposite was seen as true; well-being goes with activity, not disengagement.

Various factors, however, were found to modify the relationship between activity and well-being; health, for example. High morale seems to go with good health regardless of whether it is associated with activity or inactivity. Social factors are also seen as important in the disengagement relationships. Those subjects who are highest in socioeconomic status and those who experience a minimum of work-role change are the most likely to report both high activity and high satisfaction. Another factor is whether the person has a confidant, someone to confide in. If he does, then he can have good morale even with little social interaction. If he doesn't, he may be unhappy even with it. While most people may not be happy in disengagement, some are. Among these, the most successful, it appears, are those who are self-directed, have high self-regard, and are interested in the world but not in personal interactions with people.

In the main, psychological tests show that changes in adult personality are not marked, but those changes commonly seen are of the type that indicate disengagement. Cross-sectional studies point to a turning inward with a diminished intensity of energy and affect. Many older people tend toward depression, introversion, a seriousness of manner, and passive personality patterns. Longitudinal studies may show even less change with age. They show a decrease in excitability, especially as it relates to general activity. Older people seem to be more practical and conventional. There is a danger in generalizing about the personality of older people, however, without knowing much about them other than test scores. For the most part, the elderly are not characterized by personality disorders; they fare relatively well even in the face of severe physical and social losses. But life can hardly be pleasant if attitudes all around suggest negatives, especially when these are neither necessary nor even true. People of all ages, including old people themselves, have negative attitudes toward the elderly. Old people do not want to be considered different; often they are afraid of being pushed aside and rejected.

Old people very often are lonely. Their spouses and friends die, and their children may leave them. Loneliness may be exacerbated with retirement from work. Among many things, work is a source of social interactions. Involuntary retirement makes room for the younger worker and reduces payroll costs, but very often it does not relate to the work ability of the older person. The older worker has been seen to perform at least as well as the younger worker, and often better.

Retirement is difficult for many people. Good adjustment to retirement from work is facilitated by three important factors: whether or not there is sufficient income, health, and substituted satisfactions. Not all people shun retirement, of course. Many find it a positive part of life. Those who never liked their jobs, those who found their work taxing, those who enjoy leisure are able to relish their retirement. But people who like their jobs or who get other satisfactions from them tend to want to stay working.

There is evidence that, during the later years, the years during which most people are retired from the work force, role relationships between men and women change. Women become more accepting of their assertive, authoritative, aggressive impulses, and men become more accepting of their submissive, nurturant, and affiliative impulses. This is just the opposite pattern of sex roles typically seen in early adulthood.

REFERENCES

Ames, L.B. Age changes in the Rorschach responses of a group of elderly individuals. *Journal of Genetic Psychology*, 1960 (a), 97, 257–258.

Ames, L.B. Age changes in the Rorschach responses of individual elderly subjects. *Journal of Genetic Psychology*, 1960 (b), 97, 287–315.

Atchley, R.C. *The sociology of retirement*. New York: Wiley, 1976.

Axelrod, S., and Eisdorfer, C. Attitudes toward old people: an empirical analysis of the stimulus-group validity of the Tuckman-Lorge questionnaire. *Journal of Gerontology*, 1961, 16, 75–80.

Binstock, R.H. Aging and the future of American politics. In *Political consequences of aging. Annals of the American Academy of Political and Social Science*, 1974, 415, 199–212.

Borges, M.A., and Dutton, L.J. Attitudes toward aging. *The Gerontologist*, 1976, 16, 220–224.

Botwinick, J., and Storandt, M. *Memory, related functions and age*. Springfield, Ill.: Charles C Thomas, 1974.

Botwinick, J., and Thompson, L.W. Depressive affect, speed of response, and age. *Journal of Consulting Psychology*, 1967, 31, 106.

Britton, P.G., and Savage, R.D. The MMPI and the aged: Some normative data from a community sample. *British Journal of Psychiatry*, 1966, 112, 941–943.

Brown, R.G. Family structure and social isolation of older persons. *Journal of Gerontology*, 1960, 15, 170–174.

Busse, E.W. Psychoneurotic reactions and defense mechanisms in the aged. In P.H. Hock and J. Zubin (Eds.), *Psychopathology of aging*. New York: Grune & Stratton, 1961.

Busse, E.W., and Pfeiffer, E. Functional psychiatric disorders in old age. In E.W. Busse and E. Pfeiffer (Eds.), *Behavior adaptation in late life*. Boston: Little, Brown & Co., 1969.

Busse, E., and Reckless, J.B. Psychiatric management of the aged. *Journal of the American Medical Association*, 1961, 175, 645–648.

Butler, R.N. *Why survive? Being old in America*. New York: Harper & Row, 1975.

Butler, R.N., and Lewis, M.I. *Aging and mental health*. St. Louis: C.V. Mosby, 1973.

Calden, G., and Hokanson, J.E. The influence of age on MMPI responses. *Journal of Clinical Psychology*, 1959, 15, 194–195.

Cattell, R.B. *Personality: a systematic, theoretical, and factual study*. New York: McGraw Hill, 1950.

Chown, S.M. Personality and aging. In K.W. Schaie (Ed.), *Theory and method of research on aging*. Morgantown, W.Va.: West Virginia Univ., 1968, pp. 134–157.

Cumming, E., and Henry, W. *Growing old: the process of disengagement.* New York: Basic Books, 1961.

Douglas, K. and Arenberg, D. Age changes, cohort differences, and cultural change on the Guilford-Zimmerman Temperament Survey. *Journal of Gerontology*, 1978, in press.

Eisdorfer, C. Rorschach rigidity and sensory decrement in a senescent population. *Journal of Gerontology*, 1960(a), *15*, 188–190.

Eisdorfer, C. Developmental level and sensory impairment in the aged. *Journal of Projective Technique*, 1960(b), *24*, 129–132.

Eisdorfer, C. Rorschach performance and intellectual functioning in the aged. *Journal of Gerontology*, 1963, *18*, 358–363.

Epstein, L.E., and Murray, J.H. Employment and retirement. In B.L. Neugarten (Ed.), *Middle age and aging.* Chicago: Univ. of Chicago Press, 1968.

Erikson, E.H. *Childhood and society.* 2nd ed. New York: W.W. Norton Co., 1963.

Fozard, J.L. Predicting age in the adult years from psychological assessments of abilities and personality. *Aging and human development*, 1972, *3*, 175–182.

Gavron, E.F. Changes in Edwards Personal Preference Schedule needs with age and psychiatric status. *Journal of Clinical Psychology*, 1965, *21*, 194–196.

Goldfarb, A.I. Masked depression in the old. *American Journal of Psychotherapy*, 1967, *21*, 791–796.

Gutman, G.M. A note on the MPI: Age and sex differences in extroversion and neuroticism in a Canadian sample. *British Journal of Social and Clinical Psychology*, 1966, *5*, 128–129.

Havighurst, R.J., Neugarten, B.L., and Tobin, S.S. Disengagement and patterns of aging. In B.L. Neugarten (Ed.), *Middle age and aging.* Chicago: Univ. of Chicago Press, 1968, pp. 161–172.

Heron, A., and Chown, S.M. *Age and function.* London: Churchill, 1967.

Hess, B. Friendship. In M.W. Riley, M. Johnson, and A. Foner (Eds.), *Aging and society, Vol. 3.* New York: Russell Sage Foundation, 1972.

Hollingshead, A.B., and Redlich, F.C. *Social class and mental illness: a community study.* New York: John Wiley and Sons, 1958.

Jacobson, D. Rejection of the retiree role: a study of female industrial workers in their 50s. *Home Relations*, 1974, *27*, 477–492.

Kalish, R.A. *Late adulthood: perspectives on human development.* Monterey, Calif.: Brooks/Cole, 1975.

Kogan, N., and Shelton, F.C. Beliefs about "old people": A comparative study of older and younger samples. *Journal of Genetic Psychology*, 1962, *100*, 93–111.

Lowenthal, M.F., and Boler, D. Voluntary vs. involuntary social withdrawal. *Journal of Gerontology*, 1965, *20*, 363–371.

Lowenthal, M.F., and Haven, C. Interaction and adaptation intimacy as a critical variable. *American Sociological Review*, 1968, *33*, 20–30.

Maddox, G.L. Fact and artifact: evidence bearing on disengagement theory from the Duke Geriatrics Project. *Human Development*, 1965, *8*, 117–130.

Maddox, G., and Eisdorfer, C. Some correlates of activity and morale among the elderly. *Social Forces*, 1962, *40*, 254–260.

Neugarten, B.L. The awareness of middle age. In B.L. Neugarten (Ed.), *Middle age and aging.* Chicago: Univ. of Chicago Press, 1968, pp. 93–98, 137–147.

Neugarten, B.L., Crotty, W.F., and Tobin, S.S. *Personality in middle and late life.* New York: Atherton Press, 1964.

Neugarten, B.L., and Gutmann, D.L. Age-sex roles and personality in middle age: A thematic apperception study. *Psychological Monographs: General and Applied*, 1958, 17, Whole No. 470.

Neugarten, B.L., Havighurst, R.J., and Tobin, S.S. Personality and patterns of aging. In B.L. Neugarten (Ed.), *Middle age and aging*. Chicago: Univ. of Chicago Press, 1968, pp. 173–177.

Neugarten, B.L., Moore, J.W., and Love, J.C. Age norms, age constraints, and adult socialization. In B.L. Neugarten (Ed.), *Middle age and aging*. Chicago: Univ. of Chicago Press, 1968, pp. 22–28.

Palmore, E.B. Differences in the retirement patterns of men and women. *Gerontologist*, 1965, 1, 4–8.

Reichard, S., Livson, P., and Peterson, P.G. *Aging and personality*. New York: John Wiley and Sons, 1962.

Riegel, K.F. Personality theory and aging. In J.E. Birren (Ed.), *Handbook of aging and the individual*. Chicago: Univ. of Chicago Press, 1959.

Riley, M.W., and Foner, A. *Aging and society, Vol. 1*. New York: Russell Sage Foundation, 1968.

Riley, M. W., Johnson, M., and Foner, A. *Aging and society, Vol. 3*. New York: Russell Sage Foundation, 1972.

Rosow, I. *Social integration of the aged*. New York: Free Press, 1967.

Schaie, K.W., and Marquette, B. Personality in maturity and old age. In R.M. Dreger (Ed.), *Multivariate personality research: Contributions to the understanding of personality in honor of Raymond B. Cattell*. Baton Rouge, La.: Claitor, 1972, pp. 612–632.

Schaie, K.W. and Parham, I.A. Stability of adult personality traits;. fact or fable? *Journal of Personality and Social Psychology*, 1976, 34, 146–158.

Schaie, K.W., and Strother, C.R. Cognitive and personality variables in college graduates of advanced age. In G.A. Talland (Ed.), *Human behavior and aging: Recent advances in research and theory*. New York: Academic Press, 1968.

Sealy, A.P., and Cattell, R.B. Standard trends in personality development in men and women of 16 to 70 years, determined by 16 PF measurements. Paper read at British Psychological Society Conference, April 1965.

Shanas, E. Health care and health services for the aged. *Gerontologist*, 1965, 5, 240.

Sheppard, H.L. Work and retirement. In R.H. Binstock and E. Shanas (Eds.), *Handbook of aging and the social sciences*. New York: Van Nostrand Reinhold, 1976.

Slater, P.E., and Scarr, H.A. Personality in old age. *Genetic Psychological Monographs*, 1964, 70, 229–269.

Spangler, D.P., and Thomas, C.W. The effects of age, sex and physical disability upon manifest needs. *Journal of Counseling Psychology*, 1962, 9, 313–319.

Streib, G.F. Morale of the retired. *Social problems*, 1956, 3, 270–276.

Streib, G.F. Are the aged a minority group? In A.W. Gouldner and S.M. Miller (Eds.), *Applied sociology*. New York: Free Press of Glencoe, 1965, pp. 311–328.

Streib, G.F., and Schneider, C.J. *Retirement in American society*. Ithaca, N.Y.: Cornell Univ. Press, 1971.

Swenson, W.M. Structured personality testing in the aged: an MMPI study of the gerontic population. *Journal of Clinical Psychology*, 1961, 17, 302–304.

Tuckman, J., and Lorge, I. Attitudes toward old people. *Journal of Social Psychology*, 1953, 37, 249–260.

Tuckman, J., and Lorge, I. Old people's appraisal of adjustment over the life-span. *Journal of Personality*, 1954, *22*, 417–422.

Tuckman, J., and Lorge, I. Attitude toward aging of individuals with experiences with the aged. *Journal of Genetic Psychology*, 1958, *92*, 199–204.

Wallach, M.A., and Kogan, N. Aspects of judgment and decision making: Interrelationships and changes with age. *Behavioral Sciences*, 1961, *6*, 23–36.

Zacher, A.N. Goal rigidity as a variable in mid-life and old age depression. Unpublished doctoral dissertation, Washington University, St. Louis, Mo., 1971.

Zinberg, N.E., and Kaufman, I. Cultural and personality factors associated with aging: an introduction. In N. Zinberg and I. Kaufman (Eds.), *Normal psychology of the aging process*. New York: International Universities Press, 1963.

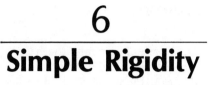

6
Simple Rigidity

It was said in the previous chapter that, in general, as people become older, they become more rigid. Actually, this is a gross over-generalization. The problem of rigidity is much more complicated than it appears at first sight, and its relation to age involves further complexity.

Rigidity, to most people, seems to mean keeping an attitude or an opinion, or the sticking to a task, despite plentiful evidence that this persistence is wrong or unrewarding. Its converse, flexibility, implies the ability to shift from one pattern of activity to another. More often than not, a person referred to as "rigid" is thought to be generally so, characterized as doggedly persisting in a variety of situations, not just a particular one. Rigidity has been thought to be a global aspect of man.

Many psychologists, until relatively recently at least, behaved as if they also had this view of rigidity. This was typified most extremely, perhaps, by the orthodox psychoanalytic view: If there is fixation at a particular stage of psychosexual development, that is, if childhood development is not complete, having stopped at a particular point in the process, the resulting adult will be stunted in effectiveness by an obsessive thought system and by an excessive rigidity of behavior. His whole "life-style" would be characterized by a constricted, unyielding narrow focus, an inability to shift to more appropriate, satisfying patterns of accomplishment.

MORE THAN ONE KIND OF RIGIDITY

Most psychologists today do not accept this notion of rigidity. Probably most psychologists would agree with Chown (1961) that, "It is hoped that . . . the myth of the 'rigid' person . . ." would be weakened, "since at least five kinds of rigidity were . . ." found.[1]

[1] For a general discussion of the problems of rigidity, the reader is directed to an earlier article by Chown (1959).

Even if we were to endorse the premise that young adults can be classified on a continuum of general rigidity, and even if we were to accept the notion that rigid personality is the result of earlier life experiences, it does not necessarily follow that rigid behavior in the later adult years arises in the same way or for the same reasons that it does in young adulthood. It may arise as a result of an entirely different "cause" and by way of an entirely different mechanism. Rigidity arising in old age may be intrinsic to the biological processes of aging. It was for this reason that in a previous review of studies on rigidity the word itself was not used; more neutral-sounding terms were used instead (Botwinick, 1959, pp. 752–757). The review centered around concepts such as shifting expectancy or set, control of inhibition, reorganization of habits and perceptions, and others.

What does this mean with regard to the commonly held belief that old people are more rigid than young people? "You can't teach old dogs new tricks" suggests, not that advanced age is associated with a lowered general ability to learn, but that advanced age is associated with a lowered ability to unlearn that which is already integrated into well-established thought and behavior systems. Old dogs, so to speak, are less likely to develop new solutions to problems and new ways of doing things. To investigate this commonly held belief properly, we ought to ask whether or not old age is associated with a greater variety of the rigidities—with new types appearing in later life. We ought to ask whether old age is associated with a greater intensity of the same rigidities found in young age. Or, perhaps, we might ask if old age is associated with a full-bloom generalized rigidity characterizing elderly people in many areas of life, even though this may not be the pattern in young adulthood.

RIGIDITY IS RELATED TO OTHER FUNCTIONS

Not all of these questions have been asked in the published research, but several of them have. The research has provided much information, not the least of it concerning the complexity and ambiguity of the problem. Whereas the study of rigidity at one time seemed relatively simple and straightforward, the view now is that this is not the case at all.

This complexity and ambiguity will be discussed in detail, but first it may be best to back off a bit and see what was reported at the occasion of the previous review, when it was possible to maintain a more simplistic view.

A Previous Review of the Literature

It was already indicated that in the previous review the word "rigidity" was avoided so that no implication could be made as to the mechanism or antecedents of rigidity in later adulthood. The concept was described as follows (Botwinick, 1959, pp. 752–757):

> . . . activities in everyday living require continuous modification of prior experience such that some tendencies are inhibited and others maintained. The susceptibility or proneness to certain behavior tendencies and the difficulty in surmounting or inhibiting them define (the problem). The contexts . . . are of various sorts and include perceptual organizations, acquired habits, inhibitory processes, and cognitive abilities.

Eleven studies were summarized in the review, and each of these was characterized by the fact that only a single measure was used. With respect to the concept, "rigidity," the best study, perhaps, was that of Heglin (1956).

Three age groups were compared in a series of problem-solving tasks, each task involving similar or repetitive operations. The groups were aged 14–19 years, 20–49 years, and 50–58 years. The tasks were so arranged that in the continuous repetition of dealing with them a technique of solution was established which, while very efficient at first, became inefficient later on because a shorter, more direct method was better. Still later in the series of tasks, the technique became totally inadequate because it could not be used to solve the problem at all.

Heglin found that the oldest group tended to stick with the original technique for solution, even when no longer very efficient. They even stuck to this when it was no longer adequate. The two younger groups did this to a lesser extent. Heglin then taught all his subjects to avoid this "rigid" pattern and found that this training benefited the oldest subjects least and the middle group, the 20 to 49-year-olds, most.[2]

Heglin's study was one of seven which reported data compatible with a hypothesis of increased rigidity in later life. Four studies were not in accord with such a hypothesis, but the natures of two of these were such that they might best not be credited to either side of the ledger. All told, then, the evidence was weighted for a belief that rigidity increases in later life.

[2] A later study by Smith (1967) did not disclose significant age differences in performances on tasks very similar to that used by Heglin. This study and Heglin's are described in chapter 14 in greater detail.

Learning and Rigidity

Since the time of the review, many other single-measure studies appeared, which—while not all designed to test the rigidity hypothesis —were relevant to it. Many of these had to do with issues involved in learning and memory. In summing up these studies, it was suggested that "the evidence for a rigidity learning deficit in later life does not seem impressive. When there was an indication of such a deficit it tended to be marginal and it was often correlated with an overall deficit in learning performance" (Botwinick, 1967, p. 193).

Human Studies. The notion that rigidity and learning ability are correlated does not in itself indicate which of these two correlates is the primary one. For example, if a subject in a learning experiment cannot acquire the information or develop the skill required by the experimenter, the subject very often is left with only a limited number of things he can do. He can do nothing, or he can repeat the same mistakes. In repeating the same wrong things, he may know that they won't work, but he may hope they might; in any case, he is doing something which may be more comfortable than just sitting in the experiment situation and not responding. Doing over and over again the same wrong thing will be labeled "rigid." Conversely, if a subject is truly rigid, he will be so set in a particular pattern that he may fail to unlearn his wrong efforts and thus appear unable to learn new things. Clinically or in real life situations, the question of which correlate is the primary one—that is, which is responsible for the other, learning or rigidity—is not important. But for the researcher, the investigator who is interested in mechanism or explanation, as well as description, the question is very important. There is the goal to understand human behavior and its underlying processes, but there is also the important goal of doing something about it all. In working with an old person, would we best put our efforts into teaching him how to learn, or how to develop more flexible attitudes?

Learning studies on rigidity have taken many different forms. One interesting form was seen many years ago. Snoddy (1926) used a mirror to reflect the image of a figure which his subjects traced. This reversed the normal, right-left relationship. Ruch (1934) also used a mirror, but his was for the purpose of reflecting a pursuit rotor target which the subjects had to track. Both Snoddy and Ruch reported that reversing these life-long right-left patterns was particularly difficult for the older subjects.

Another example of the form which studies can take is one carried out by Kay in 1951. He used a laboratory apparatus involving 10 lights and 10 response keys, each key extinguishing one light. Kay observed that his older subjects tended to repeat their learning errors; they failed to amend or unlearn their ineffective responses.

Still another type of problem was taken from a real-life situation. Entwisle (1959) investigated what took place when a company in England changed from horse-drawn vehicles to motor vehicles. Entwisle found those drivers under 40 years had no problem making the change; in fact, they were better with the motor vehicles than those of similar age who had no driving experience of any kind. However, the situation was otherwise with those over 40. Their experience with the horse-drawn vehicles was a hindrance. One problem with real-life situations is that the investigator has to take the situation as it is; he cannot order it into a perfect scientific experiment. In the Entwisle experiment, the older drivers had more years of experience with the outmoded, horse-drawn vehicles than the younger drivers. That is, they had more to overcome. Perhaps this fact, rather than the fact of their having been older, was the crucial factor in the difficulty in switching. A more perfect experiment would be one in which different age groups were identical with respect to the time spent with horse-drawn vehicles. Perhaps such an experiment would show that the age groups were similar in their rigidities; those subjects, irrespective of age, who had long years with the horse-drawn vehicles were the poorest with the motor vehicles.

These studies are but a few examples of those that have been done. In general, the studies convey the idea of a rigidity in later life, but, as already indicated, either because of the correlation between rigidity and learning ability, or because of imperfect experimental designs, the issue of rigidity in later adulthood remains open.

Animal Studies. Psychologists doing animal studies have been trained to not anthropomorphize. It is inappropriate to observe animal subjects—as, for example, rats learning a maze—and, from their performances, attribute to them the mental and feeling characteristics of man. In describing a rat as rigid, though we are using a term invested with human qualities, we are not necessarily anthropomorphizing. If we use the term "rigidity" to classify certain behaviors and not to make interpretations about such factors as unknown early life history, then we may call the rat rigid. For example, we can describe an ongoing pattern of behavior as successful for the rat in achieving food; we can describe this pattern as persisting even when no longer successful, and we can observe that, in this persistence, new and successful behavior patterns are not established. We can use the shorthand, "rigidity," to describe all of this.

There are several animal studies which have to do with the problem of rigidity in relation to age. As with the human studies, not all of these were carried out with the concept of rigidity made explicit. And, as with the human studies, not all pointed to an increased rigidity in later life. Three studies that did point to a rigidity are described here because, although they are different from one another in some ways, together they indicate the types of studies which have been done.

As long ago as 1929, Stone reported a series of learning experiments with rats of wide age range. His subjects were aged 20, 50, 100, 240, and 730 days. (Roughly, when a rat reaches two years old, i.e., 730 days, it is considered elderly, perhaps comparable to an adult of retirement age. A one-year-old rat is at full maturity and is middle-aged, and at six months the rat reaches what might be called young adulthood. At three to four months the rat has reached puberty. It is worthwhile to note that the vast majority of the very many behavioral experiments on the rat have been carried out when they were not adult. Most rat subjects are between three and four months of age, perhaps comparable to human subjects aged between 12 and 16 years.)

In his first experiment of the series, Stone (1929) used a box into which the rat was placed and from which he could escape by simply stepping onto a platform. Stone reported that the old rats developed a "door habit." They persistently kept trying to force their way through the door rather than stepping onto the platform. They repeated their errors rather than amend them—they behaved "rigidly."

A more recent study, and one typical in some ways of several aging studies, was carried out by Botwinick, Brinley, and Robbin (1962). Rats of three ages, old (22–27 months), mature (8–12 months), and pubescent (3–4 months), were trained to go either to the right or left to get some food. This was called original learning (OL). When this learning was established, the animals were trained to find food in the opposite direction. That is, if OL was to the right, the rats were trained to find food to the left. This reversal learning was called R_1.[3]

The results of this experiment may be seen in Figure 6.1. While the old animals were somewhat poorer than the younger ones in their performances of OL, they were most disadvantaged in R_1. That is, the old rats were not nearly as inferior in learning to find food in either a right or left direction, as they were inferior in learning to switch directions.

This is not the complete story, however. The data of Figure 6.1 indicate rigidity, but when rats within the three age groups were selected so that their OL performances were equal, their R_1 performances were also

[3] It need not concern us here that in this experiment the rats were retrained after R_1 to the original direction, called R_2; then retained back again, R_3; and finally retrained again, R_4.

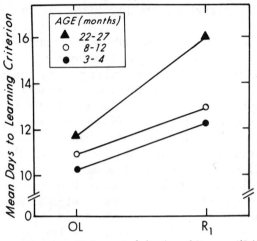

FIGURE 6.1: Learning scores in relation to the type of task. Sprague-Dawley female rats were taught to go either right or left to get food. After this original learning (OL), they were taught to reverse (R₁) and go in the opposite direction. (Data from Table 1 of Botwinick, Brinley, and Robbin, 1962.)

seen to be equal. Thus, rigidity in the older rats was seen primarily when poor learning ability was present. While a case can be made that the rigidity of the older rats is what made for poor original learning—they adhered rigidly to their incorrect choices—an equally good case can be made that poor learning ability made for rigidity. Which one is primary to the other?

A third animal study was carried out by Goodrick (1975). Again, rats were taught to run a maze, but this time the animals had to make 14 correct choices between right and left directions, not just one, before they could get the food reward at the end. An interesting observation was made when the results of this study were compared to those of a previous one, also by Goodrick (1973). In the previous study, aged rats were seen to make repetitive errors at the various choice points; the younger, mature rats did not, or they did not make as many. Thus, the aged rats were seen as rigid, making for poor learning performances.

Goodrick (1975) reasoned that if all the animals were kept from completing the wrong responses at each of the 14 choice points—if they simply were not permitted to go through the wrong doors—the more rigid older animals would not have all these "bad habits" to unlearn. In fact, rigidity of correct choices should help the aged animals to perform well.

This is exactly what happened: Rats aged 25 months were compared to rats aged 5 months in learning a 14-unit maze when all wrong turns were blocked. The animals, during training, could commit themselves to an incorrect right or left direction but they could not complete the response by entering the wrong door. Later, when the tests were made, each of the 14 doors that had been blocked were unblocked so that it was possible to go through all the doors attempted. Goodrick's hypothesis was confirmed: The older animals performed better than the younger ones, and this was attributed to taking advantage of their rigidity—of only correct responses made during training. There may be a good lesson here. Have the learners commit responses, but try to arrange it so that mainly the correct ones are ventured.

It is seen, then, that the problem of rigidity has characteristics common to both animal and human studies. While studies with animal subjects have the advantage of being able to use very simple procedures, the advantages of human studies include the richness and variety of responses unique only to people. The next section highlights this richness and uniqueness.

Dogmatism and Rigidity

"Both dogmatism and rigidity," according to Hollander and Hunt (1967, p. 160), "refer to forms of resistance to change. . . ." Hollander and Hunt made a point of conceptualizing dogmatism "as a higher-order and more complexly organized form of resistance to change." They hypothesized that dogmatism can lead to a rigidity in solving specific problems, but that rigidity cannot lead to dogmatism.

It is not necessary for present purposes to distinguish between these two concepts in terms of which is the more encompassing. It is necessary only to recognize that both are "forms of resistance to change," with dogmatism involving "the authoritarian and intolerant manner in which ideas and beliefs are communicated to others."

Riegel and Riegel (1960) were interested in both rigidity and dogmatism and gave tests of them to approximately 500 people above the age of 55, and to 120 people between the ages of 17 and 19 years. The older people were grouped into age intervals of 5 years. The rigidity and dogmatism tests were given in questionnaire forms, with each item endorsed by the subject on the basis of a five-point scale: i.e., the subject rated each item, as it applied to him, as: (1) correct; (2) partly correct; (3) neither correct nor incorrect; (4) partly incorrect; or (5) incorrect.

Personal and General Rigidity. Riegel and Riegel's rigidity test comprised 12 items. Unlike the rigidity tests discussed so far, where the subject performs in a particular way and then is required to shift and perform in a different way, these 12 items are characterized by opinions or attitudes that were held or expressed. It may be said, therefore, that this test measures an attitude-type of rigidity. Half the items on the test were expressed in the first person singular; for example, "If I could take a trip, I would prefer to go to a place where I have been before." The other half of the test was expressed in general terms: "The best way to enjoy a vacation is to plan every detail carefully before you leave."

The results of the total test indicated a consistent rise in the average rigidity scores over the whole life-span from 17 to over 75 years of age, which was particularly marked among men. Up to age 60-64 years, the sexes were similar with respect to the rigidity scores, but after this period of life the scores of men seemed to increase more than those of women. Despite the consistent age trend, the actual correlation between the individual subject's age and the rigidity score was not extremely large. It was 0.44, and half of this when only the over-55-year group was examined.

Riegel and Riegel analyzed those rigidity items framed in the first person singular separately from those items framed in general terms and found interesting results. All age groups appeared more rigid when the questions were stated in the more general contexts, but this was more the case for the older subjects. Stated in an opposite way: "If one asks an older subject what actions he would take personally in a certain situation he is less likely to express a highly rigid attitude" (Riegel and Riegel, 1960, p. 191).

Dogmatism: Anxiety, Intolerance, and Stereotypy. The dogmatism scale, like the rigidity scale, involved a series of statements, each of which was endorsed by one of five choices ranging from correct to incorrect. The data of Riegel and Riegel (1960) show little, if any, change in dogmatism with advancing age. What average age trend was seen involved a very slight increase in dogmatic attitude in those aged 70 years and over.

The Riegels then inspected the items of the dogmatism test and described three different groups of them. One group referred "to feelings of anxiety and insecurity" (e.g., "I have often felt that people say insulting and vulgar things about me"). A second group of items expressed "an intolerant attitude" (e.g., "In a heated discussion I generally become so absorbed in what I am going to say that I forget to listen to what the others are saying"). The third group of items referred "to a dogmatic and fanatic attitude in a more general way." As with the general rigidity items, these were stated in "general, stereotyped phrases" (e.g., "It is a sign of weak character to give up one's earlier convictions").

Figure 6.2 describes a surprising result. From the youngest age, 17–19 years, to the age group 55–59 years, the general, stereotypic dogmatism scores increased sharply and then increased very slightly with further advancing age, with perhaps a small drop very late in life. A nearly reverse pattern was seen with the anxiety and intolerance items of the dogmatism test: there was a sharp decline from age 17–19 years to 55–59 years, with a slight increase thereafter. Older people, the Riegels concluded, "do not frequently express feelings of anxiety and intolerance."

The data in Figure 6.2 are even more impressive when evaluated along with the correlations between the three dogmatism scores and the age of the subjects. The correlation coefficient between age and stereotypic dogmatism was 0.63; the other two coefficients were negative, −0.49 and −0.28 for intolerance and anxiety, respectively.

Independence of Dogmatism and Anxiety. Thus, the Riegels viewed dogmatism as involving several dimensions, among which are a general stereotypic dogmatism which increases with age, and an anxiety-laden dogmatism which does not. Monge (1972), dealing with a similar problem, conceptualized it differently. He asked the question whether dogmatism increased with age, and, if it does, whether an age-related anxiety could account for it.

He gave a short Dogmatism Scale, not unlike the scale used by the Riegels, to many men and women in the broad age range of 20s through the 70s. He also gave a series of anxiety scales. Monge reported that the older people were clearly the most dogmatic; test scores rose linearly from the 20s to the 70s. However, there was no systematic age pattern with respect to the anxiety test scores. Accordingly, Monge concluded that increased anxiety with age as an explanation of the increased dogmatism was not justified by his data. Both Monge and the Riegels, therefore, were in agreement with respect to the pattern that dogmatism takes in relation to age, and they were also in agreement with respect to the independence of this pattern and the age pattern of anxiety.

Correlations Between Dogmatism and Rigidity. Recognizing that in the data of Riegel and Riegel the items of the dogmatism test were so heterogeneous that they gave rise to opposite age patterns, it would not be surprising to find a low correlation between the Riegels' total dogmatism scale, i.e., the sum of these items, and the rigidity scale. Actually, the coefficient of correlation between the rigidity and dogmatism scales was higher than might be expected. Depending upon sex and specific

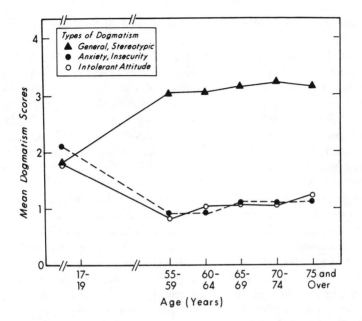

FIGURE 6.2: Dogmatism in relation to age. Three types of dogmatism were identified, one with an age pattern just the opposite of the other two. (Data from Table 1 of Riegel and Riegel, 1960.)

age group, the coefficients of correlation between the two tests ranged from 0.22 to 0.46. These low correlations between tests aimed to measure a form of resistance to change, plus the opposite age patterns seen with items from one of these tests, clearly point to the need of dispensing with what Chown (1961) calls the "myth of the 'rigid' person."

SUMMARY

Rigidity involves a personal resistance to change. The notion that a person can be characterized as rigid or as flexible, however, does not stand up under the analysis of research results. The data suggest that the concept, rigidity, is not a unitary one, there being a variety of rigidities. A person can be rigid in one area of endeavor, but not in another.

Accordingly, questions regarding rigid behavior in later life ought to be framed broadly. We ought to ask: Is old age associated with a greater variety of rigidities than is young adulthood? Is old age associated with a greater intensity of the same rigidities? Does a full-bloom, generalized rigidity occur in later life, not seen earlier? On the other hand, the question, "are older people more rigid than younger people?" is insufficient.

More than anything else, perhaps, the research on aging and rigidity disclosed how complex and ambiguous the problem is. When rigid behavior was seen in older people, it tended to be marginal. More important, it is impossible, or at least very difficult, to separate rigidity of behavior from deficits in related cognitive performances. Studies of both human and animal subjects have pointed to some difficulty in later life in shifting from one task to another, i.e., in maintaining flexible sets, but in both types of studies such difficulties vanished or were reduced appreciably when learning factors were controlled.

Dogmatism, like rigidity, involves resistance to change, but it takes the unique form of intolerance. Dogmatism, also like rigidity, apparently has many aspects. Not all aspects seem to be age-related, although some are. For example, a form of dogmatism described as general and stereotypic was seen to increase in later life. This form involves concepts such as, "It is a sign of weak character to give up one's earlier convictions." Dogmatism of the form involving anxiety, on the other hand, was not seen to increase with age. Older people do not frequently express feelings of anxiety and intolerance.

When greater dogmatism or rigidity was found in older adults than in young adults, it was seen as descriptive only. No necessary explanation was involved; the differences among age groups may be reflective of experiential rather than maturational factors.

REFERENCES

Botwinick, J. Drives, expectancies, and emotions. In J.E. Birren (Ed.), Handbook of aging and the individual: psychological and biological aspects. Chicago: Univ. of Chicago Press, 1959, pp. 739–768.

Botwinick, J. Cognitive processes in maturity and old age. New York: Springer Publishing Co., 1967.

Botwinick, J., Brinley, J.F., and Robbin, J.S. Learning a position discrimination and position reversals by Sprague-Dawley rats of different ages. Journal of Gerontology, 1962, 17, 315–319.

Chown, S. Rigidity—a flexible concept. Psychological Bulletin, 1959, 56, 195–223.

Chown, S. Age and the rigidities. Journal of Gerontology, 1961, 16, 353–362.

Entwisle, D.G. Aging: the effects of previous skill on training. Occupational Psychology, 1959, 33, 238–243.

Goodrick, C. Maze learning of mature-young and aged rats as a function of distribution of practice. Journal of Experimental Psychology, 1973, 98, 344–349.

Goodrick, C.L. Behavioral rigidity as a mechanism for facilitation of problem solving for aged rats. Journal of Gerontology, 1975, 30, 181–184.

Heglin, H.J. Problem solving set in different age groups. *Journal of Gerontology*, 1956, *11*, 310–317.

Hollander, E.P., and Hunt, R.G. *Current perspectives in social psychology*. New York: Oxford Univ. Press, 1967.

Kay, H. Learning of a serial task by different age groups. *Quarterly Journal of Experimental Psychology*, 1951, *3*, 166–183.

Monge, R.H. Age differences in dogmatism and anxiety from the 20s to the 70s. Unpublished, 1972.

Riegel, K.F., and Riegel, R.M. A study of changes of attitudes and interests during later years of life. *Vita Humana*, 1960, *3*, 177–206.

Ruch, F.L. The differentiative effects of age upon human learning. *Journal of General Psychology*, 1934, *11*, 261–285.

Smith, D.K. The Einstellung effect in relation to the variables of age and training. *Dissertation Abstracts*, 1967, *27B*, 4115.

Snoddy, G.S. Learning and stability. *Journal of Applied Psychology*, 1926, *10*, 1–36.

Stone, C.P. The age factor in animal learning: I. Rats in the problem box and the maze. *Genetic Psychology Monograph*, 1929, *5*, 1–130.

7
Multidimensional Rigidity

If the problem is one of studying rigidities rather than rigidity, clearly it is necessary to develop and use a variety of different kinds of procedures. If a variety of procedures is used, it is necessary to determine whether or not they are truly different in the sense of measuring different kinds of rigidity. It is also necessary to determine groupings or clusterings of these different kinds of rigidity. It may be that people who tend to be low in two or three types of rigidity tend to be high in two or three other types. The techniques for determining such clusterings, factor analysis and principal-component analysis, involve mathematical treatments of the correlations among the test scores so that a relatively few factors or components describe the many scores.

THREE RIGIDITIES AND I.Q.

There have been several studies of rigidity in aging involving a variety of tests and using the techniques of either factor or principal-component analysis. Probably the first among these was the study by Schaie (1958). He gave a battery of four rigidity tests to 500 men and women between the ages of 20 and 70 years. One test involved substituting capitals for lower case letters when copying a paragraph. For example, "The Duke DREW his sword" becomes "tHE dUKE drew HIS SWORD." The second test involved a list of words to which synonyms were given when the particular word was in capitals, and antonyms when the word was in small letters. The third test was a list of statements which were endorsed as favorable or not; the fourth test also involved statements, but these were in question form, such as, "Do you feel strongly inclined to finish whatever you are doing in spite of being tired of doing it?"

From these four tests, Schaie derived seven scores and subjected these to a factor analysis in order to establish the clusterings of the scores. His analyses led him to the conclusion that the data could be described by three factors or clusterings, which ". . . just about cover the gamut of psychological views on behavioral rigidity" (Schaie, 1958, pp. 3–4). His factors were labeled: (1) Motor-Cognitive Rigidity; (2) Personality-Perceptual Rigidity; and (3) Psychomotor Speed. Schaie (1958, p. 4) wrote:

> The motor-cognitive rigidity factor seems to indicate the individual's ability to shift without difficulty from one activity to another; it is a measure of effective adjustment to shifts in *familiar* patterns and to continuously changing situational demands. The personality-perceptual rigidity factor seems to indicate the individual's ability to adjust readily to *new* surroundings and change in cognitive and environmental patterns; it seems to be a measure of ability to perceive and adjust to *unfamiliar* and *new* patterns and situations. The psychomotor speed factor finally indicates an individual's rate of emission of familiar cognitive responses. A high score on this factor would seem to imply superior functioning efficiency in coping with familiar situations requiring rapid response and quick thinking.

Each of the three rigidity factor scores was related to age in his cross-sectional comparisons such that "people do become more rigid with increasing age on all the dimensions of rigidity measured" (Schaie, 1958, p. 10). The greatest decline was seen with the Motor-Cognitive Rigidity factor and the least decline was seen with the Personality-Perceptual factor.

Along with these rigidity tests Schaie also gave an I.Q. test, Thurstone's SRA Primary Mental Ability (PMA) Test. Schaie examined the relationship between I.Q. and rigidity, seeking to determine whether the extent of correlation changes with age.

He found that I.Q. and rigidity factors were related. For example, a composite of the three rigidity factors and of the PMA test correlated between .60 and .80 in each five-year age grouping except the 61 to 65-year grouping, where the correlation was only .32. The correlations between high rigidity and low mental ability were seen throughout the adult age span, but with a tendency for the correlation to decrease in the later years of life.

This still left open the question of whether those old people who show signs of rigidity do so because of lowered I.Q.s, or whether there is a relationship between rigidity and age, independent of I.Q. (It will be noted that the rigidity-I.Q. relation has the same basic characteristic as the rigidity-learning ability relation, discussed in the previous chapter.)

Schaie (1958) resorted to the statistical technique of analysis of covariance to answer the question of whether rigidity and age go together, independently of I.Q. This technique permits holding one variable "statistically constant," as, for example, I.Q., while testing for age difference in rigidity. It "statistically equates" old people with young people on I.Q. and tests them for differences in rigidity. With the analysis of covariance, Schaie found that the age groups still differed on rigidity. The older subjects made higher rigidity scores even when the effect of I.Q. was negated by statistical means.

Later in this chapter, it will be seen that Schaie and his co-workers modified this conclusion on the basis of subsequent, longitudinal studies. They found somewhat different age patterns, and these will be described in some detail under the heading, "Longitudinal Research" (see pages 109–111).

FIVE RIGIDITIES, I.Q., AND SPEED

By their very nature, studies based upon factor or principal-component analyses are very complex. Factor analysis, as already indicated, or the more exact mathematical form, principal-component analysis, involves forming into a relatively few groups a larger number of test scores. Of the complex factor and component studies on aging, the one by Chown (1961), alluded to on several occasions in the previous chapter, has special interest, since it involves two different types of factor analyses.

Chown gave 18 tests to 200 people aged 20 to 82 years. Sixteen of the 18 tests were rigidity tests, and two were intelligence tests.* These 18 tests yielded 25 scores which were analyzed in three ways:

1. The data of all the subjects were examined in one group. A principal-component analysis was carried out to "find out the structure of those rigidities in the test battery." In this analysis, age of the subject was a 26th variable. Thus, Chown (1961) was able to determine which of the rigidity factors were most closely related to age.

2. Scores on each of the tests were examined in relation to age, independent of the correlations among them. This particular analysis, then, is like those discussed in the previous chapter under the heading, "Simple Rigidity."

---

* The 18 tests and 25 scores are described in some detail on pages 354–355 of Chown (1961). The two intelligence tests were the Progressive Matrices and the Mill-Hill Vocabulary. The 16 rigidity tests, for the most part, were 10-minute pencil-and-paper types of tests. The total battery took two and a quarter hours to complete.

3. Chown carried out three separate principal-component analyses, one each on three different age groupings. Separate analyses were carried out on groups of subjects with average ages of about 26, 41, and 61 years. The purpose of these latter analyses "was to discover whether any organization of the rigidity factors occurred among older subjects."

Intelligence Is Very Important

At the expense of repetition, one of Chown's major conclusions was "that the addition of the present evidence will further weaken the myth of the 'rigid' person . . ." (Chown, 1961, p. 360). Her first analysis, the one of all the subjects together, disclosed five kinds of rigidity. None of these rigidity components, however, were very prominent; they were not nearly so prominent as the components of Age and Intelligence. The largest rigidity component was labeled Spontaneous Flexibility, and it accounted for only 7.8 percent of total variance. The Age component accounted for 9.8 percent of the variance, and the Intelligence component was nearly twice as large, accounting for 20 percent. The other rigidity components were even smaller: Personality Rigidity (5.2 percent), Speed (7.2 percent), and two Disposition Rigidity factors (with 5.5 and 4.8 percent).

Thus, 30 percent of the data, even though based upon so many rigidity tests, were attributable to the components labeled Age and Intelligence. "It is impossible to separate out age and intelligence into factors such that neither loads upon the other—just as it is impossible to separate out the two satisfactorily in real life" (Chown, 1961, p. 361). The older people tended to be both lowest in intelligence of the "problem-solving" type and highest in rigidity. Chown posed the same question with regard to intelligence and rigidity that was asked before: Is low intelligence the cause of rigidity, or is it a consequence? Her data, she said, show that the "effects of low intelligence score were more far-reaching than age itself" in accounting for the total variance (Chown, 1961, p. 362).

This complexity of results brings us again to the basic question of this chapter. In terms of component structure, are elderly persons more rigid than younger ones? Chown would answer, "Yes," but, in the main, only to the extent that their problem-solving type of intelligence is lower. Not all studies are concluded with emphasis on the importance of intelligence in rigidity. In an earlier study by Shields (1958), the emphasis was otherwise. Her study was not a factor analytic or principal-component study; it simply involved four tests of "ideational rigidity," plus a brief test of verbal intelligence. Her subjects were adult women of two ages, 30 years apart. Shields, like Chown, found that the aged subjects scored significantly higher on the rigidity tests than did the younger women, but, like Schaie, and unlike what is suggested in Chown's conclusion, Shields' two age groups remained highly different after the effects of intellectual functioning were statistically removed. Shields believed that chronological age was more important in accounting for rigidity scores than were the intelligence scores.

Age and Rigidity

Although Shields and Chown were differently impressed with the role of intelligence in rigidity, both were in agreement that rigidity as seen "in real life" increases with age. When Chown (1961) examined the performances on each of the 16 rigidity tests in relation to age, she grouped them on the basis of her five rigidity components. Six of the 16 tests were grouped by the component, Spontaneous Flexibility. This component seems to be characterized by tests which measure abilities to think in a variety of different ways, especially unique ways. Rigidity would inhibit the creative expression necessary to perform well on these tests. For example, one test in this group was "Brick Uses." The instruction is to list as many uses as possible for a brick; the score "consists of the number of times the type of use mentioned is altered." On these tests measuring Spontaneous Flexibility, average performances were found to increase from the 20s to the 40s, i.e., people became more flexible as they aged, but the scores decreased after the late 50s.

Six test scores were also represented on the Speed component. Test performances in this group were characterized by how quickly certain simple tasks were written in the usual way, then by how quickly they were written in a way different from usual (for example, backwards), and, further, how quickly the usual and unusual ways could be alternated. On these tests, Speed increased with age up to the early 60s, after which age a marked decline was noted. This age pattern is not the same as that when straight speed of performance is measured. With typical speed measures, decrement in performance is typically continuous with increasing adult age.

Four of the 16 tests displayed an age relationship, distinct from an intelligence relationship. One of these tests, "Liking for Habit," consisted of 39 questionnaire items, among which were the rigidity items. The results on this test suggested "that older people do see themselves as preferring to keep to established routine" (Chown, 1961, p. 360).

Speed, An Aspect of Intelligence and Rigidity in Old Age

It will be recalled that Chown's third analysis consisted of three separate principal-component analyses, each for a different age group. Groups were of approximate mean age 26, 41, and 61 years.

With 60 subjects in each age group, Chown believed that the sample sizes were too small to give definitive results, but they were large enough to provide clues. She reported that only in the old group did a factor emerge which was characterized by a Liking for Detailed Work. Other differences among groups were also noted, but perhaps most important was a shift from the young group where there was a distinct Speed factor, to the old group where the effects of speed were more diffuse and where they were loaded mainly on the Non-verbal Intelligence factor (but on others too). "Thus among old people, but not among the young, these speed tests became a measure of intellectual capability and of the extent of the perseveration of this function" (Chown, 1961, p. 361). Later, in chapter 12, the same quote will be made when discussing the role of speed in different contexts.

Taken together, Chown's studies demonstrate that three variables seem to go hand in hand in later life: There is a slowing of response patterns, there is a decrease in intelligence of the problem-solving kind, and there is an increase in rigidity. Which of these are the more primary? Which the most important? While old age was found to be associated with simultaneous changes in all three variables, it is well to realize that individual differences were large; Chown's data were about people, not about a particular person.

SPEED AND PROBLEM DIFFICULTY

Brinley's rigidity study (1965) was framed in the context of a person's ability to perform tasks involving shifts from one function to another, relative to his ability to perform comparable tasks not involving such shifts. Brinley was interested in tasks requiring speed of performance because a prime characteristic of old age is the slowing which occurs in a wide variety of situations. Brinley wrote:

> In general, the questions which the study was designed to answer were the following: (1) whether older individuals would behave more rigidly in shift tasks despite variations in task content; (2) whether factor analysis would reveal that some relatively independent "rigidity" factor or factors were more important in determining response rates in an

older population than in a younger one; and (3) whether the greater showing which older individuals exhibited in shift tasks would be associated with shifting *per se*, what Cattell and Tiner (1949) termed "process rigidity," or whether it might be associated with other aspects of shift tasks.

Shift and Non-Shift Tasks

Brinley's questions were straightforward, and his research method of answering them was direct. Despite this, his method involved a complexity which may be difficult to understand without Table 7.1 and its accompanying figure, which were taken directly from Brinley's report.

Brinley constructed tasks which required shifting from one operation to another (shift tasks) and tasks which did not (non-shift tasks). Both of these were made up in three forms: verbal material, arithmetic items, and perceptual items. Each combination of form and task type was given with three different kinds of instructions, requiring different operations. Thus, each subject was given nine non-shift tasks plus nine shift tasks; there were three non-shift verbal tasks, three shift verbal tasks, similar numbers of non-shift and shift arithmetic tasks, and similar numbers of perceptual tasks. All responses required a simple checking of alternatives.

More specifically, it may be seen in Table 7.1 that each non-shift task required one type of repetitive operation. The subject checked synonyms when so instructed, antonyms when so instructed, or rhymes when so instructed. Table 7.1 demonstrates example items. A correct check for the synonym "Wild" is "Savage"; the antonym for "Right" is "Wrong"; the rhyme of "Near" is "Beer."

In similar fashion, the arithmetic items involved checking choices with instructions of addition (e.g., $8 + 3 = 11$); subtraction (e.g., $9 - 4 = 5$); and multiplication ($8 \times 7 = 56$). Figure 7.1 presents one perceptual example, but in every item one face differed from the other two on the basis of its hair, eyebrows or mouth. The non-shift task involved instructions bearing on these three facial characteristics.

As indicated, the shift task parallels of these verbal, arithmetic and perceptual non-shift tasks also had three types of instructions: selections, directions, and memory. For example, Table 7.1 shows that the selection instructions of the verbal tasks involved items in which the subject had to discover whether a synonym, antonym, or rhyme was required. "Hard" could only go with "Soft"—thus an antonym was required, not a synonym or a rhyme. Similarly, in the arithmetic task, "6" "2" could only go with "8"—it is an addition instruction. The procedure, "direc-

TABLE 7.1
Examples of Verbal and Arithmetic Materials

NONSHIFT TASKS
Verbal

Synonyms Test	*Wild*	Tame ( )	Tiled ( )	Savage (✓)
Antonyms Test	*Right*	Correct ( )	Wrong (✓)	Bite ( )
Rhyming Test	*Near*	Far ( )	Close ( )	Beer (✓)

Arithmetic

Addition Test	8+3	13 ( )	11 (✓)	12 ( )
Subtraction Test	9—4	5 (✓)	4 ( )	6 ( )
Multiplication Test	8×7	54 ( )	55 ( )	56 (✓)

SHIFT TASKS
Verbal Shift Tasks

Selection Test	*Hard*	First ( )	Beat ( )	Soft (✓)
	Quiet	Better ( )	Find ( )	Silent (✓)
	Wide	Lied (✓)	Bitter ( )	Careful ( )
Directions Test	*Sweet* (opposite)	Beat ( )	Sugary ( )	Sour (✓)
	Bare (same)	Covered ( )	Naked (✓)	Wear ( )
	Bad (rhyme)	Wicked ( )	Add (✓)	Good ( )
Memory Test	*Over*	Above (✓)	Under ( )	Clever ( )
	Tiny	Small ( )	Huge (✓)	Shiny ( )
	Kind	Dined (✓)	Friendly ( )	Cruel ( )

Arithmetic Shift Tasks

Selection Test	6	2	11 ( )	5 ( )	8 (✓)
	9	2	12 ( )	18 (✓)	6 ( )
	9	7	2 (✓)	62 ( )	17 ( )
Directions Test	4—2		8 ( )	2 (✓)	6 ( )
	8+3		11 (✓)	5 ( )	24 ( )
	4×3		1 ( )	12 (✓)	7 ( )
Memory Test	6	4	24 ( )	2 ( )	10 (✓)
	7	4	11 ( )	3 (✓)	28 ( )
	8	3	11 ( )	24 (✓)	5 ( )

FIGURE 7.1: An example of the type of perceptual materials employed. (Permission to reprint this table and figure given by Brinley, 1965, and by Charles C Thomas, publisher.)

From Brinley, J. F. Cognitive sets and accuracy of performance in the elderly. In A. T. Welford and J. E. Birren (Eds.), *Behavior, aging and the nervous system.* 1965 (p. 126). Courtesy of Charles C Thomas, Publisher, Springfield, Illinois.

tions," informs the subject what the instruction is: "Sweet" (opposite) calls for "Sour" as a response; "4 — 2" calls for "2." The "Memory" procedure instructs the subject to shift from synonym, antonym, to rhyme, in the case of the verbal task; addition, subtraction, to multiplication, in the case of the arithmetic tasks.

To repeat, there were shift and non-shift tasks, each with different types of material, given with different instructions. Brinley (1965), in addition, gave three other tasks, each nearly identical with the psychomotor response features of the task in the main battery. This was for the purpose of ascertaining the strictly non-cognitive response aspect differences among subjects. These latter tests involved checking identical words and identical numbers, and copying digits.

Slowness in Shift Performances

The data were clear in indicating that the older subjects tended to spend relatively more time shifting than younger subjects, relative to the time spent in carrying out the non-shift cognitive functions of the task. The older subjects ranged in age from 59 to 82 years, with an average age of about 71 years, and the younger subjects ranged in age from 18 to 35, with an average of 24 years.

In eight of the nine tasks, the ratio of time spent doing the shift task relative to the non-shift task of the same category was significantly greater for the old. Thus, again, the older subjects were seen to be the more rigid. Giving the person step-by-step directions, that is, telling him which function to perform next, minimized the slowing in shift performance of the elderly, while the selections instruction, that is, having him discover which function to perform, maximized the age deficit in shifting.

Rigidity and Task Difficulty

Brinley then carried out an interesting analysis which bears on the question: Is the lower score of the older group a reflection primarily of rigidity or is it basically a reflection of the difficulty of the task? The fact that older people spent relatively more time on the shift tasks in comparison to non-shift tasks may be due, simply, to the fact that the shift tasks were the more difficult ones. It takes greater ability to perform well on difficult tasks irrespective of rigidity. This question is analogous to: Which is the more primary, learning and intelligence, or rigidity? Brinley concluded that it was the difficulty of the task, not rigidity, which accounted for the relative slowness in carrying out the shift procedures.

Rigidity Not More Prominent in the Old

One of the questions that Brinley set out to answer was whether a factor analysis would demonstrate that rigidity factors were more important in the old than in the young. He inter-correlated all his speed scores and carried out a principal-component analysis on the data of the young and of the old, separately. Unlike Chown (1961), Brinley found one factor in each analysis that accounted for an appreciable amount of the total data. Two smaller factors described the task content, i.e., verbal, arithmetic, and perceptual and two still smaller factors were of rigidity. His most important result, however, was that the rigidity factors were not more prominent in the old group than in the young group. The rigidity factors accounted for six percent in the old and eight percent in the young—a trend opposite to a hypothesis of rigidity in later life.

Overall, then, Brinley was not impressed with the notion that rigidity increases in later life. While he observed increased rigidity-type performance in later life, he attributed this to the fact that rigidity tasks are intrinsically more difficult than non-rigidity tasks. Brinley believed it is general ability, not ability unique to rigidity functions, which differentiates the old from the young.

LONGITUDINAL RESEARCH

All the studies on rigidity described so far were cross-sectional studies. In each of these, two or more age groups were compared during the single period of time that the study was being carried out. This means, of course, that the older or oldest people studied were born in a different era than were their younger counterparts; this fact—the fact of different cultural influences—more than the maturational fact of their being older, may have made for the results which were reported.

An interesting, possible illustration of this may be found in the study on rigidity and dogmatism by Riegel and Riegel (1960), described in the previous chapter. Riegel and Riegel reported that "a stereotyped dogmatic and fanatic attitude" increased with age. Their study was carried out in Germany during the later 1950s. This means that the subjects over 75 years were in their early 50s when Hitler rose to power. Those subjects aged 55 were in their early 30s. The subjects aged 17–19 were not yet born when Hitler was so dominant in establishing the cultural values of the early 1930s. Isn't it possible, or even probable, that the "stereotyped dogmatic and fanatic attitude" on the part of the older subjects was more a function of their cultural experiences than of their maturational age changes? If so, it is likely that the 17–19-year-olds of the study, when they are in their 70s, will not be nearly as dogmatic as were the 70-year-olds tested by the Riegels.

Longitudinal follow-up studies would help unravel this confounding between age and cultural effects because the subjects of one age are compared to themselves at an earlier age. A follow-up study involving the dogmatism data was actually carried out by the Riegels, but, unfortunately, the data were not analyzed to unravel the confounding (Riegel, Riegel, and Meyer, 1967). The only follow-up longitudinal studies of rigidity designed to do so were those based upon the original data of Schaie (1958), discussed earlier in this chapter.

Men and women in several age groups ranging from the 20s to the late 60s were tested three different times, each seven years apart, thus covering a period of 14 years (Schaie and Labouvie-Vief, 1974). They were tested with the behavioral rigidity scales discussed before providing indices of Motor-Cognitive Rigidity, Personality-Perceptual Rigidity, and Psychomotor Speed. This experimental cross-sequential design of *repeated measures* is described more fully in chapter 19. In addition to this study, an unrepeated or *independent-measures* design study was carried out (Schaie, Labouvie, and Buech, 1973). In this latter study people are tested only once. Seven years following the first testing, Schaie et al. tested a different, but comparable, sample of subjects. Still a different sample was selected for testing at the time of the third session seven years later. Both the repeated and independent measures are thought to represent different types of longitudinal research.

The results of these studies were different from what might be expected on the basis of the cross-sectional studies described earlier. While the cross-sectional components of both the repeated- and independent-measures studies reflected increased rigidity with age, the longitudinal components did not, or reflected this to a lesser and inconsistent degree. In the case of Motor-Cognitive Rigidity, for example, only the oldest group—the one aged 67—showed increased rigidity over the 14-year test period. This was in the repeated-measures study; in the independent-measures study, only the youngest group (25 years) and a group aged 53 years showed increased rigidity with age.

Personality-Perceptual Rigidity showed more change with age, but nothing dramatic. In the repeated-measures study, increased rigidity with age was seen beginning at 53 years, but not before then. In the independent-measures study, several age groups showed increased rigidity over the three test periods covering 14 years, but even here the consistency with change in relation to age was not great.

Even Psychomotor Speed Rigidity showed a less consistent age pattern than might have been anticipated. In the repeated-measures study, the oldest groups (60 and over) did show increased rigidity with increased age, as did one younger group, but again no broad generalization is possible. The independent-measures study pointed to rigidity and age in even a lesser way.

CONCLUSIONS

What can we conclude from all these data? First, the different methods of data collection and data analysis provided different results. The traditional cross-sectional methods were clear in showing increased rigidity with age. The longitudinal methods were mixed. The different age-sequences showed a complexity such that there were age-decreases as well as age-increases. Second, even when the data pointed to rigidity in old age, it is well to consider that *rigidity is not a necessary concomitant of later life*. The individual differences were enormous.

SUMMARY

After analyzing all, or nearly all, of the data to date bearing on the problem of rigidity in later life, and after reviewing these data in some detail in this and in the previous chapter, the most definitive statement that can be made is that the question of whether or not increasing age brings with it increasing rigidity is too simplistic to be answered with a clear affirmative or negative. The problem involves an ambiguity and a complexity that can be summarized only by recourse to extensive oversimplification.

The data do seem to indicate that, when elderly adults are compared to young adults, the older people are the more rigid. But, this rigidity is not, or may not be, intrinsic to maturational age changes. The rigidity is determined in part, or in whole, by cultural and experiential factors, quite independent of age itself. While the elderly of today may be seen as more rigid than their younger counterparts, the elderly of tomorrow are likely to be less rigid than present-day elderly people, and perhaps not more rigid than their junior contemporaries. The reasons for this conjecture are the results of longitudinal investigations, on one hand, and of increasingly greater opportunities for continued intellectual growth on the other.

Intellectual growth is expected to minimize rigidity because so much of the literature pointed to a tie between I.Q. and rigidity: on the average, elderly people perform less well on intelligence tests than do younger adults, and those elderly who do perform poorly also have poor scores on tests of rigidity. While some data indicated an age relation to rigidity quite independent of intelligence, the intrinsic tie between these two variables cannot be denied. When a task is difficult cognitively, as rigidity tasks tend to be, elderly people often have problems with it.

Also associated with rigidity in later life is the slowing of response patterns. One study pointed to a triad: With increasing age there was a decrease in intelligence of the problem-solving kind, there was a decrease in speed of response which in later life seemed to be part of general intelligence, and these, in turn, were related to rigidity. Which of the triad is the primary factor in the sense of its being responsible for the others? The answer is unknown, and is important mainly for theoretical analysis. In practical, every-day affairs, the question is less important than the recognition that the three variables tend to go hand-in-hand. This means that when an older person is seen to be bright and able, he, in all likelihood, will be seen also as flexible, not rigid; he will also be seen as relatively quick in pursuing his interests.

REFERENCES

Brinley, J.F. Cognitive sets and accuracy of performance in the elderly. In A. T. Welford and J.E. Birren (Eds.), *Behavior, aging and the nervous system.* Springfield, Ill.: Charles C Thomas, 1965, pp. 114–149.

Cattell, R.B., and Tiner, L.G. The varieties of structural rigidity. *Journal of Personality*, 1949, 17, 321–341.

Chown, S.M. Age and the rigidities. *Journal of Gerontology*, 1961, 16, 353–362.

Riegel, K.F., and Riegel, R.M. A study of changes of attitudes and interests during the later years of life. *Vita Humana*, 1960, 3, 177–206.

Riegel, K.F., Riegel, R.M., and Meyer, G. A study of the dropout rates in longitudinal research on aging and the prediction of death. *Journal of Personality and Social Psychology*, 1967, 5, 342–348.

Schaie, K.W. Rigidity-flexibility and intelligence: a cross-sectional study of the adult life span from 20 to 70 years. *Psychological Monographs: General and Applied.* 1958, 72, No. 9 (Whole No. 462), 1–26.

Schaie, K.W., Labouvie, G.V., and Buech, B.U. Generational and cohort-specific differences in adult cognitive functioning. *Developmental Psychology*, 1973, 9, 151–166.

Schaie, K.W., and Labouvie-Vief, G. Generational versus ontogenetic components of change in adult cognitive behavior: a fourteen-year cross-sequential study. *Developmental Psychology*, 1974, 10, 305–320.

Sheilds, E.A. Rigidity in the aged. *Dissertation Abstracts*, 1958, 18, 668–669.

8

Personality and Cognition in Cautious Behavior

> For college youth the standard of abstract right and wrong is dead. . . .
> Not only have the concepts of *sin, wickedness, piety,* and *righteousness*
> completely lost meaning for the modern young person, but the author-
> ity upon which the right and wrong standard is based—the authority
> of church, home, school, and state—is fast waning.

This quote was seen in a 1928 article (Anderson and Dvorak, 1928, p. 286), making it clear that what we now call the "generation gap" is not new at all. Rather, it is an old popular belief that attitudes, interests, and values change with the generations and that a conservative outlook and cautious behavior typify the old.

Research during the later 1920s through the 1940s focused upon age comparisons regarding attitudes, interests, and values and substantiated this belief sufficiently for Kuhlen (1959, p. 882) to write

> . . . older adults are more conservative than younger adults. They do
> not like change; they cling to older ideas and are slower to adopt new
> ones; in morals, politics and general living they are likely to be "old-
> fashioned" rather than modern and liberal. . . .

The substantiation of this belief, however, was not extensive; the empirical investigations of the 1920s through the 1940s did not disclose marked age patterns of conservatism. In fact, the studies showed that "the differences between means of age groups are frequently so slight and individual differences so great that these age trends may have little practical significance" (Pressey and Kuhlen, 1957, p. 495).

This Pressey-Kuhlen conclusion in reviewing the data to the 1950s seems correct today. Glamser (1974) questioned the wives of university faculty members regarding their opinions about controversial issues of race, law enforcement, and patriotism. None of the women were over 65 years although to this age there was a tendency, albeit a slight one, toward conservatism (the significant correlation between age and con-

113

servative opinion was $r = .28$). This tendency was manifested even when social class, education, and other factors were controlled. Obviously, factors in addition to age mold attitudes and opinions; some are even more important than age—education, for example.

Studies carried out since 1950 have been less concerned with the interests, attitudes, and values of the elderly than they have been with performances of the elderly that could be explained on the basis of some form of cautiousness. Conservatism and cautiousness have in common a disinclination to make a change or to venture a response that could result in gain if there is a risk of losing what is already in hand.

MANY CONTEXTS AND FORMS OF CAUTIOUSNESS

Some of the studies described here resorted to the concept of cautiousness in post hoc explanation of data collected for other purposes. Other studies, however, investigated cautiousness directly. Both types of study attest to the wide array of situations in which cautiousness in later life may be manifest. The studies also highlight many aspects of personality which tie in with the concept of cautiousness. The general hypothesis derived from these studies, and requiring further test, is that in later life there is discomfort with the new and the uncertain. There is a loss of self-confidence and the expectation or fear of failure, loss, and rejection. These threatening consequences inhibit venturesome behavior and result in cautiousness. The studies from which this hypothesis derives are the basis of the present chapter.

Carefulness

If the young may be compared to the hare, the old may be compared to the tortoise—slow and steady, sometimes to win the race. The old are thought to be cautious in the avoidance of mistakes; there is valuation of accuracy over speed; errors are to be eschewed at all costs.

Valuing Accuracy. Research has borne evidence making it possible to maintain this analogy of the tortoise and the hare. For example, Welford (1951) reported that in performing a psychomotor task, "the subjects in their thirties appeared to maintain the speed of those in their twenties, but at the expense of accuracy. From the forties onwards accuracy was restored at the expense of speed."

While these results are interpretable in the framework of cautiousness, Welford did not prefer to do so. In fact, he brought up the concept of cautiousness in order to refute it; he believed the determining characteristics of the slowing in performance of the elderly were not volitional. Welford suggested that the slowing in behavior, even if related to increased accuracy, was due, not to a preference, but to limitations in perceptual mechanisms and in translation mechanisms which control movement (Welford, 1958).

The unsettled controversy, therefore, is whether aged people purposely, i.e., with "free will," are careful to provide accuracy because they value it, or whether accuracy is simply a by-product of failing biopsychological mechanisms. This controversy has been cast in terms of a *motivation hypothesis* in the case of the "free will" position, versus a *consequence hypothesis* in the case of the failing mechanism position (Botwinick, 1959, p. 763). It is to be noted that, whichever hypothesis is the more correct or the more encompassing, the accuracy of the elderly is often greater than that of the young only in a relative sense. Often, as in Welford's (1951) study, the youngest subjects are both speedy and accurate.

Avoidance of Mistakes. The tendency to avoid mistakes may be called upon in explanation of the well-established observation that older people very often do not respond in a testing situation. When performances of older people are poor, often this is attributable to their failure to answer questions rather than to their answering them incorrectly. Psychologists have classed the non-response as an *omission error* and the incorrect response as a *commission error.*

Perhaps the first empirical demonstration of this phenomenon was in the classic 1928 publication, *Adult Learning,* by Thorndike, Bregman, Tilton, and Woodyard (pp. 171–172).

> We have also compared old with young . . . in respect of the proportion which omitted elements are of omitted plus wrong. If age is accompanied by an increase in caution or a decrease in impulsiveness in intellectual operations the old would be expected to write no answer rather than a wrong answer oftener than the young. . . . There are many irregularities, but the general influence of age is clearly toward a substantial increase in the percent which the number of omissions is of the number of wrongs.

Thorndike et al. demonstrated the propensity of the aged to commit the omission error more frequently than the commission error in the context of intelligence testing. The omission error by the aged has been demonstrated in other contexts as well. In learning situations, for example, Korchin and Basowitz (1957) with paired-associate procedures, and Eisdorfer, Axelrod, and Wilkie (1963) with serial learning procedures, demonstrated the omission error effect. In perceptual situations also, Basowitz and Korchin (1957) demonstrated the effect. Here, however, the effect was seen in one situation but not in another, indicating the need to specify the specific procedures or operations.

Basowitz and Korchin (1957) presented two tasks to their subjects. In one, the Gestalt Completion Test, the main ability tested is perceptual integration of fragmented parts of pictures. The subject's job is to put together in his mind the parts of the pictures which have been presented in a mixed pattern. In this task, the omission error was prominent. In the second task, Concealed Figures, the error was not prominent. The ability tested here is to identify a simple figure embedded in a complex background which masks it. It is possible, however, that the specific instructions given with this task minimized the omission error. All that was required of the subject was to simply specify whether or not the figure could be found in the background. It was not necessary to point out the concealed figure. As will be seen later, instructions such as this, in providing a circumscribed structure and direction, minimize ambiguity and, in so doing, minimize aging patterns of the cautious omission error.

Need for Certainty

It is a reasonable hypothesis that the self-confidence with which people face the world determines in part what they demand from a situation. As self-confidence decreases, more certainty is required before there is response. The omission error may stem from just such a desire for more certainty—better not respond than be wrong. It staves off failure and maximizes self-esteem. This hypothesis was implicit in the conclusions drawn from several studies, as may be seen in the following.

Confidence in Responding. In the perception study of Basowitz and Korchin (1957, p. 96) it was suggested that with increased age there is "the need for a high degree of certainty before committing oneself." In their learning study (Korchin and Basowitz, 1957, p. 68) it was concluded:

> Despite the injunction to guess, it may be that older persons require greater certainty before they are willing to report. . . . This tendency to inhibit response in the uncertain situation may reflect a more profound personality defense of the aged through which the recognition of inadequacy is avoided.

The need for certainty was indicated also in still a different type of study. Adults of two diverse ages were compared in their judgment of which of two vertical bars was the shorter (Botwinick, Brinley, and

Robbin, 1958). The two bars were presented simultaneously; sometimes the difference in their length was great and easy to distinguish, sometimes it was small and difficult to distinguish. For all practical purposes, no limit in time to view the two bars was imposed because the judgments were made in much shorter times than the actual two seconds given. The older people were generally slower than the young in making the judgments, and this was more the case with the difficult discriminations than the easy ones. Following this, both the old and young adults were driven to make their judgments more quickly by the expedient of reducing the time allowed for viewing the two bars—they were shown the bars for only fifteen one-hundreths of a second.

People of both age groups made their judgments more quickly than before, but the older people now made their judgments with a relatively large increase in speed with the difficult discriminations. As may be seen in Figure 8.1, the old people were slowest when they had a long time in which to make the difficult judgments; their speed improved greatly in judging these very same bars when they were pushed to be quicker by the experimental procedure. It was concluded that: "It is as if the older person takes a longer time with the difficult discriminations when he has this time to take, but relative to his ability to discriminate correctly, the older person may not require this added time" (Botwinick, Brinley, and Robbin, 1958, p. 6). This alleged extra time was thought to be reflective of an increase with age in "response reviewing or confidence level required before responding." The increased "confidence level required" may well be for the purpose indicated by Korchin and Basowitz, viz., to avoid the recognition of inadequacy. To minimize their own expected failures, to increase their confidence of being correct, they required more certainty from the situation.

In a follow-up of these studies, Silverman (1963) put the confidence hypothesis to a more direct test. He matched two adult age groups in their ability to recognize words shown for very brief exposures. His matching of age groups was based on their performances under instructions which forced a response, i.e., the subject had to guess the word, if necessary. Silverman (1963, p. 372) then compared the two age groups in their responses when they were under instructions to be "sure they had recognized it . . . to say nothing at all and wait for the next word if they were not sure."

In the matching procedure, Silverman obliged response regardless of whether or not the subject felt sure and wanted to respond. Choosing young and old adults who performed equally well, and then giving them the opportunity to respond only when sure, the confidence hypothesis was considered confirmed if the older group gave fewer responses than did the younger group. The older group did give fewer responses than the younger group.[1]

Self-Expression of Confidence. It would seem that if older people desire more certainty, need a higher level of confidence before responding, especially if this stems from an expectation or fear of failure, they would be aware of lacking self-confidence. An obvious way to test this is by the simple expedient of asking for expressions of self-confidence. However, because there is a gap between feeling inadequate and admitting it, simply asking may not be the best way to gain information. Nevertheless, it is a place to begin.

Elderly persons and young adults were asked to rate themselves with respect to their levels of self-confidence in responding to two types of questionnaire situations (Botwinick, 1970). In one situation no knowledge or information was required; in the other, information was involved but was not ordinarily available to the responder and was not essential for response. The "fear of recognizing their inadequacy" or "greater confidence level required" might be more a factor when information is involved than when it is not.

The no-information questionnaire was a true-false version of the 60-item Depression scale (D-scale) of the Personality test, MMPI (Hathaway and McKinley, 1956). Each item was answered true or false and, in addition, checked on a four-point scale going from "extremely confident" to "not at all confident" in the response. In similar fashion, 24 items of the information questionnaire[2] were checked on a four-point scale, going from "nearly certain" to "very uncertain."

The results of this study were not at all in accord with the expectation that the old adults would show themselves as less self-confident than the young adults. In the case of the questionnaire involving information, old and young adults were similar in their declared levels of self-confidence. In the case of the questionnaire not involving such infor-

---

[1] Silverman considered the hypothesis only partially confirmed because the level of statistically significant age differences was not great (p<.10). The t-value was 1.99 with 22 subjects in each age group. A one-tailed test of significance would be appropriate in this case; had Silverman carried out such a test, his results would show statistically significant age differences at less than the .05 level.

[2] The questionnaire was a slightly modified version of the "Band-Width" procedure used by Wallach and Kogan (1965, pp. 112–115), which was based upon "The Category Width Scale" of Pettigrew (1958).

Each item of this questionnaire started with a declarative statement, as, for example, "Most men in the world are around five feet, seven inches tall." One part asked a question regarding the maximum dimension (fastest, longest, most) and the second part asked a question regarding a minimum dimension. In the example given, the first part asked, "How tall is the tallest man in the world?" The second part asked, "How short is the shortest man in the world?"

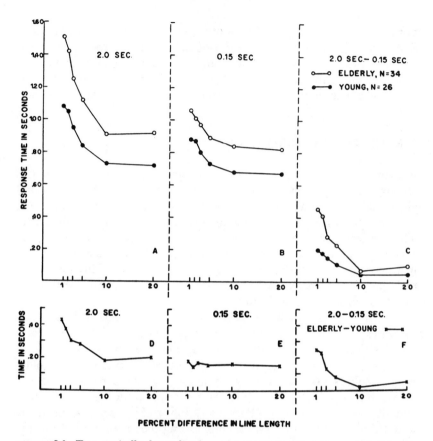

PERCENT DIFFERENCE IN LINE LENGTH

FIGURE 8.1: Two vertically drawn line-bars placed side by side were presented tachistoscopically to adults of two age groups: 67-71 years and 18-35 years. Each person had to judge which of the two bars, right or left, was the shorter. The longer bar was always 80 mm. long and the shorter bar was either 1, 2, 3, 5, 10, or 20 percent shorter than this.

Each person was urged to make the judgment as fast as possible. The line-bar pairs were presented for 2.00 seconds, then they were presented for 0.15 seconds. (Figure 1 from Botwinick et al., 1958. Permission to reprint this figure was given by *Gerontologia*, now called *Human Development*.)

mation, the two age groups were different, but it was the younger group, not the older, which declared itself to have less confidence.

Two points are clear with respect to these results. First, as already indicated, a conscious self-rating of confidence may not reflect the facts. Conceivably, it could reflect just the opposite, i.e., an effort to minimize or even deny a loss of confidence in oneself. Second, these results, especially when examined along with those of a study by Wallach and Kogan (1961), show that a notion of generalized self-confidence may not be as meaningful as a notion rooted in specific context. Wallach and Kogan found elderly men less self-confident in their responses to questionnaire items than were young men, but elderly women were not less self-confident than young women. Specific contexts allow self-confidence for some people, aging women, for example, while some contexts do not.

STRUCTURE AND DIRECTION

A clear situational structure and a clear direction minimize differences among age groups. Korchin and Basowitz (1956) presented young and elderly adults with a series of 13 pictures, the first of which was a cat that, by successive changes in the picture series, gradually became a dog. The greatest ambiguity of percept, i.e., dog or cat, was found in the middle pictures in the series. Frenkel-Brunswik (1949) first used such a picture series to investigate the now classic concept, "intolerance of ambiguity," as a "perceptual personality variable." A sample of this picture series may be seen in Figure 8.2.

When Korchin and Basowitz presented their subjects with this dog-cat series, they found that the older adults tended to shift from cat to dog later in the series than did the young adults. Moreover, they tended to vacillate more from dog to cat in the successive pictures. The older people could be said to be cautious in modifying their percept to dog.

A subsequent study based upon this one was carried out, but with a variation of the procedure (Botwinick, 1962). The variation in procedure led to a variation of results, emphasizing the importance of specifying the conditions of measurement. The same dog-cat series was presented to young and old adults, and, in addition, a 22-picture series of a triangle merging into a circle was given. In this study, the shift was made *earlier* in the series by the older people than by the younger.

In the Korchin and Basowitz study it might be concluded that the older subjects were more cautious in making the change because the ambiguous situation was fraught with uncertainty. In the Botwinick study, uncertainty was minimal. When Frenkel-Brunswik showed the pictures she asked some form of, "What is it?" This made for uncertainty with cautiousness and perseveration. When Korchin and Basowitz showed the pictures they asked, "Is it more like a cat or more like a dog?" There was more structure here, but the emphasis was not on shifting and uncertainty remained. The older people vacillated back and forth and then made the final shift late in the series. In the Botwinick study there was maximum structure: The need to shift was clearly emphasized in the instructions; the beginning and end points of the series were shown at the start of the experiment. The subjects were not given an opportunity to vacillate back to initial percepts since the experiment was terminated with the first shift.

It is suggested here that, given appropriate structure and direction rather than an opportunity to determine structure and direction by oneself, the older person will perform with minimum difficulty. As problems become harder, as certainty diminishes, perhaps as self-confidence

FIGURE 8.2: A series of 13 pictures was shown to each person, one picture at a time. Each picture was a combination of a cat and a dog, with the first picture in the series being most clearly a cat and the last picture in the series being most clearly a dog. The middle pictures in the series were the most ambiguous, being about as much cat as dog. Pictures 1, 7, and 13 in the series are presented here. (Figure 1 from Korchin and Basowitz, 1956. Permission to reprint this figure given by S. J. Korchin and the *Journal of Personality*.)

declines, as the need for change remains unspecified, the older person will fare less and less well.

Specifying directions to provide structure was seen also as helpful to the elderly in quite a different situation. As described in the previous chapter, Brinley (1965) tested old and young people in a series of mainly cognitive tasks. The tasks were given with three different instructions: (1) the subject had to discover for himself what was required (least structured); (2) the subject needed to keep in mind a sequence of instructions; and (3) called "Directions," the subject was told explicitly what the test required (most structured). The older people performed most adequately in the structured situation and least well in the unstructured one (see Table and Figure 7.1).

FACTORS RELATED TO CAUTIOUSNESS

If old age is associated with discomfort in uncertain situations, with a need for structure, with the expectation of poor accomplishments, why is this so? There seem to be three classes of reasons: factors of ability, environmental demands, and personality.

If ability declines with age, an expectation of failure is realistic. It is very important, however, to ascertain whether goals and activities based on these abilities are necessary, or even desirable. Why should an old man engage in competitive market-place activities, or sports, or even in interpersonal power relationships?

Does the social order work to the old man's advantage, or does it so structure the reward system as to make him a loser? After all, in any practical sense, a decline matters only if it is relevant to a man's needs, real or imagined.

Are personality changes associated with age contributory to cautious attitudes? Are such changes of primary importance in understanding cautiousness in later life?

These three classes of factors—ability levels, environmental demands, and personality considerations—have not been investigated very thoroughly, as they relate to cautiousness. If they were, we would have a better understanding than we do about the large individual differences in cautiousness seen even among the elderly.

Ability

Cautiousness and cognitive ability seem to be related. Cognitive ability as measured cross-sectionally declines with age. This decline of ability, however, is not equal along all dimensions. This may be seen clearly in Figure 13.2, describing the differential decline with age of intelligence test functions. It is the very type of abilities examined in this chapter which undergo the greatest age changes—the functions which have been described as perceptual integrative, involving speed of response. On the other hand, verbal abilities and stored information decline least, if at all, with age (see chapter 13).

Edwards and Wine (1963) gave an intelligence test which measures functions declining with age (the Raven Progressive Matrices), and they also gave a personality questionnaire (Comrey Personality Inventory). These two tests were given to men of a wide age range, patients in a VA hospital. Cautiousness, among other characteristics, was found to increase with age, and intelligence to decrease; but, when intelligence levels were matched for the men of different ages, cautiousness was no longer seen as age-related. Edwards and Wine concluded that cautiousness in later life was a function of intellectual decline. As in the discussion of rigidity in the two previous chapters, a reverse conclusion is also possible: Older men were lower in intelligence as a result of their cautiousness, not the other way around. Either interpretation is equally tenable from the study.

Verbal ability was also seen related to cautiousness. Wallach and Kogan (1961) observed that vocabulary test scores and an index of cautiousness were correlated in much the same way as observed by Edwards and Wine. High verbal intelligence was seen with low cautiousness, and vice versa.

Social Order

Youth, not old age, is valued in Western culture—the old try to appear young, and the young try to remain young. It is a social phenomenon against man's nature; it is a pattern destined to make man at the end part of his life feel unable, unworthy, and unwanted. As old age is reached, people tend to withdraw from other people and from activities, and become increasingly turned inward. There is a disengagement from the social scene. The theory and problem of disengagement is discussed fully in chapter 5; here, it need only be recognized that there is a point of view that this disengagement is more a function of society's response to the old person than it is a natural consequence of his being. Society is organized to meet man's aging with condemnation, with rejection, with the expectation of his failure. Man incorporates the values of society and thus, when old, accepts his own unworthiness. If this be correct, it is only to be expected that the aged would inhibit response, value accu-

omission error, vacillate, desire certainty—be cautious. It
at Edwards and Wine (1963) reported a cluster of per-
which they labeled "yielding to society."

Variables

Many facets of personality have already been seen to be intimately
tied to patterns of cautiousness. Few aging studies, however, have aimed
directly at determining the effect of a specific set of personality measures
on cautiousness. A study by Kogan and Wallach (1961), involving the
role of anxiety, is among the few. If failing abilities make for expectations of failure, if society frames human relations so that the aged are
rejected, we might expect that the ensuing cautiousness would be laden
with anxiety.

The study by Kogan and Wallach suggested instead a different role
for anxiety. Women ranging in age from 51 to 86 years were given a test
of anxiety (a group form of the MMPI, which was factor analyzed,
yielding a large factor labeled "anxiety"). Low (factor) scores of anxiety
were believed related to "satisfaction with or adjustment to one's
acknowledged 'elderly' or 'non-elderly' status . . . [it] . . . might reflect
the extent to which feeling of elderliness or non-elderliness are conflict
free" (Kogan and Wallach, 1961, pp. 124–125). Feelings of elderliness
were ascertained by what was called "subjective age." Each woman was
asked, "Do you consider yourself elderly?" A "yes" was scored as 3,
"undecided" as 2, and "no" as 1.

In addition, measures of cautiousness were made. The overall finding
was that subjective feelings of elderliness were correlated with cautiousness in the low anxiety group, but not in the high. It was suggested that
the low anxiety women, whether realistically or not, may have been rea-
sonably satisfied with their self-perceptions. If they saw themselves as
elderly, they were cautious; if they didn't, they weren't cautious. The
anxious women, on the other hand, were thought of as in conflict with
regard to their elderliness. These women were cautious in ways unrelated
to their self-perceptions.

Despite the rather complicated role anxiety played in the study of
Kogan and Wallach (1961), the more simple role suggested earlier is
not to be disregarded without evidence, i.e., anxiety may be part of the
cautiousness associated with feelings of inadequacy resulting from
declining abilities and cultural expectation. The omission error and all
the rest can be seen as a general withdrawal, perhaps attributed to—or
at least associated with—a high level of anxiety (Eisdorfer, 1965, p. 22).
Anxiety is only one of many dimensions of personality which may
relate to cautiousness.

MORE THAN ONE KIND OF CAUTIOUSNESS?

When psychologists and others first began the study of intelligence there was a quest for the measurement of overall, general intelligence. Further investigation disclosed general intelligence factors, but, in addition, pointed to a large variety of specific intellective abilities. There are many kinds of intelligence. The same was said for rigidity, except that the case for an overall, generalized rigidity factor is not as good as it is for intelligence (see chapters 6 and 7). So it may be with cautiousness: it may be that, when the study of cautiousness is more complete, more than one kind of cautiousness will be found. It may be that the notion of a generalized cautiousness factor is a myth. Evidence for more than one kind of cautiousness is seen in the next chapter.

SUMMARY

It is an old, popular belief that attitudes, interests, and values change with the generations so that older adults become characterized by a conservative outlook and a cautious behavior. Research studies during the 1920s through the 1940s substantiated this popular belief somewhat, but in the main they showed only slight age trends toward conservatism, if any at all.

Studies since then, those carried out since 1950, were less concerned with attitudes, interests, and values than they were with performances which could be explained on the basis of some form of cautiousness. Conservatism and cautiousness have in common the disinclination to make a change for the sake of gain when loss may be the result instead.

Several lines of investigation have suggested that in later life there is more cautiousness. It seems to stem from a discomfort with the uncertain, with the expectation and fear of failure. Cautiousness is thus seen as a defense for ego-saving purposes. Perhaps for the purpose of this defense, the elderly seem to value accuracy over speed; often they will avoid responding altogether, and avoid making mistakes in so doing. While there is controversy whether or not the trade-off of speed for accuracy, and the omission error for the commission error, is volitional in nature, there is little doubt that older people do not tend to risk being wrong for the sake of being right or fast.

Perhaps it is for this reason that older people seem to desire great certainty from a situation before committing themselves to a response. Certainty provides a high level of confidence in being correct. Ambiguous situations provide little information and structure, and are thus uncertain. Given clear structure and direction, the older person may be expected to perform optimally. As tasks become difficult, as ambiguity increases, as the need to change patterns of thought and behavior remain unclear, the older person may fare less and less well. It would seem, from all of the foregoing, that older people would have less confidence in their behaviors than would younger people. Moreover, it would seem that this would be so apparent that they would freely admit to it. Questionnaire data did not bear this out; perhaps the gap between feeling inadequate and admitting it negates the validity of answers to direct questioning. Low self-confidence, therefore, remains but an unconfirmed hypothesis with respect to the elderly.

Why do the elderly behave in a way suggesting that greater certainty and structure is desirable? First, there is decline in certain abilities with age, particularly those underlying the functions in which older people have shown inclinations toward cautiousness. Second, the social order values youth, not old age. Society meets man's aging with rejection and expectation of failure. It is to be expected, then, that aging man would withdraw, desire certainty, and inhibit his response to avoid mistakes. Third, other personality variables may relate to cautiousness. Anxiety, for example, thought to stem from feelings of inadequacy, may make for general withdrawal and cautious response. One study showed that congruence between cautiousness and feelings of elderliness was apparent when only a small amount of anxiety was present; when there was much anxiety, this congruence was not seen.

REFERENCES

Anderson, A., and Dvorak, B. Differences between college students and their elders in standards of conduct. *Journal of Abnormal and Social Psychology*, 1928, 23, 286–292.

Basowitz, H., and Korchin, S.J. Age differences in the perception of closure. *Journal of Abnormal and Social Psychology*, 1957, 54, 93–97.

Botwinick, J. Drives, expectancies, and emotions. In J.E. Birren (Ed.), *Handbook of aging and the individual: psychological and social aspects.* Chicago: Univ. of Chicago Press, 1959, pp. 739–768.

Botwinick, J. A research note on the problem of perceptual modification in relation to age. *Journal of Gerontology*, 1962, 17, 190–192.

Botwinick, J. Age differences in self-ratings of confidence. *Psychological Reports*, 1970, 27, 865–866.

Botwinick, J., Brinley, J.F., and Robbin, J.S. The interaction effects of perceptual difficulty and stimulus exposure time on age differences in speed and accuracy of response. *Gerontologia*, 1958, 2, 1–10.

Brinley, J.F. Cognitive sets and accuracy of performance in the elderly. In A. T. Welford and J.E. Birren (Eds.), *Behavior, aging and the nervous system*, Springfield, Ill.: Charles C Thomas, 1965, pp. 114–149.

Edwards, A., and Wine, D. Personality changes with age: their dependency on concomitant intellectual decline. *Journal of Gerontology*, 1963, *18*, 182–184.

Eisdorfer, C. Verbal learning and response time in the aged. *Journal of Genetic Psychology*, 1965, *107*, 15–22.

Eisdorfer, C., Axelrod, S., and Wilkie, F. L. Stimulus exposure time as a factor in serial learning in an aged sample. *Journal of Abnormal and Social Psychology*, 1963, *67*, 594–600.

Frenkel-Brunswik, E. Intolerance of ambiguity as an emotional and perceptual personality variable. *Journal of Personality*, 1949, *18*, 108-143.

Glamser, F.D. The importance of age to conservative opinions: a multivariate analysis. *Journal of Gerontology*, 1974, *29*, 549–554.

Hathaway, S.R., and McKinley, J.C. Scale 2 (Depression). In G.S. Welsh and W.G. Dahlstrom (Eds.), *Basic readings on the MMPI in psychology and medicine*. Minneapolis: Univ. of Minnesota Press, 1956, pp. 73–80.

Kogan, N., and Wallach, M.A. The effect of anxiety on relations between subjective age and caution in an older sample. In P.H. Hock and J. Zubin (Eds.), *Psychopathology of aging*. New York: Grune & Stratton, 1961, pp. 123-135.

Korchin, S.J., and Basowitz, H. The judgment of ambiguous stimuli as an index of cognitive functioning in aging. *Journal of Personality*, 1956, *25*, 81–95.

Korchin, S.J., and Basowitz, H. Age differences in verbal learning. *Journal of Abnormal and Social Psychology*, 1957, *54*, 64–69.

Kuhlen, R.G. Aging and life-adjustment. In J. E. Birren (Ed.), *Handbook of aging and the individual: psychological and social aspects*. Chicago: Univ. of Chicago Press, 1959, pp. 852–897.

Pettigrew, T.P. The measurement and correlates of category width as a cognitive variable. *Journal of Personality*, 1958, *26*, 532–544.

Pressey, S.L., and Kuhlen, R.G. *Psychological development through the life span*. New York: Harper, 1957.

Silverman, I. Age and the tendency to withhold responses. *Journal of Gerontology*, 1963, *18*, 372–375.

Thorndike, E.L., Bregman, E.O., Tilton, J.W., and Woodyard, E. *Adult learning*. New York: The Macmillan Company, 1928.

Wallach, M.A., and Kogan, N. Aspects of judgment and decision making: interrelationships and changes with age. *Behavioral Sciences*, 1961, *6*, 23–36.

Wallach, M.A., and Kogan, N. *Modes of thinking in young children*. New York: Holt, Rinehart & Winston, 1965.

Welford, A.T. *Skill and age: an experimental approach*. London: Oxford Univ. Press, 1951.

Welford, A.T. Psychological and social gerontology in Europe. *Journal of Gerontology*, 1958, *13*, 51–67, Supplement no. 1.

9

Cautiousness in Decision

The previous chapter disclosed patterns of cautiousness in later life in a variety of experimental contexts of cognitive and perceptual natures. The present chapter continues the discussion, focusing on decision processes. The distinction between decision processes and cognitive or perceptual ones is not absolute. Perceiving an ambiguous figure involves decision as to what it is. Learning a list of words may involve decision of whether to verbalize a half-guess. For the most part, however, these decisions are not ones we ponder; we do not consciously deliberate alternative aspects of ambiguous figures or words in learning lists.

The data of the present chapter are specifically involved with tasks that call for deliberation of alternatives. The situations involve more social and practical decisions than do those in the previous chapter.

RISK OF GAIN WITH CHANCE OF LOSS

Wallach and Kogan (1961) constructed an interesting questionnaire which they gave to young and elderly adults. This questionnaire consisted of 12 "life situations," each one involving a central character who faced a decision. The decision was whether or not to embark upon a course of action which, if successful, would bring much gain, but, if not successful, would result in serious loss. Each person responding to the questionnaire and reviewing the 12 "life situations" had to indicate how he would advise the central character in the decisions. Each person revealed something of his gambling propensities in the advising, since the decision was made on the basis of the probability of success deemed necessary to take the action.

Wallach and Kogan (1961, pp. 27–28) wrote:

As an example of the situations presented, the first item follows in its entirety:

"(1) Mr. A, an electrical engineer who is married and has one child, has been working for a large electronics corporation since graduating from college five years ago. He is assured of a lifetime job with a modest, though adequate, salary, and liberal pension benefits upon retirement. On the other hand, it is very unlikely that his salary will increase much before he retires. While attending a convention, Mr. A is offered a job with a small, newly founded company with a highly uncertain future. The new job would pay more to start and would offer the possibility of a share in the ownership if the company survived the competition of the larger firms.

Imagine that you are advising Mr. A. Listed below are several probabilities or odds of the new company's proving financially sound. *Please check the lowest probability that you would consider acceptable to make it worthwhile for Mr. A to take the new job.*

—— The chances are 1 in 10 that the company will prove financially sound.

—— The chances are 3 in 10 that the company will prove financially sound.

—— The chances are 5 in 10 that the company will prove financially sound.

—— The chances are 7 in 10 that the company will prove financially sound.

—— The chances are 9 in 10 that the company will prove financially sound.

—— Place a check here if you think Mr. A should *not* take the new job no matter what the probabilities."

Eleven other situations were presented, each in the same manner as the first one. Each was scored on the basis of the probability of success deemed necessary to take the indicated action: A score of 9 (chances in 10) represents a conservative decision—a requirement of a high likelihood that the action would lead to success. A most incautious person would be scored as 1 (chance in 10 of succeeding). Refusal to advise the risky alternative regardless of its probability of success was scored as 10 (chances in 10). The higher the score, the less risk is indicated in the choice and the more cautious the responder is taken to be.

Older People Are More Cautious than Younger People

Wallach and Kogan (1961) compared young men with older men, and young women with older women in regard to cautiousness. In both comparisons, the older group was seen as the more cautious. The analysis focused on the content of the "life situations." Both older men and women seemed to be especially cautious in decisions involving financial matters. Not surprisingly, perhaps, for them the lure of substantial financial gain was not worth the possible loss of money-in-hand. Some of the 12 "life situations" reflected cautiousness in later life in one of the sexes, rather than in both. Wallach and Kogan reported that the older men seemed more cautious than the younger men in items dealing with professional failure and with death. Older women were more cautious than younger women in items concerning defeat in a game and in unsuccessful marriage. With the possible exception of the risk-of-death item differentiating only males, and the peculiarity of the game situation differentiating the females, Wallach and Kogan suggested the results were in accord with cultural expectation.

Different Problems for Young and Old

A perusal of the 12 "life situations" indicated that they mostly involve problems and activities of young adults. The central characters go into new business ventures, play football, apply to graduate schools, marry. While some of these are activities elderly people engage in too, for the most part they typify concerns of young adults. To offset this, an investigation was carried out with "life situations" about aged central characters facing problems representative of their own age group. Would aging patterns in cautiousness be exacerbated when problems and consequences were tied more intimately to their circumstances?

In addition to the 12 "life situations" of Wallach and Kogan (1961), 12 others were written about aged people (Botwinick, 1966). A total of 24 situations were thus available, making a 24-item questionnaire. As before, each of the items called for a decision based upon a desired probability of outcome before venturing a risk: the higher the desired probability, the more cautious the responder was considered to be.

Needs, Problems, and Cultural Determination. Cautiousness was investigated in relation to the age and sex of the respondents, and also their level of education as a crude index of socioeconomic status. The different "life situations" of the young and aged central characters were taken as reflecting needs and problems of their respective generations (Botwinick, 1966).

The basic result of Wallach and Kogan (1961) was again seen in this study: The older adults responded in a more cautious manner than the younger adults; they seemed to want more assurance that the outcome would be favorable before recommending an action. Men and women were not very different in their levels and patterns of cautiousness. Neither were the education groups different in levels of cautiousness, but their patterns were different with respect to the 24 "life situations." This suggested that socioeconomic factors may determine the specific approaches to various problems, but not the overall extent of cautiousness. A similar cultural role may be indicated in regard to aging. Those elderly people in this study who were of about the same level of education as those in the Wallach and Kogan (1961) study often demonstrated their cautiousness by way of different "life situations." Since Wallach and Kogan (1961) investigated people mostly from eastern Massachusetts and Botwinick (1966) examined people mostly from central North Carolina, it was suggested that the cautiousness in later life may be manifest in culturally different contexts.

Different Responses to Different Problems. The Botwinick (1966) study yielded an unexpected result. It was thought that the "life situations" in which aged central characters coped with needs and problems of old people would bring out more cautiousness on the part of the elderly respondents. It was reasoned that elderly people are cautious and this would be especially true with problems that are "close to home."

Just the opposite resulted. Both the elderly and young adults were more cautious in their decisions concerning young adult central characters than in those concerning aged central characters, but this pattern was accentuated among the older respondents. The older respondents, more than the younger ones, seemed to devalue the lives and problems of the aged central characters. But old and young alike performed in a manner to suggest that they regarded the aged as having less to lose than the young should a risky course of action go badly; the young, having a longer life ahead of them, have more at stake and more to lose. As logical as this conclusion may appear, it is most important to recognize that alternate possibilities exist. In fact, subsequent research, described later, suggests that this conclusion is probably not the correct one.

Disinclination to Risk. It will be recalled that each respondent decided whether or not to embark upon a course of action in each of 24 "life situations," and was characterized by the average of these 24 decisions (1, 3, 5, 7, 9, or 10 chances in 10). A different method of analysis was also made. Rather than compare groups on the basis of these average probability levels, comparisons were made on the basis of the number of times each probability level was chosen. For example, one person might have chosen 1 one time; 3 two times; 5, 7, and 9 five times each; and 10 six times. The combined total of these for each respondent was 24, the number of "life situations."

Figure 9.1 shows the number of times each probability level was chosen by age, sex, and education groups. Perhaps the most prominent feature in Figure 9.1 is the tendency of elderly adults to choose the number 10 alternative—the alternative which is to not advise risk regardless of the likelihood of the success in the outcome. This tendency is clearly apparent in each of the three education groupings of men and in the middle grouping of women.[1]

Why do elderly people, possibly men more than women, shy away from risky courses of action regardless of their likelihood of success? It was suggested (Botwinick, 1966, p. 352) that older people either "were disinclined toward making decisions and taking actions, or they were more willing than young Ss (people) to continue with involvements which were far from ideal (or both of these)."

RELUCTANCE TO ACT VERSUS CAUTIOUSNESS

A distinction may be made between a type of cautiousness which takes the form of a reluctance to make decisions and to act, and a cautiousness which does not involve this reluctance but does involve behaviors which minimize risk even if it means minimizing potential gain. Is the number 10 alternative a very cautious response which minimizes risk to nearly zero, or is it something else—a reluctance to decide or to act, to be involved? In other words, is the number 10 alternative on a quantitative continuum with the other choices involving risk, or is choice of the number 10 alternative a qualitatively different phenomenon?

When Risk Cannot Be Avoided

An attempt to answer this question was made by repeating the previous, 1966 study, except that the number 10 alternative was left out altogether (Botwinick, 1969). The thinking was that, if the choice of the number 10 alternative was a very cautious response and quantitatively on the same continuum as the others, then when not available, the respondent would simply go to the next most cautious option, i.e., the choice recommending action only if there are 9 chances out of 10 that success would be the outcome. On the other hand, if the number 10 alternative was qualitatively different from the others, then the respondent would be faced with a different problem and might choose any of the options.

[1] Older women with college degrees tended less to the number 10 alternative than did the less well educated older women. This was seen with highly educated men also, but they did resort to the number 10 alternative more than did the younger men ($p<.05$). The age comparison for women of the lowest education group was based on a very small number of elderly women. Perhaps this comparison would best not be given serious attention.

The same 24-situation questionnaire was given to two age and sex groups, and this time only to the two more highly educated groups (i.e., 13 to 15 and 16-and-more years of education, not the 7 to 12-year group). The results were very different in this study than they were in the studies by Wallach and Kogan (1961) and Botwinick (1966). Age differences in cautiousness were not seen at all! The implication is quite clear: In the earlier studies, the cautiousness on the part of the elderly probably was due more to their avoidance of risk situations than to their gambling propensities when risk could not be avoided.

Another different result was seen: When obliged to face risk, when refuge in the number 10 alternative was not possible, the alleged devaluation of the lives and problems of the aged central characters by the older respondents was no longer seen. In fact, a very slight trend in the opposite direction was the case. The older respondents did not devalue their problems, so to speak, they tended to avoid decisions with respect to them.

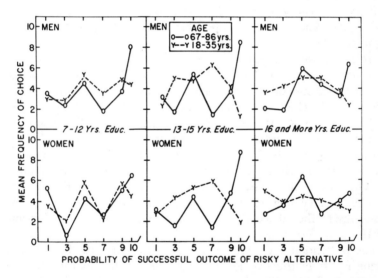

FIGURE 9.1: Mean frequency of choice among six alternatives in the decisions of young and elderly adults. Abscissa values are ordered from lesser to greater cautiousness. Alternative "1" represents a decision to follow a course of action which has a low likelihood of success. There are rewards if it does succeed, but there are negative consequences if it does not. Alternative "9" is to follow this course only if there is a high likelihood of its success. Alternatives "3," "5," and "7" are middle-value alternatives. Alternative "10" is not to follow the course of action regardless of the likelihood of success. (Figure 1 and legend from Botwinick, 1966; permission to reprint this figure was given by the *Journal of Gerontology*.)

Avoidance of Risk and Disengagement

Two Studies Compared. Some of the older people tested in this study were the same ones tested in the earlier study, some 23 to 40 months previously. Figure 9.2 provides the two sets of results: the dashed line in the figure shows the percentage (of 24 opportunities) each alternative was chosen when risk was unavoidable (Botwinick, 1969); the solid line shows the percentage when risk was avoidable by resorting to the number 10 alternative (Botwinick, 1966).[2]

The same people, responding in both situations, chose the option to not venture risk regardless of the probabilities in nearly 30 percent of the occasions, but, when not permitted this option, rather than go the next most cautious one (alternative number 9), they tended to choose the middle levels of cautiousness. This latter pattern is very similar to that of young people under comparable conditions. As already indicated in Figure 9.1, this was the pattern also of young people when the number 10 alternative was available.

Pain in Social Engagement. Why did the elderly seem to avoid making decisions when it was possible for them to do so? It is interesting to speculate.

In the previous chapter, studies on perception and learning were interpreted in terms of older people requiring a higher "confidence level . . . before responding" (Botwinick, Brinley, and Robbin, 1958), "a defensive reluctance to venture response for fear of recognizing their inadequacy" (Basowitz and Korchin, 1957, p. 96), an "increase in overall anxiety . . . may result in withdrawal from the situation" (Eisdorfer, 1965, p. 22). In each of these studies the older people either responded with latencies much longer than seemed necessary, or did not respond at all. They made the omission error (no response) rather than the commission error (wrong response, see previous chapter), and this may be analogous to the choice of the number 10 alternative (no decision of risk).

The perception and learning studies in the previous chapter are distinguished from the decision questionnaire studies in this chapter in that many of the former measure abilities or capacities while the latter measure choices or preferences. If there is suspicion of deterioration in ability and capacity, then the withholding of responses because of anxi-

---

[2] The dashed line in Figure 9.2 is higher than the solid line because the measurement is percent of choice, rather than frequency of choice as in Figure 9.1. There were only five options (in each of the 24 items) in the later study, 1, 3, 5, 7, and 9 (chances out of 10); there were six options in the earlier study, number 10 plus the others.

ety and feelings of inadequacy may be understandable. But when the situation does not involve threat to presumed deteriorating abilities, when it simply involves choice of preference, and there still is reluctance to commit oneself, how threatening life must be!

WISDOM IN CAUTIOUSNESS?

A vocabulary test was used to measure cautiousness in decision among the elderly (Okun and Di Vesta, 1976). The test-taker earned "points" by correctly defining the words of the test, earning more points for the difficult words than for the easier ones. All the words were graded in difficulty with the unique feature of the study being that the difficulty level of the word to be worked on was left to the choice of the test-taker.

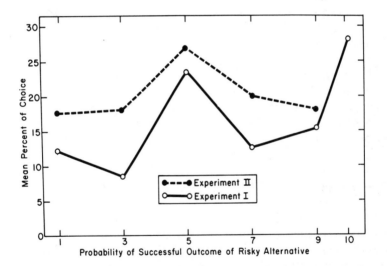

FIGURE 9.2: The same questionnaire of 24 "life situations," with one difference, was presented to elderly persons on two occasions, designated here as Experiment I and Experiment II. The one difference was that in Experiment I, six alternative choices for each situation were available, with the choice labeled "10" on the abscissa being one to avoid risk regardless of the probabilities of successful outcome. In Experiment II, this alternative was not available, leaving only five possibilities to choose among, with alternative "9" being the most cautious response and alternative "1" being the most risky. When alternative "10" was available, nearly 30 percent of the choices were for this option. When it was not available, alternative "5" was the most common choice, not "9." This suggested that gambling propensities of the elderly are similar to those of the young. (Figure 1 from Botwinick, 1969; permission to reprint this figure was given by the *Journal of Genetic Psychology*.)

That is, a hard word could be chosen, which brought more points if correctly defined, or an easy one could be chosen, which brought fewer points. Obviously there was more risk of failure in the choice of the hard word with the big point payoff.

In this study, there was no rational basis for choosing either a hard word or an easy one since the experimenter manipulated the points so that one strategy was as likely to be successful as another. In this uncertain situation the elderly again were the more cautious. They tended to choose easier words while younger adults tended to choose the more difficult ones.

A second study was different in that there was a rational basis for choosing hard or easy words (Okun and Elias, 1977). The experimental arrangements were such that sometimes it was smarter to go for a hard word (better chance of making more points) and sometimes it was a better strategy to choose an easier word. In this latter study, where there was a basis for strategy, the elderly were not found more cautious than the young. The old and young were the same—even their shifts in choice of word difficulty level according to experimental payoffs were the same.

Putting the two studies together, it would seem that the elderly may be cautious when there is no reason to be otherwise. When, however, there is reason to take risks, they seem to be no more cautious than anyone else. It may be wise to be risky only when there is a meaningful reason to be so.

PRACTICAL SITUATIONS AND CONSEQUENCES

All this has practical consequence: In at least two types of studies dealing with very practical situations, this avoidance or noncommittal pattern of the elderly was seen to play a role. One type of study involved hearing tests and the other national survey interviews.

Hearing Test

In the traditional clinical audiological examination, the examiner presents short bursts of sounds in varying levels of loudness, and records the lowest level the person tested says he hears. The examiner does this for different pitches of sound and determines hearing ability for each of these.

It is being more and more recognized that the measurement of hearing ability involves psychological factors in addition to the biological ones. When the person is presented with a very low-level sound, it is often hard to tell whether or not it was heard: a decision must be made whether it was. An older person reluctant to commit himself and say that he hears this very faint sound will score lower than necessary in the hearing test.

The traditional audiological examination does not provide opportunity for the commission error, only the omission error. A more modern procedure for measuring hearing ability provides opportunities for both types of errors. In this procedure (signal detection; Tanner and Swets, 1954) the person tested is told that sometimes the faint sound will be presented and sometimes it will not; it is necessary to decide in both these situations whether or not the sound was heard.

From all that was suggested here, it may be predicted that the older person taking the hearing test will tend to report a sound only when he is certain about it. He will tend to be wrong in saying that the faint sound was not presented when it really was, but he will tend to be right when also saying that the sound was not presented when, in fact, it was not. This prediction was borne out in studies by Craik (1969), Rees and Botwinick (1971), and more recently by Potash and Jones (1977). In fact the cautiousness of the elderly was so great in the Rees and Botwinick study that the signal detection procedure could hardly be carried out. It was concluded in that study that traditional hearing tests might overestimate the magnitude of sensory deficits in later life.

This is not to say that in all contexts do signal detection analyses disclose greater cautiousness on the part of the elderly. It will be seen in chapter 15 that in learning and memory tasks, the elderly are not always the more cautious.

Interview Behavior

The avoidance of decision situations, and preference for not being wrong more than preference for being right, has implications for a wide variety of contexts. Gergen and Back (1966) investigated national survey data, much of it of a political nature. Their results could be applied to many interview situations.

Opinionation. Gergen and Back analyzed the items of four Gallup surveys that allowed a "no opinion" response. (The "no opinion" response may well be analogous to the choice of the number 10 alternative in the Botwinick [1966] study, the "did not hear" response in the Rees and Botwinick study [1971], and the omission error in the Basowitz and Korchin [1957] and Eisdorfer [1965] studies.) Gergen and Back (1966) analyzed the "no opinion" response in relation to three groups of people interviewed: young, 20 to 39; middle, 40 to 59; and old, 60 years and over. In each of the four Gallup surveys, "the middle-aged group exceeded the young in terms of the number of items for which the percentage of 'no opinion' responses was greater . . . the difference between the old group and the middle-aged group is even more striking" (Gergen and Back, 1966, p.389). Clearly, what they referred to as "opinionation" decreased with age.

Two additional surveys were analyzed, this time only two age groups were compared: a young (18 to 25) and a middle-aged group (40 to 55 years). In these surveys, the alternative, "don't know," rather than, "no opinion," was available. Even within such a restricted age range, the frequency of "don't know" responses increased with age.

Still another type of response investigated was the "no difference" response.

> If a situation is demanding enough, and the issue is an evaluative one, a person can generally come to a decision about whether A is "better" than B, "more" than B, etc. However, . . . the path of least resistance is merely to respond neutrally, i.e., A and B are "the same" (Gergen and Back, 1966, p. 393).

Again, increasing age was associated with avoidance. The "no difference" response increased with age.

Education. It is often typical of scientific investigation that further inquiry discloses complexity, clouding or even mitigating previous, neatly packaged conclusions. Gergen and Back recognized that the older respondents were often more poorly educated than the younger ones. They found in one of the Gallup surveys that the age-opinionation relationship held for those who had a high school education or more, but it did not hold for those with less than a high school education. In fact, for the less educated, just the opposite was seen—opinionation *increased* with age.

Gergen and Back provided evidence to suggest that only when the interviewer presses for opinions do the older respondents with little formal education react as they do, i.e., give opinions. This is not the case for the better educated. When the interviewer does not press, the low-education older person reacts in a way similar to his better educated contemporary—he is less opinionated than the younger person.

Glenn (1969), apparently, was not impressed with this evidence of pressing for opinions. He re-analyzed data from 35 opinion surveys, including one that Gergen and Back examined, and concluded that, when education levels are precisely controlled between old and young, no evidence is revealed that aging is associated with low opinionation. A slight trend in just the opposite direction was seen—the older people were more opinionated.

One of several arguments which Glenn brought up as possibly negating his results is that older adults more often than younger ones refuse to be interviewed. This, of course, is avoidance in the extreme. Glenn counterargued this by referring to data which showed that people refusing to be interviewed participate no less often in political and social affairs than do people cooperating in the interviews. Whether this is a good counterargument or not, the role of education requires further examination. It will be recalled that in the questionnaire study by Botwinick (1966), education also seemed to play a role, although a different one. In that study, a very high level of education tended to reduce the avoidance type of cautiousness of later life.

SUMMARY

This chapter dealt with cautiousness as it was seen in mostly laboratory situations calling for deliberation and decision. In the first of a series of studies, elderly and young adults responded to a questionnaire of 12 "life situations," each one depicting a central character who faces a conflict. He must decide whether or not to embark upon a course of action which, if successful, brings much gain, but if not successful, brings serious loss.

Each respondent had an opportunity to be cautious or not by indicating the likelihood of success a course of action would have to have before advising the central character to embark upon it. As compared to young adults, elderly adults required greater likelihood that the action would be successful before they would advise it. Thus, the elderly were considered the more cautious.

A second study in the series took cognizance of the fact that the 12 "life situations" were of young adult central characters facing problems more unique to their age group than to an elderly group. Accordingly, young and elderly people were asked to respond to "life situations" of both young and aged central characters. The basic result was seen again, viz., the elderly adults, as compared to the younger ones, required greater likelihood that the action would be successful before they would advise it. They were more cautious.

A further examination of these data revealed an interesting result. The greater cautiousness on the part of the elderly was largely attributable to an option they often exercised—an option not preferred by the younger adults. The older respondents often chose to not recommend the course of action which could lead to gain regardless of its probability of success. A study was then carried out questioning whether this option is a cautious one in the sense of its being similar, on the same continuum as the others, or whether it is qualitatively different from the others. In other words, a distinction was made between a pattern of cautiousness taking the form of a reluctance to make decisions or to take action, and a pattern of cautiousness taking the form of doing these things, but in a manner which minimizes risk even if if means minimizing potential gain.

This latter study repeated the main parts of the previous one, except that the opportunity to avoid risk altogether was not allowed. Each respondent had to advise taking a risk, even if a relatively small one. It was argued that, if the option no longer available was on the same continuum as the others, the older people would simply choose the next most cautious alternative. If it was qualitatively different, then the task is a different one when the option is no longer available.

When some risk was unavoidable, old and young were not different in their cautiousness. Thus, what seems to differentiate the old from the young is their reluctance to be involved in decision situations in the first place, not their gambling propensities. This reluctance was seen as similar to the making of omission errors and avoidance responses. These behaviors could be interpreted as representing much self-doubt.

This response pattern on the part of the elderly was seen to have practical consequence. Two types of studies were described which demonstrated the avoidance response in contexts important in everyday life. One was a hearing test. Here, older people were so reluctant to report hearing faint sounds as to suggest that their hearing ability might be underestimated in traditional clinical examinations. Another practical context was the national opinion survey. Older adults, as compared to younger ones, gave more "no opinion" or "don't know" types of responses. This was also interpeted as avoidance. Of possible importance here was the role of education. One study indicated that older people of very high education tend less to this type of response, and another study indicated that older people of very low education also do. The role of education in the cautiousness of later life requires further investigation.

REFERENCES

Basowitz, H., and Korchin, S.J. Age differences in the perception of closure. *Journal of Abnormal and Social Psychology*, 1957, 54, 93–97.

Botwinick, J. Cautiousness in advanced age. *Journal of Gerontology*, 1966, 21, 347–353.

Botwinick, J. Disinclination to venture response versus cautiousness in responding: age differences. *Journal of Genetic Psychology*, 1969, *115*, 55–62.

Botwinick, J., Brinley, J.F., and Robbin, J.S. The interaction effects of perceptual difficulty and stimulus time on age differences in speed and accuracy of response. *Gerontologia*, 1958, *2*, 1–10.

Craik, F.I.M. Applications of signal detection theory to studies of ageing. In A.T. Welford (Ed.), *Interdisciplinary topics in gerontology*, *4*. Basel and New York: Skarger, 1969, pp. 147–157.

Eisdorfer, C. Verbal learning and response time in the aged. *Journal of Genetic Psychology*, 1965, *107*, 15–22.

Gergen, K.J., and Back, K.W. Communication in the interview and the disengaged respondent. *Public Opinion Quarterly*, 1966, *30*, 385–398.

Glenn, N.D. Aging, disengagement, and opinionation. *Public Opinion Quarterly*, 1969, *33*, 17–33.

Okun, M.A., and Di Vesta, F.J. Cautiousness in adulthood as a function of age and instructions. *Journal of Gerontology*, 1976, *31*, 571–576.

Okun, M.A., and Elias, C.S. Cautiousness in adulthood as a function of age and payoff structure. *Journal of Gerontology*, 1977, *32*, 451–455.

Potash, M., and Jones, B. Aging and decision criteria for the detection of tones and noise. *Journal of Gerontology*, 1977, *32*, 436–440.

Rees, J., and Botwinick, J. Detection and decision factors in auditory behavior of the elderly. *Journal of Gerontology*, 1971, *26*, 133–136.

Tanner, W.P., Jr., and Swets, J.A. A decision-making theory of visual detection. *Psychological Review*, 1954, *61*, 401–409.

Wallach, M.A., and Kogan, N. Aspects of judgment and decision making: interrelationships and changes with age. *Behavioral Science*, 1961, *6*, 23–36.

10

Contact with the Physical Environment

It is becoming clearer that traditional and classic studies of sensation and perception are more complete when behavioral and personality factors are taken into account. For example, in the previous chapter it was seen that, even in so seemingly simple and routine a procedure as the hearing test, personality enters to modify the results. Conversely, what a person is capable of hearing, or otherwise sensing and perceiving, may well influence his behavior and personality. If one has a suspicious nature, how much easier it must be to impart dire meaning to a barely overhead conversation than one that is clearly audible! Or, how easily discouraged and damaging to self-concept it can be when a sense defect hinders a person from coping with rapidly incoming items of information.

The existing literature on sensation, with very few exceptions, is traditional. But, what it lacks in other ways, it makes up in reliability. "Probably in no other area of psychological investigation are the findings so clear-cut and consistent: old people simply don't see, hear, or otherwise perceive as acutely . . . as do younger people" (Helson, 1968, p. 53). This decrease in sensory adequacy in later life determines in part, the world in which older people live. Artificial help such as eyeglasses and hearing aids, and compensatory adjustments learned from personal life experience, may overcome many of these limitations, but there comes a point of disability where the once-manageable environment is quite different than it had been.

The literature of sensory and perceptual decline in relation to age is both extensive and very technical. Corso (1971), in reviewing the literature, listed more than 100 references. The list grew very much longer in 1977 with Birren and Schaie's edited volume, which included four chapters on this topic alone. These chapters are recommended for details of information not given here.

SEEING

When people talk about seeing they usually mean how clear things look —how much detail can be spotted. For scientists studying visual sensation and perception, however, various aspects of seeing ability are examined.

Visual Acuity

Acuity is what most people mean when they talk about seeing ability, yet this index is among the least well documented. In fact, Corso (1971, p. 91) wrote, "Experimental data on age and visual acuity are meager." The charts used to measure acuity, the Snellen chart, for example, are used in a way that the visual object—a letter, a number—is seen by the "normal" eye over a specified distance, say 40 feet. If a person sees the object with the same reported clarity at 20 feet, but no further, his vision is reported as 20/40. There are variations of this index, but all of them are designed to measure the smallest visual angle at which the object could be correctly seen (i.e., the farther away the person is from the object, the smaller the visual angle at his eye when lines are drawn from the eye to the top and the bottom of the object). Several investigators reported the relationships betwen age and acuity, among them Chapanis (1950) and Hirsch (1960). Up to ages 40 to 50, little change in acuity has been noted, but after this time there is marked decline. By age 70, without correction, poor vision is the rule rather than the exception.

Accommodation

In addition to the decline in visual acuity at far distances, there is loss in ability to focus on near objects (Duane, 1931; Friendenwald, 1952; Hofstetter, 1954). This becomes apparent to most everyone sooner or later. Due mainly to the loss of elasticity of the lenses of the eyes, people become farsighted, i.e., they do not see well those things up close; they find it hard to read. This is called presbyopia. Bifocal eyeglasses take care of this problem by minimizing the need for the lenses of the eyes to change shape.

While most everyone recognizes this decline in later life, many do not realize that the loss of accommodation is gradual, beginning very early in childhood. However, the greatest decline in close distance vision comes about for most people between the ages 40 to 55, as determined by longitudinal study (Brückner, 1967). It declines thereafter at a lesser rate.

Cataracts and Glare

A problem for many old people is cataracts; perhaps 20-25 percent of those in their 70s have this problem. The lens of the eye becomes clouded so that rays of light are scattered in making their way through the visual system. When the clouding is severe and sight is much impaired, the lens has to be removed surgically. This has become a very commonplace procedure, which greatly increases the person's ability to see. Glasses or contact lenses must then be used as a replacement for the natural lens that has been removed.

One negative feature of the cataract removal is that things look bigger than they are, but there is also an added benefit. With cataracts, the scattering of light rays makes for glare, which is uncomfortable as well as an obstacle to seeing well. Maybe this is the reason so many of the elderly seem to prefer dark, even dingy sitting rooms rather than bright sunny ones. When the opaque lens, the cataract, is removed, glare problems diminish, if not disappear altogether (Fozard et al., 1977).

Illumination

If too little light reaches the retina, it is hard to see. People adjust to this automatically by simply raising the level of ambient light. When this is done, elderly people are helped relatively more than are younger people, although their vision never reaches the same level of acuity (Weston, 1949). Older people need greater levels of illumination than do younger people. Various reasons are seen for this—one reason might be that older people have smaller eye pupils than do younger people (Birren, Casperson, and Botwinick, 1950); it is through the pupil that light reaches the retina. There is an approximate linear decrease in the amount of light reaching the retina from age 20 to age 60 years (Weale, 1965).

The need for greater illumination is seen in many circumstances. For example, shadows, driving at night, these are not the safest situations for the elderly. Depth perception is impaired in later life and this is exacerbated when there is low illumination. Not seeing a street curb because it is in shadow may lead to falls.

There is conflict here. It was indicated that glare is uncomfortable, makes for poor sight and, it seems, elderly people avoid illuminated areas to reduce the glare. A practical solution in the conflicting needs between glare reduction and more illumination is to leave the control of lighting as much as possible to the individual. It has been suggested that environments should be lit for the "older eye," or at least the "average-age eye," rather than for the "young eye" as is now the practice (Fozard et al., 1977, p. 582).

Adapting to the Dark

There are two dimensions to dark adaptation: (1) how long it takes to develop maximum seeing ability, and (2) how good a level is eventually reached. There is little doubt that the level reached by the old is not nearly as good as that reached by the young. Birren and Shock (1950) showed this, as did McFarland and Fisher (1955), and Domey, McFarland, and Chadwick (1960) among others. This relationship between age and the final level of dark adaptation is so clear that rarely in psychological work are correlations so consistently high. McFarland, in several of his studies, reported correlations of approximately 0.90.

The other dimension of dark adaptation is more controversial: Does is take longer for the old to reach their own level of adaptation in the dark than it does the young? Birren and Shock's data suggested not—only the level was displaced with age. The old saw less well in the dark, but, given this as a base line, they got to this level at the same rate as did the young. On the other hand, Domey et al. concluded from their study and from the literature overall that the rate of dark adaptation as well as the final threshold level decreases with age. They concluded that the old not only see less well when finally dark-adapted, but it takes them longer than the young to get their optimum level.

Dark adaptation has important practical significance. Birren (1964, p. 92) referred to automobile driving at night, and McFarland (1968, p. 18) to piloting airplanes in overcast skies as tasks that could be both difficult and dangerous for older people.

Color Vision

Colors are different for old and young—some seem to be almost as clear and vivid and as easily told apart by old people as they are by younger ones, while some colors are not so clear. The lenses of the eyes yellow with age and this makes for a filtering of the shorter wave lengths of light. The shorter wave lengths of light are the blues and violets, while the longer lengths are the yellows and reds. This yellowing of the lenses may not be the whole reason for the aging effect on color vision, but it seems to be the main one.

Several studies have shown that with increasing age there is special difficulty in discriminating among the blues, blue-greens, and the violets, with much greater success in discriminating among the reds, oranges, and yellows. Gilbert (1957) showed this in a rather straightforward way. She tested people of wide age range in a task of matching chips of various colors. People aged 10 to 19, perhaps surprisingly, were not as good in this matching as were people in their 20s. People in the 20s were best in this task; after this age, there was a gradual decline in color matching ability. While the decline was seen in all colors, including the red part of the spectrum, the decline was greatest for the blue part.

A difficulty in distinguishing between blues and greens, or such similar colors, can make for special problems if not recognized. For example, if a physician prescribes medication in the form of pills—two green ones in the morning and three blue ones in the evening—there must be some basis for distinguishing the two kinds of pills. Color coding of home appliances, of power tools and the like, ought to be arranged with color vision abilities of the elderly in mind.

Brightness Discrimination

Various brightnesses, like colors, are not as discernible in later life as they are in earlier adulthood. Weiss (1959) pointed out that, while only few studies are available to document this fact, there is evidence showing that contrast sensitivity does decline with age. This can also have practical consequence. Referring to an old study by Zinner (1930), Weiss reported that astronomers over age 50 could not differentiate as many brightnesses among stars as could their younger colleagues.

Brightness is not only a dimension of white, it is a dimension of all colors. It would not be unexpected, therefore, that elderly people would have difficulty in discriminating brightnesses of various colors, as well as white. Increasing the level of illumination is helpful in making finer discriminations among differing brightnesses.

HEARING

The decline in hearing ability with age has been documented many times both in the laboratory and in the clinic. Yet the extent of this decline may be overrated as judged from two aging studies that were concerned with non-sensory personality factors which contribute to measured hearing loss. Craik (1969) and, as already indicated in the previous chapter, Rees and Botwinick (1971), while finding clear evidence of hearing loss in old age, also found that the old were more cautious in that they were inclined to report hearing things only when they were fairly sure they had heard them. When not so sure, they said they did not hear the sound, and, thus, they were judged to be hard of hearing.

Another dimension of hearing ability is attention. Apart from decreased sensory adequacy, the ability to concentrate and to focus attention on the sound plays an important role in hearing it. Evidence suggests that the older person is more likely than the younger one to be inattentive and to concentrate poorly. This also will appear as an auditory deficit.

Pitch-Threshold

The hearing loss in old age is not equal across all frequencies of sound. High pitch tones, such as those a soprano can reach, are progressively less audible for the elderly while those of lower pitch are better heard. So many studies have documented this by now that several of the more recent reports have taken to combining the various studies. For example, Kryter (1960) compared the results of five studies and Spoor (1967) compared the results of eight. The problem of high tone disability (presbycusis) is depicted in Figure 10.1, extracted from the report by Spoor.

The "normal" human ear can hear sounds ranging in pitch from 20 vibrations per second to 20,000 per second. The very bass sounds or the very soprano sounds, however, have to be much louder than the middle frequency sounds if they are to be heard. In the measurement of hearing ability, a wide range of frequencies is presented and the loudness level (measured in decibels, db) necessary to hear each frequency is recorded. When it is said that the old suffer presbycusis, it means that the sounds have to be made progressively louder as the frequencies are increased.

Figure 10.1 shows that the decline with age is relatively slight with tones of frequencies less than 1,000 vibrations per second (Hz). A 1,000 Hz tone is similar to that heard on the piano when a note two octaves above middle C is played. While the decline with age in hearing tones lower than 1,000 Hz is slight—it is only about five db from age 25 to 50 years—it is progressive; that is, the decline is somewhat greater, for example, between ages 75 and 85 than it is between 25 and 35.

Presbycusis becomes really apparent after age 50 with pitches above 1,000 Hz. As the frequencies are increased, loudness levels must be raised progressively for the older person to hear the tones at all. For men at age 50, with tones approximately 4,000 Hz (the highest note on the piano), the hearing loss is 17 db or more; at age 75, the loss is more than

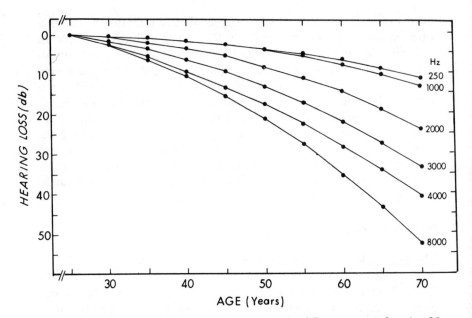

FIGURE 10.1: Hearing loss in relation to age of men for different tone pitches. Age 25 years is taken as the base line, i.e., no hearing loss. (Selected data from Table 3 of Spoor, 1967.)

47 db. At age 60, it is typically difficult to hear a tone one octave higher than the highest one on the piano (8,000 Hz); the loss with age is about 35 db. The higher the frequency and the older the person, the louder will the tone need to be to be heard. For practical, everyday purposes, however, high-tone deafness for frequencies above 3,000, perhaps 4,000 Hz, is not too important.

For some reason, this aging pattern is more pronounced with men than with women. It has been suggested that men are subject to greater "noise pollution" than are women because their jobs more often provide such hazards. This suggestion receives more support in a series of studies which showed that where the environment is low in such hazards the percentage of old people who are poor hearers is lower than otherwise (Rosen, Bergman, Plester, El-Mofty, and Sath, 1962; Rosen, Plester, El-Mofty, and Rosen, 1964; Bergman, 1966). This indicates that at least part of the problem of presbycusis is environmental. Causes for presbycusis are multiple, encompassing age changes all the way from the inner ear to the auditory cortex. While deterioration has been demonstrated in the auditory sense organ (the cochlea), this has not been seen as sufficient to account for the loss in hearing sensitivity. Higher nervous system centers are also involved.

Pitch Discrimination

If older people hear tones of varying pitch less well than do younger people, it may not be surprising to find that they also discriminate among tones less well. More, it may not be surprising to find that the tones which are least well discriminated are those that are heard with most difficulty. On the other hand, all this might not necessarily follow if each of the tones to be discriminated is made as functionally loud for the old as it is for the young.

The fact is that older people do have difficulty in discriminating among pitches, even when the tones are made as functionally loud for them as for young people. Konig (1957) presented people with tones 40 db above their own individual thresholds. While such tones do not seem very loud to the person tested, they are designed to be loud enough to be easily heard. Konig found that from ages 25 to 55, discrimination ability decreased slightly, but after 55 the decrease was marked. The age decline in pitch discrimination was relatively small with tones 500–1,000 Hz, but with tones of frequencies above 1,000 Hz, the age decline was greater. Thus, it is seen that the age curve for pitch discrimination follows a trend similar to that of pitch threshold.

Weiss (1959) speculated that these changes may affect speech comprehension. The comprehension of speech, very obviously, governs conversation and communication. In the next chapter it will be seen that speech comprehension does seem to be impaired with increasing age. For the present it is only necessary to note that difficulties arise when there are background noises. If there is a noisy air conditioner or traffic sounds, for example, the older listener may have much trouble communicating. Not that background distractions are necessarily more confusing to the old than to the young, but starting as the elderly do with high tone problems and pitch discrimination problems, the added burden of background noise can be most inconveniencing (see Corso, 1977, pp. 545–547).

TASTE AND SMELL

Vision and audition are more easily investigated than the other senses and thus there are many more reliable reports of them. In fact, the data on human sensation other than vision and audition are sparse and often of limited generality.

Taste and smell tend to go together experientially, as evidenced by the lack of taste of foods when the nose is clogged. There is evidence for decreased ability to taste in later life, but the evidence is not unequivocal. The basic tastes are salty, sweet, bitter, and sour. In one study carried out with 100 people aged 15 to 89 years, changes in each of the four tastes were minor, if at all, up to the later 50s; after this time, there was decline in ability to taste substances with these attributes (Cooper, Bilash, and Zubek, 1959). In an earlier study (Bourlière, Cendron, and Rapaport, 1958), elderly people were less able to detect sweet substances than were young adults. Old men also showed deficiency in detecting salty tasting substances but old women did not. This sex difference, however, was not observed by Cooper et al.

Taste ability is governed by many factors. Some studies, but not all, showed that smoking is a factor—it diminishes ability to taste. Attitudes toward food and eating are important. For this reason, perhaps, plus those of the difficulty of measurement, the results of studies vary. For example, Cohen and Gitman (1958) found no significant age decline in taste sensitivity to salty, bitter, sour, or sweet stimuli.

The data on smell are even sparser than those on taste—most of the evidence of age decline is indirect or of a clinical nature. The results of two recent laboratory studies suggest smell sensitivity does not decline (see Engen, 1977, pp. 556–557). However, one of these studies was of unusually superior people and the other of very few subjects. The data are thus still to be collected in this very difficult area of research.

PAIN

There is much clinical evidence that old people do not feel pain as intensely as do younger people. Severe internal diseases of the aged do not seem nearly as painful to them as they would to younger adults. Minor surgery can often be performed on old people without inflicting severe pain; coronary thrombosis occurs often without the agony found in young people. Paradoxically, however, subjective sensory complaints are very common in old age.

Weiss (1959, p. 530) reviewed the literature on pain thresholds in later life and concluded that, while the aged seem to be spared many of the agonies of disease and surgery, the "statistics as to the incidence of these clinically observed changes are few." The fact is, the laboratory data are not only few, they often show no age change in pain sensation at all. Part of the inconsistency in the literature lies in the difficulty of measuring pain. The feeling of pain, and certainly the reporting of it, appears to be related to personality and to cultural influences.

One of the better older studies, one that does corroborate clinical experience, was reported by Schludermann and Zubek (1962). Radiant heat was applied with a projector to five different parts of the body while the subject lay on an air mattress. Each person was told that the procedure was not a test of the ability to endure pain but of the ability to perceive the first trace of it. He was given a stop watch which he started when the heat apparatus was turned on, and which he stopped when he first felt pain.

It was found that the time it took to be aware of the pain stimuli increased slightly with age up to 60 years; after this age the increase was more noticeable. A more recent study, also using a method of radiant heat, investigated sex differences as well as differences between young and middle-aged adults (Clark and Mehl, 1971). A signal detection analysis disclosed that men of these two age categories were not different in detecting heat stimuli, but women were. Middle-aged women seemed to decline in ability to feel thermal pain. The middle-aged men, more than the middle-aged women, endured greater pain than the younger adults before reporting it.

Harkins and Chapman (1976) electrically stimulated the pulp of teeth to induce pain, also applying a signal detection analysis. Unlike the data based on radiant heat, young and elderly men were similar in their ability to detect the pain stimulus, i.e., electrical shock. However, when two shocks were applied, one more noxious than the other, the older men were not as able to discriminate between them as were the younger men. Thus, pain sensitivity was seen to undergo a decline with age.

As in the Clark and Mehl study, the older people were less willing to report the sensation as pain, but this time only when the pain stimuli were relatively mild. When the electrical shocks to the tooth pulp were preceived as strong, the elderly were not reluctant to report pain.

These studies are similar in some ways to those that measure hearing. If older people, as compared to younger ones, want to be more sure of pain before reporting it (as older people want to be more sure of hearing the tone stimulus), the noticeable increase in pain threshold after age 60 may be in part due to this reason.

TOUCH

The threshold of touch, like that of pain, varies with the part of the body stimulated. Perhaps even more than with pain, the "data are noticeably absent in the area of tactile sensitivity with age effects" (Corso, 1971, p. 101). Birren (1964, p. 101) concluded, "touch sensitivity remains unchanged from early adulthood through about age fifty to fifty five, with a rise in threshold thereafter."

This conclusion was based largely on experiments of stimulating different parts of the body with very fine bristle-like stimuli. More complex stimuli, however, also reflect decreased sensitivity with age. Thompson, Axelrod, and Cohen (1965) had subjects aged 18-34 years and 60-77 years palpate, without looking, a variety of differently shaped forms made of masonite. The task was to identify these forms with those represented on a visual display. The older group identified the forms less well than the young group, but this was attributed as much to deficits in searching the visual display as to deficits in touch sensation.

Another sensation that has been investigated is seen as closely aligned with touch—the ability to sense vibration. Weiss concluded that the clinical and experimental findings are in good agreement here: vibratory sensitivity diminishes with age. Again, the thresholds are very dependent upon the specific part of the body that is stimulated.

SUMMARY

Probably in no other area of psychological investigation are the findings as clear-cut as they are in sensory age changes. Old people do not see or hear as well as young people do, and decline in sensitivity is present also in taste, smell, and touch.

The ability to see detail at far distances declines with age, although up to the 40s and 50s this decline is very slight. More apparent, and beginning very early in life, is the decline in ability to see things well that are up close. Other visual processes also change, e.g., the ability to differentiate colors and brightnesses, the ability to see in the dark, and probably the time it takes to adapt to the dark. Raising the level of illumination is especially helpful to older people.

Hearing ability also declines with age, but the loss is not equal across all frequencies of sound. High pitch tones are progressively less audible for the elderly while those of lower pitch are better heard. The decline with age is relatively slight, however, before age 50, or with tone frequencies less than 1,000 Hz. There is evidence that this auditory change is at least partly due to environmental insult rather than inevitable maturational age change.

Old people have difficulty in discriminating among pitches, especially the higher ones, as well as in hearing them. The high pitches are the consonants and the lower ones the vowels. These changes probably affect the very important daily business of speech comprehension and communication.

The data on human sensation other than vision and audition are more sparse and lend themselves less well to making generalizations. In studies of taste the basic stimuli are described as salty, sweet, bitter, and sour. The ability to sense these tastes seems relatively well maintained up to the later 50s, but after this time there is decline. The data on smell are even sparser than those of taste—most of the evidence of age decline is indirect or is of a clinical nature.

There is much clinical evidence that old people do not feel pain as intensely as do younger people, but, paradoxically, subjective sensory complaints are very common in old age. The scientific studies on pain thresholds in later life are few and often show no age change in pain sensation at all, but the more recent literature shows little change to age 60, with increased pain thresholds thereafter.

The threshold of touch, like that of pain, varies with the part of the body stimulated. Perhaps even more with pain, the scientific data are noticeably absent. And, as with pain, touch sensitivity seems to remain relatively unchanged from early adulthood through later middle age, with a rise in thresholds thereafter.

The pattern for all the senses seems to be relative maintenance of function until late middle age with decline in later life.

REFERENCES

Bergman, M. Hearing in the Mabaans. *Archives of Otolaryngology*, 1966, *84*, 411–415.

Birren, J.E. *The psychology of aging.* Englewood Cliffs, N.J.: Prentice-Hall, 1964.

Birren, J.E., Casperson, R.C., and Botwinick, J. Age changes in pupil size. *Journal of Gerontology*, 1950, *5*, 216–221.

Birren, J.E., and Schaie, K.W. *Handbook of the psychology of aging.* New York: Van Nostrand Reinhold, 1977.

Birren, J.E., and Shock, N.W. Age changes in rate and level of visual dark adaptation. *Journal of Applied Physiology*, 1950, *2*, 407–411.

Bourlière, F., Cendron, H., and Rapaport, A. Modification avec l'age des seuils gustatifs de perception et de reconnaissance aux saveurs salée et sucrée chez l'homme. *Gerontologia*, 1958, *2*, 104–111.

Brückner, R. Longitudinal research on the eye. *Gerontologia Clinica*, 1967, *9*, 87–95.

Chapanis, A. Relationships between age, visual acuity and color vision. *Human Biology*, 1950, *22*, 1–33.

Clark, W.C., and Mehl, L. A sensory decision theory analysis of the effect of age and sex on d', various response criteria, and 50% pain threshold. *Journal of Abnormal Psychology*, 1971, *78*, 202–212.

Cohen, T., and Gitman, L. Studies in the gastrointestinal tract in the aged. *Journal of Gerontology*, 1958, *13*, 441 (abstract).

Cooper, R.M., Bilash, I., and Zubek, J.P. The effect of age on taste sensitivity. *Journal of Gerontology*, 1959, *14*, 56–58.

Corso, J.F. Sensory processes and age effects in normal adults. *Journal of Gerontology*, 1971, *26*, 90–105.

Corso, J.F. Auditory perception and communication. In J.E. Birren and K.W. Schaie (Eds.), *Handbook of the psychology of aging*. New York: Van Nostrand Reinhold, 1977, pp. 535–553.

Craik, F.I.M. Applications of signal detection theory to studies of ageing. In A.T. Welford (Ed.), *Interdisciplinary topics in gerontology, 4*. Basel and New York: S. Karger, 1969, pp. 147–157.

Domey, R.G., McFarland, R.A., and Chadwick, E. Dark adaptation as a function of age and time: II. A derivation. *Journal of Gerontology*, 1960, *15*, 267–279.

Duane, A. Accommodation. *Archives of Ophthalmology*, 1931, *5*, 1–14.

Engen, T. Taste and smell. In J.E. Birren and K.W. Schaie (Eds.), *Handbook of the psychology of aging*. New York: Van Nostrand Reinhold, 1977, pp. 554–561.

Fozard, J.L., Wolf, E., Bell, B., McFarland, R.A., and Padolsky, S. Visual perception and communication. In J.E. Birren and K.W. Schaie (Eds.), *Handbook of the psychology of aging*. New York: Van Nostrand Reinhold, 1977, pp. 497–534.

Friedenwald, J.S. The eye. In A.I. Lansing (Ed.), *Cowdry's problems of aging, 3rd ed*. Baltimore: Williams and Wilkins, 1952.

Gilbert, J.G. Age changes in color matching. *Journal of Gerontology*, 1957, *12*, 210–215.

Harkins, S.W., and Chapman, R.C. Detection and decision factors in pain perception in young and elderly men. *Pain*, 1976, *2*, 253–264.

Helson, H. Comments on McFarland's paper. In K.W. Schaie (Ed.), *Theory and methods of research on aging*. Morgantown, W.Va.: West Virginia Univ., 1968, pp. 53–55.

Hirsch, M.J. Data cited by Weymouth, F.W. Effect of age on visual acuity. In M.J. Hirsch and R.F. Wick (Eds.), *Vision of the aging patient*. Philadelphia: Chilton, 1960.

Hofstetter, H.W. Some interrelationships of age, refraction, and rate of refractive changes. *American Journal of Optometry and Archives of the American Academy of Optometry*, 1954, *31*, 161–169.

Konig, J. Pitch discrimination and age. *Acta Oto-Laryngologica*, 1957, *48*, 473–489.

Kryter, K.D. Damage-risk criteria for hearing. In L.L. Beranek (Ed.), *Noise reduction*. New York: McGraw-Hill, 1960.

McFarland, R.A. The sensory and perceptual processes in aging. In K.W. Schaie (Ed.), *Theory and methods of research on aging*. Morgantown, W.Va.: West Virginia Univ., 1968, pp. 9–52.

McFarland, R.A., and Fisher, M.B. Alterations in dark adapation as a function of age. *Journal of Gerontology*, 1955, *10*, 424–428.

Rees, J., and Botwinick, J. Detection and decision factors in auditory behavior of the elderly. *Journal of Gerontology*, 1971, *26*, 133–136.

Rosen, S., Bergman, M., Plester, D., El-Mofty, E., and Sath, M. Presbycusis study of a relatively noise-free population in the Sudan. *Annals of Otology*, 1962, *71*, 727–743.

Rosen, S., Plester, D., El-Mofty, E., and Rosen, H.V. High frequency audiometry in presbycusis: a comparative study of the Mabaan tribe in the Sudan with urban populations. *Archives of Otolaryngology*, 1964, *79*, 18–32.

Schludermann, E., and Zubek, J.P. Effect of age on pain sensitivity. *Perceptual and Motor Skills*, 1962, *14*, 295–301.

Spoor, A. Presbycusis values in relation to noise induced hearing loss. *International Audiology*, 1967, *6*, 48–57.

Thompson, L.W., Axelrod, S., and Cohen, L.D. Senescence and visual identification of tactual-kinesthetic forms. *Journal of Gerontology,* 1965, 20, No. 2, 244–249.

Weale, R.A. On the eye. In A.T. Welford and J.E. Birren (Eds.), *Behavior, aging and the nervous system.* Springfield, Ill.: Charles C Thomas, 1965.

Weiss, A.D. Sensory functions. In J.E. Birren (Ed.), *Handbook of aging and the individual.* Chicago: Univ. of Chicago Press, 1959, pp. 503–542.

Weston, H.C. On age and illumination in relation to visual performance. *Transactions of the Illuminating Engineering Society* (London), 1949, 14, 281–297.

Zinner, E. Die Reizempfindungskurve Ztschr. *Psychol. Sinnesphysiol.,* 1930, 61, Abt. II, 247–266.

11

Processing Sense Information

It is impossible to separate the processes of sensation from perception except by some quasi-arbitrary decision. This is so because all measurements are based upon the response of the subject, and, in this response, a multitude of factors interact continuously. By convention, perception is usually taken to include more interpretation of the external stimulus than is sensation. The more complex, ambiguous and emotion-arousing the stimulus, the more the room for interpretation. Thus, operationally, more often than not the distinction between sensation and perception is made on the basis of the nature of the stimulus.

It is through sensation and perception that the person interacts with his environment. If, with age, there is impairment in these processes, the person's effectiveness is either limited or must otherwise be compensated. Studies which include analyses of age changes in compensatory adjustments resemble studies in personality or cognition as much as they do perception. Some of the former were seen in two earlier chapters (8 and 9) dealing with cautious response.

SEQUENTIAL INTEGRATION

If a person responds to a stimulus and then responds to a second one shortly afterward, the second response is often different from the first one, even if the two stimuli are identical. One theory explaining this is that the first stimulus, in its neural representation, must be "cleared through the nervous system" before the second stimulus can be responded to as was the first one. Before the nerve impulses are so cleared through, before neural transmission is complete, the person is not optimally ready to process the input of the second stimulus. The trace of the first stimulus persists, so to speak, leaving the responder either relatively refractory to subsequent stimulation or, more often, responsive but in a different way.

As a theory or a model, much data can be explained by this notion of stimulus persistence. As a theory or a model, there is reason to believe that stimulus traces persist longer in the nervous systems of old people than of young ones. For example, Welford (1969, pp. 4–5) referred to a study by Jeeves in which speed of response was measured to each of two stimuli separated by brief time intervals. The task was a four-choice reaction task. When the two stimuli were very close in time, the response to the second stimulus was slower than to the first one. Welford reported that for adults aged 18-33 years, it was not until about 300 milliseconds elapsed between stimulus-response sequences that the response to the second stimulus was as fast as to the first. But for older adults aged 58-71 years, about 500 milliseconds were necessary for this to be the case. The inference here is that the neural impulses of the first stimulus, together with those of the associated response, persisted longer in the older group than in the younger, and left them less prepared for the second stimulus.

This idea of stimulus persistence is a theory or a model more than it is a fact, but many facts seemed to fit the model. For this reason, the model is useful. The fit of perception data to the model was suggested by Axelrod (1963) and was expressed succinctly in a later report:

> In the senescent nervous system, there may be an increased persistence of the activity evoked by a stimulus, i.e. . . . the rate of recovery from the short-term effects of stimulation may be slowed. On the assumption that perception of the second stimulus as a discrete event depends on the degree to which the neural effects of the first have subsided, the poorer temporal resolution in senescence would then follow (Axelrod, Thompson, and Cohen, 1968, p. 193).

The concept of stimulus persistence also receives support in the psychophysiological literature. Mundy-Castle (1953) observed that EEG aftereffect activity to photic stimulation is more enduring among older adults than among younger ones. This physiological support, however, must be regarded as tentative because stimulus persistence theory is applied here in *post hoc* fashion, i.e., the study was not done to test the theory, but the theory was used after the fact to explain the data.

Stimulus Fusion

Critical Flicker Fusion. A classic and frequently used measure of visual efficiency is critical flicker fusion (CFF). A flashing light is presented to the viewer and the duration and the frequency of the flashes are very well controlled. If the flashes follow one another in rapid order they appear to fuse for the viewer, and are perceived as a steady light.

The exact rate of flashing at which they will appear fused depends on a variety of factors including the level of illumination, the duration of both the on and off periods of the lights, and of course, the frequency of the flicker, i.e., how quickly the light flashes come one after the other.

Among the better replicated findings is that the fusing point comes sooner for older people than it does for younger people. It takes a higher rate of on-off flickering for the young to perceive a steady state than it does for the old. Weale (1965) reviewed several studies and concluded that between 20 and 60 years the mean decline in CFF is about seven cycles per second. Young adults perceive fusion when the light flickers about 40 cycles per second (Misiak, 1947) and old people perceive it at slower rates.

There is little doubt that CFF threshold is related to peripheral, preretinal factors, especially the thickening of the lenses of the eyes and the reduction in pupil size. But, largely on the basis of a study by Coppinger (1955), who showed that an increase in illumination makes for fusion sooner in the young than in the old, Weiss (1959) concluded central factors are implicated in CFF thresholds as well as the peripheral. Other evidence implicates central factors too. In reviewing the literature, Corso (1971, p. 94) concluded, "whenever the general efficiency of the central nervous system is reduced due to pathology or age, both CFF and certain intellectual functions will also be depressed."

Stimulus persistence theory may explain these results. If the trace of the first flash persists longer in the older person's nervous system than in that of the younger person, it has the same effect as a longer duration flash, and, as such, will fuse with the subsequent trace of the external flash which soon comes. McFarland, Warren, and Karis (1958) presented data which could be interpreted in this manner. As they varied the procedure so that the on-off interval was taken up more and more with the light on, fusion of the flashes came about more readily, i.e., thresholds for CFF were lowered. When there was long light-on time, the old and young were relatively similar in CFF threshold; it is as if the stimulus made for a persisting trace in all subjects regardless of age. But, when there was little light-on time, and fusion was not readily perceived by any age group, it was the old group, much more than the young group, that perceived fusion. For the old, when the light was on only 10 percent of the time, stimulus persistence made the effective stimulus duration longer and their CFF thresholds relatively lower than those of the young.

Letter Fusion. Rather than light flashes as in CFF, the letter O was flashed (Walsh and Thompson, 1977). In addition, rather than emphasizing the steady state of fusion, the focus of concern was in detecting the disappearance of the O, i.e., detecting flicker when the time between successive flashes of the letter O was increased. The results of this study, unlike those of CFF, did not support the stimulus persistence notion. In fact, the results were just the opposite although Walsh and Thompson maintained that CFF and letter fusion are different processes. In the latter study, it was with the young, not with the old, that fusion occurred with greater time spacing between letter O appearances.

This study by Walsh and Thompson and some of those described later are among only several that put the theory of stimulus persistence to a test, rather than use it to explain existing data in *post hoc* fashion. This study, thus far, is the sole one, or at least one among very few, that shows effects just contrary to the stimulus persistence concept.

Click Fusion. CFF thresholds are measures of the perceptual fusing of discrete visual stimuli. The young perceive these inputs as discrete more readily than do the aged—their perceptions are more in keeping with objective reality. An auditory analogue of this visual fusion was seen in studies utilizing sound clicks (Weiss and Birren, reported by Weiss, 1959, p. 523; and Weiss, 1963).

Two sound clicks were presented in rapid order to both ears of a subject, who tried to determine whether it sounded to him as two clicks or a fused one click. The difference between a young age group and an over-65-year age group was not great, but tended to a pattern similar to that of CFF: Fusion of the two clicks came about more readily for the old. Again, the young perceived objective reality better than did the old.

The subjects also were given a train of clicks, 1 to 10 in number, and these were varied in the rate of delivery. "On the whole, older subjects reported significantly fewer clicks than younger subjects" (Weiss, 1959, p. 523). It was as if the persistence of the stimulus trace of the earlier part of the train of clicks fused with later parts to make differentiation more difficult.

Weiss (1963) later compared young men to each of two groups of men over 65 years, differing in their states of health. One group of the older men was what is typically called "normal" healthy and the other group was of men of extraordinary health—no sign of disease whatsoever. The comparisons were of the time between clicks in which fusion was perceived. The young and extraordinary elderly groups were not different from each other, but the young and "normal" healthy groups were different in accord with the stimulus persistence model: The old perceived fusion with more time between clicks. Perhaps it is the combination of age and ill health that makes for stimulus persistence.

Fusion of Discrete Shocks. Axelrod et al. (1968) stimulated the fingers of the hand with mild shocks. The threshold for being able to perceive the shocks as the discrete stimulations they were was measured with two groups of people aged 21-34 and 65-75 years. Each subject was told that sometimes the shocks would be applied simultaneously and sometimes successively. The task was to judge whether the stimuli were presented together or separately.

The successive shocks were applied in four different ways, but two are of interest here. One way was with the mild shocks applied to one hand and the other was with the shocks applied to both hands, i.e., the first stimulus to one hand and the second stimulus to the other.

In line with the stimulus persistence model, the old fused the successive presentations more readily than did the young. The temporal thresholds were higher for the bimanual stimulations than for the unimanual ones, and this was more the case for the old than for the young. That is, fusion took place more readily with the stimulation of one hand than two, and this was even truer for the old than the young. Axelrod et al. explained the higher temporal thresholds of the bimanual stimulation on the basis that there are contralateral projections to the brain from each hand, and with two hands there is interhemispheric interaction involving synapses. Thus, with the aged, especially when additional synapses are involved, there might be "greater persistence of evoked activity [than with the young, giving] rise to a greater increase in temporal threshold . . ." (Axelrod et al., 1968, p. 193).

Stimulus Masking and Stimulus Enhancement

There is a type of experiment that bears relationship to fusion experiments. Instead of investigating steady-state stimulation arising from a series of discrete but identical stimuli, masking of the first stimulus (or enhancement of it) is investigated as a result of a second but *different* stimulus. In the masking study the first stimulus (called the test or target stimulus) is masked by a second stimulus (called masking stimulus) presented shortly afterward. In the enhancement study, the second stimulus is integrated with the first one, providing a new dimension.

In the fusion experiments, as in CFF, the trace of the first stimulus is presumed to persist long in old age and to combine with an identical stimulus trace formed soon afterward. The thinking is the same in the masking and enhancement studies: The effect of the first stimulus is long lasting in old age. Stimulus persistence theory receives confirmation when older people experience the effects of the first stimulus for a relatively long while after it has terminated. If the trace of the first stimulus takes long to "clear through" the nervous system (even when the physical stimulus is no longer present), then the second stimulus will mask the first one, or enhance it, depending on its nature.

The studies in this section properly test the stimulus persistence notion rather than use it to explain existing data.

Masking Digits. The first study in the series was by Kline and Szaf-ran (1974) who masked digits with an array of short horizontal and vertical line segments (visual noise). Both the target digit stimuli and the masking visual noise stimuli were presented to the same eye (monoptic stimulation). In a later study, Kline and Birren (1975) presented the first target stimulus to one eye and the second masking stimulus to the other (dichoptic stimulation). Both studies showed similar results: Older people were more susceptible to the masking than younger people. That is, after the target stimulus was no longer physically present, the second stimulus masked the perception of the first one after time durations longer for the old man than for the young. These studies were in confirmation of stimulus persistence theory, indicating that it takes the old longer to process a stimulus than the young.

Masking Letters. A series of studies was carried out where the target stimuli were letters of the alphabet presented in straight line strokes; the masking stimuli were patterned line segments (Walsh, 1976; Walsh, Till, and Williams, 1978; Walsh, Williams, and Hertzog, 1978). Again, stimulus persistence theory was confirmed, although Walsh et al. did not discuss their data in these terms. Instead, they discussed them in terms of speed of perceptual processing—old people being slower than young.

Stimulus persistence, apparently, can be modified with training. In one study, practice was given to reduce the amount of time needed to process the target stimulus. Both young and old reduced their times, and to a similar extent (Hertzog, Williams, and Walsh, 1976). The ability to modify stimulus persistence effects is all the more interesting if the effects are thought to have neurophysiological bases. It seems especially important to replicate these results.

Corresponding Stimulus Halves. Letters of words were constructed from a series of dots. Half the dot-letters of a word were presented as a first stimulus and the other half as the second stimulus. In this way, rather than interfere with or mask the target stimulus, the second stimulus added a meaningful dimension to the first one by forming the whole word. Whereas in the masking studies stimulus persistence theory predicts greater masking on the part of the old, the theory in the word-half enhancement studies predicts greater word idfentification on the part of the old. The persistence of the first half of the word fuses with that of the last half.

Contrary to stimulus persistence theory, the young, not the old, showed higher word identification (Kline and Baffa, 1976). However, the investigators considered the fact that old people tend to have difficulty making sense of such poorly structured material as dot arrangements for words. Also, they thought that the lighted background on which the stimuli were presented may have carried over and reduced the visibility of the stimuli. Accordingly, the study was repeated, this time using straight white horizontal and vertical line segments on a black background, instead of black dots on a white background.

With the study redone in this way, the results were otherwise. With half the word given as the first stimulus and the other half as the second one, the older adults identified *more* total words than the young, in "strong support for the stimulus-persistence model . . ." (Kline and Orme-Rogers, 1977).

Stimuli Reflecting Common Experience

Judging Weights. A different type of study, one involving comparisons between weights rather than fusion thresholds of successive stimulation, was reported by Landahl and Birren (1959). In the fusion experiment, the performances of the young, more than the old, were seen as keeping the inputs relatively discrete perceptually. In the masking experiment, the performances of the young were seen as reflecting relative escape from masking at shorter intervals between stimulation. In the word-half study, more readily fused word halves on the part of the old made for better identifications. In all these instances, the performances of the young were thought superior to the old in that they reflected more nearly the objective physical reality.

In the weight judgment experiment of Landahl and Birren, good performance was seen as the ability to perceive which of two lifted weights was the heavier. Stimulus persistence theory could explain the results of this weight comparison study but not as well or as easily as the results of the fusion studies.

Subjects of two age groups, 18-32 and 58-85 years, were presented with a standard weight of 100 grams and a comparison weight of either 100, 105, 110, or 115 grams. There were a variety of comparisons, but the important ones here were: (1) the standard weight was placed in one hand and a comparison weight in the other simultaneously; and (2) the standard placed in one hand and a comparison placed in the same hand after the standard weight was removed.

With the stimulus persistence model, the prediction might be that the successive comparisons would be better for the older subjects than the younger, relative to the simultaneous comparisons. It could be speculated that the older subjects should be aided in making successive weight comparisons by having the trace of the standard (first) stimulus persist in the nervous system so that either its presence or more recent "clearance" would provide an adequate standard of comparison when the second weight is being judged. On the other hand, for the young, the course of neural transmission having further progressed makes for a trace less available for adequate comparison. The outcome of the Landahl-Birren experiment could be interpreted in this way but, again, it must be emphasized that the experiment was not carried out for the purpose of testing the model, and this interpretation may be less direct or good than other interpretations. Moreover, as already indicated, the correct test of the model must be made of predictions that the model generates (as in the masking and corresponding stimulus halves studies), not *post hoc* interpretations of existing data. The model is used here mainly to suggest an organizing scheme to integrate a great variety of diverse studies.

In the Landahl-Birren study, when the two weights were presented simultaneously, one in one hand and one in the other, discrimination performance of the older group was less good than that of the young group. If we accept this as a baseline for further age comparisons, an interesting result is seen. When the two weights were presented successively in one hand, first the standard and then the comparison weight, the two age groups performed very similarly. If we start with the proposition that the old perceive weights less well than the young (as in the simultaneous condition, when the trace of the standard stimulus is in the nervous systems of both the old and the young) we can speculate that the old are benefited relatively, when only they have a persisting or recent comparison trace and the young do not. This interpretation becomes more interesting when it is recognized that short-term memory is involved in the successive condition and not the simultaneous one. Later in this book it will be seen that short-term memory performance tends to be poor in old age. On this basis alone, the prediction might be of relatively better weight judgment on the part of the elderly in the simultaneous condition where memory was not involved. As indicated, it was the other way around.

Visual Figures. It was seen that not all evidence is explained equally well by the stimulus persistence model. In the lifted weight experiment, the model had to be applied in a complicated way and a total support for the model was not actually achieved. With the explanation used, a total support might have been seen had the older group been superior to the younger group in the successive weight comparison condition, rather than not being poorer. A study by Wallace (1956) on visual perception must be interpreted in a manner similar to that of the lifted weight study if the stimulus persistence model is to be applied. In addition, another idea is useful, although perhaps not crucial, in applying the model. This idea will also be used in the next section on the perception of speech. Under certain conditions, if the second stimulus is the same as the first, as in the simple case of CFF, they appear fused. If the two stimuli are similar and do not come too rapidly together, and the two must be compared, the trace of the first can aid in judgments of the second. However, if, as in speech, the new input is different from the old and the two come in close temporal order, comparison is not possible, only a type of fusion. In this case, the fusion makes for confusion. With these ideas, Wallace's data can receive a stimulus-persistence interpretation, although they tax the theory considerably.

Wallace presented, sequentially, visual information to an under-30 age group and to an over-60 age group. She used four groupings of stimuli, varied in complexity. As an example, going from simple to complex, she used a triangle, a five-pointed star, a side-view silhouette of a child walking holding a flower, and, as most complex, a pictorial representation of a policeman holding the hands of two children while walking with them. This latter stimulus included shadows for perspective and a major background item. From simple triangle to a complex picture, Wallace had a wide range of meaningful complexity.

Wallace had each subject look through a narrow opening in a box and, in so doing, the subject could see only a small part of the particular stimulus on display. To start, only the lowest portion of the stimulus was seen, soon the next part above it, and slowly—in the course of two to three seconds—the top part was seen. At any one moment only a small portion of the stimulus was visible, but, in time, the whole of it was successively revealed. Correct identification of the displays depended upon integrating material perceived serially over the period of time.

With the simple stimuli, the performances of the two age groups were nearly equal; with increasing complexity of stimuli, the older subjects were increasingly slower than the young in making correct identifications.

Referring to the interpretations suggested above, it may be concluded that, with the complex stimuli, each new sequence of visual trace was "confused" with the previous one. For the old, fusing comes about more readily than for the young, and the fusing of complex, incompatible visual sequences is detrimental to correct perceptual identification. With the simple triangle, however, fusion could be helpful, not detrimental. The successive trace sequences are compatible so their fusion forms a perception that is congruent with the actual physical stimulus. As if in partial support for such hypothesizing, Wallace (1956, p. 292) indicated, "one possible reason for incorrect identification by older people is given by comparing successive replies . . . there was evidence of a 'set' being formed by older subjects, the contents (or supposed contents) of one display influencing the response to the next. . . ." What was cognitively perceived influenced the perception of what followed.

It should be pointed out that, as in the weight comparison study, the old were not better in perception than the young with their more advantageous condition. They were not worse relative to a baseline of larger age differences with more complex stimuli. And, again, this *post hoc* interpretation may not be the most appropriate one. Wallace provided a cue as to how the elderly may be helped to improve their sequential integrations. The more time spent viewing the sequences, and the greater the amount of sequence that was viewed, helped all people, but it helped the older ones most of all.

Speech Perception. With advancing age, speech intelligibility is decreased (Pestalozza and Shore, 1955; Farrimond, 1961). While there is little doubt that much of this problem is attributable to the hearing loss of the high frequency sounds, an analysis of the literature by Corso (1971, p. 97) suggested to him that "reduced speech perception in the aged seems to be due in part to the increase in time required to process the information in the higher auditory centers."

The intelligibility of speech is a function of the rate at which it is spoken. Calearo and Lazzaroni (1957) reported that, for people over 70, speaking louder can compensate for poor intelligibility of fast speech, but the compensation is not very successful if the rate is 350 words a minute. Not all types of speech decline in intelligibility for the aged. Bergman (1971) reported little decrease with age in hearing ordinary speech, but when there are distortions or competing noises, large decrements are noted with age.

Overall, the data show that it is when the spoken words follow one another in rapid sequence, and when the conditions are poor to cull meaning from the words, that the older person becomes disadvantaged over and beyond what problems he may have with high frequency sounds. The explanation of this, based on stimulus persistence theory, was already suggested: With the elderly, the longer persisting auditory trace of one word or sound in a sentence interferes with the processing of the next word. If we refer to the fusion experiments, particularly Weiss' click experiments, we can hypothesize that there is an "earlier fusing" of words or sounds on the part of the elderly than the young, and that this makes for greater unintelligibility.

Sustained Attention

A Continuous Sound. An interesting auditory illusion was used in a study of the aged by Warren (1961). This illusion may present a very exaggerated aspect of what has just been interpreted as a basis for poorer speech perception on the part of the elderly.

Tape recordings were made of single words such as "police" and "tress," and one recording was made of a short phrase. Each of these was continuously repeated; until the tape recorder was turned off, there was an endless repetition of the particular word or phrase. The illusion was that, as the word was continuously heard, it seemed to change. For example, as the word "tress" is heard over and over, it may change to "press," "trez," and others, and back again to these.

Aged adults were less susceptible to this illusion than the young, and they did not report as many changes in word sounds. Warren did not carry out his study to test the stimulus persistence notion, but his data could be explained by it, even if in the *post hoc* way it has been used here. For the aged, the trace of the initial word stimulus persists longer than for the young, and thus has greater effect over very similar traces associated with the new and different parts of the repeating word inputs. The fusion with very similar—almost identical new inputs—would tend to maintain the initial perception and not modify it.

Vigilance. The more complicated and demanding the task, the more are vigilance and attention required. But even in so simple a task as CFF, attention is necessary, for without it the stimulus would not be perceived, or would not be perceived well, and the measured thresholds might be different. A watchful, attentive orientation is necessary for a great variety of perceptual activities, and an impaired ability to pay attention and be vigilant would certainly set limits to the adequacy of performance of many of them.

There have been several investigations of vigilance performance in relation to age, and two of them will be discussed here as prototypes. Each shows that vigilance behavior declines with age, and crucial in this decline is the rate of information change.

Thompson, Opton, and Cohen (1963) presented a series of numbers to people aged 18 to 35 years and 65 to 75 years. Each person had to push a key when he perceived either two consecutive even numbers or two consecutive odd numbers. The numbers were presented in varied speeds, either one, two or four seconds between them. At the slower rates of speed, the two age groups were similar in their performances. A marked decrement in performance was seen, however, with the older group when the consecutive numbers came rapidly.

A conceptually similar study was reported by Talland (1966). He had eight electronic tubes in a circle and a ninth one in the center. Each tube presented a number from 0 to 9, lighting up and turning off instantly before presenting another number. Each subject was instructed to watch the changing display and to press a key each time he saw the number 4 flash in any one of the nine tubes. Talland tested 40 men in each decade between 20 and 69 years.

At slower rates of display change, the performances did not decline much up to age 60, but, as in the Thompson et al. study, at faster rates ability to watch for and detect the signal, i.e., the number 4, showed more decline. The decline was seen with each age decade. "The aging effect observed is attributed to a slowing down of scanning and decision processes which match the incoming message with a model" (Talland, 1966, p. 114).

Can the stimulus persistence model explain vigilance data? It possibly can, but it may not be the best model to use for it. If the item to be detected (the signal) is regarded as but one of a sequence of stimuli, and the others in the sequence being the non-signal (noise), then the longer persistence of one of these (signal or noise) in the older person's nervous system may be thought to interfere with the processing of the subsequent inputs. As with speech perception, and as with Wallace's visual sequences, a slowing of the rate of incoming information permits the neural trace to "clear through" and not merge with new inputs. The older subject is then free to process new information.

Figural Aftereffect. If the stimulus persistence model is to be maximally effective it should be able to explain and predict results of aftereffect experiments where it gets its most direct test. Unfortunately, the model falls down badly here, but it still remains possible to salvage something for it.

The aftereffect experiment is of this form: If a person is stimulated with a first stimulus which is taken away, the perception of a second stimulus will be made in relation to the aftereffect of the first one. If the stimulus trace persists longer in the older nervous system than in the younger one, the aftereffect of the first stimulus should be greater in the old than in the young.

There are very few studies of aftereffects in relation to age, but these indicate that the old do not seem very susceptible to the aftereffect, and, when it is present, it is not long sustained—a damaging blow to the stimulus persistence model. Perhaps, however, more complete and adequate data are yet to be collected, which might tell a different tale. Not only are there few studies bearing on this, but of those few, several are not appropriate to test the model because both young and old adults had not been compared. One that could have been appropriate was reported by Axelrod and Eisdorfer (1962). They first reported results on both a visual and a kinesthetic aftereffect, concluding that people aged 60-76 years were no different from those aged 18-34 either in susceptibility to, or duration of, the figural aftereffects. Later, however, Eisdorfer and Axelrod (1964) found that one of the data collectors had been suffering from a neurological disorder which affected the results. A re-analysis proved the kinesthetic aftereffect data invalid, but the visual aftereffect data proved interesting.

In the measurement of the figural aftereffect, each person visually fixated on a dot with a black rectangle placed to the left. After this, the rectangle was removed and another one was placed to the left of where the first rectangle had been. Having fixated on the first rectangle and dot, the aftereffect of this made the new rectangle look farther to the left of the dot than it really was. How far away was measured by the person attempting to set a movable rectangle placed on the right of the fixation dot the same distance away from it as the rectangle on the left appeared to be.

The re-analysis by Eisdorfer and Axelrod (1964) supported previous contentions that the elderly are less susceptible to the aftereffect than are the young; they tended to not experience the aftereffect very readily. However, another part of their findings was in support of stimulus persistence theory. Once the aftereffect was established, at a lower level for the old than for the young, it was better maintained by the old than it was by the young. As may be seen in Figure 11.1, from the test made immediately after removing the fixation stimulus to the test made 120 seconds after removing it, the aftereffect diminished rapidly in the young and only slowly in the old. This relative diminution was such that, as seen in Figure 11.1, after 120 seconds, a greater aftereffect was measured with the old than with the young. In terms of statistical significance, the age difference was seen only immediately after removing the fixation stimulus, but the significantly greater persistence of the aftereffect in the old, and the crossover of curves, leaves the door open for the stimulus persistence model. The next experiment discussed also concerns aftereffect. This one also allows leaving the door open.

TEMPORAL INTEGRATION
OF NON-SEQUENTIAL INFORMATION

Up to now the discussion has centered around stimuli which come to the perceiver one at a time or parts at a time. The present section deals with complex stimuli which are not sequential. Even here, however, the perceiver must integrate information. There are different parts of the stimulus, and if the stimulus is very large or very complicated, it is neces-

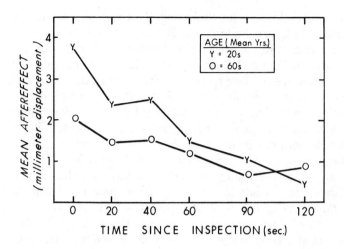

FIGURE 11.1: Magnitude of figural aftereffect as a function of the time since inspection. (Drawn from Figure 4 of Eisdorfer and Axelrod, 1964.)

sary to scan it and process the different sections, as in sequential information. If processing continues for very long, i.e., if the perceiver focuses very long on such stimuli, illusions can develop.

Spiral Aftereffect

It was said that a serious challenge to stimulus persistence theory comes from studies of aftereffects. Perhaps the most serious challenge comes from the study of spiral aftereffects. A spiral is drawn on a disc, beginning at the center and spiraling out to the edge. The spiraled disc is then rotated by motor, placed in such a way as to be vertical with respect to the perceiver. As the spiral rotates for a time, say 30 seconds, and a person fixates on it, an aftereffect of a spiraling image continues after the motor is turned off and the actual spiraling stops.

If the nervous system of the older person is to be thought of as being a longer-term stimulus persistence mechanism than that of the younger person, the old should have a longer duration aftereffect. The few studies bearing on this tend to show that the reverse is true—the old have shorter spiral aftereffects than the young. Again, however, as with the Eisdorfer-Axelrod report depicted in Figure 11.1, all the evidence may not yet be in. Griew and Lynn (1960) reported that with fixations of 30 seconds on the rotating spiral, the duration of the aftereffect was briefer for the old than for the young. This was seen again in a subsequent study by Griew, Fellows, and Howes (1963).

In this later study, however, the duration of fixation was varied. As may be seen in Figure 11.2, after 15 seconds, 30 seconds, and 45 seconds of focusing on the rotating spiral, the aftereffect of the old (60-81 years) was less than that of the young (18-25). But, as shown in the figure, after 60 seconds of viewing the rotating spiral, the older subjects had *longer* aftereffects than the younger subjects, not shorter! The crossing of curves in both this figure and in Figure 11.1 warrant further investigation. Both these figures suggest that, for whatever reason, the old are not as susceptible as the young to aftereffects but, once the aftereffects are established, they persist longer. They persist longer at least relative to their initial levels, and they may persist longer irrespective of initial levels. If this be true, stimulus persistence theory is not invalidated by the data of aftereffect studies, and only the difficulty in establishing the effect remains unexplained.

Color Afterimage

It has long been known that if a person focuses on a patch of color presented on a neutral background, then takes his eyes off the color and focuses on a neutral background without any color on it, the person will

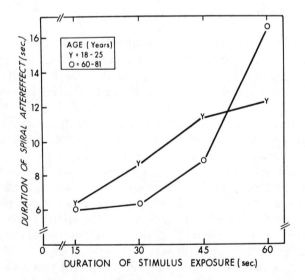

FIGURE 11.2: Duration of spiral aftereffect as a function of stimulus exposure duration. (From Table 1 of Griew et al., 1963.)

see an image of color that is close to the exact color complement of what had been looked at. For example, fixating on a green patch will make for a red afterimage. Within limits, the longer the eye fixates on the stimulus color, the longer the afterimage lasts. Stimulus persistence theory predicts that the afterimage would be sustained longer by the old than the young.

Kline and Nestor (1977) found just such a result. They presented a green patch on a red background to enhance the formation of the image. They had exposure durations of 30, 60, and 90 seconds, and unlike the spiral aftereffect findings of Griew et al. in Figure 11.2, the afterimages persisted longer among the old than the young at each of the three exposure durations, a direct confirmation of the theory.

Time to Perceive Complex Stimuli

Why is it difficult to establish aftereffects with the older person? The data of Figure 11.2 may give us a clue. Perhaps the reason is simply that it takes longer with older people for external physical events to be tranformed into nervous energy and be processed than it does with younger people. There is evidence to support such an idea.

Eriksen, Hamlin, and Breitmeyer (1970) carried out two experiments in which they compared three adult age groups, none of them old (30-35, 40-45, and 50-55 years). In the first experiment, ability to visually identify forms was measured when the stimulus was exposed for varying times. Even with the narrow age range and even after equating subjects on visual acuity, it was found that it took progressively more time with increased age to perceive the stimulus. This is a typical finding. For example, it was found with a variety of form perception tests (Crook, Alexander, Anderson, Coules, Hanson, and Jeffries, 1958), with the perception of meaningful words (Riegel, Riegel, and Wendt, 1962), and in a variety of other studies.

The Eriksen et al. study was carried further. With the same three age groups of subjects, the stimulus materials were equated in difficulty for each person. The size and the details of the stimuli were adjusted so as to allow for each person 70 percent correct identifications of forms, at a particular exposure duration and brightness level. In this way, the three age groups responded to their own particular stimuli, different in terms of physical dimension but equal in difficulty in terms of their own perceptual abilities.

Using these stimuli, Eriksen et al. then varied their exposure durations as in the first experiment, but this time they co-varied with it the intensity of illumination. In this way the light energy reaching the retina remained constant in each of the different stimulus exposure durations. (Eriksen et al. called this the critical duration of time-intensity reciprocity.)

Keeping the stimuli equated among age groups for perceptual difficulty, and keeping the stimulus energy constant, the results were such that they

strongly suggest that the critical duration or time unit over which light energy is integrated does increase with advancing age. This lengthened integration period would account for the ability of the aged Ss [subjects] when given longer exposure durations, to achieve the acuity performance of younger Ss. The older Ss can compensate on this task for their heightened sensory threshold for light by integrating energy over a longer time period, thus effectively increasing the intensity of the stimulus. While the increase in the sensory threshold with advancing age may reflect impairment in the sense organ, the change in the integration period would definitely point to a more central locus for age changes (Eriksen et al., 1970, p. 356).

In terms of the stimulus persistence model and the aftereffect data, this conclusion of Eriksen et al. can be brought to bear as follows: With increasing age, more difficulty is encountered in processing inputs, and it takes more time to do so. But once they are incorporated into the perceptual system of the older person, they persist longer and result in a variety of effects. Very often these effects are detrimental, but there are instances where they can be beneficial.

Illusions

A variety of experimental illusions have been studied by psychologists and, while many of these illusions appear similar or otherwise seem to involve similar perceptual processes, by and large, performance on one illusion task does not tend to correlate well with performances on others. Possibly the unreliability of the measurements of illusions explains the low correlations among them.

Necker Cubes. Several illusions have already been discussed. Warren's "continuous sound" is an example of an illusion based upon sequential inputs. Aftereffects are illusions. Another illusion investigated in relation to age was the Necker cubes (Heath and Orbach, 1963). In this illusion sketches of cubes are drawn in such a way that there is perceptual oscillation of what is in the foreground and what is in the background. As in the "continuous sound" illusion, a count may be made of the number of these oscillations.

Heath and Orbach reported that of 31 people aged 65-90 years tested with the Necker cubes, only six were able to report measurable oscillations; of these six, four had scores "clearly below those expected of normal young adults." It is seen once again, therefore, that, for whatever the reason, be it time to perceive the stimulus or for some other reason, the old are not as susceptible to illusion as the young. These Necker cube findings could be interpreted in the same way as Warren's "continuous sound" was interpreted: The trace in the older nervous system persists, making for fusion with newer aspects of the stimulus which might befall the retina, thus maintaining percepts, not modifying them.

Retinal Rivalry. Another illusion is called retinal rivalry. Here, with the aid of a stereoscope, one eye views one color (e.g., green), and the other eye views another color (e.g., red). There are three types of perceptions that have been recorded with this procedure: (1) the visual field oscillates from green to red and to green again; (2) the colors fuse and a gray field is seen, with no oscillation; (3) there is no complete fusion, but there is no oscillation either.

It was found in one study that the frequency of oscillation systematically decreased with increasing age from 40 to 93 years, with fusion to gray being more characteristic of the older subjects than the young (Jalavisto, 1964). A total lack of oscillation was found in the oldest age categories. While the frequency of oscillation depends upon the intensity of the stimulus and thus upon peripheral eye factors, "the phenomenon of age dependent decrease in retinal rivalry oscillation frequency is connected primarily with brain function and only in a less degree in retinal conditions" (Jalavisto, 1964, p. 6).

The results of this study may be interpreted from a stimulus persistence model in the same way as was the Necker cubes study—a persisting stimulus trace fuses with newly sensed dimensions of the stimulus.

SPATIAL INTEGRATION

Up to now the discussion has centered on the processing of stimuli where considerations of threshold and sequential patterning are important. Now the discussion will center on stimuli which are difficult to perceive because they are either spatially spread out, or their parts are spatially dissociated or disguised.

Part-Whole Relationships

Dissociated Stimulus Parts. There is a test called the Street Test. It is composed of pictures of objects and animals in segmented form with missing parts. Each picture looks as if it would be in solid black silhouette if it were not segmented and if no parts were missing. The task, very simply, is to identify the picture, e.g., dog, airplane, and so on.

Crook et al. (1958) gave this test, among others, to subjects aged 20 to 50 years. The ability to perceive the forms of each picture did not change in this limited age period, but, when the exposure time of each picture was very much reduced, decline with age in the ability to recognize the forms was prominent. Whether it was, again, the time to perceive the stimulus complex, or the difficulty in integrating the stimulus parts which declined with age is not clear from this study. An indication that it may be at least partly the latter may be surmised from other sources.

There is a test called the Hooper Visual Organization Test (Hooper, 1958) which was devised to help in the diagnosis of organic brain pathology. The test presents the subject with drawings of simple objects which have been cut into parts and the parts rearranged so that each drawing can appear as a type of jigsaw puzzle. The subject's job is to name the object, which can be done only by a spatial reorganization and integration of the parts.

According to Hooper, the test is "particularly sensitive to the decrement in abilities which appear with physiological changes in the cortical structures." Hooper reported that, while the test performances are relatively unrelated to sex, education, normal intelligence levels, and age of young adults, the performances are related to the age of young and elderly adults together. Thus, it is seen that, with increased age, there tends to be a decreased ability to spatially integrate information.

Parts Embedded in Confusing Backgrounds. Other evidence points to this decreased ability also. For example, Crook et al. gave their subjects a version of the Gottschaldt test. This test is of two-dimensional geometric figures that are to be identified when embedded or hidden in a confusing complex of other figures and lines. Many abilities are involved in this task, one of which seems to be spatial rearrangement of the forms. The results of this study were not reflective of age decline; instead, there was much individual difference. But, with a test of these figures given to people of older age (a mean of 78 years), Basowitz and Korchin (1957) found their performances much poorer than those of younger people (see chapter 8).

Hidden figures were also used by Axelrod and Cohen (1961); they used both a visual version and a tactile version. The tactile version involved examining figures by touch and finding them by touch when embedded in more complex contexts. Here too, with both the visual and the tactile versions, the old were found to have greater difficulty than the young in identifying the figures. Axelrod and Cohen also measured touch sensitivity to determine if this could account for their results. Touch sensitivity was not related to tactile embedded figure performance and it was thus concluded that the latter was a "higher-order" (nervous system) function than was tactile acuity.

It is doubtful whether stimulus persistence theory is very helpful with data of the type discussed in this section. If it is, it would probably take a form similar to that applied to sequential processing as in Wallace's visual perception study. The persisting trace of one part of the stimulus is helpful to the older person in forming correct percepts only when it can be fused with traces of other parts of the stimulus that are very similar both in physical aspect and in spatial arrangement. Since, in tasks of embedded figures or dissociated parts, fusion of the contiguous stimulus elements would not make for correct percepts, the persisting trace serves to hinder good performance.

Modification of Percepts

Stimulus persistence theory, if it is to be rooted in physiological mechanisms, is most meaningful when the time sequences are very short, a matter of milliseconds or even less. However, as a model, predictions can be made for much longer term processes. If complex sensory information takes a long time to process and, in so doing, engages the stimulus-response mechanisms, new information would have relatively little impact on the perceiver, or it would be responded to in less than adequate fashion. It becomes possible with this reasoning to explain rigidity-type behavior in later life. Since older people are engaged longer in perceiving and responding to items of information, they will not be as responsive to new information and will respond to it inadequately. The old, therefore, may seem less modifiable to new experience and appear rigid. Several sets of data fit this model, but, again, this model may not be the most expedient for this purpose.

Structural Sets. In 1956, Korchin and Basowitz published what was to be one of the better known studies of the effect of aging on perceptual modification, i.e., the inclination or ability to switch from one percept to another when the conditions warrant it. A subsequent study based upon this one was reported by Botwinick (1962). These two studies were discussed in some detail in chapter 8, which deals with the problem of cautiousness in relation to age. It may be recalled from that discussion that old and young adults were presented with a series of 13 sketch-drawings, the first of which was a cat and the last of which was a dog (see Figure 8.2). From the first to the last drawing, each was modified gradually until the cat became the dog, with the middle drawings in the series being part dog and part cat.

Korchin and Basowitz found that the young subjects shifted percepts (from cat to dog) earlier in the series than did the old. With quite different instructions and with a different procedure, Botwinick found just the opposite: The old shifted earlier in the series. It was pointed out that, unlike the earlier Korchin-Basowitz study, the procedure in the Botwinick study emphasized the need to shift, and the nature of the shift was made very clear. With this very structured direction, the older adults did not have difficulty modifying the percept; they seemed to have difficulty only when the structure lacked certainty and direction. Problems seem to become difficult for the elderly when there is an unspecified need to change set. This idea is compatible with the impression that elderly persons tend to function best in familiar environments. A new input which is incompatible with a previous one is responded to less adequately by the elderly than by the young unless, perhaps, differences between inputs are clearly differentiated beforehand.

Perceptual Span. The first cat-dog study suggested that the elderly tend to hold on to a percept and are less inclined than the young to modify it. Two later studies, very similar to one another, supported the notion of difficulty in later life in the modification of perceptions, but other interpretations are possible too (Botwinick, Robbin, and Brinley, 1959; Botwinick, 1965).

An ambiguous figure was used in the first of these studies, which has been referred to as "my wife" and "my mother-in-law" because both a young woman and an old woman could be seen in it (Boring, 1930; see Figure 11.3 [A]). Male subjects aged 19-34 and 65-81 years were presented with this figure, and they were asked to tell what they saw. If either the "wife" or the "mother-in-law" was seen by the subject, he was told that "another picture" could be seen also. If he could not perceive the other "picture" in this figure, a more stable version of it was shown to him (the "wife," Figure 11.3 [B]; or the "mother-in-law," Figure 11.3 [C]). If the subject could not see the percept in this form, the facial and other features were pointed out. Following this, the ambiguous figure (11.3[A]) was presented again without indicating that it was the one he had already seen. The subject was then asked what he saw.

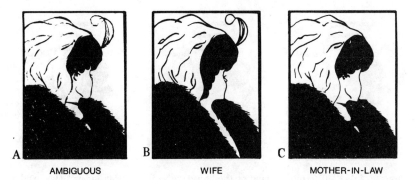

FIGURE 11.3: Photograph drawings of the "wife" (B), "mother-in-law" (C), and figure comprising both (A). Permission to reprint these was given by the *American Journal of Psychology* (Boring, 1930) and the *Journal of Gerontology* (Botwinick et al., 1959).

The elderly men tended to report the alternate percepts less frequently than did the young men, and it was concluded that they could not or did not reorganize the initial percept as readily—they were less modifiable—they showed a type of stimulus persistence.

This study also concluded that, since 78 percent of the younger subjects and 94 percent of the older group reported seeing the "wife" first (Figure 11.3 [B]), the "mother-in-law" (Figure 11.3 [C]) may have been a more difficult percept to organize than the "wife" and perhaps too difficult for the older subject. That is, to perceive the "mother-in-law" required a spatial integration of more stimulus parts than did perceiving the "wife." If this was too difficult a task for the older subject, then this reason, more than reasons of modifiability, could explain the results.

Accordingly, a more balanced ambiguous figure was developed (Botwinick, 1961)—a "husband" and "father-in-law" (see Figure 11.4), and this was presented to old and young subjects of both sexes. The results of this study were similar to those of the earlier one: the young modified the initial percepts readily, and the old did not. This was true for both men and women.

Although this newer figure was a more balanced one than Figure 11.3(A), the elderly subjects still tended to report the younger percept, i.e., the smaller part of the total. Again, therefore, the ability to integrate spatially spread-out parts may have been the prime factor in the results. To see both the "wife" and the "mother-in-law" in one figure, and the "husband" and "father-in-law" in the other, may require a perceptual span greater than many old people have.

FIGURE 11.4: Photograph drawing of the "husband" (B), "father-in-law" (C), and a figure comprising both (A). Permission to reprint these was given by the *American Journal of Psychology*, (Botwinick, 1961).

ANOXIA, ANOTHER MODEL

Much of the foregoing has been framed around a model of a stimulus persistence. This model may or may not reflect a psychoneurological reality, but, in either case, its main utility is to aid in organizing a collection of diverse findings and to enable predictions of what might be found. If the model is rooted in psychoneurological reality, so much the better; perhaps it can point the way to useful research on this level.

The model has been seen as very useful in some areas and less so in others. Should future research prove the model very much more limited in usefulness than here suggested, should it be seen that it was over-ambitiously and incorrectly applied, should a much better one be evolved, only the model will be discarded, not the data it is meant to explain. The data discussed in this chapter could be represented on their own without the model and, in fact, this is how it has typically been done. As to the model itself, it can only be tested properly with experiments carried out with respect to it as the more recent studies have done. These studies have lent credence to the model.

There are other theories or models, and one in particular is extraordinarily good. It is a model expressed mainly by McFarland (e.g., 1968, p. 40) and it takes the form of "oxygen want." Many similarities were noted by McFarland between aging and oxygen want, particularly in regard to sensory and perceptual performances. McFarland wrote:

> most sensitive tests for [high] altitude [where oxygen is less present] give essentially the same results in regard to aging. Although one cannot assume identical causal mechanisms, the striking similarity in

changes in performance and on the physiological processes . . . suggests that impairment may reflect interference with the normal metabolic processes within the individual cells.

In perception, the afferent nerves conduct sensory messages of environmental stimulations to higher brain centers. These centers integrate the messages and relate them to what already is in memory. If the cells of the brain or lower centers are deprived of oxygen and thus do not function optimally, deficit performance would certainly be anticipated.

COMPENSATORY ADJUSTMENTS

When in later life there is decrease in sensory acuity and in the adequacy of perceptual processing of information, there are compensatory adjustments that are possible. Some of these appear as changes in personality characteristics and, as already indicated, often take the form of a cautiousness, discussed in earlier chapters. There are other types of adjustments that are also possible and these, unfortunately, have hardly been studied at all. It is here, perhaps more than in other areas, where good work can be very important both for basic science and for helping people.

For the hard of hearing, for example, the prescription is slow speech, louder speech and, very important, close attention to the person talking. As important—and in many cases more important—the prescription is to watch the lips of the person talking. This provides an additional, and sometimes crucial, source of information, corroborating and supplementing the main information source, and when necessary, supplanting it.

Bisensory compensatory adjustments sometimes are automatically made, often without an awareness. A famous neurologist, for example, once described his observation that young people tend to drink water from a glass without any apparent visual attention to the glass. The kinesthetic and proprioceptive cues are sufficient to carry out the drinking. However, some older people, particularly the impaired aged, tend to monitor their drinking by a close, visual watch.

A more experimental analysis of the relative benefit for older people of looking at what they are doing was made by Szafran (1951). He had industrial workers of widely varying ages locate targets with a pointer under two conditions: (1) when direct vision was permitted; and (2) when the use of goggles made it possible to see the general display but not the targets or pointers. Szafran reported that when unable to make use of vision the older workers had great difficulty. They tended to make postural adjustments, turning their heads and often their bodies in the direction of the particular target to be located. Without the maximum sensory opportunities, the old fared poorly indeed; they were at a special disadvantage.

SUMMARY

If a person responds to a stimulus and then responds to a second one which follows very shortly afterward, the second response is often different from the first one, even if the two stimuli are identical. It is as if the trace of the first stimulus persists, interfering with the processing of the trace of the second stimulus. An aspect of this theory or model is that stimulus traces persist longer in the nervous systems of old people than of young ones. While this is more a theory than a fact, much data may be explained in this way.

Stimulus persistence theory explains well the fact that discrete, simple stimuli coming in rapid order fuse more readily for the old than for the young. This was seen for visual stimuli (CFF), auditory clicks, and shocks to the hand. Stimulus persistence theory not only explains but also seems to be validated by the data of studies on backward masking and corresponding stimulus half presentations. Stimulus persistence theory is less satisfactory in explaining more complex perceptual processing. For example, two studies were described, one in which lifted weights were compared, and another in which visual percepts had to be formed. In the weight comparison study, when two weights were presented simultaneously, one in one hand and one in the other, discrimination performance of the older group was not as good as that of the young group. But, when the two weights were presented successively in one hand, first the standard and then the comparison weight, the two age groups performed very similarly. In the visual perception study, pictures were shown such that the parts of each were seen in sequences: At first only the lowest portion was seen, then the next part above it, and last the top part was seen. With simple stimuli, correct identification of the visual display was nearly equal for old and young adults but, with increasing complexity of stimuli, the older subjects were increasingly poorer than the young. Stimulus persistence theory was used to explain both the weight comparison data and the visual perception data by indicating that persisting stimulus traces might be helpful in sequential integration of information when the stimuli are simple, but, when the stimuli are complex, stimulus persistence may interfere with perception. With simple stimuli, the persisting trace may fuse with new traces or be used as a comparison making for correct perceptions. Fusing complex traces, however, makes for incorrect perceptions.

A similar interpretation was made with results showing that meaningful speech can become less intelligible for elderly people when the speech is rapid. With old people, the longer persistence of the auditory trace of one word or sound in a sentence might interfere with the processing of the next word; with young people this would happen at more rapid rates of speech.

In all these perceptual tasks, vigilance and attention are required. There have been several investigations of vigilance performance in relation to age, and they tend to show that vigilance behavior declines with age and that crucial in this decline is the rate of information change. As in speech, the faster the speed with which inputs follow one another, the greater the age decrement. In differentiating the "signal" from the "noise," the persistence of the trace of one of these (signal or noise) may be thought to interrupt the processing of the subsequent ones.

Most studies of perceptual aftereffects and other illusions, but not all, show that aged adults tend not to be susceptible to them. Moreover, when they are established, they are often reported less sustained in later life than in young adulthood. Such reports argue against stimulus persistence theory for, if in the old nervous system traces persist longer than in young nervous systems, aftereffects and illusions should be sustained longer. However, the reports may be misleading. The literature shows that when figural and spiral aftereffects are developed after long and thorough periods of stimulus viewing, and tests of aftereffects are carried out for long periods afterward, they might be seen lasting longer in the old than in the young. One reason it may be more difficult to establish an aftereffect in the old than in the young may be that it takes more physical energy of the external event to make an impact on them. Once the energy of stimulation is increased, the old often perform as well as the young. If two modalities are stimulated simultaneously, the elderly may perform even better. A study on color afterimages was different in that it was not especially difficult to initiate the images among the elderly. The afterimages lasted longer among the elderly than the young, confirming stimulus persistence theory.

Quite another type of stimulus processing involves spatial integration. Old subjects were seen to have difficulty with spatially integrating dissociated stimulus parts and finding them in complex backgrounds. They also seemed to have difficulty in modifying percepts once established. Stimulus persistence theory was applied here too, but only with great stress on the theory.

Thus stimulus persistence theory has been useful in explaining much of the data of perception studies. The theory has been used to organize data already reported in the literature and has been put to a test by studies carried out for just that purpose. While the stimulus persistence notion seems useful, it is well to keep in mind that this is not the only theory that is considered effective. There are other theories, and one in particular which is extraordinarily good takes the form of "oxygen want." Many similarities were noted between aging and oxygen deprivation, particularly in regard to sensory and perceptual performances.

REFERENCES

Axelrod, S. Cognitive tasks in several modalities. In R.H. Williams, C. Tibbitts, and W. Donahue (Eds.), *Processes of aging*, Vol. 1. New York: Atherton Press, 1963, pp. 132–145.

Axelrod, S., and Cohen, L.D. Senescence and imbedded-figure performance in vision and touch. *Perceptual and Motor Skills*, 1961, *12*, 283–288.

Axelrod, S., and Eisdorfer, C. Senescence and figural aftereffects in two modalities. *Journal of Genetic Psychology*, 1962, *100*, 85–91.

Axelrod, S., Thompson, L.W., and Cohen, L.D. Effects of senescence on the temporal resolution of somesthetic stimuli presented to one hand or both. *Journal of Gerontology*, 1968, *23*, 191–195.

Basowitz, H., and Korchin, S.J. Age differences in the perception of closure. *Journal of Abnormal and Social Psychology*, 1957, *54*, 93–97.

Bergman, M. Changes in hearing with age. *Gerontologist*, 1971, *11*, 148–151.

Boring, E.G. A new ambiguous figure. *American Journal of Psychology*, 1930, *42*, 444–445.

Botwinick, J. Husband and father-in-law—a reversible figure. *American Journal of Psychology*, 1961, *74*, 312–313.

Botwinick, J. A research note on the problem of perceptual modification in relation to age. *Journal of Gerontology*, 1962, *17*, 190–192.

Botwinick, J. Perceptual organization in relation to age and sex. *Journal of Gerontology*, 1965, *20*, 224–227.

Botwinick, J., Robbin, J.S., and Brinley, J.F. Reorganization of perception with age. *Journal of Gerontology*, 1959, *14*, 85–88.

Calearo, C., and Lazzaroni, A. Speech intelligibility in relation to the speed of the message. *Laryngoscope*, 1957, *67*, 410–419.

Coppinger, N.W. The relationship between critical flicker frequency and chronological age for varying levels of stimulus brightness. *Journal of Gerontology*, 1955, *10*, 48–52.

Corso, J.F. Sensory processes and age effects in normal adults. *Journal of Gerontology*, 1971, *26*, 90–105.

Crook, M.N., Alexander, E.A., Anderson, E.M.S., Coules, J., Hanson, A., and Jeffries, N.T., Jr. *Age and form perception*. USAF School of Aviation Medicine, Randolph AFB, Texas, 1958, Report No. 57-124.

Eisdorfer, C., and Axelrod, S. Senescence and figural aftereffects in two modalities: A correction. *Journal of Genetic Psychology*, 1964, *104*, 193–197.

Eriksen, C.W., Hamlin, R.M., and Brietmeyer, R.G. Temporal factors in visual perception as related to aging. *Perception and Psychophysics*, 1970, 7, 354–356.

Farrimond, T. Prediction of speech hearing lóss for older industrial workers. *Gerontologia*, 1961, 5, 65–87.

Griew, S., Fellows, B.J., and Howes, R. Duration of spiral aftereffect as a function of stimulus exposure and age. *Perceptual and Motor Skills*, 1963, 17, 210.

Griew, S., and Lynn, R. Constructive "reaction inhibition" in the interpretation of age changes in performance. *Nature*, 1960, 186, 182.

Heath, H.A., and Orbach, J. Reversibility of the Necker cube: IV. Responses of elderly people. *Perceptual and Motor Skills*, 1963, 17, 625–626.

Hertzog, C.K., Williams, M.V., and Walsh, D.A. The effect of practice on age differences in central perceptual processing. *Journal of Gerontology*, 1976, 31, 428–433.

Hooper, H.E. *The Hooper visual organization test—Manual*. Beverly Hills, Calif.: Western Psychological Services, 1958.

Jalavisto, E. The phenomenon of retinal rivalry in the aged. *Gerontologia*, 1964, 9, 1–8.

Kline, D.W. and Baffa, G. Differences in the sequential integration of form as a function of age and interstimulus interval. *Experimental Aging Research*, 1976, 2, 333–343.

Kline, D.W. and Birren, J.E. Age differences in backward dichoptic masking. *Experimental Aging Research*, 1975, 1, 17–25.

Kline, D.W. and Nestor, S. The persistence of complementary afterimages as a function of adult age and exposure duration. *Experimental Aging Research*, 1977, 3, 191–201.

Kline, D.W. and Orme-Rogers, C. Examination of stimulus persistence as the basis for superior visual identification performance among older adults. *Journal of Gerontology*, 1978, 33, 76–81.

Kline, D.W. and Szafran, J. Age differences in backward monoptic visual noise masking. *Journal of Gerontology*, 1975, 30, 307–311.

Korchin, S.J., and Basowitz, H. The judgment of ambiguous stimuli as an index of cognitive functioning in aging. *Journal of Personality*, 1956, 25, 81–95.

Landahl, H.D., and Birren, J.E. Effects of age on discrimination of lifted weights. *Journal of Gerontology*, 1959, 14, 48–55.

McFarland, R.A. The sensory and perceptual processes in aging. In K.W. Schaie (Ed.), *Theory and methods of research on aging*. Morgantown, W.Va.: West Virginia Univ., 1968, pp. 9–52.

McFarland, R.A., Warren, B., and Karis, C. Alterations in critical flicker frequency as a function of age and light : dark ratio. *Journal of Experimental Psychology*, 1958, 56, 529–538.

Misiak, H. Age and sex differences in critical flicker frequency. *Journal of Experimental Psychology*, 1947, 37, 318–332.

Mundy-Castle, A.C. An analysis of central responses to photic stimulation in normal adults. *Electroencephalography and Clinical Neurophysiology*, 1953, 5, 1–22.

Pestalozza, G., and Shore, I. Clinical evaluation of presbycusis on basis of different tests of auditory function. *Laryngoscope*, 1955, 65, 1136–1163.

Riegel, K.F., Riegel, R.M., and Wendt, D. Perception and set. *Acta Psychologica*, 1962, 20, 224–251.

Szafran, J. Changes with age and with exclusion of vision in performance at an aiming task. *Quarterly Journal of Experimental Psychology,* 1951, 3, 111–118.

Talland, G.A. Visual signal detection as a function of age, input rate and signal frequency. *Journal of Psychology,* 1966, 63, 105–115.

Thompson, L.W., Opton, E., Jr., and Cohen, L.D. Effects of age, presentation speed, and sensory modality on performance of a "vigilance" task. *Journal of Gerontology,* 1963, 18, 366–369.

Wallace, J.G. Some studies of perception in relation to age. *British Journal of Psychology,* 1956, XLVII, 283–297.

Walsh, D.A. Age differences in central perceptual processing: a dichoptic backward masking investigation. *Journal of Gerontology,* 1976, 31, 178–185.

Walsh, D.A. and Thompson, L.W. Age differences in visual sensory memory. *Journal of Gerontology,* 1978, in press.

Walsh, D.A., Till, R.E., and Williams, M.V. Age differences in peripheral perceptual processing: a monoptic backward masking investigation. *Journal of Experimental Psychology: Human Perception and Performance,* 1978, in press.

Walsh, D.A., Williams, M.V. and Hertzog, C.K. Age-related differences in two stages of central perceptual processes: the effects of short duration targets and criterion differences. *Journal of Gerontology,* 1978, in press.

Warren, R.M. Illusory changes in repeated words: differences between young adults and the aged. *American Journal of Psychology,* 1961, 74, 506–516.

Weale, R.A. On the eye. In A.T. Welford and J.E. Birren (Eds.), *Behavior, aging and the nervous system.* Springfield, Ill.: Charles C Thomas, 1965.

Weiss, A.D. Sensory functions. In J.E. Birren (Ed.), *Handbook of aging and the individual.* Chicago: Univ. of Chicago Press, 1959, pp. 503–542.

Weiss, A.D. Auditory perception in aging. In J.E. Birren, R.N. Butler, S.W. Greenhouse, L. Sokoloff, and M.R. Yarrow (Eds.), *Human aging: a biological and behavioral study.* P.H.S. Publication No. 986. Washington, D.C.: U.S. Government Printing Office, 1963.

Welford, A.T. Age and skill: motor, intellectual and social. In A.T. Welford (Ed.), *Interdisciplinary topics in gerontology,* 4. Basel and New York: S. Karger, 1969, pp. 1–22.

12

Slow Response to Environmental Stimulation

It was seen how the environment becomes functionally altered when aging causes the sensory and perceptual processing of information to change. As change occurs, differences in response are noted, but, as investigated in the laboratory at least, the differences are more quantitative than qualitative. Among the more frequently investigated quantitative behavioral differences is the slowing down of the responses of older people.

It is difficult to separate this slowing of response from changes in perceptual abilities that also occur in later life, because both are assessed from the same type of information. For example, response is slower when the intensity of stimulation is lower, but one measure of the ability to perceive the stimulus is the time it takes to recognize it. The tie between perception and response speed is so close that the previous chapter, dealing with perceptual processing of information, was introduced with a brief discussion of a four-choice reaction time task. Conversely, in introducing the topic of speed of response, Birren (1964, p. 107) wrote: "One difference in the perceptual performance of older and younger subjects . . . is that of speed" of response.

For some it might seem that the study of speed of response in later life is a trivial pursuit; not so, however, for many psychologists studying aging. It is thought so important, in fact, that Birren (1964, pp. 111–112) concluded, "the evidence indicates that all behavior mediated by the central nervous system tends to slow in the aging organism. . . . In the view favored here, slowness of behavior is the perceptual manifestation of a primary process of aging in the nervous system." This view, in varying forms, is examined in this chapter with evidence which supports it and evidence which does not. An extensive analysis of the problem, but with a different focus, may be seen in a comprehensive chapter by Welford (1977).

INPUT AND PERIPHERAL MECHANISMS

If the loss of speed with age is due mainly to alterations in the sense organs, in the neuromuscular pathways—any aspect of peripheral nerve conduction—it would not be of much importance. The loss of speed would not have much bearing on processes such as cognition and perception. If, however, the loss of speed is mainly due to alterations of the central nervous system, then the consequences could be substantial.

Ruling Out Sensory-Perceptual Factors

Perceptual Difficulty. Birren and Botwinick (1955) presented adults of two age groups (19-36 and 61-91 years) with a task of judging which of two vertical bars was the shorter. These were drawn on a card and presented tachistoscopically. The difference between the bars was varied so that, when it was most difficult to tell them apart, there was only a one percent difference in length between them; when it was most easy, there was a 50 percent difference—one bar was twice the height of the other. The subject's job was to report by saying "right" or "left" as quickly as possible, indicating the shorter bar of the two. (The results of a subsequent but similar study may be seen in Figure 8.1.)

As might be expected, the response time became slower as it became more difficult to differentiate the lengths of the two bars, and this was more so for the old than for the young subjects. Of interest here, however, is that the old were slower than the young at every level of discriminative difficulty. Beginning at a point where there was a 15 percent difference in the lengths of the bars and going to the 50 percent difference point, the speeds of response were no longer determined by the perceptual difficulty in making discriminations; this was as true for one age group as for the other. Thus, the slowness of the older group in responding to the easy discriminative stimuli was not seen as related to perceptual factors—it was related to other factors.

Stimulus Intensity. A similar conclusion was reached in later studies where more direct tests were made. The concept of perceptual difficulty as used in this study of bar lengths was more akin to the concept of sensation than it was to higher-order perceptual responses involving discriminations. The concept of perceptual difficulty was used more in terms of the intensity of input than in terms of making judgments. Perhaps it would have been more appropriate to refer to the differences in bar length as "sensory difficulty" or "stimulus difficulty" or even "stimulus intensity."

A test was made of the proposition that the loss of speed with age is due mainly to functional stimulus intensity, i.e., sensory ability differences between old and young (Botwinick, 1971). Knowing that speed of response is slower when the intensity of stimulation is weaker, and knowing that sensory ability diminishes with age, could it be that the poorer hearing and seeing ability of the old makes the typical laboratory stimuli functionally weaker for them and, as a result, they react more slowly to the stimuli than do younger people?

The reaction times (RTs) of young adults (17-22 years) were compared with those of older adults (64-79 years) in three ways. One, a loud tone stimulus was used, the same one for all subjects (approximately 81 db). This is the type of tone typically used in laboratory studies of RT. Two, a weak sound was used, but different for each subject. By the method of limits, the lowest intensity tone heard by each subject 100 percent of the time was determined. This intensity, different and individual for each subject, was then used to measure RT. Three, the lowest intensity tone heard by each subject approximately 75 percent of the time was determined and used for measuring RT. In this way, each subject was measured for RT with three intensities of tone stimuli, two which were low and unique to the individual based upon his reported hearing ability, and one which was loud and the same for everyone.

If the slowing with age is primarily a problem of sensing the stimulus, then equating this factor between age groups should solve this problem. If sensing the stimulus is not the reason for the slowing, then the old should have RTs slower than the young.

Figure 12.1 presents the results of this study. Not only did the equating of stimulus intensity fail to do away with the slowing of the old age group, it maximized it. This study, then, provided no support for the proposition that the aged are slow because of problems in sensing inputs.

Equalizing stimulus intensity was not expected to increase the differences between age groups in RT. It was thought it might either decrease it or not affect it, but there was no expectation that it would increase it. In this study, the equated stimulus intensities that were used in the RT measurements were very low. As indicated, the tones were so low as to be of threshold intensity. This may have put a burden upon the elderly that was not intended. The perception of very low-intensity tones requires an attention or concentration which is a central process; perhaps the effort made to aid the older subject by equating effective loudnesses became a burden to him instead. Accordingly, a follow-up study was carried out in which young (18-21 years) and older subjects (54-71 years) were compared in RT with the intensity of stimulation also based upon individual hearing ability, but this time, louder suprathreshold tones were used. The stimuli were 10 and 30 db above the subject's own 100 percent "absolute threshold" (Botwinick, 1972).

The results of this study showed that the elderly subjects were still slower than the young. Both age groups were quicker with the louder stimulus of the two, but one age group not more so than the other. The results of this study, together with those of the previous one, suggested that the slowing in later life is not attributable to input or sensory factors. A third study in the series (Botwinick and Storandt, 1972) indicated that it is not until the same physical intensity of stimulation is quite low for the old to hear and still very adequate for the young to hear that input factors are important in the slowing with age.

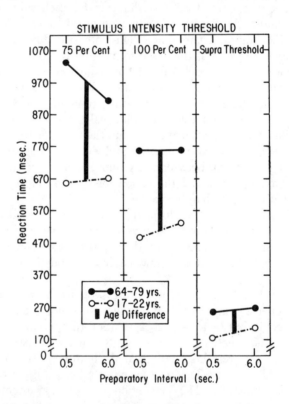

FIGURE 12.1: Differences with age in simple reaction time as a function of stimulus intensity. The loudest stimulus intensity was approximately 81 db, the same for each subject. The two less intense stimuli were different in db for each subject, but similar in terms of their reported loudness, i.e., they were of individual subject threshold measurements.

Speed of Nerve Conduction

In the previous chapter much of the data of studies on perception was explained on the basis of a theory of stimulus persistence, i.e., stimulus traces persist longer in nervous systems of old people than young ones. The neurological counterpart of this psychological theory is that the speed of nerve conduction, especially in the central nervous system, is faster in the young than in the old. Is there evidence that this is so? There is some, but the evidence for increased central nervous system transmission times with age is indirect, and most often interpreted from negative results.

Length of Neuromuscular Pathways. If the slowing of responses with age is not attributable to input factors, may it be attributed to peripheral neuromuscular factors? If so, then older people should be slower than younger people to the extent that such factors are involved in the measurement of response speed.

To investigate systematically the role of neuromuscular pathway, RT was measured for each of three response modalities, each different in effector length (Birren and Botwinick, 1955). The long pathway should make for slower RT than the short pathway to the extent that their lengths are different, and to the extent that the speed of neural conduction via these pathways contributes to RT. Comparison between young and old subjects of such differences in RT due to pathway length could tell something of the contribution of these peripheral mechanisms to the slowing in later life.

RTs for the foot (longest pathway), jaw (shortest), and finger of the hand (middle length) were measured in men aged 18-36 and 61-91 years. For a confirmation of the hypothesis that the slower RTs of the old are attributable to conduction speeds of peripheral neuromuscular pathways, the RTs of the old would have to be increasingly slower than those of the young as we go from jaw to finger to foot.

The results of this experiment provided no support for the hypothesis: The magnitude of difference in RT between old and young was essentially the same for each of the three response modes. Thus, the neuromuscular transmission speeds were not seen to explain the overall age difference in RT.

Two points make this conclusion less certain. First, this study reported a negative result, i.e., no difference with age due to pathway length. An inference regarding central nervous system functioning is implicit from this, but it is a dubious practice to draw positive conclusions from negative results. From studies to be discussed shortly, even when reporting positive results regarding peripheral mechanisms, inferences of central functioning are also drawn. While this may be the best that could be done at present, it is still a dubious practice, and such inferences may best be kept tentative. Second, while the RT study showed no contribution to the slowing with age of the length of the pathway, the actual results were not in accord with expectations. The RT of the jaw was longer than that of the finger. The shorter pathway of the jaw should have resulted in quicker RTs. This result was attributed to details of the procedure of measurement with the indication that, while these prohibit comparisons between the modes of response, they do not prohibit comparisons between age groups with respect to the modes.

Transmission Time. Several studies have been carried out to determine the differences, if any, among age groups in conduction velocities of various peripheral nerves. These studies attempted, in a different way, to examine some of the same factors investigated in the study just described.

Norris, Shock, and Wagman (1953) measured speed of impulse conduction in peripheral motor nerves of both reflex and voluntary behavior. Later, Hügen, Norris, and Shock (1960) measured plantar reflex latencies and abdominal reflex latencies as well as voluntary RT. In the earlier study, peripheral nerve conduction time of the reflex was found decreased with adult age, but in the second study it was not. In neither study, however, were the measured periphereal latencies large enough to account for the slowing with age of the voluntary RTs.

A similar result and conclusion based upon the albino Norwegian rat was reported by Birren and Wall (1956). The conduction velocity of the sciatic nerve was found constant from age 300 days to age 650 days and older. As did the investigators of human subjects, Birren and Wall concluded that conduction velocities of the peripheral sciatic pathway are not long enough to account for age changes in RT. The implication is that central factors account for RT.

One study was different from these in that both motor and sensory nerve conduction velocities were measured (LaFratta and Canestrari, 1966). This was done with human subjects ranging in age from 23 to 91 years. The wrist (median nerve) was stimulated and action potentials were recorded of the index finger (digital nerve) and the area of the hand below the thumb (*abductor pollicis breves* muscle). The action potential measurements showed that both sensory conduction time and motor conduction time declined with age, but the decline of the latter was not as great nor as related to age as was the former. Both the sensory and the motor velocities from the wrist to the hand or fingers were very brief—on the order of less than three to just more than five milli-seconds. Again, the values are small in relation to voluntary RT which may be of the order 130 to 250 milliseconds or more.

Taken together, these studies suggest that peripheral nerve transmis-sion speeds, while perhaps taking longer in the old than in the young, are minor contributions to the total time needed to execute voluntary reactions. Such reactions require translation of the input and association to correct response.

CENTRAL MECHANISMS
Synaptic Delay in the Spinal Cord

"It seems reasonable that because of aging there might be a general slowing of integrative processes in the central nervous system due to pro-longed excitation of synapses." With this in mind, Wayner and Emmers (1958, p. 403) compared young and aged rats in the delay in transmis-sion of a monosynaptic reflex through the spinal cord. They found that it took longer for impulses to be transmitted across this simple synapse in old rats than in young ones. With hooded rats categorized within five age groups, from 117 days to 822 days, the synaptic delays rose systemati-cally from 0.97 to 1.86 milliseconds.

These transmission times are miniscule compared to total RT, and Wayner and Emmers concluded that additional information is necessary to relate them to it. It has been suggested by some that if the results of Wayner and Emmers are representative of the very many synapses in the central nervous system, and if changes with age in the delays across all the synapses are summative, this could account for much of the slowing with age in total RT.

Premotor Time

Weiss (1965) was able to segment RT into two parts, a motor compo-nent and a premotor component. He did this by recording muscle potentials (electromyograms, EMGs) from the responding forearm muscle (*extensor digitorum communis*) of the subject performing an RT task. Weiss recorded the time the stimulus was presented, when the forearm muscle fired, and when the finger lift response was made. In this way, he had records of the total RT and that part of RT taken up from muscle firing to the finger lift. This latter part he called motor time (MT). Subtracting MT from total RT, he was left with what he called premotor time (PMT). Thus, $RT = PMT + MT$.

In a subsequent study, Botwinick and Thompson (1966) corroborated and extended Weiss' findings, measuring PMT and MT of young adults (18-35 years) and elderly ones (68-87 years) while varying conditions of preparatory set or expectancy. Both PMT and MT were slower in the older group than in the younger one but, in both age groups, PMT was the more important component in RT. It constituted approximately 84 percent of total RT, while MT constituted only 16 percent. This corroborated much of the work done on transmission rates of peripheral pathways in showing that MT is relatively unimportant in total RT.

Stimulus Expectation and Response Preparation

The PMT is made up of sensory transmission time, central interpretation time, and time to associate these to response. Sensory transmission time, i.e., the time from sense organ to brain, is probably the smallest segment of the PMT and is probably least important in accounting for the slowing with age. The major component of PMT slowing in later life seems to rest in the central nervous system, beginning after sensory nerve conduction is completed and ending before the peripheral, neuromuscular system is activated. One dimension of the PMT component is what typically is called RT "set" or "expectancy."

RT set is short-hand for saying that the response is most adequate, RT is quickest, when it is known exactly what the stimulus is and when it will occur. This permits correct expectation and allows for response preparation. If the stimulus comes too soon, if it comes as a surprise, or if it provides too little time for the preparing of responses, RTs are slow. RT set is manipulated experimentally by a variation of the foreperiod or preparatory interval (PI). The PI is that period of time between a warning signal, informing the subject that the stimulus will appear shortly, and the stimulus itself.

The data show that PMT, and not MT, is varied by the PI (Botwinick and Thompson, 1966). Variations in the PI are thought to affect PMT, and thus RT, by making for variations in states of readiness for the stimulus and in the time available to prepare or organize the response.

The data also show great individual differences, with men and women seemingly different with respect to these states of readiness as they reflect on RT. With men, at least, increasing age is associated with relatively poor ability to maintain set for quick response. It is also associated with the need for relatively long periods of time to recover from the effects of incorrect stimulus expectations. Old men seem to find it difficult to organize quick response when the time allowed for this is very brief, but this is largely overcome with practice. It is thus possible for older people to act quickly if they have a chance to learn how to do so.

Psychophysiological Correlates

If central factors are antecedent to RT, and if set, as manipulated by the PI, is important in RT, it is reasonable to expect that variations in psychophysiological indices of central functioning should be reflected by variations of the PI and, in turn, should reflect variations in RT. This expectation has only minimally been substantiated. Two major psychophysiological processes have been examined; one is the alpha wave function of the electroencephalogram (EEG), and the other is cardiac rhythm, as it is thought to influence brain stem activity.

EEG. When with environmental stimulation the alpha waves of the EEG are blocked, the person is said to be aroused, activated, or alert. This concept may not be unlike the concept of RT set, expectancy, or readiness, which is manipulated by PI variations. If blocking or other change of the alpha wave represents an activated state of the responder, then it might be expected that this would be associated with quicker response and with PI variations.

There are various measures of changes in the alpha wave of the EEG that could be used. Thompson and Botwinick (1968) measured change in EEG amplitude to analyze activation patterns in both young adults (19-35 years) and in older ones (62-87 years). This pattern was examined in relation to different PIs in both regular and irregular series, with the finding that the two age groups were very different in their EEG activation patterns. From these results it would have been very tempting to explain the RT slowing with age on the basis of EEG activation had it not been for an additional finding. In this study, RT and EEG activation were unrelated. Thus, EEG activation was not seen as an explanation of the slowing with age.

Quite a different conclusion was reached by Surwillo (1961, 1963). He analyzed alpha period (the inverse of frequency) as a correlate of RT. Surwillo did not intend to vary PI and, in fact, did not utilize a warning signal—he used only a stimulus. But he varied the time between stimulations and thus effectively had a type of irregular RT series. Surwillo also had, during the end part of his procedure, a condition which he called "high vigilance, high motivation." This condition was of a stimulus duration much shorter than he had used earlier in the study.

In this "alerted" condition, the mean RT and the mean alpha period were computed for each subject and found to be highly correlated (r = .72). Surwillo (1963, p. 112) concluded, "It appears, therefore, that frequency of the EEG is the central nervous system factor behind age-associated slowing in response time." The conclusion, while possibly correct, does not fit his finding that the correlation between age and RT was very low. This fact will be emphasized in a later section.

Cardiac Functioning. The results relating RT to cardiac rhythms have been as uncertain as those involving EEG. Cardiac-RT relationships had been examined because of presumed mechanisms not unlike those of EEG activation. There is reason to think that contractions and relaxations of the heart produce variations in blood pressure which, in turn, produce variability in brain excitability (by way of neural connections in the cardiovascular system, especially the baroreceptors of the carotid sinus).

Birren (1965) reported that RT was related to cardiac functioning in young adults, but not older ones. For young adults, if the stimulus occurred during the heart's contraction (R-wave) the RT was slower than when it occurred during different phases of the heart cycle. For old adults, this was not observed.

Botwinick and Thompson (1971) tested this result by indicating that it is very difficult to examine relationships between RT and stimulation during different phases of the cardiac cycle unconfounded by the PI. It was argued that, since RT is a function of the PI, any variation in the PI, however slight, if systematically linked with the different phases of the cardiac cycle, may result in spuriously high relationships between RT and cardiac phase. Accordingly, a study was carried out testing for the RT-cardiac phase relationship while keeping the PI constant from phase to phase. No relationship between RT and cardiac rhythm was found.

If RT is unrelated to cardiac rhythms, at least among the old, RT does appear related to the status of overall heart functioning. Abrahams and Birren (1973) compared simple and complex RT of men behaviorally predisposed to coronary heart disease with those of men not so disposed. The predisposed men were found slower in response. In a somewhat similar manner, Botwinick and Storandt (1974a) compared elderly and young adults in simple RT after categorizing each person in terms of his response to a questionnaire designed to assess cardiovascular well-being. Those who reported more cardiac symptoms were slower in response, but the extent of the sympton-RT relationship was not great.

Moreover, the relationship held no more so for the old than for the young, indicating that while cardiac function was involved in speed of response, it did not account for the slowing with age.

With little or no exception, these are the sum total of studies testing for psychophysiological correlates of RT in relation to age. They are equivocal, or they account for little of the variance, or they are negative but, in the end, it is only reasonable to expect that, whatever slowing of responses there may be in later life, it has to be referred to psychophysiological functioning. This is especially so if the slowing really is a direct consequence of central nervous system functioning.

COMPLEX STIMULI AND RESPONSES

Up to now we have been considering stimuli and overt responses which are very simple—possibly more simple than any other. What bearing do these have on more complex stimuli and responses?

There are several ways that this question can be investigated and two will be considered here. One way is to keep the stimuli and responses simple but to vary their number, thus requiring the responder to make a choice. A second way is to determine relationships between speed of response and other types of behaviors that are also under central control —behaviors such as perception and cognition.

Choice RT

As the RT situation becomes more complex and requires more difficult choice, responses become slower. The question is this: Is there anything unique in the slow responses seen in the complex choice situations that is not set down or determined by RT in the simple situation? The old are slower than the young in the simple situation, and they are even more so in the complex situation—is there anything unique in their slowness of making choices that is not determined by their slowness in making simple responses to a simple stimuli?

Disproportionate Slowing. In comparison to that of the young, if RT of the old is slowed *disproportionately* as the complexity of the task increases, this disproportionate slowing could be attributed to an age-related difficulty in making choices, not to simple RT. While it might seem that the analysis of disproportionality should be straightforward, the fact is that this is not the case. The matter hinges on the concept "disproportionate." For example, an early study by Goldfarb (1941) was given different, although not opposite, interpretive emphases by Birren (1964, p. 120) and by Welford (1959, p. 572). Goldfarb measured simple RT of five different age groups of subjects and he also measured their two-choice and five-choice RTs. He found that RT became slower as the number of choices increased and that the extent of this slowing was more evident in the older groups than in the younger ones. Birren wrote:

> Were slowing only a matter of involving the overt response it would be expected that older persons would become more like younger persons when the stimulus conditions are made more complex. The results do not bear this out, and whatever the ultimate neurophysiological nature of slowing with age involved in simple reaction time, it seems to become increasingly involved in complex choices and associative processes.

With different emphasis rather than disagreement, Welford concluded that the rise with age in choice RT as the number of choices increased was not disproportionate: ". . . the effect of choice is to add a constant to the reaction time at all ages." Birren's emphasis was on the older group's progressive slowing with choice, while Welford's emphasis was on the constant RT increment with choice for old and young alike.

The difference in emphasis rests with the concept "disproportionate." Welford resorted to information theory and analyzed RT complexity in logarithm terms. For example, the difference in complexity between an eight-choice RT task and a four-choice task is considered the same as the difference in complexity between a four-choice task and a two-choice task (the progression here is in doubling the number of choices). Goldfarb's RT data, investigated in logarithm terms, made for functions similar for old and young. There was overall slowing of the old (level and intercept were different for old and young) but the rate of slowing with increased choice (slope of function) was similar for all ages. In this sense, what difference there was between old and young in the time taken to make choices was established by the differences between them in the time taken to make simple responses. Thus, both Welford and Birren placed a lot of importance on the slowing with age in simple RT, but each highlighted different aspects. As if in corroboration of this importance, Waugh, Fozard, Talland, and Erwin (1973) concluded from their study that the older person's longer choice RT reflects impaired efficiency in initiating responses rather than in selecting them.

Brief versus Long Duration Stimuli. Early in the present chapter, and in chapter 8, a study was described where vertical bars, two at a time, were presented to young adult and elderly subjects. One bar was shorter than the other and the subject had to tell which one it was, the right or the left. There were two conditions of measurement, one with a long stimulus exposure and one with a very brief exposure. Figure 8.1 of chapter 8 shows that, when the stimulus exposure was of long duration, the old were differentially slow in making the difficult stimulus discriminations, but with the brief exposure, the old were not differentially slow (Botwinick, Brinley, and Robbin, 1958). It was concluded that the old may be more cautious than the young in that they seem to take more time than necessary to make the difficult discriminations.

Welford (1960) subjected these data to an information theory (logarithm) analysis and concluded that perceptual discrimination time, in common with choice reaction time, slows with age but not disproportionately—the rate of slowing with perceptual difficulty and choice RT is established by the general slowing with age. It seems that it is only when the older person has time to review the stimulus, and personality factors are thus allowed to modify the time required to make discriminations and choice, that he shows unique slowing over and beyond simple RT.

Stimulus exposure duration is thus seen as an important factor in choice RT and, unless it is systematically varied, it may not be clear whether the increased slowing with age in relation to increased RT complexity is disproportionate or not. For example, Suci, Davidoff, and Surwillo (1960), unlike Welford, reported disproportionate slowing with age as the number of choices in the RT task were increased. But they permitted up to 5 seconds for a response, during which time the stimulus was exposed. This is quite a long stimulus exposure duration and perhaps these data might reflect the same processes as those inferred from the data of Botwinick et al. (1958). There was one study in which the stimulus exposure duration was varied, just for the purpose of testing the hypothesis of disproportionality with long exposures and not with short ones (Griew, 1959). It was concluded from this study that the hypothesis is tenable.

A Central Role of RT

The implication of much of the foregoing is that the slowing of responses with age underlies a great number of cognitive and other important life activities. This is not the typical formulation of most psychologists. Most measure performances in terms of accuracy or of speed, or some combination of these two, and then make inferences regarding the specific function tested. The formulation here—the formulation of several behavioral gerontologists, most notably, perhaps, Birren—is very different. It is radical in suggesting that age-related deficits in cognitive and perceptual abilities are a result of the slowing with age or, at least, share a common antecedent with it. This is implicit in statements such as that made at the beginning of this chapter, "slowness of behavior is the perceptual manifestation of a primary process of aging in the nervous system."

If the proposition is that RT or RT-type behavior underlies cognitive and perceptual performance, or that these are controlled by a common, central mechanism, the most direct test of the proposition is to determine correlations between them. This has been done on various occasions, but usually for reasons other than testing the proposition. The results of these tests have been varied; reported correlations ranged from zero to a high in one case of .60. The data, taken as a whole, offer some support, but not a whole lot, for the proposition that RT is important to, or a reflection of, cognitive and perceptual ability in later life.

Clusters of Correlations. But this does not tell the whole story. The clustering of correlation coefficients—principal component or factor analysis—highlights a more important role for speed of response.

A comprehensive factor analysis involving RT and pencil-and-paper speed tests was carried out by Birren, Botwinick, Weiss, and Morrison (1963). They gave 32 tests to elderly people, most of the tests being of sensation-perception and cognition, with 11 of the latter represented by the subtests of the Wechsler Adult Intelligence Scale (WAIS). Not only was RT relatively independent of the perceptual and cognitive performances, but it was also not correlated highly with performances on the pencil-and-paper speed tests thought to involve essentially the same type of function.

Despite this, when the data were analyzed by principal components, a fourth factor was disclosed, where RT was represented with a loading of .40, and a non-verbal, non-speed test of intelligence (Raven Progressive Matrices, Raven, 1938) was represented with a loading of .30. This means that this component, involving many measurements each contributing small amounts to the total, was about as much a component of intelligence as it was of RT. While these loadings are small, i.e., .40 and .30, only one other of the 32 variables contributed more.

When the age range of subjects covers young adulthood through old age, the important role of speed of response is more apparent. A study by Botwinick and Storandt (1974b) demonstrated this. A variety of tests were given to men and women across the age range 20 to 79 years. Among these tests were simple pencil-and-paper speed tests and tests of brain function (typically used in the clinic to measure brain integrity). The latter measure perceptual and cognitive abilities. Several principal component analyses were carried out with one of them indicating a factor encompassing age, speed, and brain function. Increased age was associated with decreased speed and decreased scores on these tests. Other analyses showed somewhat different results, but all of them pointed to a central role for speed. It was suggested that speed of response is related to "central intactness," but mainly in regard to the ability to process incoming sequential information quickly (see Botwinick and Storandt, 1974b, pp. 68-77 and 170-177).

The role of speed in cognitive and perceptual functioning was seen also in other studies. Jalavisto (1965, p. 358) reported test loadings of a factor analysis based upon 91 men and women aged 40 to 93 years. More than 25 tests were given and among these were RT, tapping speed, memory, abstraction ability, and others. A comparable picture emerged: As age increased, speed decreased as did memory and abstraction ability. Jalavisto labeled this first factor, "Aging, Speed, Memory."

In concluding this section it is well to point out that not all cluster studies suggest an important role for RT. Botwinick and Storandt (1973) correlated RT performances with those on pencil-and-paper speed tests and with two subtests of the WAIS—the Digit Symbol and Vocabulary. A principal component analysis disclosed two factors, one of speed and one of cognition. RT scores, predictably, were high for the Speed factor, but they were near zero for the Cognition factor. It was essentially the same for the pencil-and-paper speed tests.

Overall, then, the factor analytic studies tend to point to an important role for RT and speed performances, but not all studies do.

Age Differences in Correlation Clusters. In these studies, the age range of subjects was broad, and age was used as a variable for intercorrelation. Another technique that has been used is to carry out factor or principal component analyses separately for different age groups of subjects.

The study by Chown (1961), based mostly on rigidity tests, and discussed in chapter 7, did just this. With the rigidity tests, Chown gave tests of speed and intelligence. It was with her young subjects (average age = 26.4 years) where the "speed tests formed their own unique factor . . . ," not the old subjects (60.7 years). The uniqueness of speed was maintained to a lesser extent in the middle group (average age = 40.7 years), but in the old group, the speed scores loaded most highly on the Nonverbal Intelligence factor. Chown's conclusion is most supportive of the proposition that the loss of speed in later life is important to other central functions. Chown wrote, "Thus among old people, but not among the young, the speed tests became a measure of intellectual capability and of the extent of the perseveration of this function."

JUST HOW IMPORTANT IS RESPONSE SLOWING?

Perhaps too little distinction has been made in this chapter between RT and the speed of carrying out specified tasks. RT is a measure of the speed with which responses are initiated, and the latter are measures of a great many different kinds of performances. Even though the literature includes studies differentiating the two, the distinction in the literature has been underemphasized and this fact is reflected here.

Just how valid is the contention that the slowing with age of RT and other speed of response performances is central and antecedent to the life processes of cognition and perception? The evidence, it seems, is equivocal. RT and speed functions should be highly correlated with cognition and perception, because they are thought to govern these functions, or they should be highly correlated with them because they are thought to share a common destiny as a result of their common antecedent of central nervous system functioning. The fact is that many studies show little or no correlation between these two sets of variables. On the other hand, when broader-based concepts are evolved, concepts of clusters of correlated functions, RT or speed measures do seem to contribute to these together with cognitive-perceptual measures.

Even if we were to accept these investigations as giving support to the contention that speed of response is important to cognitive and perceptual functioning, there are other types of data which indicate that this importance must be viewed with much qualification. The important role attributed to speed of response implies a generality or universality of slowing with age, and it also implies an inevitability. It also suggests a slowing that is largely insensitive to volitional and experiential factors. What are the facts with respect to this?

Exercise

While hardly a study in which age groups are compared in RT fails to show that older people are slower than are younger ones, some studies do. Botwinick and Thompson (1971), for example, did not observe a difference in RT between men aged 68-86 years and men aged 18-22 years. This, it was indicated, could be attributed to the poor habits of exercise of many of the younger subjects. In that study, and in an earlier one (Botwinick and Thompson, 1968a), the young subjects were divided into two groups based upon whether or not they were athletic and exercised regularly. It was with the athletes that RT differences between old and young were most apparent; with young non-athletes, RT age differences were not observed.

These studies suggested that it may be necessary to qualify the generality, or at least the extent of slowing with age, on the basis of personal experience, such as habits of exercise. A subsequent study, however, showed otherwise. In that study both the old and young were categorized on the basis of how much exercise they did (Botwinick and Storandt, 1974a). Within each of the age groups, people were classed into one of four categories ranging from no exercise at all to exercising appreciably. A significant correlation between exercise level and RT ($r = .44$) was found among the young only; no significant correlation was found among the elderly. Thus what influence exercise may exert on RT seems to be limited to the young. There was no suggestion that exercise will enable older people to react more quickly. Left unresolved, however, is the question of exercise habits over a lifetime as contrasted to exercising in late life without prior history of exercise. Perhaps physical exercise throughout life would enable people to respond quickly when old and permit them to maintain high levels of mental abilities.

Individual Differences

The foregoing implies great variability and individual differences in RT. This, in fact, is the case. First, to attain RT measurements that are stable, many must be averaged or otherwise grouped. Second, once grouped, the range of individual differences is not only large, but larger for the old than for the young. This was reported by Miles (1931), Obrist (1953), Botwinick and Thompson (1968b), and others. The extent of individual difference is so great that many older subjects perform more quickly than younger ones. In one study where RT and age were correlated, rather than, as is done in most studies, simply comparing two or more age groups in RT, the coefficient of correlation was only .19. Only about 4 percent of the variation of RT could be accounted for by the age of the responder (Surwillo, 1963). This is hardly a basis for so much emphasis on the slowing of responses in later life.

Practice

To the extent that RT differences are minimized or done away with as a result of practice, the important role for RT must be extended to include learning factors. There are several studies that show that much of the age-related RT slowing seen in conditions of very short duration PIs could be reduced with just a little bit of practice.

Murrell (1970) carried out an experiment in which the RT practice was extensive. He sought to determine the effect on RT over a course of

20,000 measurements. While he tested only three subjects, no other study tested subjects as extensively. There were three women subjects aged 57, 18, and 17 years. They were tested for simple RT, two-choice RT and eight-choice RT, all with a PI of 1 second. Fifty responses were measured each day with each of these procedures.

A study based on so few subjects makes conclusions based upon age comparisons tentative. This is a price for data based upon so many measurements. Murrell (1970, p. 273) concluded:

Age differences shown when Ss [subjects] were naive were largely eliminated by practice in this experiment. . . . The amount of practice required to eliminate age differences seems to be related to the complexity of the task [i.e., number of choices]. . . . Younger Ss seem to start improving almost from the outset, but older Ss may take up to 300 responses before improvement starts.

Motivation

If experience and practice minimize age-related slowing, and if this reflects on the importance of the central role of RT in aging, so do motivational factors. Different sets of data indicated that heightened motivation on the part of the elderly may reduce their response slowing (Botwinick, Brinley, and Robbin, 1959a, b).

A rather crude technique of increasing motivation to respond quickly was applied to adult men of two age groups. A mild shock to the wrist of the responder was given for responses slower than his own individual median RT, as determined in a previous series of measurements. Subjects aged 18-37 years were compared to older subjects aged 65-79 years in the improvement in their RTs with this shock motivation. It was found that both old and young were quicker with this motivation than without it, but the extent of the improvement was the same for the old and the young. This suggested that motivation was not an agent in the slowing of RTs in later life.

In this study irregular PIs were used. The study was repeated and similar results were found. Then, other PIs were used in irregular series and the results were essentially the same. When, however, the PIs were regular, the older subjects improved their RTs more than did the younger subjects. The older subjects were not as fast as the young with the shock motivation, but there was less difference between them than there was without it. It was seen, therefore, that both experience and motivation modify the typical slowing in later life as measured in the laboratory. Again, this could be seen as either diminishing the theoretical importance of the slowing in later life or requiring a broader view of it.

Conclusions

In the present chapter issues regarding the role of the slowing in later life were raised and evidence was presented which supports contentions that this slowing is important to cognitive and perceptual abilities, but evidence was also presented that questioned this contention. This disparity reflects the equivocal state of the work to date. On the side of importance, the following may be counted: (1) the slowing with age is a general phenomenon; in almost every study, the old are seen as slower than the young. To an extent, this seems to be independent of culture and perhaps of health status. Animals lower than man also slow with age as, for example, the laboratory rat (Birren, 1955); (2) RT slowing is central; it is independent of the sensory modality stimulated and the type of response measured; (3) and very important, the slowing with age does relate to vital functions, even if indirectly.

On the negating side the following can be counted: (1) habits of exercise and different opportunities for learning may minimize the slowing with age; (2) motivational patterns can reduce the slowing; (3) individual differences are so great that many old people are faster than young people; (4) and most important, many, but not all, of the direct correlations between response slowing and vital life functions tend to be low.

SUMMARY

Evidence was examined that bears on the proposition that the slowing of responses in later life is a reflection of altered central nervous system functioning. Evidence was also examined to test the contention that the slowing is important to perceptual and cognitive skills, either becuse it controls them or because all these variables together are controlled by the altered central nervous system.

Much of the evidence points to the central nervous system as the antecedent of the slowing in later life but, for the most part, the evidence is indirect and based upon negative results. First, sensory mechanisms have been judged unlikely as the basis of the slowing, since the old remain slower than the young when the intensity of stimulation is functionally equated between age groups. Also, the old are slower to respond than the young when the stimulus is of sufficient strength as to not be an issue. Second, peripheral neuromuscular mechanisms have been judged unlikely as the basis of the slowing as determined by the speed of impulse conduction via peripheral nerves. These are so rapid and take so little time as to be unable to account for the slowing with age of voluntary behavior.

More direct tests of the role of the central nervous system in the slowing with age were made on several levels. On the most simple level, delays in transmission across a simple synapse in the spinal cord were measured in five age groups of rats. The delay increased systematically with age, suggesting that, if this were the case for most of the many synapses in the central nervous system, and if these delays were summative, then the slowing with age might be accounted for on this basis.

More complex analyses involved human subjects. Reaction time (RT), as a prototype of the slowing, is largely accountable by events occurring prior to motor involvement. These events are partially controllable by the experimental manipulation of the preparatory interval (PI) in the RT experiment. The PI is thought to manipulate the state of the responder—states such as set or stimulus expectancy and response preparation. With men, at least, increasing age is associated with relatively poor ability to maintain set for quick response. Also, elderly men seem to find it difficult to organize quick response when the time allowed for this is very brief, but this is largely overcome with practice.

If the slowing of response with age is of central origin, it may be important to performances based upon perception and cognition. Two types of studies have been carried out to test this possibility. One is to keep the stimuli and responses simple but to vary their number, thus requiring the responder to make a choice, and a second is to determine relationships between speed of response and behaviors of perception and cognition.

It has been found in the choice RT situation that older people become disproportionately slower than younger ones as the number of choices increases. The disproportionate increase in response time, however, is seen mainly or solely when the exposure duration of the stimulus is long. Older people seem to take more time than is necessary in order to make a choice, suggesting that this might be indicative of cautiousness. When the stimulus exposure duration is brief, and time is thus not allowed for such personality characteristics to affect decisional processes, an increase in the number of choices affects RTs of the old in a manner very similar to that of the young.

When speed of response is examined for its relationship with perceptual and cognitive processes, the relationship, most often, is found to be small or near zero. When, however, the relationship is examined by way of factor or principal component analyses, speed of response and perceptual-cognitive performances contributed together to broader configurations of measured behavior.

While the data, overall, point to the central nervous system as the antecedent of the slowing with age, the implications for higher level functioning remain equivocal. Whatever the implications, however, they must be qualified by the following: It is possible that life habits of physical exercise reduce the extent of slowing with age; increased motivation may do this too. Practice reduces the extent of slowing; and extended practice may eliminate it completely. Finally, it is most important to recognize that, whatever the significance of the slowing with age, the magnitude of individual differences is very great. Very many old people are quicker in responding than many young adults.

REFERENCES

Abrahams, J.P., and Birren, J.E. Reaction time as a function of age and behavioral disposition to coronary heart disease. *Journal of Gerontology*, 1973, 28, 471–478.

Birren, J.E. *The psychology of aging.* Englewood Cliffs, N.J.: Prentice-Hall, 1964.

Birren, J.E., and Botwinick, J. Age differences in finger, jaw, and foot reaction time to auditory stimuli. *Journal of Gerontology*, 1955, 10, 429–432.

Birren, J.E., Botwinick, J., Weiss, A.D., and Morrison, D.F. Inter-relations of mental and perceptual tests given to healthy elderly men. In J.E. Birren, R.N. Butler, S.W. Greenhouse, L. Sokoloff, and Marian R. Yarrow (Eds.), *Human aging.* H.E.W., P.H.S. Publication No. 986, Washington, D.C.: U.S. Government Printing Office, 1963, chapter 10, pp. 143–156.

Birren, J.E., and Wall, P.D. Age changes in conduction velocity, refractory period, number of fibers, connective tissue space and blood vessels in sciatic nerve of rats. *Journal of Comparative Neurology*, 1956, 104, 1–16.

Botwinick, J. Sensory-set factors in age difference in reaction time. *Journal of Genetic Psychology*, 1971, 119, 241–249.

Botwinick, J. Sensory-perceptual factors in reaction time in relation to age. *Journal of Genetic Psychology*, 1972, 121, 173–177.

Botwinick, J., Brinley, J.F., and Robbin, J.S. The interaction effects of perceptual difficulty and stimulus exposure time on age differences in speed and accuracy of response. *Gerontologia*, 1958, 2, 1–10.

Botwinick, J., Brinley, J.F., and Robbin, J.S. Maintaining set in relation to motivation and age. *American Journal of Psychology*, 1959(a), 72, 585–588.

Botwinick, J., Brinley, J.F., and Robbin, J.S. Further results concerning the effect of motivation by electrical shock on reaction-time in relation to age. *American Journal of Psychology*, 1959(b), 72, 140.

Botwinick, J., and Storandt, M. Sensation and set in reaction time. *Perceptual and Motor Skills*, 1972, 34, 103–106.

Botwinick, J., and Storandt, M. Speed functions, vocabulary ability, and age. *Perceptual and Motor Skills*, 1973, 36, 1123–1128.

Botwinick, J., and Storandt, M. Cardiovascular status, depressive affect, and other factors in reaction time. *Journal of Gerontology*, 1974(a), 29, 543–548.

Botwinick, J., and Storandt, M. *Memory, related functions and age*. Springfield, Ill.: Charles C Thomas, 1974(b).

Botwinick, J., and Thompson, L.W. Components of reaction time in relation to age and sex. *Journal of Genetic Psychology*, 1966, 108, 175–183.

Botwinick, J., and Thompson, L.W. Age difference in reaction time: An artifact? *Gerontologist*, 1968(a), 8, 25–28.

Botwinick, J., and Thompson, L.W. A research note on individual differences in reaction time in relation to age. *Journal of Genetic Psychology*, 1968(b), 112, 73–75.

Botwinick, J., and Thompson, L.W. Cardiac functioning and reaction time in relation to age. *Journal of Genetic Psychology*, 1971, 119, 127–132.

Chown, S.M. Age and the rigidities. *Journal of Gerontology*, 1961, 16, 353–362.

Goldfarb, W. An investigation of reaction time in older adults and its relationship to certain observed mental test patterns. Contributions to Education, No. 831. New York: Teachers College, Columbia University, 1941.

Griew, S. A further note on uncertainty in relation to age. *Gerontologia*, 1959, 3, 335–338.

Hügen, F., Norris, A.H., and Shock, N.W. Skin reflex and voluntary reaction times in young and old males. *Journal of Gerontology*, 1960, 15, 388–391.

Jalavisto, E. The role of simple tests measuring speed of performance in the assessment of biological vigour. A factorial study in elderly women. In A.T. Welford and J.E. Birren (Eds.), *Behavior, aging and the nervous system*. Springfield, Ill.: Charles C Thomas, 1965, pp. 353–365.

LaFratta, C.W., and Canestrari, R.E. A comparison of sensory and motor nerve conduction velocities as related to age. *Archives of Physical Medicine and Rehabilitation*, 1966, 47, 286–290.

Miles, W.R. Measures of certain human abilities throughout the life span. *Proceedings of the National Academy of Science*, 1931, 17, 627–633.

Murrell, F.H. The effect of extensive practice on age differences in reaction time. *Journal of Gerontology*, 1970, 25, 268–274.

Norris, A.H., Shock, N.W., and Wagman, I.H. Age changes in the maximum conduction velocity of motor fibers of human ulnar nerves. *Journal of Applied Physiology*, 1953, 5, 589–593.

Obrist, W.D. Simple auditory reaction time in aged adults. *Journal of Psychology*, 1953, 35, 259–266.

Raven, J.C. *Progressive matrices*. London: H.K. Lewis, 1938.

Suci, G.J., Davidoff, M.D., and Surwillo, W.W. Reaction time as a function of stimulus information and age. *Journal of Experimental Psychology*, 1960, 60, 242–244.

Surwillo, W.W. Frequency of the "alpha" rhythm, reaction time and age. *Nature*, 1961, 191, 823–824.

Surwillo, W. The relation of simple response time to brain-wave frequency and the effects of age. *Electroencephalography and Clinical Neurophysiology*, 1963, 15, 105–114.

Thompson, L.W., and Botwinick, J. Age differences in the relationship between EEG arousal and reaction time. *Journal of Psychology*, 1968, 68, 167–172.

Waugh, N.C., Fozard, J.L., Talland, G.A., and Erwin, D.E. Effects of age and stimulus repetition on two-choice reaction time. *Journal of Gerontology*, 1973 28, 466–470.

Wayner, M.J., Jr., and Emmers, R. Spinal synaptic delay in young and aged rats. *American Journal of Physiology*, 1958, 194, 403–405.

Weiss, A.D. The locus of reaction time change with set, motivation and age. *Journal of Gerontology*, 1965, 20, 60–64.

Welford, A.T. Psychomotor performance. In J.E. Birren (Ed.), *Handbook of aging and the individual.* Chicago: Univ. of Chicago Press, 1959, pp. 562–613.

Welford, A.T. The measurement of sensory-motor performance: survey and reappraisal of twelve years' progress. *Ergonomics*, 1960, 3, 189–230.

Welford, A.T. Motor performance. In J.E. Birren and K.W. Schaie (Eds.), *Handbook of the psychology of aging.* New York: Van Nostrand Reinhold, 1977, pp. 450–496.

13

Intelligence

The slowing of responses with age was discussed in the previous chapter, and its role in cognitive functioning was indicated. The slowing, it was said, may be a reflection of higher mental functioning, but it is certainly a limiting factor in the behavioral expression of it. In the present chapter, the emphasis is on intelligence, with the role of speed of response again indicated, but this time in a different manner.

CONTROVERSY

A previous review of studies on intelligence in later life was introduced with this statement: "In the study of aging, no problem has received greater attention than that of intelligence; yet in spite of the abundance of research data gathered, many questions remain" (Botwinick, 1967, p. 1). The fact is, many more questions are asked now than were then, years ago. There is even controversy and heated debate. The older literature of mainly cross-sectional studies raised questions but was unequivocal in pointing to age decline in intellectual performance. The newer literature, involving more longitudinal research, pointed to less decline with age and, in instances, even no decline. The controversy may be seen in a variety of places, but none more apparent than the heated exchange in the well-known journal, *American Psychologist*. Responding to a variety of publications saying no decline with age but, perhaps, mainly to one by Baltes and Schaie (1974) entitled, "Aging and IQ: The Myth of the Twilight Years," a strong position for decline was struck by Horn and Donaldson (1976) in their article, "On the Myth of the Intellectual Decline in Adulthood." A rejoinder to this, maintaining no decline, was soon forthcoming from Baltes and Schaie (1976) carrying the title, "On the Plasticity of Intelligence in Adulthood and Old Age: Where Horn and Donaldson Fail." This was answered in yet

208

another article, "Faith Is Not Enough: A Response to the Baltes-Schaie Claim that Intelligence Does Not Wane" (Horn and Donaldson, 1977).

The controversy is not resolved and probably will not be resolved, not because different data are examined, but because the same data are interpreted differently. There was, however, an analysis that brought the polarized positions together, even if to a limited extent (Botwinick, 1977). The analysis indicated that decline with age for many intellectual functions does not begin until relatively late in adulthood—50, 60, or later—and, moreover, that these declines tend to be small. For other intellectual functions, however, particularly those involving speed of response and perceptual-integrative functions, decline may be seen before then.

Unlike many areas of study, the greatest part of what is known about the intelligence of the aged is not new. Much of it has been known for about as long as there has been a focus on the study of aging because of the inherent interest in the question, "Does intelligence decline in old age?" With some exceptions, most of the older cross-sectional literature may be read in great detail in previous reviews (e.g., Jones, 1959; Botwinick, 1967).

WHAT THE TEST MEASURES

Intelligence and achievement tests have come under attack in recent years, mostly on the basis that what is measured often is not relevant to the purpose for which the test is used. There is little argument, for example, that to the extent that the values of young, white middle-class people are implicitly sought, intelligence tests are suitable to measure skills in accord with these values. Conversely, to the extent that the person tested is not part of the majority culture, the test may be unfair and not a measure of intrinsic ability or intelligence. The argument is that using these tests to compare people of different cultures makes little sense.

It was with thoughts related to these that Demming and Pressey (1957) asserted that tests used to measure intelligence of older people should deal with problems indigenous to them. Traditional intelligence tests often involve items more indigenous to children or very young adults. Accordingly, Demming and Pressey constructed a test comprising information items very practical in nature, items more related to the needs of adults. They reported results of a test based "on use of yellow pages of a telephone directory, on common legal terms, and on people to get to perform services needed in everyday life" (Demming and Pressey, 1957, pp. 144–145). They found a *rise* in scores through middle and later years with this test, even with the same people who declined in their test scores with the conventional tests. Tests that measure ability need to be made with reference to the purpose for which the test is administered in the first place. Very much more research is necessary to clarify the important factors in making a test relevant to older people.

Some related research has already established important facts. For example, the level of education and the scores on tests of intelligence are correlated. This will be discussed in more detail later, but for the present it is well to recognize that this correlation does not tell us whether people of superior intelligence tend to go further in school, whether people who go further in school end up with higher intelligence, or whether both take place simultaneously. What does seem clear is that education is intimately linked with intelligence and if one assesses the ability of a person with low education, the test score may be more a measure of this then of intelligence *per se*.

Similarly, research data suggest that mental abilities of adults are very much a function of socioeconomic status. For example, Pressey and Kuhlen (1957) reported that scores on general ability tests were markedly different for men of different types of occupations. "One must not promptly conclude," they suggested, "that most people in this country rise to the occupational level of which they are capable." They pointed to data which showed that 10 percent of machine operators scored above the median for lawyers. Their contention was that school and job training increase the ability of adults to score well on tests. The implication of this contention is that people will more nearly approach the height of their intellectual potential as they are given better opportunities in their socioeconomic world.

Older adults tend to be more poorly educated than younger adults, and they tend to be of lower socioeconomic levels. Inferences based upon test scores comparing the old and young need to be made with these considerations uppermost in mind.

AGE DECLINE

There are many tests of adult intelligence, but probably the test most widely used today is the Wechsler Adult Intelligence Scale (WAIS). The test comprises 11 subtests, each reflective of different, although related, aspects of intellective life (Wechsler, 1955).

Wechsler (1958, p. 135) had a very clear opinion about what happens to intelligence with age:

Beginning with the investigation by Galton in 1883 . . . nearly all studies dealing with the age factor in adult performance have shown that most human abilities . . . decline progressively, after reaching a peak somewhere between ages 18 and 25. The peak age varies with the ability in question, but the decline occurs in all mental measures of ability, including those employed in tests of intelligence.

The Age Factor in I.Q.

The role of age is so dominant in the measurement of intelligence that the whole concept of I.Q. has a factor of age built into it. In the Wechsler scoring system, for example, if a 25-year-old man and a 75-year-old man each makes the same I.Q. score, the actual performance of the older man is poorer than that of the younger one. The reason is that the I.Q. has an age correction as part of its definition. It is average (i.e., "normal") for old people to perform less well than young people on this test, and the I.Q. is constructed to reflect this "normal" process. If in one man's lifetime there is neither decline nor improvement in his test performance, his measured I.Q. will go up as he gets older.

Figure 13.1 demonstrates this: The curve was constructed on the basis of the scores made by people in various age groups, each group having an I.Q. of 100 (Wechsler, 1955). The scaled scores were arbitrarily set at approximately 110 with the group aged 20-34 years, and the scores of the other age groups scaled from this reference point. These scores were then converted to I.Q.s of 100, the average. This conversion means that the youngest group in Figure 13.1 had 10 *points subtracted*, and the oldest group had approximately 32 *points added*, in order to result in "normal" I.Q.s of 100 (Wechsler, 1955, pp. 82–97).

Meaning of I.Q.

In a practical sense, what does all this mean? Does it mean that older people should be kept from the most important jobs, the jobs of great responsibility? Does it mean that 20-30-year-olds, the group of highest test performance, ought to be the only ones to maintain executive roles? Decidedly not. First, the data in Figure 13.1 are group data, a statistical representation of populations; a given old man may have extraordinarily high intelligence when compared to anyone. Correlations between

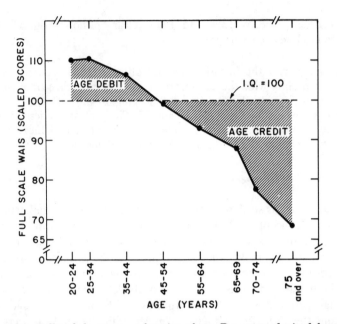

FIGURE 13.1: Full scaled scores as a function of age. Data were obtained from Table 18 of the WAIS Manual, 1955, (pp. 82-97) by culling scaled scores of I.Q.s of 100. The broken line represents the conversion of the scaled scores to I.Q.s. (Reprinted from Figure 1 of Botwinick, 1967.)

chronological age and intelligence tend to be below .50, often much below, explaining only about a quarter of the variance, at most. Thus, predictions of I.Q. when knowing age alone, while better than chance, are hardly useful for any but the most gross purpose. A second reason why older people ought not to be excluded from important jobs is that, even if test scores and age were more highly correlated, intelligence is only one of the important ingredients necessary in carrying out responsibility. To be a successful executive, for example, wisdom, patience, courage, social adeptness, and a variety of skills, not just intelligence, are important. While it may be desirable to reorganize our social patterns so that more young people can be placed in power positions and more old people in counseling positions, it would be a tragic mistake to think that people of any age can be successfully evaluated for responsibility by test scores alone.

Why bother with the description of age decline in intelligence if it is so limited in what it conveys? First, this information, though limited, is important. Intelligence is an essential ingredient of much successful behavior. Second, tests are useful for research purposes. We want to learn which abilities change with age; which of these change primarily because of a changing biology, and which are more the result of a changing environment. But the fact remains: There are no studies, there are no data, telling what test decline means in a practical way in the daily routines of older adults. There is the belief that decline on intelligence tests is indicative of behavioral difficulties, but this belief is not founded on analysis of what the skills and functions are that older people need for practical purposes. In short, there is a dearth of information about what constitutes a valid test for older people.

AGE-SENSITIVE AND AGE-INSENSITIVE MEASURES
A Classic Aging Pattern

Intelligence is not a unitary quality; there are intelligences. These vary with age in different ways and to different extents. There is a general classic pattern of aging decline; verbal abilities show relatively little, if any, deficit with advancing age, but psychomotor abilities decline appreciably. In the Wechsler test, this takes the form of scores on Verbal subtests as compared to Performance subtests. The aged do relatively well on the former and more poorly on the latter. In this sense the latter are "sensitive" to the processes of aging and the former are "insensitive." The sensitivity refers to the ability to discriminate among age groups.

This classic aging pattern of Verbal and Performance scores has been demonstrated many times and now constitutes one of the best replicated results in the literature. Few, if any, studies fail to find this pattern. Eisdorfer, Busse, and Cohen (1959) reported that the pattern held for each five-year age period from 60 through 75 years and over, for men and women, for white and black subjects, for different levels of socioeconomic status, for people over and under I.Q.s of 100, and for both people who resided in the community and who resided in mental hospitals.

Differential Decline

The Verbal scores of the WAIS comprise the six subtests of Information, Comprehension, Arithmetic, Similarities, Digit Span, and Vocabulary; the Performance grouping comprises the five subtests Digit Symbol, Picture Completion, Block Design, Picture Arrangement, and Object Assembly. The classic aging pattern is explained more fully by an analysis of these specific subtests in relation to age. Figure 13.2 is a summary of such an analysis, based upon ten aging studies with the WAIS, or its predecessor, the Wechsler-Bellevue test (WB).

In each of the ten studies, the eleven subtests were ranked according to how elderly people performed on them: A rank of 11 represented the best score and 1 the poorest score. Figure 13.2 shows the average ranks of the ten studies.*

This figure shows that the subtests Information, Vocabulary, and Comprehension are the three highest ranked, and that Block Design, Picture Arrangement, and Digit Symbol are the three lowest ranked. These rankings are remarkably similar within each of the ten studies. They reflect the "classic aging pattern"; the functions referred to as "Verbal" tend to be maintained with increasing age, and the functions referred to as "Performance" tend to not be maintained. The bottom-ranked tests, therefore, are the most age sensitive in showing changes; the top-ranked are least sensitive.

The Role of Speed

If the subtests of Figure 13.2 are examined from the vantage point of the person taking the test, it becomes clear that, in the main, the bottom-ranking tests involve speed of responding and the top-ranking tests do not. This observation became central to a controversy regarding the significance of loss of speed in old age. Older people are slower in their behaviors than young people, and they perform less well on the speeded tests. One view of this maintained that the slowing is only a matter of the muscles and thus of no importance to cognition. Psychometrically, therefore, speeded tests are unfair and inappropriate for testing the elderly. The opposing view held that speed of response is a reflection of central nervous system functioning and, as such, it is most important in cognition. Proponents of this view held that speeded tests are both appropriate and necessary in testing the elderly.

The controversy was largely resolved with the study by Doppelt and Wallace (1955) and more recently by Klodin (1975) and Storandt (1977). They gave the WAIS, both with and without time limits, and found the age patterning of scores essentially the same in both conditions, i.e., speed made relatively little difference. From a psychometric viewpoint, therefore, the controversy centering upon speeded tests no longer seemed of great importance. From the point of view of understanding the loss of speed with age, however, questions remained. Research centering on loss of speed was described in the previous chapter.

* The ranks within each of the ten studies and descriptions of the people tested may be seen in Table 1 of Botwinick, 1967, p. 9.

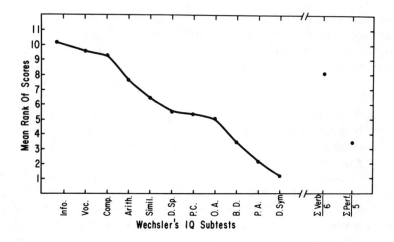

FIGURE 13.2: A rank of 11 indicates the best performance by the elderly on the WAIS or the W-B, and a rank of 1 indicates worst performance. The ordinate represents the mean ranks of 10 studies. (Based on the data of Table 1 of Botwinick, 1967, and published as Figure 2 of Botwinick, 1970.)

Achievement and Perceptual-Integrative Skills

It was said that the top-ranked subtests in Figure 13.2 measure verbal abilities and the bottom-ranked tests measure psychomotor abilities. With the aid of the highly mathematical technique of principal component analysis, Birren, Botwinick, Weiss, and Morrison (1963) elaborated the description. They indicated that tests similar to the top-ranked ones measure achievement and are related to general experience in our culture. This achievement and experience can be regarded as "stored information." Tests such as the bottom-ranked ones in Figure 13.2 involve manipulative skills, perceptual functions, and the processing of new information.

Even these descriptions, as helpful as they are, do not go as far as we would like. The WAIS Vocabulary subtest, for example, requires the person taking it to give the meaning of words. The more "stored information" he has, and the more words he knows, the higher will be his score. This function is well-maintained in later life. Does this mean that such stored verbal information in later life is useful in judgments and in making decisions? Does it mean that knowing words is helpful in social relations? It is one thing to know the subtle nuances of words and to use them in creative ways; it is another thing to carry on "already programmed" conversation such as, "I am fine," when asked, "How are you?" The point here is simply that tests which do not show changes with age, while they may reflect "stored information" and achievements, may not necessarily reflect the usefulness of the "store." Two recent studies indicated that the maintained verbal store of older adults, at least as represented by vocabulary test responses, may not be at as high a level qualitatively as seen with younger adults (Botwinick and Storandt, 1974; Botwinick, West, and Storandt, 1975).

In similar fashion, questions can be raised about the bottom-ranked subtests in Figure 13.2, the subtests which are sensitive to aging processes. As indicated, these subtests measure manipulative skills, the ability to process new information. The lowest ranked subtest in Figure 13.2, the one in which older people do least well, is Digit Symbol. This subtest involves a display of numbers from 1 to 9, each associated with a symbol. The job is to write the appropriate symbol under the particular number whenever it appears on a test paper. It is one thing to say that the function measured by the Digit Symbol subtest involves the processing of information; the person taking the test perceptually searches, he matches number with symbol, and he translates his findings into written forms—this involves coding, an aspect of memory (Storandt, 1967). It is another thing to say, however, that the subtest measures abilities that have relevance to the complex needs of everyday life. A person's test score needs to be matched with his job or other important life activity in order to determine the social importance of the test.

Normal and Psychotic Functioning

Differences in Decline Patterns. Whatever the intrinsic meaning of the differential decline seen in Figure 13.2, the subtests reflect a "normal" aging pattern; again, elderly people tend to do poorly with tasks such as the Digit Symbol subtest and relatively well with tasks such as the Vocabularly subtest. Figure 13.3 shows that this pattern is seen not only with normal elderly people, but, in general, is seen also with elderly psychotics (Botwinick and Birren, 1951).

A close analysis of the data in Figure 13.3, however, will disclose that the most age-sensitive subtests are not necessarily the most sensitive ones in discriminating between the intellectual deficits of psychotic and non-psychotic elderly. Figure 13.3 is based upon a comparison of non-psychotic people in their 60s with institutionalized patients of the same age. The latter were diagnosed as having either senile psychosis or psychosis with cerebral arteriosclerosis. In Figure 13.3 the control group was designated as "normal" and the psychotic group as "senile."

The mean scores of all subtests were lower for the senile psychotic group than for the control group. But, as already said, the sensitivity of a subtest to measure normal age decline is not to mean that it is also sensitive in differentiating between senile and normal control samples. For example, Figure 13.3 shows that the Information subtest was within the first two ranks in both groups; thus, this test showed little age decline. However, it showed maximum differentiation between the non-psychotic and the psychotic elderly. This was true whether the index of differentiation was in terms of mean difference (4.17 weighted score points) or in terms of this mean difference in relation to the standard deviation (2.46) of the "normal" group. On the other hand, the Vocabulary subtest, which also ranked within the first two positions in the differential subtest decline, was seen as a poor subtest in discriminating between psychotic and control groups. The Digit Symbol subtest, in ranking last, was also a poor discriminator between groups. Figure 13.3 suggests that, if the choice of subtests is for the purpose of comparing psychotic and non-psychotic elderly people, the subtests Information and Comprehension would be first choices, with Arithmetic and Object Assembly next.

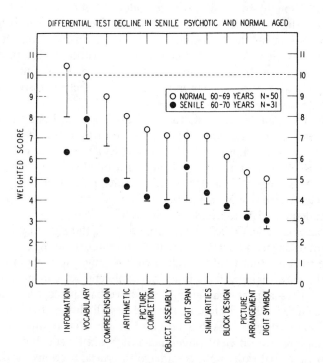

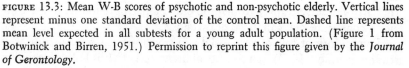

FIGURE 13.3: Mean W-B scores of psychotic and non-psychotic elderly. Vertical lines represent minus one standard deviation of the control mean. Dashed line represents mean level expected in all subtests for a young adult population. (Figure 1 from Botwinick and Birren, 1951.) Permission to reprint this figure given by the *Journal of Gerontology.*

The Picture Arrangement subtest, while not discriminating the two groups in terms of mean difference, was among the better ones in terms of mean difference in relation to the standard deviation of the control group. This subtest also has the virtue of being sensitive to normal aging. Thus, a test battery designed to assess intellectual functioning of normal and psychotic elderly might do well to include the Picture Arrangement subtest.

Is Psychosis of the Senium Inevitable? Probably because of the changing age of our society, there is now an interest in problems associated with psychoses of the senium, an interest that was not nearly as great just a few years ago. There are various terms used to designate states of psychosis—senile dementia, organic brain disease, chronic brain syndrome, psychosis with cerebral arteriosclerosis, and others. In the main, these represent diagnoses that differ in two broad ways. Psychoses are thought to originate primarily either from brain cell loss or from such vascular problems as obstructions in the blood vessels. While the latter are thought to result in more sudden onset of psychotic symptoms than the psychoses of neural origin, the fact is that it is often very hard to distinguish the two kinds of psychoses. In fact, from a behavioral point of view, if not a biomedical one, it is not always possible to differentiate these from non-organic depressive psychoses in later life. Often, only after spontaneous improvement in the depressive case can the two types of psychoses be told apart.

Thus, behaviorally at least, the goal is first to distinguish between normal and abnormal aging, that is, to identify organic brain disease. There are two opposing views: One is that senile psychosis is an inevitable end point of the normal aging process if one lives long enough. The other view is that it is a degenerative state quite apart from normal aging. This latter view seems to be the one gaining favor although there are not adequate data to decide conclusively.

Verbal and Non-Verbal Skills. Figure 13.3, the study by Botwinick and Birren, suggests that the verbal skills, those tending to hold with age, are the ones that tend to decline with organic psychosis in later life. From the view that psychosis is an inevitable end state of normal aging, it would thus appear that after the non-verbal, perceptual-integrative skills decline, further decline in the verbal skills brings the person to a state of inability called psychosis. From the view that normal and abnormal aging are two different phenomena, it could be concluded that disruption of verbal skills reflects damage to crucial sections of the brain that in themselves, apart from problems of perceptual-integrative functions, constitute the main basis of psychosis.

The important role of verbal skills in psychosis was seen also in other studies. Orme (1957) gave a vocabulary test (Mill Hill Vocabulary

Scale) and a non-verbal test of logical analysis (Progressive Matrices) to three groups of older adults—one that was healthy, one suffering from senile dementia, and one from depression without symptoms of organic problems. The depressive group was similar in performance to the healthy group, both groups showing relatively poor scores on the non-verbal test. The dementia group, however, showed decrement in both the verbal and non-verbal performances. These results corroborate the main pattern of Figure 13.3.

Two later studies point in the same direction. Overall and Gorham (1972) compared old and young normal adults and then compared old normal adults with old chronic-brain-syndrome patients. In part similar to Figure 13.3, it was reported that, "Pattern differences are suggested by the relatively poorer Information and Vocabulary subtest scores for the chronic brain syndrome group." Further, these "are the two subtests on which least decrement associated with [normal] aging was observed."

In similar manner, Goldstein and Shelly (1975) compared groups of both old and young normals and old and young brain-damaged patients. Factor analyses of many performance scores resulted in four factors: non-verbal memory, language ability, motor ability, and psychomotor problem solving. The WAIS Information and Vocabulary subtests were prominent in the language ability factor and the Picture Arrangement and Digit Symbol subtests in the psychomotor factor.

In keeping with the earlier research findings, the language ability factor did not reflect decline in normal aging. In fact, the normal old performed *better* than the normal young. However, both young and old brain-damaged people performed less well than their normal counterparts. The results were otherwise in regard to psychomotor problem solving. Both the old normal and the old brain-damaged people performed less well than their younger controls. In all, then, the "classic pattern" was seen in the comparison of the normal age groups, and added decrement in verbal skills was seen with organic brain syndrome.

Survivorship

Birren (1968, p. 211) made a comparison of test scores between elderly men who survived five years following the testing period and men of similar age who did not survive. The men and tests are described briefly in a later section of this chapter, under the heading Health.

It is interesting that Birren's conclusions regarding survivorship are not unlike those involving psychoses. He wrote that the original measurements that most distinguished between the subsequent survivors and non-survivors were those tests that contained verbal information. However, the measurements involving speed of response, known to be associated with age, did not show significant differences between them. The implication is that behavior slows with advancing age, and this is independent of disease. "In contrast, the relative intactness of the brain . . . likely closely reflects the presence or absence of vascular disease and influences the amount of stored information."

Those still surviving some 11 years later, now of average age 71 years, were again compared to the non-survivors in regard to their original test scores (Granick, 1971, pp. 55–57). This time both initially low Verbal and Performance scores were associated with earlier death; however, the Verbal scores were still somewhat more apparent in the differentiation.

Not many studies had been carried out making such analyses, and among those few that did, differing results were reported (see Botwinick, 1977, pp. 601–603). Thus, it seems best to keep conclusions regarding survivorship tentative, even though testable speculations are worth considering. Perhaps decline in verbal skills reflects both the states of organic brain disease and impending death. It may well be that brain deterioration hastens death and in this way both are reflected by decrement in verbal language skills.

ORGANIZATION OF ABILITIES

When there are many tests and many people tested with them, it becomes exceedingly difficult to organize the great mass of data and to impart meaning to it. There are mathematical methods of organizing data into structural groupings, based upon the degree of correlation among the different test scores. These methods, factor analysis and principal component analysis, result in groupings (factors or components) which are relatively independent of each other and are few in number, certainly fewer than the number of tests that were used. These methods, therefore, help determine constellations of mental abilities that are sufficiently sizable to account for, and describe much of, the individual differences in scores on a test battery.

There have been two general goals implicit in the aging studies that have utilized such methods of organizing intelligence test data. One is simply to describe what constellations of intelligence characterize older groups of people; the other is to determine whether or not these constellations change with age.

The studies are very difficult to summarize because of their diversity, but several concepts seem to persist throughout. The single most important element in the organization of intelligence is general ability. It is overall ability, rather than any one specific ability, that most distinguishes one person from another. This is about as true for old people as it is for young, but there is a difference of opinion as to whether the general abilities of old and young are made up of the same type of test score organizations. For reviews of these studies and details not presented here, see Botwinick (1967, pp. 13–20) and Matarazzo (1972, pp. 261–276).

Memory

In addition to general ability, most studies have identified Verbal and Perceptual factors. However, it is a factor related to memory that seems to be the most interesting. It seems that, when differences in intellectual organization are found in people of different age, the differences tend to center around memory. In advanced age, much more than in earlier life, individual differences in memory ability account for the degree of success on a variety of tasks. Individual differences in memory of younger people are less important in accounting for success, not because memory ability is less important in the young than in the old, but that younger people are more similar to each other in memory function and, thus, differences among them are too small to account for differences in success with other tasks.

Education

One of the studies on the organization of intelligence in relation to age was particularly important because it focused upon the role of education in intelligence, and it turned up a result related to the "classic aging pattern." Birren and Morrison (1961) were able to re-analyze the WAIS standardization data, based upon the scores of people in the age range 25-64. Rather than compare factor groupings of several age groups, they analyzed the 11 WAIS subtests along with both age and education in the same matrix of correlations. That is, the age and education of each person were intercorrelated with the WAIS subtest scores just as if age and education were scores themselves. Birren and Morrison extracted a large component of general intelligence which accounted for approximately half of the variance; but of greater interest to the study of aging, the age of the person was not at all important to this component. The education level was very important to this component, and it contributed as much to it as did any one of the 11 subtests. Age was very important in their second component which accounted for approximately 11 percent of the total variance. Birren and Morrison referred to the second component as an Aging component which contained subtests "positively related to age, e.g., vocabulary, and a group negatively related to age, e.g., digit symbol." They wrote that, "This aging component may have within it at least two concurrent, independent processes operating in opposite directions" (Birren and Morrison, 1961, p. 368). This is another aspect of the "classic aging pattern," i.e., the age-sensitive and age-insensitive test groupings.

These results suggest that the educational level of a person is more important than his age in regard to his mental ability. It is very clear, then, that in studying the effects of age, it is important to evaulate the effects of education. Birren and Morrison (1961) emphasized that the failure to control or remove the effects of education by statistical or experimental means exaggerates the decremental effects of aging since older people tend to have fewer years of schooling .

Fluid and Crystallized Intelligence

Factor analysis has suggested a dichotomy of tests, which measure functions thought to be based, on one hand, primarily on the neuroanatomic integrity of the central nervous system, especially the brain (fluid intelligence), and on the other hand, on learning and experience (crystallized intelligence). Horn and Cattell (1967) tested people aged 40 to 61 years and concluded that fluid intelligence declines with age, not crystallized. Since the fluid tests appear similar in many ways to the WAIS Performance tests, and the crystallized to the WAIS Verbal tests, it may be concluded that the fluid-crystallized dichotomy reflects the "classic aging pattern."

INITIAL AND LATER LEVELS OF ABILITY

Do the initially more able people—people who go far in school when young, perhaps—end up more able in later life? In other words, do people of high initial ability decline less in old age than do people of lower initial ability? Obviously, the way to answer these questions is by longitudinal research where people of different ability levels are followed from young to old age.

Equally obvious, this is not easy to do. There are, however, some longitudinal data, even if severely limited. Also, there are educated guesses that can be made on the basis of cross-sectional studies.

First, the longitudinal data: Owens (1959) located people who 30 years previously had been given the Army Alpha intelligence test on entering college. He retested them with the same test and thus had data at two points in the life cycle—ages 19 and 49 years. While these ages hardly involve elderly adults, the study indicated that, to middle age at least, initial ability was not a factor in subsequent decline or improvement. A similar conclusion was reached by Baltes, Nesselroade, Schaie, and Labouvie (1972) for adults of all ages through the 70s. The limitation of this latter study, however, was that the time period of change was only 7 years.

The cross-sectional studies are more comprehensive but, again, they provide suggestions more than observed age changes. In cross-sectional studies, the major difficulty in investigating the relationship between initial level and later level of intelligence is that of determining what the initial level was. Unless we follow a large number of people over many years of testing, the determination of what the initial level was may be so based upon tenuous assumptions as to involve criteria of initial level that are less than completely satisfactory. For example, the highest completed grade in school, or the occupation of the person tested, has been used as an index of initial level. It was already indicated that these indices are not always adequate because intelligence may not find expression in opportunities to go to school or to get good jobs.

The usual way of examining the relationship between initial and later levels of mental ability has been to test many people of different ages and to group them according to the criteria of initial level, i.e., education, occupation, or some other such index. One of the earliest studies which used this method was that of Miles and Miles (1932), using a speed test of intelligence (Otis Intelligence Test). Miles and Miles concluded that the initially more able remain more able in later life, but they decline, nevertheless. Those scoring initially in the 93rd percentile were estimated to drop to the 50th percentile in the eighth decade of life. Those scoring in the upper quartile were estimated to drop to the 33rd percentile, and those who are about average, to the 6th percentile.

Other studies used occupational status as an index of initial ability. Vernon (1947) reported the greatest decline in intelligence with "the least intelligent occupations"; in similar fashion, Gilbert (1941) reported that the more intellectual occupations had a positive effect in the maintenance of ability.

A most comprehensive set of data dealing with the problem of initial level and subsequent decline was seen in the reports by Foulds and Raven (1948) and by Foulds (1949). Foulds and Raven gave both a non-verbal test of logical reasoning (Progressive Matrices) and a vocabulary test (Mill Hill Vocabulary Scale, which is similar to the WAIS Vocabulary subtest). Their sample size was very large, and they were able to plot the test scores in relation to age for different percentiles, i.e., ability levels at each age grouping. Foulds and Raven found that, with the non-verbal test, decline with age was seen at every ability level. Moreover, the lower the initial level, the greater the decline. With the verbal test, they only found decline with age when the initial level was low. When the ability level at early life was average, the age decline was seen as minimal. On the other hand, when higher ability levels were examined, the verbal function *increased* with advancing years. These conclusions are similar to those that can be drawn from a more recent study based on very different tests (Riegel and Riegel, 1972).

These results may be reframed as follows: In later life, high level elderly people are characterized by very high verbal ability independent of age; they are characterized by high non-verbal intelligence, however, only when compared to others of the same age. With low ability people, both functions decrease in later life and are low by any comparison. People of average ability maintain verbal ability with only slight decreases, if any, but they show appreciable decrements in non-verbal intelligence.

The cross-sectional and longitudinal studies thus yielded conclusions that may seem apart but are not—they can be resolved by referring to the two questions raised at the start of this section: Initially high level people tend to end up high level relative to other members of their cohort. This seems particularly true for verbal skills. However, the extent of decline or improvement seems unrelated to initial ability levels. Another way of saying this is that a high level person may be seen to decline more than a low level person, but still end up at a higher level.

CROSS-SECTIONAL AND LONGITUDINAL STUDIES
A Common Belief

There is a common belief that cross-sectional studies show decline in intellectual abilities in later life but that longitudinal studies do not. The fact is, such a belief is both overly simplistic and mainly wrong. There are two related reasons why this belief is prevalent. First, longitudinal studies tend to reflect lesser decline than cross-sectional studies, and they often show decline starting later in life. This is so largely, if not totally, because the initially less able are not as available for subsequent retesting as are the initially more able. This produces a biased sample at later longitudinal retests. As will be seen in more detail later, recent analysis showed that even when longitudinal research had indicated decline, continued longitudinal testing obfuscated the decline pattern seen previously because of the dropout of the initially less able people (Botwinick, 1977, pp. 589–591, 593–595).

The second reason why it is often believed that cross-sectional studies show decline and longitudinal studies do not has to do with the type of subjects dropping out of the longitudinal study and the type remaining in. A large number of the dropouts are people who had died in the course of the study, or people who had become ill. Riegel and Riegel (1972) suggested that if only the healthy survivors are considered, not the sick or deceased, decline is not observed. Age decline, this suggestion would have it, is observed only with those test-takers who are in the process of dying. Those in full health do not show decline.

This may be true. But, with little exception, it is not possible to tell in advance who is to become sick or who is to die. Retrospective considerations make for highly artificial analyses; by definition, aging is living and dying, and this is part of longitudinal research. Longitudinal research provides information similar to cross-sectional research, at least insofar as intellectual performance is concerned. What differences are seen in the findings between the two methods of research are of magnitude, not type. As indicated, longitudinal research tends to reflect lesser decline, starting later in life.

Major Longitudinal Studies

In one study, people of wide age range were tested with several procedures, the main one being The Primary Mental Abilities Test (Schaie and Labouvie-Vief, 1974). They were then retested seven years later and, again, seven years afterward. In the 14-year period involving three testings, overall decline was seen only among those people aged 53 or older at the time of initial testing. Moreover, the decline was not great; it was less than seen in comparable cross-sectional studies.

A result similar to this 14-year longitudinal study, but one showing more decline, was reported with a method thought similar in principle to that of longitudinal research (Schaie, Labouvie, and Buech, 1973). Instead of testing the same people at times 1, 2, and 3 as in the longitudinal study, different people of the same cohort were tested at time 2 and still different ones at time 3. In other words, it is as if a cross-sectional study were carried out but instead of testing different age groups at one period of time, the different age groups were tested at different periods of time—the older the age group, the later in time it was tested. The results of this study (called independent measures method) were more in line with those of cross-sectional studies than they were with the longitudinal study. The reason for this, probably, is that selective subject dropout in independent measures research is not as great a problem as in longitudinal (repeated measures) research.

Another longitudinal study was reported in two parts—after 10 years of testing (Eisdorfer and Wilkie, 1973) and after 15 years (Wilkie and Eisdorfer, 1973). People of average age 64 and 72 were tested four times in the course of 10 years and it was seen that both age groups declined in their performance over this time. Part of these data may be seen in

Figure 20.1. The study was continued for five more years with three additional testings. Decline was apparent in the later years, but of special interest was the first 10-year longitudinal period of the 15-year study. The demand of seven testings over a 15-year period left remaining only those most intellectually able, and these people showed no decline in the next 10 years. The total original group, those tested only over 10 years, did show decline.

There are other important studies, for example a 20-year retest of people aged about 65 at the start (Blum, Fosshage, and Jarvik, 1972) and a 35-to-40 years retest of people aged in the 20s and 30s at the start (Gilbert, 1973). From all these and other studies, it can be concluded that there is decline with age, but the decline is not great until very late in life. The decline is mainly with the perceptual-integrative tasks, especially when speed is involved. Verbal skills are maintained, except in very advanced old age. And, very important, individual differences are great at all ages, and become greater with advancing age. These results, it will be recognized, are similar to those seen in cross-sectional studies.

BIOLOGICAL MECHANISMS

Regardless of the type of organization of intelligence in later life, whatever the role of environment in mental abilities, it is logical to assume that biological mechanisms mediate the behaviors we class as intelligent. Investigations of aging mechanisms are few and constitute just a beginning.

Health

A gross assessment of the role of these mechanisms was implicit in a study which attempted to examine older men who were so unusually healthy as to be atypical or non-representative of people of their ages (Botwinick and Birren, 1963). They were selected to meet the requirement of no apparent disease of any kind even after intensive medical examination. First, there was a general medical screening, and the unhealthy subjects were disqualified. Then, there was a second, intensive medical examination, during which several men (Group II) were medically separated from the highly select sample (Group I). Actually, Group II was composed of men who were much healthier than those normally seen in a representative sample of similar age. "The abnormalities in this group were mild, but did not inhibit the physical or social functioning of the subjects, and were generally asymptomatic. These subjects were believed to approximate more closely the usual medical concept of a 'normal' aged group" (Lane and Vates, 1963, p. 16).

The men of both Groups I and II were given the 11 WAIS subtests along with 12 other tasks, most of which were cognitive in nature. Although statistically significant differences were found with only six of the 23 tests, the actual scores were poorer for the less healthy group than for the optimally healthy group in all but two tests. The Performance tests more than the Verbal tests differentiated the two groups. These results suggested that even slight alterations of optimum health of the elderly can adversely affect their intellectual functioning.

This study by Botwinick and Birren was compatible with that of a later study in which less healthy people were examined (Correll, Rokosz, and Blanchard, 1966). In this later study, health ratings were made, and these were correlated to a moderate or low extent with intelligence scores. Of greater interest, however, it again was the more age-sensitive measures which correlated with health status, rather than the less age-sensitive, verbal measures.

Brain Function

Health status is a broad catch-all category and it does not tell which organ systems, what mechanisms relate to changed intellectual functioning with age. It would seem logical to expect that the central nervous system would be one such system. Obrist, Busse, Eisdorfer, and Kleemeier (1962) studied brain wave patterns (electroencephalograms, EEG) of older people and related them to their Wechsler intelligence test scores. No relationship was found with people residing in the community, volunteering to be examined. When, however, the same study was repeated with people who were mental hospital patients, and with people who were residents in an old age home, small, but significant, correlations were found. Diffuse slowing of the brain pattern and a slow alpha rhythm were associated with low intelligence test scores. It would seem that this association, found with people having arteriosclerosis and not with people relatively free from this pathology, is attributable to the poorer nourishment to the brains of the former group. A faulty circulation of blood due to a damaged cardiovascular system may result in deprived brains, making for both EEG slowing and lower test scores.

Cardiovascular Function

This interpretation of the results of Obrist et al. received support in an interesting and important study by Wilkie and Eisdorfer (1971). This study is a unique one in that it tried to explain intellectual loss over a 10-year period among elderly people.

Wilkie and Eisdorfer hypothesized that since hypertension increases with age and is related to a variety of behavioral functions, intellectual decline over time would be related to heightened blood pressure. They measured the former with the WAIS and the latter by standard technique of the diastolic pressure. Two types of WAIS scores were recorded —the scores made at time 1 and at time 2, ten years later; and delta scores, the difference between scores made at time 1 and time 2.

While their study, initially, was not designed to test this hypothesis, the longitudinal nature of their program permitted it. The people tested initially were divided into two age groups, one 60-69 years (at the time of initial testing) and the other, 70-79 years. They were further divided into groups of normal pressures, borderline pressures, and high diastolic pressures.

Wilkie and Eisdorfer reported that in the younger group (60-69) the three levels of blood pressure were related to different extents of intellectual change. Delta scores on the overall WAIS and on the Performance part (again the subtests sensitive to normal aging) were greatest for the high blood pressure group: intellectual decline was greatest for the group with highest diastolic pressure. None of the three blood pressure groups showed significant changes in the Verbal part of the WAIS.

Interestingly, while the normal blood pressure group also showed decline in total WAIS and in the Performance part (although not as great a decline as the high blood pressure group) the borderline blood pressure group, the middle group, showed improvement over the course of the years. In explanation of this result, Wilkie and Eisdorfer (1971, p. 962) referred to a contention by Obrist (1964): "mild elevations of BP (blood pressure) may be necessary among the aged to maintain adequate cerebral circulation."

The data based upon those aged 70-79 years at the start of the study were marred by the fact that none of the high blood pressure group completed the 10-year study. Both the normal and borderline groups declined in their test performances over this period of time, with perhaps a greater decline for the borderline group. The fact that the younger borderline subjects improved their intelligence scores during the 10-year period, and the older ones did not, suggested to Wilkie and Eisdorfer (1971, p. 962):

. . . that even in the face of mild elevations of BP (blood pressure) other factors may be operating to compromise cerebral circulation. Perhaps the duration of cardiovascular disease, with consequent structural change or other interacting pathology relating to more advanced age, may intervene.

Taken together, the studies of this section suggest what might have been anticipated from knowledge of the relationship between brain functions and cardiovascular functions. Older people of good health, with relatively undamaged cardiovascular systems, with, perhaps, enough mild elevation of blood pressure to nourish the brain in face of some natural-occurring arteriosclerosis, tend to maintain their intellectual abilities better than their less healthy counterparts. This augers well for the future, when more medical control will be possible over the states of our vasculatures.

This is not to say that the cardiovascular system is the whole explanation of intellectual performance. In the data of Wilkie and Eisdorfer, for example, the older group, 80-89 when last tested, declined from the period 10 years earlier irrespective of their levels of blood pressure. The brain loses cells, other body systems change, and these too, it may be expected, are important to intellectual functioning.

Hearing Loss

It is not necessary to refer to global biological factors such as brain and cardiovascular functions to see relationship with intellectual performance—specific and relatively simple sensory functions also are important. A study demonstrating this dramatically with hearing loss was reported by Granick, Kleben, and Weiss (1976).

They correlated measured hearing ability and intellectual performance in two samples of people: One comprised the atypically healthy men discussed under "Health" above; the other comprised aged women, each with some significant medical problem but free of emotional pathology. Both the atypically healthy men and not-so-healthy women showed the typical age decline in auditory function of high tone loss. In both groups, however, these declines were in the normal range for people of their ages (mean about 76 years).

Hearing losses were correlated with cognitive test performances, including those on the WAIS. The results showed associations between hearing losses and test scores for both samples such that the greater the loss, the poorer the performance. Unlike the data of health status differences, the Verbal tests reflected this more than the non-Verbal tests. In particular, performances on the Information and Vocabulary tests, the tests more resistant to normal aging (see Figure 13.2), were among those most related to heraring loss. It was concluded that "aged subjects may be more intellectually capable than their test performances suggest..." (Granick, Kleben, and Weiss, 1976, p. 434).

SUMMARY

Intelligence and achievement tests have come under attack in recent years, largely on the basis that many of the present tests are inappropriate for many of the population groups and for many of the purposes for which they are used. Tests for the aged might be best if they dealt with problems indigenous to the lives of older people.

The adult test most widely used today is the Wechsler Adult Intelligence Scale (WAIS). This measures I.Q. which, in part, is defined by the age of the person taking the test. For example, if a young man and an old man each make the same I.Q. score, the actual performance of the young man is superior to that of the older one. Intelligence, however, is not a unitary quality; there are intelligences, and these vary with age in different ways. Some abilities decline sharply with age and some do not decline at all. Overall decline is not great and is hardly apparent until about age 50 or later. Those tests measuring decline may be said to be age-sensitive. The sensitivity refers to the ability to discriminate among age groups. The age-sensitive tests measure psychomotor skills, especially those involving speed and perceptual integrative functions. The age-insensitive tests measure stored information and general verbal ability.

The subtests that are especially sensitive to normal aging are not necessarily the ones that are accurate in assessing psychosis in later life. A test sensitive to psychosis in later life must be able to detect deficit over and beyond that seen in normal aging, or to detect deficit when in normal aging there is none. It is the age-insensitive test that tends to do this.

Often, it is exceedingly difficult to organize great masses of intelligence test data and to impart meaning to them. Factor analysis and principal component analysis have been found helpful in this regard. Aging studies using these techniques have tended to show that the single most important element in the organization of intelligence is a general ability. It is overall ability, rather than specific abilities, which most distinguishes one person from another. The amount of education a person has contributes more to this general ability than does his age. Level of education is clearly related to ability levels of young adults. The literature suggests that people of high initial level retain their verbal abilities when old and, while they decline in their perceptual-integrative abilities, the extent of decline still keeps them at a level above their initially less able age peers.

It is logical to assume that intelligence is mediated by biological mechanisms. The study of these mechanisms in relation to age is only in its beginning stages. Data to date suggest that brain states are adversely affected by cardiovascular pathology and, in turn, affect behavior adversely. For example, one recent study showed that people in their 60s with high blood pressure declined over a 10-year period in intelligence to an extent over and above that of persons with lower blood pressure. Not only broad biological mechanisms, but simple sensory loss relates to intellectual performance. Good hearing ability enhances performance.

Taken together, the aging literature points the way for future research —research focusing upon the description and explanation of age changes in intelligence. It has not yet pointed the way to tests that are completely appropriate for the elderly in content and in interest.

REFERENCES

Baltes, P.B., Nesselroade, K., Schaie, K.W., and Labouvie, E.W. On the dilemma of regression effects in examining ability-level-related differentials in ontogenetic patterns of intelligence. *Developmental Psychology,* 1972, *6,* 78–84.

Baltes, P.B., and Schaie, K.W. Aging and IQ: The myth of the twilight years. *Psychology Today,* 1974, *7,* 35–40.

Baltes, P.B., and Schaie, K.W. On the plasticity of intelligence in adulthood and old age: Where Horn and Donaldson fail. *American Psychologist,* 1976, *31,* 720–725.

Birren, J.E. Increment and decrement in the intellectual status of the aged. *Psychiatric Research Report,* 1968, *23,* 207–214.

Birren, J.E., Botwinick, J., Weiss, A., and Morrison, D.F. Interrelations of mental and perceptual tests given to healthy elderly men. In J.E. Birren et al. (Eds.), *Human aging: a biological and behavioral study.* Washington, D.C.: U.S. Government Printing Office, 1963.

Birren, J.E., and Morrison, D.F. Analysis of the WAIS subtests in relation to age and education. *Journal of Gerontology,* 1961, *16,* 363–369.

Blum, J.E., Fosshage, J.L., and Jarvik, L.F. Intellectual changes and sex differences in octogenarians: A twenty-year longitudinal study of aging. *Developmental Psychology,* 1972, *7,* 178–187.

Botwinick, J. *Cognitive processes in maturity and old age.* New York: Springer Publishing Co., 1967.

Botwinick, J. Adult development. In W.S. Griffith and A.P. Hayes (Eds.), *Adult basic education: The state of the art.* Washington, D.C.: U.S. Government Printing Office, March 1970.

Botwinick, J. Intellectual abilities. In J.E. Birren and K.W. Schaie (Eds.), *Handbook of the psychology of aging.* New York: Van Nostrand Reinhold, 1977, pp. 580–605.

Botwinick, J., and Birren, J.E. Differential decline in the Wechsler-Bellevue subtests in the senile psychoses. *Journal of Gerontology,* 1951, 6, 365–368.

Botwinick, J., and Birren, J.E. Cognitive processes: mental abilities and psychomotor responses in healthy aged men. In J.E. Birren et al. (Eds.) *Human aging: a biological and behavioral study.* Washington, D.C.: U.S. Government Printing Office, 1963.

Botwinick, J., and Storandt, M. Vocabularly ability in later life. *Journal of Genetic Psychology,* 1974, 125, 303–308.

Botwinick, J., West, R., and Storandt, M. Qualitative vocabulary test responses and age. *Journal of Gerontology,* 1975, 30, 574–577.

Correll, R.E., Rokosz, S., and Blanchard, B.M. Some correlates of WAIS performance in the elderly. *Journal of Gerontology,* 1966, 21, 544–549.

Demming, J.A., and Pressey, S.L. Tests "indigenous" to the adult and older years. *Journal of Counseling Psychology,* 1957, 2, 144–148.

Doppelt, J.E., and Wallace, W.L. Standardization of the Wechsler Adult Intelligence Scale for older persons. *Journal of Abnormal and Social Psychology,* 1955, 51, 312–330.

Eisdorfer, C., Busse, E.W., and Cohen, L.D. The WAIS performance of an aged sample: The relationship between verbal and performance I.Q.s. *Journal of Gerontology,* 1959, 14, 197–201.

Eisdorfer, C., and Wilkie, F. Intellectual changes with advancing age. In L.F. Jarvik, C. Eisdorfer, and J.E. Blum (Eds.), *Intellectual functioning in adults.* New York: Springer Publishing Co., 1973, pp. 21–29.

Foulds, G.A. Variations in the intellectual activities of adults. *American Journal of Psychology,* 1949, 62, 238–246.

Foulds, G.A., and Raven, J.C. Normal changes in the mental abilities of adults as age advances. *Journal of Mental Science,* 1948, 94, 133–142.

Gilbert, J.G. Memory loss in senescence. *Journal of Abnormal and Social Psychology,* 1941, 36, 73–86.

Gilbert, J.G. Thirty-five year follow-up study of intellectual functioning. *Journal of Gerontology,* 1973, 28, 68–72.

Goldstein, G., and Shelly, C.H. Similarities and differences between psychological deficit in aging and brain damage. *Journal of Gerontology,* 1975, 30, 448–455.

Granick, S. Psychological test functioning. In S. Granick and R.D. Patterson (Eds.), *Human aging II: An eleven-year followup biomedical and behavioral study.* Washington, D.C.: U.S. Government Printing Office, 1971, pp. 49–62.

Granick, S., Kleben, M.H., and Weiss, A.D. Relationships between hearing loss and cognition in normally hearing aged persons. *Journal of Gerontology,* 1976, 4, 434–440.

Horn, J.L., and Cattell, R.B. Age differences in fluid and crystallized intelligence. *Acta Psychologica,* 1967, 26, 107–129.

Horn, J.L., and Donaldson, G. On the myth of intellectual decline in adulthood. *American Psychologist,* 1976, 31, 701–709.

Horn, J.L., and Donaldson, G. Faith is not enough: A response to the Baltes-Schaie claim that intelligence does not wane. *American Psychologist,* 1977, 32, 369–373.

Jones, H.E. Intelleigence and problem-solving. In J.E. Birren (Ed.), *Handbook of aging and the individual: psychological and biological aspects.* Chicago: Univ. of Chicago Press, 1959.

Klodin, V.M. The relationship of scoring treatment and age in perceptual-integrative performance. *Experimental Aging Research,* 1976, *2,* 303–313.

Lane, M.G., and Vates, T.S., Jr. Medical selection, evaluation, and classification of subjects. In J.E. Birren et al. (Eds.), *Human aging: a biological and behavioral study.* Washington, D.C.: U.S. Government Printing Office, 1963.

Matarazzo, J.D. *Wechsler's measurement and appraisal of adult intelligence* (5th ed.). Baltimore: Williams and Wilkins, 1972.

Miles, C.C., and Miles, W.R. The correlations of intelligence scores and chronological age from early to late maturity. *American Journal of Psychology,* 1932, *44,* 44–78.

Obrist, W.D. Cerebral ischemia and the senescent electroencephalogram. In E. Simonson and T.H. McGavack (Eds.), *Cerebral Ischemia.* Springfield, Ill.: Charles C Thomas, 1964.

Obrist, W.D., Busse, E.W., Eisdorfer, C., and Kleemeier, R.W. Relation of the electroencephalogram to intellectual function in senescence. *Journal of Gerontology,* 1962, *17,* 197–206.

Orme, J.E. Non-verbal and verbal performance in normal old age, senile dementia, and elderly depression. *Journal of Gerontology,* 1957, *12,* 408–413.

Overall, J.E., and Gorham, D.R. Organicity versus old age in objective and projective test performance. *Journal of Consulting and Clinical Psychology,* 1972, *39,* 98–105.

Owens, W.A., Jr. Is age kinder to the initially more able? *Journal of Gerontology,* 1959, *14,* 334–337.

Pressey, S.L., and Kuhlen, R.G. *Psychological development through the life span.* New York: Harper and Brothers, 1957.

Riegel, K.F., and Riegel, R.M. Development, drop and death. *Developmental Psychology,* 1972, *6,* 306–319.

Schaie, K.W., and Labouvie-Vief, G. Generational versus ontogenetic components of change in adult cognitive behavior: A fourteen-year cross-sequential study. *Developmental Psychology,* 1974, *10,* 305–320.

Schaie, K.W., Labouvie, G.V., and Buech, B.U. Generational and cohort-specific differences in adult cognitive functioning: A fourteen-year study of independent samples. *Developmental Psychology,* 1973, *9,* 151–166.

Storandt, M. Speed and coding effects in relation to age and ability level. *Developmental Psychology,* 1976, *12,* 177–178.

Storandt, M. Age, ability level, and method of administering and scoring the WAIS. *Journal of Gerontology,* 1977, *32,* 175–178.

Vernon, P.E. The variation of intelligence with occupation, age, and locality. *British Journal of Psychology,* (Stat. Sec.), 1947, *1,* 52–63.

Wechsler, D. *Manual for the Wechsler Adult Intelligence Scale.* New York: Psychological Corporation, 1955.

Wechsler, D. *The measurement and appraisal of adult intelligence* (4th ed.). Baltimore: Williams and Wilkins, 1958.

Wilkie, F., and Eisdorfer, C. Intelligence and blood pressure in the aged. *Science,* 1971, *172,* 959–962.

Wilkie, F., and Eisdorfer, C. Intellectual changes: A 15-year follow-up of the Duke sample. Unpublished manuscript read at the 26th Annual Meeting of the Gerontological Society, Miami, Florida, 1973.

14
Problem Solving

Laboratory investigations of problem solving often do not differentiate among the various processes that go into successful performance. More often than not, what is assessed is the combination of processes—the forming of ideas, the testing of them for adequacy, the accepting and rejecting of them. Investigations of thinking sometimes are limited to the formation of ideas. This includes both the ability to differentiate among stimulus elements and the ability to develop organizing concepts to encompass them. Defined in these ways, problem solving includes thinking, but measures of thinking do not necessarily include problem solving.

COGNITIVE FACTORS
Intelligence

To the extent that intelligence declines in later life, it would seem reasonable to expect that the ability to think and solve problems would decline also. Actually, this expectation receives only partial support in a very sparse literature.

It is obvious that some minimum intelligence is necessary to solve problems, but, given this, is the level of intelligence sufficient to account for the different ability levels in solving problems? Studies by Young (1966, 1971) and by Arenberg (1968, 1974) suggested that the answer may well be, "No," but most other studies suggest otherwise.

Age-Sensitive Tasks. Young (1966) compared older people (54-76 years) with younger ones (29-45 years) in their efforts to solve complicated problems and found that the older people did less well. She inquired whether intelligence levels could explain her findings and answered this by testing her subjects with the Progressive Matrices test. This test is age-sensitive, i.e., it discriminates among age groups. Despite the fact that the Progressive Matrices test has been described as measuring "intelligence of the problem-solving variety" (Chown, 1961, p. 360), Young found that, while the age groups differed in the problem-solving scores, they did not differ in their intelligence test scores. Thus, intelligence was not seen as related to the problem-solving performances. Most probably, Young selected her subjects very carefully so that they would be able to work on her complicated problems; perhaps for this reason, there was much similarity between the age groups in their intelligence test scores. This similarity makes her findings of problem-solving difficulty in later life especially significant.

Age-Insensitive Tasks. Arenberg (1968) investigated the relationship between problem solving and vocabulary test scores. Thus, as will be recalled from the previous chapter, unlike Young who tested with an age-sensitive intelligence test, Arenberg used an age-insensitive one. Vocabulary function in later life is more a function of what had been achieved than of cognitive integrative or synthesizing abilities. People aged 60-77 years had higher vocabulary scores than younger people aged 17-22, yet the younger people performed better on the problem-solving task.

This task (see Table 14.1) was different from the one that Young used, but Arenberg (1974) found the same thing when he carried out a later study with a problem-solving task very similar to Young's. The task will be described later under the heading "Training for Orderly Search." The task demanded much ability and so, like Young, Arenberg had to select only subjects of high intellectual ability. This may have hidden what relationships do exist between problem solving and intelligence.

This later Arenberg study is unique. It is the only one on problem solving that made both cross-sectional and longitudinal age comparisons, the latter averaging almost seven years. The subjects were between 24 and 87 years at the start; cross-sectionally, those under 60 years performed better than those over 60 years, but longitudinally the results were otherwise. Only with those aged over 70 at the start was decline seen. Selective subject dropout was given as the reason for this (see chapter 13). The longitudinal analysis, Arenberg pointed out, was limited to a very select, superior performing sample of problem solvers because only those who were able to solve the tasks during both test and retest sessions could be included in the analysis. Thus, a wide range of ability levels was not tested.

While Arenberg did not observe a relationship between vocabulary test scores and problem-solving ability, Brinley, Jovick, and McLaughlin (1974) did among some of their subjects, but not among all. The difference in results between studies probably rested in the fact that the subjects in the latter study were more typical of the general population than were Arenberg's highly educated subjects. Also, the tasks were different —Arenberg's were much harder.

Brinley et al. tested subjects of wide age range and found vocabulary level related positively to problem-solving ability among the middle aged but not among the young (21-35 years) or the old adults (66 and over). Thus, the generally high performances of the young and the generally low of the old were outside the range of the predictive value of intelligence test scores in regard to problem solving.

Other studies also showed relationships, some indirectly, some clearly. An indirect relationship may be seen in the study by Wetherick (1964).

Equating Age Groups. While much of the literature suggests that problem-solving performance declines in old age, Wetherick did not find this. He presented subjects with a panel of four switches, each of which could be moved to any one of three positions. The subject had to discover the positions of the switches which illuminated lamps upon pressing a button. Wetherick found that the oldest subjects (60-70 years) performed better than either his young (21-30 years) or middle-aged subjects (42-47 years) on the last and most difficult of the three problems he presented. The age groups were similar on the first problem, but the oldest group was poorest on the second one. Wetherick concluded that the oldest subjects learned from their experiences on the second problem.

Of interest here is that Wetherick matched the three age groups on the basis of their scores on the Progressive Matrices test. He equated subjects by the intelligence test results, which, in effect, was comparable to the subject selection procedure that Young used. Equating subjects in intelligence tests scores, either by the method of Wetherick or Young, runs the danger of equating on very nearly the same basis on which later test comparisons are made. That is, if intelligence test scores and problem-solving scores are based upon the same processes, equating people on the former may, in effect, preclude the possibility of discovering differences in the latter. While this did not occur in Young's data, it may very well have been the case in Wetherick's data.

The more important role of intelligence was seen in another study. Wetherick (1966, p. 66), again using the Progressive Matrices test, but this time using quite a different test of problem solving, reported a rank order correlation between the two of 0.66. He did not relate either the intelligence or the problem-solving measure to age, but with three adult age groups not equated for intelligence, a slight diminution in problem-solving scores was seen.

Overall Test Scores. A more direct test with positive results was made by Bromley (1956). He demonstrated a relationship between intelligence and thinking of the type needed for problem solving. Bromley gave a modified Shaw test to people of four age groups (17-35, 35-51, 51-66, and 66-82 years). He presented them with four wooden blocks which could be arranged in a variety of different ways, e.g., according to height, weight, position of notch, and others. In addition to 15 relatively high-level concepts, called Grade A concepts, the blocks could be arranged in many other, less adequate ways.

Bromley found that the quantity of Grade A concepts declined with age and, importantly, the pattern of this decline was similar to that seen with the Wechsler intelligence test. When Bromley equated subjects on the basis of intelligence test scores and then compared them in their scores of thinking, the age-thinking association was reduced considerably. The correlation between age and the frequency of Grade A responses was —0.52 at first. When Wechsler intelligence scores were partialled out, the correlation dropped to —0.19.

Conclusion. All the above suggests that some types of intelligence are related to some types of problem-solving ability, but not all. This was seen more clearly in a study based on the problem-solving tasks of Piaget (Storck, Looft, and Hooper, 1972). Five Piaget-type tasks were given to older adults: Two of these were fairly typical of problem-solving tasks often used (multiple classification and seriation), two might be thought of as perceptual reasoning (weight and volume conservation), and one as social perception (egocentrism).

Along with these, two intelligence tests were given: The age-sensitive Progressive Matrices and the age-insensitive vocabulary test. Since all subjects had perfect scores on the weight conservation task, this was excluded from the analysis relating intelligence to problem solving. Storck et al. found that performances on the vocabulary test were unrelated to any of the problem-solving performances. On the other hand, Progressive Matrices performances were related to all but that of social perception.

Thus, it is seen that intelligence is a factor in problem solving in that only certain types of intelligence correlate with certain types of problem solving. Further, the range of problem-solving ability that is measured is a factor in the intelligence–problem-solving relationships. At very high levels (as, for example, the subjects of Young and Arenberg) and perhaps at very low levels (as in the oldest subjects of Brinley et al.) the relationship may not be seen. Therefore, to the extent that an aged person does not possess some minimum level of relevant test intelligence, problem-solving performances may be expected to fail. To the extent that the relevant intelligence is very high, exact levels of problem-solving ability may not be predictable, but it can be expected that the ability will be generally high and probably will not decline until very late in life.

Memory

Other cognitive factors may also be important in problem solving. For example, in the study by Young (1966), the two age groups that were found different in their problem-solving performances were different also in their short-term memories, the older group performing less well in both. An analysis of the problems she used disclosed that memory was involved in various phases of solving them.

Inglis (1959) also found that memory was important, but he demonstrated this in quite a different way. Inglis, like Bromley (1956), used the Shaw test. He compared elderly patients suffering from memory disorders with patients of like age and intelligence who did not manifest such disturbances. The group without memory disorder was clearly superior to the group with the disorder in their Shaw test performances. Thus, evidence was provided to show that memory ability is important in problem-solving thinking.

But the most direct demonstration of the bearing memory has on problem solving, and the best, was seen in the study by Brinley et al. They started out with the idea that even simple reasoning involves remembering what is first learned about the situation, which then has to be related or integrated with what is learned next. They presented reasoning problems and varied these in complexity; all the problems, however, were easier than those used by Young (1966) and by Arenberg (1974). Brinley et al. also varied the amount of information placed in front of the subject necessary to solve the problems. Thus, this information could be viewed rather than remembered and in this way the demand on memory was varied.

From age 21 to 35 years, problem-solving ability was high, but beginning at age 36 it began to decline, with more decline apparent from age 50 onward. This decline seemed due, at least in part, to one aspect of memory. It was not due to remembering that a particular item of information was important in solving the problem, but it was due to recalling the information from memory and utilizing it. In other words, when all the relevant information for solving the more complicated problems was available for viewing, the older person performed relatively well. When, however, the relevant information-to-be-remembered for solving the problems was not available for viewing, but had to be retrieved from memory, the older person performed less well.

ABSTRACT AND CONCRETE THOUGHT
Meaningfulness of the Task

The thought processes underlying the solution of problems typically used in the laboratory are of an abstract nature. Abstraction is high level mental functioning, whereas concrete thought can be little more than automatic response to environmental pressures. While many studies have pointed to a diminution with age in abstraction behavior, only one study pointed to the role played by the task itself. Arenberg (1968), in an insufficiently emphasized demonstration, reported that old people may be able to carry out abstract reasoning with concrete tasks, even when they are not able to carry out this same reasoning with abstract tasks. He thus demonstrated that old people may be seen as unable to think at high levels, when in fact this may not be the case at all.

Arenberg presented subjects with nine stimuli grouped in three categories. At first he worked with the categories of form, color, and number. For example, for form he might have used a square, a circle, and a triangle; for colors he might have used red, blue, and yellow; and the number might have been 1, 2, or 3. There were thus three elements, in each of three categories.

Arenberg presented the subject with one element from each category at a single time. This constituted a trial and there were several trials from which the subject would try to learn which element of the nine Arenberg had in mind. The subject did this by examining the elements of each trial along with the information, "Yes" or "No," that Arenberg provided. By the process of logical elimination based upon this information, the concept (element) could be attained.

Arenberg found this task so difficult for the older people that only a few could do it. However, Arenberg himself was a problem solver and came up with an ingenious solution which enabled older people to carry out the task. Instead of abstract categories of form, color, and number, he used food items: beverage, meat, and vegetable, which consituted meals instead of trials. One of the meal items was poisoned so that instead of the information, "Yes," the information, "Died," was given. If none of the food items was poisoned, the information, "Lived," was given. An example used by Arenberg may be seen in Table 14.1. In this example, having a meal of coffee (beverage), lamb (meat), peas (vegetable) caused death because one of these three foods was poisoned. Another meal of coffee, veal, and peas also caused death; thus, coffee and peas remained as possibly poisoned. A meal of coffee, lamb, and corn, in not causing death, left peas as the poisoned food. In this example, coffee is a negative instance in that, although death does not occur

TABLE 14.1
An Example of a Poisoned Food Problem

Step	Meals (Instances)	Lived or Died	Possibly Poisoned Foods
1.	Coffee, Lamb, Peas	Died	Coffee, Lamb, Peas
2.	Coffee, Veal, Peas	Died	Coffee, Peas
3.	Coffee, Lamb, Corn	Lived	Peas

Note: If after Step 2, the problem proceeded with the meal of coffee, beef, peas with the information, "Died," or with the meal of milk, beef, and rice with the information, "Lived," no solution would yet be possible because these meals provide redundant information. (From Table 1 of Arenberg, 1968.)

with it, important information is learned, nevertheless. The example could have included as a last meal tea, veal, and peas with death resulting. Here peas is an example of a positive instance; it is the only food item which caused death when appearing with others that did not. Negative instances are more difficult than positive instances from which to draw conclusions, and older people have been seen to have difficulty with them.

Arenberg's study will be discussed more fully later, but the important point here is simply that when the problem with the same logic characteristics was framed in both the abstract (form, color, number) and the concrete (poisoned foods), the older people could do it much more readily in the latter case. This is not to say that in all problems concrete stimulus materials will make for better performances than abstract materials. One study, for example, did not find this (Rogers, Keyes, and Fuller, 1976). Problems very different from those of Arenberg were presented in both abstract and concrete forms, utilizing foods in the latter case (the problems were of reversal and nonreversal shift). Performances by elderly adults were about the same with the two types of stimulus materials, i.e., concrete and abstract. Thus, the rule does not always apply, but it would seem that there are at least times when it is best to frame tasks for older people in ways that are personally meaningful and concrete.

Solution Preferences

At times, older people not only prefer tasks that are concrete to those that are abstract, they also—more than younger adults—tend to perform in concrete fashion. Actually, performance can be described on a continuum of abstract to concrete, and Bromley (1957) did just this in giving tests of logical inference and generalization to people aged 17 to 82 years. The tests were made up of proverbs which required interpretation.

There were two types of proverb tests. In the first, there were 14 proverbs which were scored on the basis of the continuum: a principle was abstracted and generalized; a principle was not abstracted but a relevant explanation was given; the interpretation was hardly more than the literal statement of the proverb itself, i.e., a concrete response. The second test was one of multiple choice. It consisted of 10 proverbs, each with three explanations: again the generalized, functional, and concrete. Each person was asked to record the "best," "next best," and "worst" explanation.

When the subjects were divided into three age groups of approximate mean age 27, 47, and 67 years, it was found that increased age was associated with a decrease in both the tendency to form the higher order generalization (first test), and to choose it when given an opportunity to do so (second test). The rejection of the higher order concept when not required to generate it by one's own thought seems particularly important. Either such a concept is not recognized for what it can do, or if it is, it is not as preferred as sticking close to the specific detail. This adherence to the concrete can be very limiting.

The preference for the concrete was seen also in a study by Allen (described by Welford, 1951, pp. 84–94; 1958, pp. 192–198). People were presented with a series of statements which had certain logical connections or inconsistencies. The task was to draw deductions from these statements, or to point out the fallacies in them. The results of the study were much like those of Bromley. The subjects under 35 years (mean = 24.8) tended to succeed in the task of logical analysis, but those over 35 (mean = 49 years) did not. The older subjects tended to introduce supplementary premises or, more concretely, tended to confine themselves to comments about the statements, rather than to draw logical conclusions from them.

Education seems to play a role in the preference for the concrete in later life—at least those who earlier in life were able to take advantage of higher education were seen as not quite so limited in their response repertoires. Welford (1958, p. 497) reported that, while even those subjects over 35 years who were university teachers and researchers tended to comment rather than to draw deductions, this tendency was not as great for them as it was for less well-educated subjects. Thirteen out of 14 clerical and secretarial workers commented rather than drew deductions, while only 10 out of 18 university people performed in this manner.

A more dramatic role of education was implicit in a study by Cijfer (1966). He attempted to replicate Welford's finding with subjects who were physicians from the Netherlands. The results were very different. There were no significant differences between the two age groups; in fact, the older group (35-74 years) performed non-significantly better than did the younger one (27-34 years)—the older subjects made more logical, abstract inferences than did the younger ones. Several reasons were offered to account for the differences in results between the two studies, and among them was the nature of the subject populations. Cijfer (1966, p. 168) suggested that medical training and practice equipped the physician to perform well on the test; the ability to diagnose involves logical inference.

INFLEXIBILITY

A test of "critical thinking" was given by Friend and Zubek (1958) to almost 500 people ranging in age from 12 to 80 years. From some of the items of this test, indices of "objectivity" and "inflexibility" were derived. It was found that scores on critical thinking declined with advancing adult age, and this decline was partly a result of lessened objectivity and increased inflexibility of thought. Inflexibility in this instance was the inclination to choose absolutes of true and false rather than to consider other possibilities.

The study of inflexibility—or to use its other term, rigidity—in later life is important in a variety of contexts, not only thinking and problem solving. In fact, two chapters in this book, chapters 6 and 7, are devoted to it.

Einstellung Effect

In the first of these two chapters, a study by Heglin (1956) is described which has been frequently referenced when describing inflexible response in later life. Heglin focused upon set-inducing tasks based upon Luchins' (1942) water-jar problems, sometimes called the "Einstellung effect." A series of tasks is encountered by the subject which can be solved in a certain way. This way becomes well-learned and is effective in its repetitiveness until a similar-appearing task, but one best solved by a different principle, is encountered. The induced method of solution becomes totally ineffective later on when yet a different task, also appearing similar, is presented. For example, a set-inducing task may be of this type: End up with exactly 100 quarts of water, given three jars; jar A of 21-quart capacity, jar B of 127, and jar C of 3 quarts. The Einstellung pattern is to fill jar B, pour this to fill jar A once, and jar C twice (B-A-2C). A problem in which the set is appropriate but not efficient is: A = 23, B = 49, C = 3, with the goal to end up with 20. The set solution again is B-A-2C, but the most efficient solution is A-C. An example where the set solution is not appropriate at all is: A = 28, B = 76, C = 3, with the goal to end up with 25 quarts.

Heglin also used another Einstellung task of alphabets in jumbled order—both tasks were similar in their effects. Heglin found that the oldest subjects (50-85 years) showed more susceptibility to the induced set and a greater difficulty in overcoming it than did two groups of younger subjects (14-19 and 20-49 years). The older subjects tended to use the induced solution pattern in solving the problems which were best solved by a shorter and more direct method. They also tended to stick to this pattern even when it did not work at all. When the subjects were taught to avoid the induced set pattern of solving problems, the older subjects benefited least from the instruction.

While Heglin's study is well known and frequently referred to, a later study by Smith (1967) is less well known and probably has never been referred to in the aging literature. Smith's results were very different from Heglin's.

Water-jar problems were also used by Smith. Women aged 16-18 years were compared to women aged 54-67 years, both in their susceptibility to the set-induced solution and to the effect of variations in the amount of training which induced the solution. Subgroups within each age were given either 0, 1, 2, 5, or 10 demonstrations of how to solve the water-jar problems—all these demonstrations were of the kind that induced the Einstellung effect. All subjects were then tested on five problems that could be solved either by the Einstellung formula or by the more direct method; one problem solvable only by the direct method, followed by two problems solvable by either method.

No significant age difference in set susceptibility was obtained; there were no measured signs of greater inflexibility on the part of the older women. Nor were the effects of the amount of training differentially related to age, although the greater the amount of training, the greater the Einstellung effect independent of age. Smith concluded that previous studies showing Einstellung effects with age may have had poor experimental control of related cognitive factors. Level of intelligence, for example, was again seen as important in ascertaining dimensions of problem-solving ability in later life.

Concept Attainment

Another study of problem solving did disclose disinclination or inability to change sets, and here intelligence could not be brought to bear in the explanation. Wetherick (1965) presented subjects with cards, each with four letters on them, e.g., CFJP. The subject's job was to find out whether the card should be placed in one category or another. For example, one category could be cards having the letter C and another category could be cards without the letter C. A different problem could involve two letters, for example, cards with both the letters C and J would be in one category and those cards without both letters could be in another category. Wetherick informed the subject after each categorizing response as to whether it was correct or not.

As soon as the task was completed, i.e., as soon as the concept was attained, the next task was introduced with the instruction that a different letter or pair of letters were important to the solution. Four tasks were employed with the subject learning one concept and having to shift to another until all four were learned. The subjects were aged 21-30 years, 42-47 years, and 60-70 years, and they were matched on the basis of the Progressive Matrices test scores—they were the same subjects reported in the earlier study by Wetherick (1964).

"Despite the equation on the basis of non-verbal intelligence, all four tasks showed evidence of a disinclination in old subjects to change an established concept even where it was demonstrably wrong" (Wetherick, 1965, p. 94). To the extent that this type of concept shifting is analogous to the Einstellung effect, Smith's contention regarding control of ability levels of the subjects of differing ages does not appear tenable.

However, if inflexibility is a factor in solving concept attainment problems, it may not be a factor that is general to all types of problems. Rogers et al. (1976), in their reversal and nonreversal shift problems, discounted the role of inflexibility or rigidity. They argued that rigidity suggests a perseveration of initial solutions, and their data indicated a quick tendency on the part of older subjects to new solution attempts. Successful solution simply rested in the ability to solve the new problems.

Negative Instance

Wetherick (1965) also emphasized that old subjects found it very difficult "to make proper use of negative instances." Depending upon the context and previous experience with the particular problem, a negative instance can be as informative as a positive one. The information, "No, not C," can convey as much information as "Yes, it is C." As was seen previously, in Arenberg's "poisoned food" study, "coffee" was a negative instance and "peas" a positive one, but from either one it could be inferred equally well that "peas" was the poisoned food.

For older people, the difficulty may be less with negative instance problems as such than with problems where both negative and positive instances (mixed instances) are present. Wetherick (1966), in describing three experiments, found that the older subjects were characterized by their errors in applying the operation appropriate to the positive instances to mixed instances or vice versa. In a later report, Wetherick (1969) hypothesized that even in the world outside the laboratory this inappropriate application makes it difficult or impossible to draw proper conclusions from evidence that is present. Thus, older people often appear rigid or unwilling to change their ways when, in fact, it may be nothing other than their inability to profit from negative instance information in the context of mixed instance situations. The mixed instance situation is characteristic of most life contexts.

Not all data support this view, however. Arenberg (1968, p. 281) examined the negative instance problem as one of shift or change from a positive instance. Based upon Wetherick's (1965) results, he hypothesized that "the old would be more likely than the young to continue a previous mode of operation." Arenberg found that, while concept attainment—what he called "reasoning performance"—was not as good in his 60-77-year-olds as compared to his 17-22-year-olds, the negative instance problem was not differentially difficult for them when it followed a positive instance problem. The results, therefore, did not confirm the hypothesis of special difficulty in later life in changing or shifting concepts, or in drawing conclusions from negative instances in a mixed context. Arenberg attributed the differences between his results and those of Wetherick (1965) to a considerably greater memory load needed for the correct solution of Wetherick's problems. "It is not unreasonable," Arenberg (p. 281) concluded, "that negative instances, which are seldom rich in information, are likely to be forgotten or inadequately processed when memory is taxed."

REDUNDANCY
Irrelevant Information

An instruction or a directive may include items or material which are irrelevant and uninformative. Such material often do more than just get in the way, they are often the source of misdirected behavior. Arenberg's (1968) "poisoned food" study pointed this out. In Table 14.1, knowing that either coffee or peas is poisoned but lamb is not, a meal of coffee, beef, and peas with the information, "Died," is redundant (by the rules of the procedure additional poisoned foods are not introduced). A meal of three other foods such as milk, beef, and rice, with the information, "Lived" (none of these items is poisoned), is similarly redundant.

Arenberg found that such redundancy made for errors on the part of the older problem solvers when it hardly made for errors at all on the part of the young. This was even more apparent in two studies where the amount of irrelevant information was varied and age groups were compared in their performances. In both studies the performances of the elderly became disproportionately poor as the amount of irrelevant information increased.

In the first of these studies, Rabbitt (1965) compared old (65–74 years) and young (17–24) in a task related to problem solving but best described as visual search. Cards had to be sorted into piles depending upon the letters (A, B, etc.) on them. Also on these cards were other letters, irrelevant ones, that had to be ignored. The older subjects, more than the younger ones, were slower in carrying out this task in direct relationship to the number of irrelevant letters. Thus, this study showed that older people are more disadvantaged than younger people by irrelevant information.

Another sorting task, but one closer allied to problem solving, was carried out by Hoyer, Marx, and Rebok (1978). Like Rabbitt, Hoyer et al. had their subjects match cards to a standard, but here one dimension (color, form, number, *or* position) was relevant to the matching and the others were irrelevant. (These dimensions in more typical problem-solving tasks have to be discovered by the subject in the process of sorting, matching, or selecting. This discovery problem is frequently called the concept identification task or the concept attainment task, and is thought to involve logical reasoning. When the task involves card sorting it is often called categorization or classification.)

Hoyer et al., like Rabbitt, observed that the elderly were disproportionately slower in matching the concepts or dimensions as the number of irrelevant items increased. This relative inability to ignore irrelevant information is seen as an important factor in the general behavior of older adults (Rabbitt, 1977) and certainly in perceptual behavior (Layton, 1975).

Inquiry

Welford (1958, pp. 202–205) reported a study by Bernardelli who presented subjects with an electrical problem meant to simulate the servicing of radios. The apparatus consisted of a small number of boxes each with six terminals on top, connected underneath by resistors. The subject was given one such box along with a resistance (ohm) meter, and a circuit diagram. The diagram showed the connections between the terminals in the box, but it did not show which terminals in the diagram corresponded to which ones on the box. The subject's job was to deduce the correspondence.

Welford reported that it was necessary for older adults to make more inquiries, i.e., to take more meter readings, than did the younger ones. There was greater redundancy in their inquiry. Welford interpreted these results as indicating that the older subjects had more difficulty in giving meaning to their meter readings than did the younger subjects, and they had more difficulty in remembering this information when it was later necessary to apply it in the final solution.

A conceptually similar problem was carried out by Clay (Welford, 1958, pp. 205–209), but instead of a context of electrical connections, the problem was cast in terms of a horse race in one case, and in terms of automobiles on a road in another. These tasks called for finding a button which corresponded to a light.

With increased age decades from the 20s to the 50s, subjects performed progressively poorer in solving these problems. Again, the number of apparatus readings increased with age. Welford noted that many subjects wrote notes to help themselves recall and interpret the information, minimizing the need for an excessive number of inquiries. This tendency to write notes was correlated with good performance, and it decreased with increasing age.

The frequency of redundant inquiry in later life was corroborated by Jerome (1962). He presented subjects with an apparatus named the "Logical Analysis Device" which enabled the presentation of problems ranging from extremely easy to extraordinarily difficult. Jerome (1962, p. 814) found that the performances of the older subjects (mean age, 66 years) were "strikingly inferior" to those of the younger (mean age, 23 years), and the most prominent feature in their poor performances was the redundancy of their information-seeking behavior. For successful solution of Jerome's tasks, it was necessary to elicit information piece by piece for later integration. This seemed to be the crux of the difficulty as judged by the fact that the older person tended to ask for the same information over and over again. As did Welford, Jerome thought that this could be a consequence of a failing memory. Accordingly, he tried to minimize the factor of memory by teaching and encouraging the subjects to take notes. Jerome reported that, while the younger subjects seemed to find the notes helpful, the older subjects said that they could not make use of notes and saw no reason for writing them. Their notes tended to be indecipherable, even to themselves.

ORDER IN THE SEARCH FOR INFORMATION
Following Goal Plans

This crux of the difficulty was expressed with quite a different type of task almost a decade earlier (Clay, 1954, p. 12):

> [The old] were unable to build a solution in a logical way with the more complex problems. Confusion was apparent. They could see their errors, but were unable to make the necessary connections between errors to arrive at a correct solution. The younger subjects encountered similar difficulties in coping with the increased data, but were methodical in dealing with them. They followed their initial plan more closely, whereas the older subjects became muddled and then neglected some parts of the task.

Jerome's (1962) conclusions were very similar. He saw that the older subjects did not have explicit knowledge of the goal of the particular problem until very late in the exploratory effort. Thus, their inquiries—their search for information—was characterized by a lack of order, by a considerable fluctuation and haphazard questioning rather than by a concentration on a single path to the goal. This unordered search made for information obtained only randomly, making it difficult to distinguish the relevant from the irrelevant. Before long, the older subjects were overwhelmed by the multitude of irrelevant facts and this, together with their inability to benefit from note taking, made for frequent repetition of the redundant questions.

Training for Orderly Search

Young (1966) was impressed with this lack of order on the part of older people to solve Jerome's logical analysis problems, and she made an effort to train them so that redundant inquiry and disorderly progress toward uncertain goals would be minimal. She also made an effort to minimize the memory burden of the problem by teaching special techniques.

In the logical analysis problem that Young (1966) and Arenberg (1974) used, there were three types of relationships that had to be learned in order to solve the problem of turning on a center-placed light. One relationship was an *effector* relationship: one light must be on for one or more others to go on. A second relationship was called *combinor*: two lights must be on for another to go on. And, three was a *preventor* relationship: one light on prevents another from being on. To solve the problem of lighting the center light, these three relationships must be learned, and they must be integrated into a correct and efficient sequence.

First, Young (1966) gave information about the equipment and about these three relationships. Along with this, she showed the subjects how to make notes to record what they had learned and what was necessary in order to proceed. Next, with her help, each subject solved a practice problem and was told again of the important details necessary for successful solution. Finally, the test problem was given. If solved within 30 minutes, the next problem was given. If successful solution was not achieved, the correct pattern was illustrated with the failed problem, using a procedure "designed to impose order on the search of information" (Young, 1966, p. 506). This procedure involved item-by-item correction when necessary and a monitoring of the related note taking. There were approximately nine one-hour practice sessions, each reviewing the last problem solved or attempted, and each presenting a new problem with appropriate training when necessary.

A maximum of 12 test problems were given with three forms of the same problem at each of four levels of difficulty. The subjects were of two groups, one aged 29-45 years and the other 54-76 years. At every difficulty level, fewer older than younger subjects achieved solution. At every level, the older subjects made at least twice as many inquiries as did the younger ones. Again, it was concluded that this could be indicative of the difficulty the older people had in giving meaning to the information which was elicited.

At the conclusion of the study, Young asked whether her emphasis on note taking and the intensive training to impose orderly search improved the problem-solving performance of the older subjects. She compared her results to those of Jerome (1962) and indicated that there was success with the training, but it was quite limited. Young (1966, p. 508) concluded:

Although the difficulties of the old Ss (subjects) appear to be due in part to inability to ignore irrelevant information, memory deficit, and unorganized search for a solution, the chief difficulty was the inability to learn, to apply, or to realize the utility of the solution strategy which was painstakingly and repeatedly demonstrated.

SEX DIFFERENCES

High school and college males, on a wide variety of problem-solving tasks, perform better than their female counterparts. This is less true when the problem involves verbal rather than mathematical or perceptual material and, in fact, some studies pointed to female superiority in verbal problem-solving tasks. By and large, the available data relating to adults past college age suggest that there are no sex differences. The studies by Brinley et al. (1974), Denney (1974), Cicirelli (1976), and Hoyer et al. (1978) point to this.

One study was an exception in that it did find a sex difference, and the difference was of an interesting nature. Young (1971) tested 40 married couples, aged 41-76 years, which included three subjects who were in their 70s. These people were categorized in groups aged in the 40s, 50s, and 60s, with the three oldest people placed in the 60s group.

There were three classes of problems similar in some ways to the problems Young used previously (1966). Class I had problems in which one light had to be *on* to turn a target light green, otherwise it turned red. The task was to determine which one of the 8 or the 16 lights present was the one controlling the target light. Class II problems were reversed; one light had to be *off* to turn the target light green. Class III problems were more difficult in that they were composed of irregular sequences of Class I and II problems with the subject not knowing which of the two types was being given. Class III problems were thus similar to the mixed instance problems of Wetherick (1966).

Young's subjects had to determine which type of problem it was (i.e., Class I, II, or III) and which one light of several present controlled the target light. The results of this study may be seen in Figure 14.1. Men were superior to women in solving the problem, but, most important, this held only through the 50s; during the 60s, this was no longer true. Aging patterns for men and women were different. The efficiency of performance of the women differed little with increasing age, but that of men declined with age.

Men were superior to women in their 40s but inferior in their 60s. The decade of the 50s saw men and women as very similar. Young (1971, p. 335) speculated that men in thier 50s may experience cognitive difficulties resulting from "physiological changes associated with aging, especially those related to cerebral circulation." Men in their 50s performed as well as men in the 40s on the simpler problems, but their performances resembled those of the men in their 60s as the problems became more difficult. Men in their 60s never performed as well as the others, and they profited least from their experience on the problem-solving task. Women, on the other hand, did not suffer these ravages of age, although they did not benefit earlier in life from superior performance.

It is well to recall at this time that most studies did not find older men and women different in their problem-solving abilities. Young's study may be an exception.

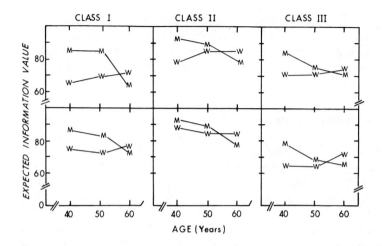

FIGURE 14.1: Men (M) and women (W) in age decades 40s, 50s and 60s were compared with respect to solving problems of determining which one of several lights present controlled a target light. The top three graphs refer to problems with 16 lights present, the bottom three graphs refer to problems with 8 lights present. Class I problems were those where one particular light had to be on to turn the target light green; Class II problems were reversed in that the light had to be off to do this; Class III problems included irregular presentations of Class I and II problems. The ordinate is a derived measure reflecting efficiency of problem solving. Note the cross-over of curves in each of the six groups. (From Table 3 of Young, 1971.)

ANOTHER VIEW
Making the Task Do-able

The evidence points to a decline with age in problem-solving ability, yet the evidence also makes it clear that situations and contingencies can be arranged to minimize this and even negate it. First, Arenberg's (1968) study showed that framing task and solution conditions in concrete rather than abstract forms can be helpful for the elderly. The study by Brinley et al. (1974) showed that reducing the memory load, i.e., keeping all that is necessary for problem solution in view, makes for better performance on the part of the elderly. Hoyer et al. (1978) and others demonstrated that by reducing irrelevant information, the aged benefit. And Rabbitt (1965) showed that the reduction of redundancy together with reduction of the amount of relevant information that the problem solver needs to cope with, is especially useful in matching situations and skills of older people. Moreover, it is well to keep in mind that not all studies showed poorer performances of the elderly. Wetherick (1964) did not find age differences and, more importantly, Arenberg's (1974) longitudinal study, the only longitudinal study reported, showed age change only after 70. This was seen with a select group of intellectually superior subjects able to carry out extremely difficult problem-solving tasks.

Modification Studies

A most significant development is a series of investigations teaching older people how to solve problems that are typically hard for them. The purpose of these studies is to demonstrate that the elderly are plastic—that they can carry out these tasks successfully if they are provided with special training focusing on the steps involved in the solutions. These studies are not only encouraging as to the capabilities of the elderly, they are also helpful in ascertaining training techniques that seem beneficial to the elderly.

At least three studies, each based on a form of the concept identification task, demonstrated problem-solving plasticity with age. In the first, an elaborate training procedure was begun with an extraordinarily simplified version of the task to be solved (Sanders, Sterns, Smith, and Sanders, 1975). The task was so simple as hardly to be a task of problem solving, but the main feature for solution was part of it. Sanders et al. then presented more difficult tasks, which included additional principles underlying successful solution. They provided practice opportunities and gave the correct answers when not known. They built up the difficulty level of the problem sequentially to a point where the problems were quite hard. They did this gradually and with much patience.

Sanders et al. trained two groups of elderly people in this way, giving one of them special rewards for correct identifications. Both groups were equal in their performances, each being superior to groups that had not been trained in this way. Considering the difficulty of the tasks that some of the subjects mastered, and considering that such tasks, even easier ones, are of the type that many older people fail to solve, the training procedure seems powerful for its purpose. Sanders et al. (1975, p. 828) indicated that the subjects "expressed strong feelings of intrinsic reinforcement and increased self-confidence because of the frequent success they achieved during training."

An even more difficult problem-solving task utilizing the same kind of training procedure was reported by Sanders, Sanders, Mayes, and Sielski (1976). Success again was seen. The investigators concluded that "a training procedure combining operant and cumulative learning hierarchy principles effectively promotes" the use of appropriate problem-solving strategy on the part of elderly people.

A third study was Labouvie-Vief and Gonda (1976). The specifics of the task were different from those above, but shared with them the need of finding the rule or concept necessary for correct solution of the problem. This study, like the other two, consisted of training and then testing, but it had two added features: One, there was a period of delayed testing (10-28 days later) to see whether the training was longer-lasting than just during the period of initial examination. Two, the study also tested with a task different from that of training, but related to it. This was for the purpose of seeing whether the training effects could be generalized to other tasks.

Women aged 63-95 years were divided into four groups and each provided with different experiences. One group had no training, another was given opportunity to work with the problems but nothing else. This group was seen as having "unspecific training." Another group was taught how to plan and guide themselves in solving the problems, and a last group was taught this also but, in addition, they were taught how to overcome anxiety and cope with failure.

The results were partly expected, partly not. They showed that the special training, both with and without the anxiety reduction, made for better test performances than no training. But for delayed testing—tests made about two weeks afterward—and for tests with different problems to see how generalizable the training procedures were, the results were mixed. Sometimes one training procedure was seen as better, sometimes another. The biggest surprise was that unspecific training, while not seen as helpful in immediate testing, was the only procedure seen as helpful in both delayed and generalized testing. Labouvie-Vief and Gonda (1976, p. 331) concluded that "The finding of *any* training effects offers an argument against the traditional implication . . . that intellectual aging decrements are irreversible." Further, they indicated that "there may be a good deal more plasticity to the intelligence in old age than has been acknowledged thus far."

No issue ought to be taken with these conclusions—only encouragement. This study, however, and the other "modification studies," those discussed above, suggest that if problem-solving performances can be improved by training or practice, then the origin of the initial difficulty must be experiential, rather than biological. This is incorrect—these studies show reversibility, or more correctly, they show improvement, but they do not show what the origin of difficulty is. It could be experiential, biological, or both.

These modification studies may well be forerunners of others to come; they show the way to future studies, which may be most useful.

CREATIVITY

Outside the laboratory, in the world of work and career, problem solving takes many forms. Over the course of many years, with the work of extraordinary people, it takes the form of publicly recognized creativity.

Creativity in Relation to Age

Lehman (1953) provided information regarding the effect of age on creativity in the sciences, medicine, philosophy, arts, practical invention, and other areas. His work dealt mainly with deceased persons of earlier centuries, but some of his later work focused specifically upon the still living (e.g., Lehman, 1963). Lehman's general method was to tabulate by age groups the frequency with which quality productions were listed in expert historical accounts. For example, in examining the creative years of chemists, Lehman referred to a written history of chemistry in which the names of several hundred chemists and the dates on which they made their contributions were listed. Often, he brought such expert historical listings to university teachers for further evaluation.

Lehman's general finding was that, within most fields of endeavor, the maximum production rate for quality work occurred during the age decade 30–39 years. The rate of creative production did not decline rapidly after the peak years, but was gradual at nearly all ages. For less distinguished work, the peak years were later and the decline was even more gradual. Lehman found the specific relations between creativity and age dependent upon not only the types of measures used (i.e., quantity vs. quality), but also upon the field of endeavor investigated. In some fields the peak years were earlier than in others. But in all fields individual variations were so great that Lehman found it necessary to emphasize that man's usefulness is not limited by his age. The more recent data of Zusne (1976) for psychologists are similar. He investigated the age at which eminent psychologists published their one most significant work. The age pattern coincided remarkably with that of Lehman.

Artifact in Method? Lehman's work was criticized by Dennis (1956a, 1958). Dennis leveled many arguments, but the most cogent one was that Lehman combined information pertaining to men of different longevities, and, in so doing, exaggerated or even manufactured the age decrements which he reported. Since all the significant contributions of short-lived people occurred only in the early decades, while those of the long-lived people occurred during both their early and late decades of life, the practice of combining longevities made for artifacts. To demonstrate this, Dennis (1956b, 1966), in two studies, analyzed only the creations of people who lived long lives. The results of both these studies were different from those typified by Lehman. Dennis showed that peak performance years were found throughout most of the adult life-span.

Dennis' analyses were based upon quantity of output and Lehman's work emphasized superior quality output. Lehman (1956, p. 324; 1958) argued that because older people put out relatively few high-quality products, the effect of combining information pertaining to men of different longevities was small. Dennis (1966, p. 6) recognized that the difference in emphasis between quality and quantity may be the key to the difference in results between his and Lehman's studies, but he contended that it is difficult to arrive at an unbiased evaluation of quality (Dennis, 1956b). His point was that an analysis of quality through biographies and citations contains systematic errors favoring man's early work, artificially making for the data Lehman reported. Dennis suggested that, first, an historian of science may be more likely to mention a young man's pioneering work than his subsequent investigations which develop and validate the earlier ones. Second, critics and historians find it harder to evaluate recent work than older work and tend not to designate the more recent work (i.e., the work of later life) as masterwork. Third, because of the increased number of creative workers from one generation to the next, competition increases, making it difficult for a man's later work to be evaluated as superior. Dennis (1958) provided data which he believed demonstrated his contention of systematic errors in the analysis of quality through biographies and citations, but Lehman maintained that all Dennis showed was that great contributions have been increasing at a slower rate than have lesser ones.

Nobel Prize Winners. The data of Manniche and Falk (1957) may be important to these considerations. They investigated the age during which Nobel Prize winners did their award-winning work. They also investigated the age trends in carrying out this work from the year 1901 to 1950. The data of Manniche and Falk and those of Lehman were similar in many respects, although there were some differences. In medicine, for example, the Nobel Prize work was done later in life, peaking in the late 40s and dropping more gradually. From 1901 to 1950 no age trend in chemistry and physics was clear.

Individual Differences and Social Planning

It was emphasized that individual variation is so large, and rate of decline sufficiently gradual, that a grave mistake would be made if any one person was discouraged from continuing his endeavors because of age. Not only would it be a grave mistake, but it could be a great loss for society. For example, Pressey and Pressey (1967) reported a study of ten remarkable men from Michelangelo to Churchill whose careers continued into their 80s. In addition, two groups of professional people past 70 were studied and some of them continued their careers well into old age. Pressey and Pressey concluded that all these long-working, successful, older adults had characteristics in common. They all had: (1) significant purpose, (2) "mellowed wisdom," and (3) role and status to nurture continuing their work.

Thus, Lehman's data are important *only* in their implications with respect to group trends—implications that are important in social planning. Lehman (1953, p. 220) made an analogy between his data and life expectancy tables of life insurance companies. Most of us expect to outlive the average life expectancy, and we arrange our lives for this possibility. But many of us also recognize the meaningfulness of the group averages and prepare for these contingencies too.

Even accepting some artifacts of method and social restrictions which unfairly suggest that older people are not as creative as younger ones, the group averages seem to point to diminution with age in creative productivity. Just as there are personal consequences to this, there are broader social ones too.

Means must be found to start young people on their creative careers earlier in life than heretofore. There seems to be a trend forming at the present time to do just this and, if so, it is all to the good. More and more training is required in most fields and the actual period of fruit-bearing is delayed well into mid-adult life. Effort must be made to shorten this training by continuously reviewing it for unnecessary requirements.

There is a lag in the time between when creations are completed and when there are rewards for this work. For example, Manniche and Falk (1957) reported that the time intervals between carrying out the Nobel Prize work and the awarding of the prize ranged from nearly zero to 37 years. And, Lehman (1953, pp. 162–178) reported that rewards in the form of leadership positions as found in government, professional, religious, and other branches of work tend to be held by men appreciably older than those performing quality creative work. The practice must be changed so that rewards come sooner in life, and these rewards must be appropriate in keeping the creative worker flourishing.

SUMMARY

While the ability to solve problems depends upon a variety of cognitive abilities, in themselves these abilities are not sufficient to insure success. Other factors are involved in problem solving too. Some evidence, but not all, suggests that elderly people have greater difficulty than younger people in solving laboratory problems, largely because these problems require abstract thought. Older adults prefer the more concrete tasks and work in more concrete fashion than younger adults. Education plays a role in the preference for the concrete such that the greater the education of the older person, the less the tendency to prefer and to think in concrete terms. Some evidence also suggests that people who are very superior intellectually, and who can solve very difficult problems, show no age decline until relatively later in life—not before age 70.

Problem-solving ability can be impaired when there is rigidity or inflexibility of thought. To solve problems it is often necessary to be flexible in going from one type of thought to another. The literature is conflicting as to whether rigidity underlies the difficulty older people have in solving problems. In many of life's situations, this ability to shift from one type of problem to another is taxed most when there is both information indicating a correct direction to take and when there is information indicating what direction not to take. The former is called a positive instance and the latter a negative instance. When both positive and negative instances are part of the same problem, and the relevant instance is left unspecified, the older person appears to be at a special loss.

Redundant information—as may be given in an instruction, for example—is also a source of difficulty in problem solving. Such information is not only irrelevant and uniformative, but it often is the source of misdirected behavior. Redundancy has been seen as a special difficulty for older problem solvers.

Redundancy is seen in inquiry as well as in given information. To solve problems, it is usually necessary to acquire information from the task itself. Older adults, in attempts to gain this information, tend to make more inquiries than do younger ones, and they often make the same inquiry over and over again. It is as if the older adults have difficulty in giving meaning to the information gained from their inquiries and, once understood, have difficulty in remembering it.

The frequency of redundant inquiry in later life is a most prominent feature in the poor performances of the elderly. For successful solution of many tasks, it is necessary to elict information piece by piece for later integration. Before this can be accomplished, explicit knowledge of the goal must be had; older people often do not have this knowledge until very late in the exploratory effort. Thus, their inquiries—their search for information—tend to be characterized by a lack of order with considerable fluctuation and haphazard questioning. Efforts to teach old people to search for information in orderly ways, and other efforts designed to teach effective strategies of problem solving have met with only very limited success.

The data suggest that men and women past college age are similar in their problem-solving abilities. One study, however, found a sex difference. The men were superior, but this was so only in the 40s. The sexes were about equal in the 50s, with the women being superior in the 60s. Age changes and sex differences in cerebral circulation have been suggested as an important element in the decline.

What may be a new trend in the study of age and problem solving was seen in a series of studies making effort to train older people in the very areas they seem to have difficulties. The purpose of these studies is to demonstrate a plasticity that older people have that is not often seen in typical laboratory studies. These training studies, called "modification studies," have already shown much promise.

Problem solving, outside the laboratory, in the world of work and career, takes many forms. Over the course of many years, with extraordinary people, it takes the form of publically recognized creativity. If problem-solving ability declines with age, it might be expected that creativity does too. There is evidence that it does, but the evidence is more equivocal than that of laboratory problem solving because of alleged artifacts of method. For extremely high-quality work in the arts, sciences, and humanities, the age of peak production has been determined as 30–39 years, with gradual decline thereafter. A most important dimension to the reported decline in creativity with age is the great extent of individual variation. Many, many creative contributions throughout the ages have been made very late in life.

REFERENCES

Arenberg, D. Concept problem solving in young and old adults. *Journal of Gerontology*, 1968, *23*, 279–282.

Arenberg, D. A longitudinal study of problem solving in adults. *Journal of Gerontology*, 1974, *29*, 650–658.

Brinley, J.F., Jovick, T.J., and McLaughlin, L.M. Age, reasoning, and memory in adults. *Journal of Gerontology*, 1974, *29*, 182–189.

Bromley, D.B. Some experimental tests of the effect of age on creative intellectual output. *Journal of Gerontology*, 1956, *11*, 74–82.

Bromley, D.B. Some effects of age on the quality of intellectual output. *Journal of Gerontology*, 1957, *12*, 318–323.

Chown, S.M. Age and the rigidities. *Journal of Gerontology*, 1961, *16*, 353–362.
Cicirelli, V.G. Categorization behavior in aging subjects. *Journal of Gerontology*, 1976, *31*, 676–680.
Cijfer, E. An experiment on some differences in logical thinking between Dutch medical people, under and over the age of 35. *Acta Psychologica*, 1966, *25*, 159–171.
Clay, H.M. Changes of performance with age on similar tasks of varying complexity. *British Journal of Psychology*, 1954, *45*, 7–13.
Denney, N.W. Classification abilities in the elderly. *Journal of Gerontology*, 1974, *29*, 309–314.
Dennis, W. Age and achievement: a critique. *Journal of Gerontology*, 1956(a), *11*, 331–333.
Dennis, W. Age and productivity among scientists. *Science*, 1956(b), *123*, 724–725.
Dennis, W. The age decrement in outstanding scientific contributions: fact or artifact? *American Psychologist*, 1958, *13*, 457–460.
Dennis, W. Creative productivity between ages of 20 and 80 years. *Journal of Gerontology*, 1966, *21*, 1–8.
Friend, C.M., and Zubek, J.P. The effects of age on critical thinking ability. *Journal of Gerontology*, 1958, *13*, 407–413.
Heglin, H.J. Problem solving set in different age groups. *Journal of Gerontology*, 1956, *11*, 310–317.
Hoyer, W.J., Marx, S.D., and Rebok, G.W. Effects of varying irrelevant dimensions on problem solving: adult age differences. *Developmental Psychology*, 1978, in press.
Inglis, J. Learning, retention and conceptual usage in elderly patients with memory disorder. *Journal of Abnormal and Social Psychology*, 1959, *59*, 210–215.
Jerome, E.A. Decay of heuristic processes in the aged. In C. Tibbitts and Wilma Donahue (Eds.), *Social and psychological aspects of aging*. New York: Columbia Univ. Press, 1962, pp. 802–823.
Labouvie-Vief, G., and Gonda, J.N. Cognitive strategy training and intellectual performance in the elderly. *Journal of Gerontology*, 1976, *31*, 327–332.
Layton, B. Perceptual noise and aging. *Psychological Bulletin*, 1975, *82*, 875–883.
Lehman, H.C. *Age and achievement*. Princeton, N.J.: Princeton Univ. Press, 1953.
Lehman, H.C. Reply to Dennis' critique of age and achievement. *Journal of Gerontology*, 1956, *11*, 333–337.
Lehman, H.C. The influence of longevity upon curves showing man's creative production rate at successive age levels. *Journal of Gerontology*, 1958, *13*, 187–191.
Lehman, H.C. Chronological age versus present-day contributions to medical progress. *Gerontologist*, 1963, *3*, 71–75.
Luchins, A.S. Mechanization in problem solving. *Psychological Monographs*, 1942, *54*, 1–95.
Manniche, E., and Falk, G. Age and the Nobel prize. *Behavioral Science*, 1957, *2*, 301–307.
Pressey, S.L., and Pressey, A.D. Genius at 80; and other oldsters. *Gerontologist*, 1967, *7*, 183–187.
Rabbitt, P. An age-decrement in the ability to ignore irrelevant information. *Journal of Gerontology*, 1965, *20*, 233–238.
Rabbitt, P. Changes in problem solving ability in old age. In J.E. Birren and K.W.

Schaie (Eds.). *Handbook of the psychology of aging*. New York: Van Nostrand Reinhold, 1977.

Rogers, C.J., Keyes, B.J., and Fuller, B.J. Solution shift performance in the elderly. *Journal of Gerontology*, 1976, *31*, 670–675.

Sanders, J.A.C., Sterns, H.L., Smith, M., and Sanders, R.E. Modification of concept identification performance in older adults. *Developmental Psychology*, 1975, *11*, 824–829.

Sanders, R.E., Sanders, J.A.C., Mayes, G.J., and Sielski, K.A. Enhancement of conjunctive concept attainment in older adults. *Developmental Psychology*, 1976, *12*, 485–486.

Smith, D.K. The Einstellung effect in relation to the variables of age and training. *Dissertation Abstracts*, 1967, *27B*, 4115.

Storck, P.A., Looft, W.R., and Hooper, F.H. Interrelationships among Piagetian tasks and traditional measures of cognitive abilities in mature and aged adults. *Journal of Gerontology*, 1972, *27*, 461–465.

Welford, A.T. *Skill and age*. London: Oxford Univ. Press, 1951.

Welford, A.T. *Aging and human skill*. London: Oxford Univ. Press, 1958.

Wetherick, N.E. A comparison of the problem-solving ability of young, middle-aged and old subjects. *Gerontologia*, 1964, *9*, 164–178.

Wetherick, N.E. Changing an established concept: a comparison of the ability of young, middle-aged and old subjects. *Gerontologia*, 1965, *11*, 82–95.

Wetherick, N.E. The inferential basis of concept attainment. *British Journal of Psychology*, 1966, *57*, 61–69.

Wetherick, N.E. The psychology of aging. *Occupational Therapy*, 1969, *32*, 15–17.

Young, M.L. Problem-solving performance in two age groups. *Journal of Gerontology*, 1966, *21*, 505–509.

Young, M.L. Age and sex differences in problem solving. *Journal of Gerontology*, 1971, *26*, 330–336.

Zusne, L. Age and achievement in psychology. *American Psychologist*, 1976, *31*, 805–807.

15

Learning and Performance

This chapter together with the next three form a sequence on learning and memory. Learning and memory are two sides of the same coin. This can be recognized by considering the obvious fact that if a man does not learn well, he has little to recall. Conversely, if his memory is poor, there is no sign of his having learned very much. Learning has to do with how information "gets in," and memory has to do with how this information gets "filed away" and later retrieved or "brought up" for use. This distinction between learning and memory, however, is easier made conceptually than operationally. In fact, operationally, distinctions can be made only by convention. In the laboratory, a subject is given something to learn and a test of learning is made on the basis of recall—memory. Or, tests of memory are given, but first some learning has to have taken place. If the learning was poor, memory test scores will be poor.

HISTORICAL TRENDS: EPISODIC AND SEMANTIC INFORMATION

American psychology of the 1940s and 1950s was largely a psychology of learning. In the 1960s, the emphasis shifted to memory and, in the 1970s, to information processing. The shift, however, did not change the fact that the distinction between learning and memory is hard to make. It is hard because, according to Craik (1977, p. 385), " 'learning' and 'memory' must rely on the same underlying mechanism. . . ."

A distinction is nevertheless made, largely because of convenience. Tulving (1972) suggested two categories of memory, one of which may be thought of as learning. *Episodic memory*, as the name may suggest, is memory for specific aspects of episodes, events, or items: "What words did you learn yesterday?" Memories based on such learning do not last long. If one of the words you learned was "table," there is no doubt that you know and will long remember the meaning of "table," but you may

261

not remember that it was one of the words you learned. Remembering the meaning of "table" is called *semantic memory*, remembering that it was one of the words is episodic memory. Episodic memory is rote learning. Semantic memory involves meaningful organization of information and relating it to what is already known. Such processing makes for much longer-lasting memory.

Thus, much of American psychology of the 1940s and 1950s was of the episodic type—rote learning or stimulus-response learning. The 1960s emphasis on memory was also largely of this type but moving toward semantic memory studies. In the main, it was not until the 1970s, with emphasis on information processing, that semantic memory came under study. As the studies progressed from learning to memory to information processing, a greater role was given to the subject. In episodic memory studies, the subject is seen as a passive responder to stimulations directed to him. In semantic memory studies, the subject is active, organizing, integrating, working on what he finds in his environment.

The aging literature follows that of general psychology, and in following, there is now only a start to studies of semantic memory. This chapter, more than chapters 16, 17, and 18, is of episodic memory studies. The subject is relatively inactive and is governed more by the information to be learned and the experimental context than by what he does to this information.

EXPRESSING WHAT IS LEARNED

In studies of episodic memory, and in studies of learning, it is often concluded that learning ability declines in later life. This may not be true. It is true, however, that learning performances tend to be poorer in later life than during young adulthood. To understand this it must be recognized that a necessary distinction is made between learning as an internal process and performance as an external act. We see only the act and not the process; we infer that learning ability is poor when we observe only a little or no improvement in some performance. It is possible to be wrong about this inference because what may have made for the poor performance was not learning ability as such but the non-cognitive elements surrounding the act. The observer may not be aware of this. For example, only a small or no improvement in a task may be due to poor motivation or to a lack of confidence or to factors such as poor conditions in which the learning takes place. To the extent that we have information about such factors, we are more nearly likely to be correct in our inferences regarding the learning.

These non-cognitive factors are especially important in studies with the aged. Much of what in the past had been regarded as a deficiency in learning ability in later life has more recently been seen as a problem in the ability to express the learned information. In other words, much of what had been thought of as a deficiency in the internal cognitive process is now seen as a difficulty older people have in adapting to the task and in demonstrating what they know.

STIMULUS PACING

More than thirty years ago Gilbert (1941) carried out an extraordinarily well-controlled study that demonstrated decline in performance with age on a variety of learning and memory tasks, but one type of task, especially, showed such decrement—a type which involved the formation of new associations—the paired-associate task. This task has remained prominent in the experimental study of learning in relation to age. (The paired-associate task involves a series of paired stimuli, very often words or letters. For example, one study paired the letters TL with the word INSANE, as one of the several paired associates in a list that was to be learned. After exposure to this and the other paired associates, a person having learned them will respond with the word, INSANE, when presented with the stimulus TL.)

Many times since Gilbert's study the paired-associate task has been shown to be specially difficult for older people. It had become accepted, on the basis of such studies, that learning ability—at least of the paired-associate kind—declines in later life. In recent years, however, this conclusion was opened to doubt. It was clear that in the studies of paired associates, performance declined with age, but did this mean that learning ability declined? Several investigators argued that experiments in paired-associate learning typically involve stimulus material so rapidly presented that the older person is required to rush his learning performances; the pacing is inappropriate to his normal speed of response patterns and, therefore, the studies are not adequate to judge learning ability.

Self-Pacing

Among the first studies demonstrating this was one carried out by Canestrari (1963). He presented older adults (60–69 years) and younger ones (17–35 years) with paired associates for learning, and he presented these with three different stimulus-pacing schedules. He had a fast pace where the stimuli were presented at the rate of 1.5 seconds, a medium pace where the stimuli were paced at 3.0 seconds, and a condition in which the subject paced himself. In the latter schedule, the subject was taught to control the apparatus so that he could get as much time for studying the stimulus and for responding to it as he desired.

Canestrari reported that in comparing the old and young adults, the old were relatively poorest in their learning performances with the fastest stimulus pacing, and they showed least deficit with self-pacing. These results demonstrated that much of the age deficit in the ability to form new associations, as seen in previous studies, is attributable to stimulus pacing factors.

Canestrari (1963, p. 167) wrote:

The most obvious feature of the self-paced schedule is that it allows the subject to spend as much time as is necessary in studying the pair as well as in making a response . . . both groups of subjects utilized the time in making the response to the stimulus word rather than in studying the pair . . . no young subject and only eight of the [30] older subjects [and then only rarely] stopped the drum in order to gain additional time to study the pair. It seems evident that an important determinant of the enhancing effect of self-pacing is the amount of time available for making a response to the stimulus word.

Canestrari's study, therefore, demonstrated that it takes more time for older people than for younger ones to express their newly learned information. They need more time to show what they have learned; otherwise, it appears as if they have not learned it well, or have not learned it at all.

Canestrari demonstrated yet another dimension of this extra time needed by older people. It has been seen in several prior studies that, when older people make errors, very often it is the result of not responding in the situation (errors of omission) rather than by responding incorrectly (errors of commission). In other chapters in this book, the errors of omission have been discussed in the context of a cautiousness on the part of elderly people. The omission error from a different perspective will be discussed later, again under the heading "Cautiousness," but regardless of the interpretation that may be given this type of error, Canestrari reported that slower stimulus pacing schedules reduce this type of error of the elderly, not their errors of commission.

Interaction between Inspection and Anticipation Intervals

The notion that older people perform poorly in quickly paced experimental tasks because of "response time" limitations rather than "studying time" limitations was explored with serial learning tasks as well as with the paired-associate tasks. (The serial learning tasks involves separate stimuli, often words, presented one after another. After the list of stimuli has been presented one or more times, the person learning the list is required to respond by anticipating and supplying the next stimulus in the sequence, the one not yet presented by the experimenter.) The conclusions based upon serial learning were compatible with those based upon paired-associate learning (Eisdorfer, Axelrod, and Wilkie, 1963; Eisdorfer, 1965).

Eisdorfer varied the exposure durations of the stimulus words (i.e., the time available for inspecting the stimulus), and he also varied the interval between the stimulus words (i.e., the time available for anticipating the next stimulus and responding before it appears). It was clear that the older subjects benefited from both the longer periods allowed for inspection and for anticipation.

A more recent study—a paired-associate study carried out by Monge and Hultsch (1971)—was designed to determine the relative importance of the time periods used for learning and the time periods for responding. They co-varied each of these periods in the same way: the learning period (inspection interval) and the response period (anticipation interval) were each presented in durations of 2.2, 4.4, and 6.6 seconds. Thus, nine conditions were had in the experiment—the quickest paced condition had both inspection and anticipation intervals at 2.2 seconds, or 4.4 seconds combined; the slowest paced condition had both intervals at 6.6 seconds or 13.2 seconds combined. The remaining seven conditions included all the possible remaining combinations of the three covariations of both intervals.

Table 15.1 shows the results of this study. In agreement with much of the previous conclusions, Monge and Hultsch reported that a longer period of time to inspect or study the stimulus helped both the young (20-39 years) and the older subjects (40-66 years), but not one age group more than the other. Most important, they reported that there is no interaction between the two types of intervals.

. . . the total time available per item [i.e., the sum of the anticipation and inspection intervals] is not differentially important to people of different ages. Only that portion of the total time allotted to the anticipation interval [response time] makes for age differences (Monge and Hultsch, 1971, p. 161).

Learning Ability

The Total Time Principle. While Monge and Hultsch concluded that the only factor making for the poorer performances on the part of the older subjects was the time allotted for response (anticipation inter-

TABLE 15.1
Mean Trials to Learn a Paired-Associate List

	INSPECTION (STUDY) INTERVAL, (SEC.)					
	2.2		4.4		6.6	
Age (Years):	20-39	40-66	20-39	40-66	20-39	40-66
Anticipation (Response) Interval, (Sec.)						
2.2	10.0	24.9	9.0	24.5	6.0	19.8
4.4	11.0	12.6	7.0	10.4	7.9	7.2
6.6	6.8	11.4	5.0	6.2	5.0	5.4

Data in this table from Monge and Hultsch (1971, p. 159, Table 2).

val), others disagreed, maintaining that it was the total time involved in learning, not the time allotted to responding. In fact, investigators of one study reached this conclusion after reworking the Monge-Hultsch data (Winn and Elias, 1975). Their argument rested on the idea that when stimuli were rapidly paced, more trials to learn the procedure were necessary than when the stimuli were paced more slowly. They suggested that presenting stimuli rapidly for many learning trials is equivalent to presenting stimuli at slower pacing for fewer trials. Accordingly, they reanalyzed the Monge-Hultsch data, converting trials to learn the task to total time for stimulus presentations; they found that time to learn increased with increasing age.

This was shown in more direct experimental fashion by Kinsbourne and Berryhill (1972). They kept the response (anticipation) interval constant at 2 seconds, and varied the learning interval (2, 4, or 6 seconds). Unlike other studies, however, they also varied the number of learning trials. Thus, as their study was carried out, a stimulus rate of 2 seconds with 6 trials was allotting the same total time for learning as a stimulus rate of 4 seconds with 4 trials, or a stimulus rate of 6 seconds with 3 trials.

Kinsbourne and Berryhill found with this analysis that learning was similar with each of the stimulus rate variations. Moreover, elderly people (60-85 years) learned more slowly than younger adults of college age, and important for the principle of total time, this could not be attributed to the rate of stimulus pacing apart from the number of trials. It was a matter of slower learning on the part of the elderly, and not slower responding time.

Study Time. An impressive array of studies have appeared which—

despite their emphasis on stimulus pacing—show age decrements in the slowest, even the self-paced conditions. For example, the following studies showed age decrements at all pacing rates: Canestrari (1963); Eisdorfer, Axelrod, and Wilkie (1963); Arenberg (1965); and Taub (1966, 1968—where stimulus pacing effects were not differentially important in regard to age, although only relatively fast rates were used). In fact, of all the learning studies carried out in ways in which age groups could be compared, we are aware of only the study by Monge and Hultsch (1971) and a study by Taub (1967) in which an age decrement in all the pacing conditions was not observed. Further, in the former study, the main one for the present purposes, the older subjects ranged in age from 40 to 66 years, with a mean of 49.4 years and a standard deviation of 6.5. This is hardly a group that is typically referred to as "old" or "aged."

Perhaps more important, an examination of Table 15.1 shows that, given a short amount of time to learn (an inspection interval of 2.2 seconds), even a long period within which to demonstrate what has been learned (an anticipation interval of 6.6 seconds) makes for relatively poor learning performances of the older group (11.4 versus 6.8 trials to criterion—see cell in lower left of Table 15.1). While not statistically significant, the percentage difference is large and in the same direction as the other two cells involving the longest anticipation interval.

A similar argument for a learning deficit in later life is seen in the study by Arenberg (1965). Elderly adults (60-77 years) and younger ones (18-21 years) learned paired-word associates by a procedure in which paced and self-paced trials were alternated. One sub-group of each age experienced fast-pacing trials (1.9 seconds) alternated with self-pacing trials, and a second sub-group of each age experienced slow-pacing trials (3.7 seconds) alternated with the self-pacing trials.

The crucial test in this study involved the comparison of error scores during the self-paced trials which followed the experimenter-paced trials. The thinking behind this crucial test was that if the older subjects learned the task during the fast-paced trials, but did not have time enough to respond, they would make poor scores during this fast pacing but good scores during self-pacing. However, if the older people did not learn well during the fast-paced trials, then their performances would be poor during self-pacing. Arenberg found that the older group was disproportionately poorer than the younger group during the self-paced trials when these followed fast pacing than when these followed the slow pacing. The conclusion, therefore, was that the poorer performance of the old group during the fast pacing could not be attributed totally to an inadequate amount of time to perform the correctly learned response.

MOTIVATION

Just as the speed with which an older person can demonstrate his knowledge limits his performance, but in itself is not regarded as a cognitive factor, so is it with motivation. Opinion has it that older people are less motivated than younger ones, certainly so in the laboratory situation where there is little of relevance to them. It is commonly believed that this lowered motivation on the part of the elderly can explain their poorer learning performances.

Actually, this opinion may be wrong. What sparse data are available suggest that, on the contrary, older people are more involved in the experimental situation than younger people. They are sometimes inappropriately involved. This tends to decrease their level of performance.

Autonomic Responsivity

Powell, Eisdorfer, and Bogdonoff (1964) carried out a serial learning study. Blood samples were taken of the subjects prior to the presentation of the learning task, during it, and afterward, and the samples were analyzed for free fatty acids (FFA). The level of FFA is thought to reflect the level of activity of the autonomic nervous system and of the adrenal medulla. Thus, it is considered a measure of "degree of arousal." Concepts such as "degree of arousal" and "level of activation" refer to psychophysiological states of the type which energize or spur people on in an undifferentiated, overall way.

The older subjects (over 60 years) had higher levels of FFA than the younger subjects (20-48 years) throughout the experiment. Thus, the older subjects were thought to be more highly aroused than the younger ones. More important in this study, however, was what happened after the learning procedure was terminated. The younger subjects dropped in their FFA arousal levels, but the older subjects continued to rise. The overall conclusions were "that the aged individual rather than being less involved in the task (and, therefore, not paying attention), is more involved and therefore experiencing a greater degree of autonomic activation" (Powell et al., 1964, p. 194). To the extent that this interpretation is correct, the continued rise in FFA levels of the older people after the experiment was terminated suggested that their highly activated states not only failed to help bring their performances to the levels of the younger adults, but also that the activated states were not always appropriate to the occasion.

Furchgott and Busemeyer (1976) did not agree with this interpretation although their data had one important aspect in common with those of Powell et al. Furchgott and Busemeyer measured heart rate and skin conductance; both can be considered indices of arousal. Three age groups were examined (23–39, 40–59, and 60–87 years) and the elderly were not seen as more aroused than the young, nor was the arousal-learning relationship different for old and young subjects. Of special interest, however: "During intertrial rest periods (of free recall) young but not old subjects showed HR (heart rate) returns to basal levels." Again, it appears that the elderly may not always be activated appropriately to the occasion.

A more direct test of the proposition that elderly people are highly involved in the experimental task, and that this involvement is often detrimental to their performing well, was made by Eisdorfer, Nowlin, and Wilkie (1970). A drug (Propranolol, commonly called Inderal) was given to elderly men (60–78 years) in the course of the serial learning task. This drug is believed to partially block the "autonomic end-organ response." By blocking neural transmission in the peripheral end organs it "largely mitigates most physiological concomitants of central nervous system arousal" (Eisdorfer et al., 1970, p. 1327). This drug, therefore, was thought to not involve the central nervous system but to suppress autonomic activity at its origins, the peripheral end organs.

Some subjects were given this drug and some a placebo; based upon the FFA study, the hypothesis under test was that when the autonomic activity of the elderly was suppressed by the drug, learning performances would improve. This was borne out; the placebo group made more errors than the drug group, suggesting that at least part of the performance deficits of older people could be explained on the basis of the function of systems other than the central nervous system. FFA levels were also measured in this study. The FFA levels were elevated with the placebo during the experimental procedure and were depressed with the drug, providing added credence to the role imparted to the drug: Propranolol acts to block autonomic responsivity.

These investigations open new directions in the study of learning in later life—they can help in our understanding of the dynamic interplay between cognitive and motivational factors. Two obvious lines of research remain untapped. One line involves the Eisdorfer et al. (1970) study. This must be carried out with a young adult control group in order to know whether the extent, and perhaps the type, of the drug effect is unique to older people. It is possible, for example, that both young and old will improve their learning performances with the drug, but not to the same extent. In such a case, we would have the means of improving performances, but we would not be able to attribute the age deficit in learning performances to factors apart from central nervous system functioning.

The other line of needed inquiry is less straightforward. This involves the relationship, if any, between the very important undifferentiated arousal functions of the autonomic nervous system, and the more volitional, goal-directed desire to achieve high scores on laboratory tests. A series of studies manipulating volitional states of motivation, perhaps by variations in instructions, or by variations in rewards and punishments, in conjunction with age studies of psychophysiological arousal, may be expected to provide a comprehensive picture of the relationship of learning and performance factors in relation to age.*

Arousal and Response Limitations

Eisdorfer (1968) considered two sets of conclusions: One, referring to an earlier study in which older people performed better in a serial learning task when the exposure duration was long, i.e., 10 seconds, as compared to a shorter 4 seconds, he suggested that fast pacing, i.e., the 4-second exposure, made for anxiety or otherwise inhibited response. Two, referring to the FFA study described earlier, the heightened autonomic arousal of the elderly subjects similarly may have served to inhibit response. The omission error was seen as an index of this inhibited response.

Thus, both the overall laboratory situation (situational anxiety, especially when needles are inserted as in FFA determinations) and the specific inhibiting character of the fast pacing of the stimuli (perhaps also anxiety producing) work together to decrease the performance levels of older people. This was tested as a hypothesis in the following way: A group of elderly subjects was tested for serial learning both with a 4-second stimulus exposure duration and a 10-second exposure. The total error scores were 84.3 and 31.9, respectively. Then, on the next day, the experiment was repeated, but this time the subjects were "autonomically aroused" by the needle-FFA procedure. The respective error scores were then 82.0 and 63.2; performance deteriorated with the longer exposure duration—the one in which performance without the "situational anxiety" had been good. The implication is that the response inhibition due to the stress of the noxious FFA procedure was maximum when response inhibition due to stimulus pacing was minimum. This pattern was reversed in a subsequent condition when the subjects became "adapted" to the FFA procedure.

Whether or not response inhibition (due to anxiety) is a reasonable interpretation, it would be of value to repeat these studies, comparing

* Not all indices and experimental situations point to a greater autonomic responsivity on the part of older people. See footnote in the next chapter.

older and younger adults. Are the response inhibition tendencies of the old so much greater than those of the young that they can account for poorer cognitive performance?

Cautiousness

The Omission Error. Autonomic responsivity, arousal or anxiety, may relate to a type of error older people make. It was said earlier that Canestrari and others found that when older people make errors in such tasks as paired-associate learning, the errors tend to be those of not responding rather than of responding incorrectly. Errors of omission along with what seem to be related types of behavior had been highlighted in chapters 8 and 9 in the context of cautiousness or the fear of being wrong.

Leech and Witte (1971) capitalized on this tendency to develop an important study. The typical teaching pattern is to reward correct responses and not wrong ones. Animal trainers, parents, teachers, and others know this and try to do this. Leech and Witte however, reasoned that if the elderly do not respond—if they make the omission error—for fear of being wrong or otherwise, then it would be hard for them to learn. Unless responses are committed, learning tends to be poor.

Accordingly, all responses made by the older subjects were rewarded, right or wrong. But, the correct responses were given greater reward than the wrong ones. In the face of all learning theories, the results showed that the old subjects getting rewards for both correct and incorrect responses learned quicker and better than those subjects who were rewarded in the traditional way only for correct responses. These data showed that what may seem like a learning deficit on the part of the elderly may not be that at all. It may be a response or performance characteristic limiting the expression of what is learned.

These results need to be repeated because the concept is so important. It is worth noting that Taub (1967) attempted to reduce the omission error by instructing the subjects to respond to every item. This was not successful; omission errors continued at about the same rate as with those elderly who had no such instruction. The monetary incentive of Leech and Witte seems to be the difference.

Response Bias in Learning and Memory. Chapter 9 discussed hearing tests and indicated that signal detection analyses disclosed that elderly people often are cautious in reporting the presence of barely audible sounds. Similar analyses have been applied to learning-memory tests where the subject indicates whether a word or another item of information that he is now shown is one among those in a list he had previously learned. Saying "yes," that it is one previously learned, is thought comparable to saying "yes, I hear the sound"; the subject, however, may be right or not in either instance. The hearing test data would suggest a disinclination on the part of the older person to say "yes" when in fact he had learned the word, but the results suggest otherwise, or perhaps more correctly, suggest a complexity of relations.

In one study adults of two different ages were asked to identify both words they had recently learned and historical facts they had learned long ago (Perlmutter, 1978). No difference with age in response bias was observed, i.e., the age groups were similar in their inclination to say "yes." A similar result was found by Gordon and Clark (1974a) whose subjects learned the content of a paragraph of prose. Thus, in a variety of learning-memory situations, response bias was not seen as characteristic of the elderly. As indicated, however, the results are more complex. The latter investigators carried out another study where a list of meaningful words had to be learned and also a list of nonsense syllables (Gordon and Clark, 1974b). The learning lists and tests of recognition of these words that followed were given twice, designated as trial 1 and trial 2.

On trial 1, the older group had higher response bias scores with the meaningful words—they were more cautious in saying "yes, I learned that word before." However, with the nonsense syllables, they were less cautious. No differences in response bias were seen in trial 2.

It may be concluded from this that "The elderly do not, as has been suggested, invariably set a high or cautious criterion . . ." (Gordon and Clark, 1974b, p. 665). Thus, it seems, the data of learning-memory studies and of hearing studies appear different. It may also be concluded that what age-related differences are observed in response bias in learning-memory studies are not a factor in learning-memory performances. The young performed better than the old with both nonsense and meaningful material even when the age-related response bias was opposite for each of these.

TASK MEANINGFULNESS

It was seen how speed of response factors and motivational factors are related to performance decrements in later life. Another factor, the meaningfulness of the task, may similarly be related; the general conception being that, since many of these laboratory procedures are not relevant to the personal needs of the subjects, they do not bring out the best performances of older people.

Personal Relevance and Task Difficulty

The opinion that older people are disadvantaged when the laboratory task is not relevant is not unlike the common opinions regarding motivation, i.e., old people are presumed to be less involved than younger adults with the laboratory task. It was just seen that data are available to indicate just the opposite—elderly adults may be more involved than younger adults.

The tie between involvement in the task and the meaningfulness of the task was seen in at least three studies. Two of these do not involve learning, but the third does. The two studies not of learning serve to point out that autonomic arousal as measured by FFA determination, for example, and suppressed by the drug, Propranolol, discussed previously, may not be the same as "involvement in laboratory situations" which are meaningful and relevant to the subject. It would seem that in the case of autonomic arousal the personal involvement is general and undifferentiated; in the case of relevant material, the personal involvement is specific to the task at hand.

In the first of the two studies, Shmavonian and Busse (1963) measured galvanic skin responses (GSRs) which were spontaneously emitted in the context of various types of stimulation. These GSRs, like the FFAs, were thought to be reflective of states of arousal on the part of the subject. Older men (60-70 years) emitted fewer of these GSRs than younger men (20-24 years) and were thus thought to be less involved in the laboratory situation, not more. This age comparison, however, was made with stimuli of simple tones; when the same comparison was made with meaningful spoken phrases, the differences between age groups in the GSRs were much diminished, although they did not disappear altogether. The implication was that the older people were disproportionately less involved in the laboratory task when it was less meaningful to them.

The second study will be discussed very briefly because it was reviewed in detail in the previous chapter dealing with problem solving and concept formation. Arenberg (1968) presented tasks that required the identification of concepts by logical analysis. Arenberg provided information based upon the abstract dimensions of color, form, and number, with the intent of monitoring the pattern of solution strategies. He found that the older subjects had so much difficulty with this task that many could not even understand what was required. When, however, Arenberg translated the abstract information to concrete meaningful terms ("poisoned foods" in this case) his results were very different.

The old subjects could understand what to do and solved many of the problems, although their overall performances were not at the same level as those of the young subjects.

A more direct example of "task involvement" was reported by Hulicka (1967). She attempted to teach a paired-associate task in which response words such as INSANE, were paired with stimulus letters such as TL. Hulicka reported that the attrition rate of elderly subjects (65-80 years) reached 80 percent. "Many refused . . . to exert themselves to learn 'such nonsense,' and others complained they could not read the small print . . ." (Hulicka, 1967, p. 181). The older subjects found the task very difficult.

Accordingly, Hulicka changed the task and made it more meaningful. Instead of letters such as TL, the stimulus components were occupations, such as BANKER. Surnames of four or five letters were the response associates, as, for example, MILL and SLOAN. When the task was so changed, the older people carried it out readily. As in the poison-food study by Arenberg, however, the performances of the older subjects were not as good as those of the younger controls.

One aspect of Hulicka's report needs to be emphasized—an aspect which is implicit in all considerations of stimulus meaningfulness. By changing the task from paired associates such as TL-INSANE to BANKER-SLOAN, the task was not only made more meaningful or relevant, it was also made easier. It was made easier for both young and old; it is possible that what Hulicka reported was simply that difficult tasks more readily distinguish between the performances of the young and the old than do easy tasks. The goal, therefore, in comparing tasks of different meaningfulness or personal relevance is to do this while keeping constant their levels of difficulty. Recognizing that it may not be possible to accomplish this completely because personal relevance, in part, defines task difficulty, a study described shortly (Wittels, 1972) demonstrates that an approximation in achieving this goal is possible.

Familiarity of the Task

The relevance or meaningfulness a task has for the individual is not identical to the familiarity of the task, but it is related to it. While there are very few studies relating to meaningfulness or relevance, there is a growing literature on task familiarity.

Strength of the Paired Associates. Some words go together more than others; for example, TABLE goes with CHAIR more than it does with GLOVE. The associative strength of TABLE-CHAIR is said to be higher than that of TABLE-GLOVE; it is more familiar than TABLE-GLOVE. In this sense, it may be said, the higher the strength of the paired associates in the list, the more familiar, perhaps meaningful, the list.

Several studies compared older and young adult subjects in their ability to learn lists varied with respect to their associative strength (Canestrari, 1966; Kausler and Lair, 1966; Zaretsky and Halberstam, 1968). In each of these studies, the older people were relatively disadvantaged with the lower association-strength pairs. One study varied the associations in three levels with adults of wide age range (Botwinick and Storandt, 1974). No difference among the age groups was seen in learning the high association pairs (e.g., ocean-water), decline was seen beginning in the 40s with the medium pairs (e.g., table-music), and steeper decline with the least meaningful associates (e.g., RW-sugar).

The implication of these results is that the unfamiliar, "meaningless" tasks often used in laboratory investigations may well be an explanation of poor performance levels of older people. However, it will be seen next that task familiarity defined in other ways does not support this proposition.

Generational Differences. Wittels (1972) hypothesized that even meaningful stimuli are not necessarily equally meaningful for old and young, especially if the stimuli are verbal materials. Meanings of words change over time and thus have different generational connotations and usages. She hypothesized further that the difficulty older people have in paired-associate learning performance is due, in part, to the fact that the stimulus materials, often verbal in nature, may be more meaningful for the young than for the old. The typical stimulus materials are developed by young adults for young adults.

Wittels devised three types of tests of paired associates: one list type was unique to the individual, irrespective of age; another list type was designed to be familiar or appropriate to subjects of their own generation; a third list type was designed to be appropriate to subjects of a generation different from their own. She devised these lists in the following way. Each person in two age groups was asked to provide ten of his own response associates to each of 15 meaningful stimulus words. The fifth response associate to each of the 15 stimulus words was singled out and used as the paired associate to that stimulus word. In this way a list was derived, different for each person, which had stimulus words in common to other lists but response associates unique to the responder. The assumption in using this personal list was that, while different from person to person, the lists were the same for all responders in regard to their familiarity (strength of the associations—all paired associates involved the fifth response associate of the individual responder).

This type of list was called the *personal list.* It was given not only to the person for whom it was devised, but it was also given to a different person of the same age, i.e., of the same generation, one who would be expected to share a more common language system than a person of a different generation. When the personal lists were given to people of the same age, they were called the *generational list*.

When the personal lists were given to people of a different generation, they were called the *cross-generational list*. Giving a list based upon the responses of people in one generation to people of a different generation was assumed to provide a context of a relatively unfamiliar language system, a context of less stimulus familiarity because of generational differences.

Wittels' hypothesis was that elderly people would perform relatively well with the generational list and disproportionately poorer on the cross-generational list. It was expected that they would do best with the personal list. This hypothesis was not confirmed—elderly subjects (60-82 years) performed more poorly than younger subjects (18-24 years) with each of the three lists. The implication is that task familiarity as Wittels explored this dimension, was not an explanation of the poor performances of the elderly in paired-associate learning.

Senseless and Senseful Stimuli. While Wittels reported no effect of task familiarity with respect to the differences in performance of old and young learners, Heron and Craik (1964) did find some evidence of a difference—but in an opposite direction: The old were seen disadvantaged by familiar material!

Heron and Craik tested English subjects in digit span, but the digits were presented in the Finnish language. (Each subject was given a list of digits in serial order and tested for the maximum number of digits that could be repeated correctly.) In this way, the English subjects were tested for the recall of auditory stimuli which to them were equivalent to nonsense stimuli. Young adults (20–35 years) and adults in their 60s were matched such that, on the average, both age groups repeated correctly 3.6 Finnish digits. These matched subjects were then given an English digit span test (senseful stimuli) and the two age groups were compared. The younger group repeated correctly 8.3 digits on the average, and the older group repeated only 6.8 digits.

These results were attributed to a reduced efficiency with age in a "coding" process, i.e., in the ability to organize incoming information, with semantic memory suffering more than episodic memory. Meaningful material can more easily be organized than nonsense material and, thus, any deficiency in the organizing process would be more apparent with senseful than with senseless stimuli.

Corroboration of this analysis was seen in a later study by Craik and Masani (1967). Three types of verbal material were presented to people ranging in age from 20 to 79 years. The first was meaningful sentences, the second was color names, and the third was proverbs with the word order scrambled. It was assumed that in the case of meaningful sentences, the material was amenable to organization, and in the case of scrambled proverbs it could also be organized but with a different system; but in the case of color names, they "merely had to be stored in relatively uncoded (unorganized) form." The hypothesis, therefore, was that aged subjects, as compared to younger ones, would show less ability with the meaningful and scrambled words (semantic memory), but do relatively well with the color names (episodic memory). This hypothesis was borne out by the results.

In a second experiment, Craik and Masani varied task meaningfulness by manipulating "the degree of contextual constraint between words." They presented five lists of words to be learned, each list different in its approximation to standard English. List 1 was of words randomly chosen; list 5 was of meaningful text, and lists 2, 3, and 4 were in between. The prediction was that aged people will be relatively disadvantaged as the list becomes more meaningful (list 5). While both young and old performed better with the meaningful lists than with meaningless ones, the difference between age groups was largest with the meaningful material. Further analysis, however, showed that this result was seen mostly with people of less than superior verbal facility. They had difficulty in semantic memory.

Taken all together, these studies give credence to the notion that, to the extent that material is meaningful and can be organized for learning and retention, the older person (while doing better than with nonsense material) will show up less well than younger persons. As seen here and as will be seen in the next chapter, this appears especially true for older people of lower level verbal facility. However, also seen here was quite an opposite role for task meaningfulness in relation to adult aging. When meaningfulness is defined in terms of associative strength and in terms of personal relevance, older people do relatively well. The role of task meaningfulness, therefore, is seen as multidimensional and complex, and generalizations in regard to aging must be referred to the specific situation or class of situations. Perhaps it must be specific to the extent that the information to be learned can be processed.

SUMMARY

A necessary distinction is made between learning and performance. The disctinction is based upon a cognitive ability in the case of learning and an ability to express what is known in the case of performance. There is little disagreement regarding performance decrements in later life, but there is disagreement whether there is decline with age in learning ability.

It is in the context of verbal learning studies in which there is quick stimulus pacing that the argument for performance deficits in later life, rather than learning deficits, receives its greatest support. The research strategy has been to vary both the amount of time the stimulus is available for study and the amount of time that is available for response. The general finding is that elderly people need more time for responding than typically is provided; they are disadvantaged when this time is not available. When sufficient time for response is available, the performance of elderly people is only slightly inferior, or not inferior at all, to that of young people. The controversy of whether or not learning ability decreases in later life remains unsettled, however, largely on the basis of some data which show that, given a long period of time for response but a rushed period for studying the material, older people perform relatively poorly. The implication is that it takes longer for older people to learn material than it does for younger people.

Just as the speed with which an older person can respond limits his ability to demonstrate what he has learned, but in itself is not regarded as a cognitive factor, so is it with motivation. Motivation in learning is important, but it is a factor apart from learning ability. It is often presumed that older people are less motivated than younger people to perform well in laboratory situations where there is little that is meaningful to them. Such a lack of motivation could explain performance deficits in later life.

Actually, there are more data which argue an opposite position than there are data which support this belief; the definition of motivation is important here. One definition includes a general involvement in the laboratory situation. The more aroused a person is psychophysiologically, the more involved he is thought to be. Studies of arousal states suggest that older people are often inappropriately and overly aroused, and their performances suffer accordingly. When these arousal states are reduced by drugs or by adaptation to the laboratory situation, their performances have been seen to improve.

Older people also seem to be reluctant to respond if they think they may be wrong—they make the omission error. This reluctance can make them appear poor in learning when it is not so. One study showed that by rewarding all responses, right or wrong, and thus discouraging the omission error, the elderly improved their learning rates.

When motivation is defined, not in terms of a general arousal state or a reluctance to respond, but in terms of a specific interest in the given task, the role of motivation in later life is less clear. The meaningfulness of the task is a factor in this type of motivation. The more meaningful the task, the more personally relevant, the higher the motivation is expected to be.

It is sometimes overlooked that laboratory investigations tend to involve highly abstract tasks which are not meaningful to older people. They may not even comprehend what is required. The tie between task meaningfulness and motivation was seen, for example, in a study in which many of the older subjects simply refused to exert themselves to learn the "irrelevant" experimental task.

The more meaningful tasks tend to be the more familiar ones. In paired-associate learning tasks, the more familiar the pairings (the greater the association strength), the more it is to the advantage of the older learner. However, when the task involves learning information which is presented one item at a time as, for example, learning a list of several different digits, familiarity does not work to the relative advantage of older people. In fact, it has been seen to work in the opposite direction. The important factor here seems to be the ability to organize the incoming information. Words, for example, can be organized into sentences, making them easier to learn. Several studies suggest that elderly people, compared to younger ones, are poor in such organizing, and thus, while they perform better on some types of meaningful and familiar tasks than on strange nonsense tasks, they often show up relatively poorly on meaningful tasks requiring organization.

Taken altogether, the learning studies reviewed here point to a variety of conclusions regarding the learning versus performance controversy as it involves aging processes. It is not until the issues of motivation and task meaningfulness are defined with greater specificity than heretofore that resolution of these conclusions will be reached. Perhaps the concept of semantic processing will be found useful in this regard.

REFERENCES

Arenberg, D. Anticipation interval and age differences in verbal learning. *Journal of Abnormal Psychology*, 1965, 70, 419–425.

Arenberg, D. Concept problem solving in young and old adults. *Journal of Gerontology*, 1968, 23, 279–282.

Botwinick, J. and Storandt, M. *Memory, related functions and age*. Springfield, Ill.: Charles C Thomas, 1974.

Canestrari, R.E., Jr. Paced and self-paced learning in young and elderly adults. *Journal of Gerontology*, 1963, 18, 165–168.

Canestrari, R.E., Jr. The effects of commonality on paired associate learning in two age groups. *Journal of Genetic Psychology*, 1966, 108, 3–7.

Craik, F.I.M. Age differences in human memory. In J.E. Birren and K.W. Schaie (Eds.), *Handbook of the psychology of aging*. New York: Van Nostrand Reinhold, 1977.

Craik, F.I.M., and Masani, P.A. Age differences in the temporal integration of language. *British Journal of Psychology*, 1967, 58, 291–299.

Eisdorfer, C. Verbal learning and response time in the aged. *Journal of Genetic Psychology*, 1965, 107, 15–22.

Eisdorfer, C. Arousal and performance: experiments in verbal learning and a tentative theory. In G.A. Talland (Ed.), *Human aging and behavior*. New York: Academic Press, 1968, pp. 189–216.

Eisdorfer, C., Axelrod, S., and Wilkie, F. Stimulus exposure time as a factor in serial learning in an aged sample. *Journal of Abnormal and Social Psychology*, 1963, 67, 594–600.

Eisdorfer, C., Nowlin, J., and Wilkie, F. Improvement of learning in the aged by modification of autonomic nervous system activity. *Science*, 1970, 170, 1327–1329.

Furchgott, E. and Busemeyer, J.K. Heart rate and skin conductance during cognitive processes as a function of age. Presented at the 29th Annual Meeting of the Gerontological Society, New York, October 1976.

Gilbert, J.G. Memory loss in senescence. *Journal of Abnormal and Social Psychology*, 1941, 36, 73–86.

Gordon, S.K., and Clark, C. Application of signal detection theory to prose recall and recognition in the elderly and young adults. *Journal of Gerontology*, 1974(a), 29, 64–72.

Gordon, S.K., and Clark, C. Adult age differences in word and nonsense syllable recognition memory and response criterion. *Journal of Gerontology*, 1974(b), 29, 659–665.

Heron, A., and Craik, F.I.M. Age differences in cumulative learning of meaningful and meaningless material. *Scandinavian Journal of Psychology*, 1964, 5, 209–217.

Hulicka, I.M. Age differences in retention as a function of interference. *Journal of Gerontology*, 1967, 22, 180–184.

Kausler, D.H., and Lair, C.V. Associative strength and paired-associate learning in elderly subjects. *Journal of Gerontology*, 1966, 21, 278–280.

Kinsbourne, M., and Berryhill, J.L. The nature of interaction between pacing and the age decrement in learning. *Journal of Gerontology*, 1972, 27, 471–477.

Leech, S., and Witte, K.L. Paired-associate learning in elderly adults as related to pacing and incentive conditions. *Developmental Psychology*, 1971, 5, 180.

Monge, R.H., and Hultsch, D. Paired-associate learning as a function of adult age and the length of the anticipation and inspection intervals. *Journal of Gerontology*, 1971, 26, 157–162.

Perlmutter, M. What is memory aging the aging of? *Developmental Psychology*, 1978, in press.

Powell, A.H., Jr., Eisdorfer, C., and Bogdonoff, M.D. Physiologic response patterns observed in a learning task. *Archives of General Psychiatry*, 1964, 10, 192–195.

Shmavonian, B.M., and Busse, E.W. The utilization of psychophysiological techniques in the study of the aged. In R.H. Williams, C. Tibbetts, and Wilma Donahue (Eds.), *Process of aging—social and psychological perspectives*. New York: Atherton Press, 1963, pp. 235–258.

Taub, H.A. Visual short-term memory as a function of age, rate of presentation, and schedule of presentation. *Journal of Gerontology*, 1966, 21, 388–391.

Taub, H.A. Paired associates learning as a function of age, rate, and instructions. *Journal of Genetic Psychology*, 1967, 111, 41–46.

Taub, H.A. Age differences in memory as a function of rate of presentation, order of report, and stimulus organization. *Journal of Gerontology*, 1968, 23, 159–164.

Tulving, E. Episodic and semantic memory. In E. Tulving and W. Donaldson (Eds.), *Organization of memory*. New York: Academic Press, 1972.

Winn, F.J., and Elias, J.W. The total time principle as a substitute for the pacing variable in paired-associate tasks with the aged. *Experimental Aging Research*, 1975, 1, 307–312.

Wittels, I. Age and stimulus meaningfulness in paired-associate learning. *Journal of Gerontology*, 1972, 27, 372–375.

Zaretsky, H.H., and Halberstam, J.L. Age differences in paired-associate learning. *Journal of Gerontology*, 1968, 23, 165–168.

16

Aids and Types of Learning

It was said at the very beginning of the previous chapter that learning and memory are operationally indistinguishable but that a distinction is made nevertheless because it is convenient to do so. It is made on the basis of how much organization is involved in processing the information, i.e., on how much meaning is derived from the material to be learned. An example was given of the word "table." It will long be remembered what the word means, what categories of events or items relate to it (semantic memory), but remembering whether it was one of the words in a list recently seen (episodic memory) is not long-term. The present chapter focuses on how to process information or fix memories for longer-term recall. Thus, the present chapter continues with the mainly episodic studies of the previous chapter and emphasizes how to shift from episodic to semantic memory.

It was seen in the previous chapter that, in typical laboratory studies of learning, elderly people perform less well than do younger people. It was also seen that the experimenter could help the older person to perform better by doing several things: he could slow the pacing of the experimental events; he could reduce, when indicated, the subject's level of autonomic arousal; and he could present more relevant and meaningful tasks.

The present chapter focuses on additional factors which aid the elderly in their performances. The discussion then continues with a description of studies that demonstrate the large variety of learning situations that show age trends from which important inferences may be drawn.

AIDS IN RECALL: ORGANIZATION OF INFORMATION

The concept of organization is a broad one, which covers a variety of techniques from categorizing information in both intentional and incidental ways, to associating or integrating the learned information with what is already well known, to simple noting of the information in special and varied ways.

Categorization

Differential Benefits for the Elderly. The studies of Heron and Craik (1964) and of Craik and Masani (1964), described in the previous chapter, indicate that elderly adults are disadvantaged relative to younger ones when a learning task is amenable to organization. As the units of information within a task can be integrated into larger units, the task becomes easier to learn, but elderly people are not always able to take advantage of this. It was hypothesized, therefore, that older people do not organize incoming information very well, and this makes for their relative disadvantage.

Hultsch (1969) sought to investigate this hypothesis by providing instructions (cues) to categorize or organize the information that was to be learned. He presented subjects with a long list of words, each word presented one at a time. The lists were presented several times with the instruction after each complete presentation to write down as many of the words as had been learned, in any order desired. Subjects of three age groups were tested, but none were of the age that is typically referred to as "elderly" or "old." The three age groups were 16–19, 30–39, and 45–54 years.

Each of these three groups was divided into three subgroups. One subgroup of each age was given the task in standard fashion, i.e., the subjects were simply instructed to write down as many words as they could. A second subgroup was instructed to do this but advised to "try and organize your recalled words in some way . . . people who organize their words . . . do better." A third subgroup was instructed, "Organize your recalled words alphabetically . . . note their first letters, and make an attempt to associate the word with the letter" (Hultsch, 1969, pp. 674–675).

Hultsch found that with people of low verbal facility, the oldest age group and the middle age group were poorer than the youngest group with the first two types of instructions, i.e., the ones least helpful in organizing the material. However, when the instructions were most explicit in how to best organize the material, these age group differences were no longer seen. This confirmed the hypothesis that the aged who are poor performers are so partly because of poor approaches or efforts in organizing incoming information. When helped in these efforts, however, they show good ability to learn.

These results, however, were not all that were reported by Hultsch. The older people of high verbal facility were not benefited differentially by the instruction which provided aid in organization. Apparently, when highly verbal people reach older ages, they do not suffer in their efforts to organize information. These results are compatible with those of Craik and Masani (1967), discussed in the previous chapter.

A later study by Hultsch (1971) again pointed to the role of organization in learning. He tested subjects in three age groups, this time people in their 20s, 40s, and 60s. Half the people of each age were given a sorting task and half a different task, and then all were given a learning task. The sorting task provided information on how to organize the information in the learning task which followed, but the non-sorting task did not do this.

It may be seen in Figure 16.1 that, for each age group, the sorting task was helpful in the learning of the task which followed, but it became more helpful as age increased. It may be concluded from this that information on how to organize material for learning and recall is relatively more important for older people than for younger ones because younger people may develop such information on their own, without help from the experimenter.

This was seen in yet another study by Hultsch (1975) who presented 40 words for learning, four from each of 10 different categories. The

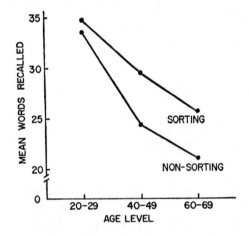

FIGURE 16.1: Mean number of words correctly learned and reported as a function of age. Prior to learning, one-half the subjects carried out a sorting task which was designed to be helpful in organizing word lists, and the other half of the subjects were involved in a non-sorting task. (Figure 1 from D. Hultsch, *Developmental Psychology*, 1971, 4, 338-342. Copyright 1971 by the American Psychological Association. Reprinted by permission.)

words were presented to men and women of three age groups, 18–34, 50–64, and 65–83 years. He asked half the people in each age group to recall the words after providing them with the category names. The other half were also asked to recall the words, but the categories were not provided. As in Figure 16.1, the oldest group benefited most from the category names; the names served to organize the information and served as cues in recall.

Differential Benefits for the Young. Thus, it seems the elderly can benefit from organizational strategies and, in some contexts, benefit more than the young when opportunity and direction are provided. While some studies show benefit to the elderly, not all show differential benefit that is to their advantage. For example, Taub (1968) did not observe differential benefits, and Walsh (1975, p. 146) found differential benefits in favor of the young. In a pilot study, Walsh provided various opportunities to organize or process the information and found that "the older were particularly poor at recall, as compared to the young when meaningful processing was required." The elderly performed better with such organizing cue instructions than otherwise but it was the young who benefited more.

Results similar to these were found by White (described in Craik, 1977). Instructions were varied in regard to opportunities for meaningful processing. Again, the older subjects benefited in recall from the more meaningful, "deeper" processing, but not as much as did the young. It is interesting to compare the results of Walsh and White with those of Craik and Masani (1967), discussed in the previous chapter. In the latter study, cues or instructions for organizing the information were not given; instead, information was varied in terms of their meaningfulness, i.e., in terms of their organization potential. The young, to a degree more than the old, were able to take advantage of the meaningful organization.

Spontaneous Organization. This suggests that the young spontaneously categorize or organize information and the old do not, or do not to as large an extent. This notion was substantiated in a study by Hultsch (1974). He tested subjects of wide age range, giving them two lists of words to learn. Each list was given in 10 study-and-test trials, thus permitting him to plot learning curves (improvement in learning-recall performances over 10 trials). Hultsch had two measures of organization that the subjects spontaneously applied to the items they learned. One measure was of order—how faithfully the subjects followed in their recall performances the order in which the words were presented. The second measure was also of order, but of a different kind. It assessed similarity of the order of recall of words in one trial (of the 10) in list 1 with that in the same trial of the second list. Hultsch found that with both measures, spontaneous "organization showed an overall age effect. As chronological age increases, less organization of material is exhibited" (Hultsch, 1974, p. 306).

Denney (1974) concluded in similar fashion. She presented two lists of words for learning to two age groups, 30–60 years and 70–90 years. One list had similar words in it (e.g., ocean and sea) and the other list had complementary words (e.g., music and piano). Denney's interest was to measure the amount of "clustering"—the amount of organization —i.e., the extent of recall of words from the same category consecutively.

Like Hultsch, Denney found that the younger subjects had more spontaneous organization in the recall; they clustered more than the older subjects. "In fact, not one of the elderly subjects clustered significantly . . ." (Denny, 1974, p. 474). In this study, learning ability was highly correlated with clustering.

As is so often the case, not all studies point in one direction. For example, Laurence (1966) did not find age differences in spontaneous organization, nor did Gordon (1975). The results of the former study can be explained by the use of a measure of organization that Hultsch (1974) claimed unduly penalized the organizational performances of the young. Gordon's results, based on meaningful sentences, could be explained on the basis that both the elderly and the young were highly educated and thus of high verbal facility. It will be recalled that Hultsch (1969) found that older people of high verbal ability were not benefited differentially by the instruction that provided aid in organization, only those of low facility were benefited. It was said that when highly verbal people reach older ages they do not seem to suffer in their efforts to organize information.

Studies on organization hold much promise; they have the virtue of being relatively translatable to practical daily-life affairs, and the translations need not require much time, effort, or cost.

Mediational Techniques

Closely related to organizational plans are a class of aids called mediational techniques. Organizational plans are designed to index and categorize, and mediational techniques are designed to highlight and associate. While a distinction is made on this basis, the two mnemonic devices are not always easily distinguished. Both are used to help in the acquisition and retention of new information.

A most instructive discussion of mediational techniques in relation to adult aging was provided by Canestrari (1968, pp. 173–185). He surveyed the literature and found evidence that excellent, really extraordinary, performances in paired-associate learning may be seen when subjects are told to "form a mental picture" to connect each word-pair associate. Such linkages or mediators may take the form of syntactical or verbal characteristics (e.g., sentences), or of visual imagery (such as the mental pictures).

Verbal and Visual Imagery. The data bearing on mediational techniques are not unlike much of the data on categorizing. Hulicka and Grossman (1967) reported that older people, unlike younger ones, do not tend to make use of such mediational techniques, unless instructed to do so. When instructed on these techniques, however, they improve considerably. In fact, when Hulicka and Grossman compared elderly people (mean age 74 years) with young ones (mean age 16 years) in paired-associate learning, they found the elderly improved more than the young when instructions in mediational techniques were given, although they did not reach the same level of performance. Hulicka and Grossman (1967, p. 50) believed that, "Part of the learning deficit observed in old . . . subjects . . . may be due to the failure to use mediational techniques spontaneously." Not all studies point to this (e.g., Bruning, Holzbauer, and Kimberlin, 1975; Nebes and Andrews-Kulis, 1970), but most do (e.g., Rowe and Schnore, 1971).

Perhaps the reason that older people do not use such techniques spontaneously is because they tend not to be very able in forming mediators and in integrating them with the material to be learned. As Canestrari suggested, older people—as judged from their performances on a variety of different types of tests—show an "associative impoverishment." Older people not only find it harder than do younger ones to form mediators, it takes them longer. It is not surprising, therefore, that they use them less often.

In the data of Hulicka and Grossman, there was a suggestion that when older people do use mediators, they tend to use verbal ones rather than visual imagery mediators. This was also seen in a more recent study by Whitbourne and Slevin (1978). Verbal mediators are often not as effective as visual image ones. Canestrari (1968) examined this suggestion by providing his subjects with both kinds of mediators. When he did this, he expected that the visual ones would help the older subjects more than would the verbal ones.

Canestrari gave subjects in two age groups (16–27 years and 50–73 years) a task of paired-associate words. Along with this learning task he presented the verbal and visual mediators. The two age groups were each divided into three subgroups. One subgroup of each age was given the paired-associate task in a standard way. A second subgroup of each age was provided, along with the word pairs, a visual mediator of a sketch drawing that illustrated both words of the pair. A third subgroup of each age was provided with a verbal mediator for each word pair—a short phrase that contained both words of the pair, e.g., "a short box" (the last two words being the paired associates). In the presentation of the paired-associate list, the mediators were used only when the word pairs were presented, not when the stimulus word was presented alone with the response word to be supplied by the subject.

The results of this study may be seen in Figure 16.2; they were very clear. The old benefited greatly from the mediators, and the young were benefited hardly at all. The young subjects made very few errors in the course of learning, irrespective of the experimental variation. Perhaps the list was too easy for them, perhaps they supplied their own mediators. The older subjects, however, made almost twice the errors in the standard condition as they made in the conditions in which mediators were used. Contrary to expectation, the two types of mediators, verbal and visual, were very similar in their effectiveness for the older subjects.

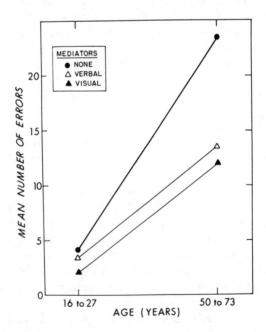

FIGURE 16.2: Mean number of errors made in learning paired associates as a function of age. The task was learned in a standard way, with verbal mediators and with visual mediators. (Data from Figure 1 of Canestrari, 1968.)

Again, despite the aid that the mediators provided the older subjects, they performed more poorly than did the young ones in all conditions.

Further analysis suggested that the elderly subjects were aided by the mediators in their errors of omission, not commission. Among the interpretations that Canestrari offered was that if the error of omission reflects a cautiousness such that the older persons will not make a response unless confident of its correctness, the mediators might have raised their levels of confidence.

Canestrari's oldest subjects were aged 50 to 73 years. A study by Mason and Smith (1977) suggests that it may be the younger people in the age bracket who benefited most from mediation. They tested three age groups (20–39, 40–59, and 60–80) for free recall of words in a list, and only the middle-aged benefited from instructions to use visual imagery. The investigators conjectured that the young use mediators spontaneously, while the old are less willing or less able to do so. Mediation instruction may well be most useful for the middle-aged.

A study by Treat and Reese (1974) suggested that instructions to use mediators may be as helpful, or even more helpful, to the elderly as providing the mediators for them. They tested two groups of people, one aged about 30 and the other about 70 years. There were three subgroups of each age: One had to learn paired-associates with no instruction regarding mediators; another group was told to generate their own image-mediators; and a third group was given the mediators for learning. Unlike Canestrari, it was seen that both the young and the old benefited from instruction. The older subjects benefited from their own image-mediators, not those provided by the experimenter. In this study, stimulus pacing schedules were varied (see chapter 15). The self-generated imagery was useful in learning by the elderly when there was a sufficiently long period of time allowed for response, not when the pacing schedule was very rapid.

For other details regarding mediation, the review by Elias, Elias, and Elias (1977, chapters 8 and 9) is recommended.

The Method of Loci. Entertainers on the stage have been seen to demonstrate great feats of memory. They have been seen to call for a long list of items and later repeat these items perfectly and in the order they were brought up. One of the techniques the entertainers use is called "the method of loci," a technique known to the ancient Greeks. This technique was used by Robertson-Tchabo, Hausman, and Arenberg (1976) in studying older people.

They carried out two studies, both with similar results. First, people mostly in their 60s and 70s were given a list of 16 nouns to learn and remember in any order they chose. Their performances were recorded.

Next, they were asked to picture in their minds the interior of their homes and take an imaginary walk through them, stopping at 16 places —places such as the entrance foyer, rooms, furniture, or anything else in the rooms. The only rule was that these locations must be sites that would be reached in succession on their imaginary walk.

When this progression of loci was well rehearsed and fixed in mind, the subjects associated each of 16 noun-words with each of the 16 loci. The subjects were asked to picture the word and the stopping places together, "for example, an 'alligator' in the 'entrance hall.' " The word could be pictured in any way, even silly ways, just so long as it was pictured with the site. Rehearsal of sites and associated noun-words was carried out in each of three days, with a test of the noun-list following. The elderly subjects recalled more of the 16 words after their "walks" through their homes than they had at first without the aid of the method of loci. Further, they recalled more than a control group who had not been taught by the method of loci.

On the day following, when tests were again made, it was found that the subjects did not resort to this mnemonic, unless instructed to do so. Thus it seems the method of loci can be helpful to the aged, but it is not one that is used by them spontaneously.

Note Writing

Mediation techniques hold much promise, as do the organizational plans. They help in integrating material so that it can more easily be managed. The common technique of note writing is also very helpful in integrating material, and it is most useful in lightening the burden of recall. It would seem that writing notes for oneself would be a natural aid that older people would use frequently, simply because it is so easy, so obvious, and helpful. This does not appear to be the case. While note writing has not been investigated systematically, there are data showing that as useful as this aid could be, older people as a group either do not or cannot take advantage of it.

There appear to be only three specific, even though brief, references to note writing; many more studies would be useful. These references were discussed in the chapter on problem solving. The first was by Welford (1958, pp. 205–209) who reported that good performance was correlated with note writing as self-aids. Both performance levels and frequency of note writing were seen to decrease with age. The second reference was by Jerome (1962). He tried to teach and encourage his subjects to take notes, to write them down. He found that younger subjects found notes helpful, but the older subjects did not. The older subjects could not make use of their notes and, moreover, saw no reason for writing them. When they did write notes, often they were indecipherable, even to themselves. Young (1966), the third reference, followed up Jerome's study with similar results.

How universal is this finding? What factors underlie it? What methods would succeed in teaching older people to avail themselves of so simple yet so effective a technique? This brief section is more for the purpose of emphasizing an important and potentially fruitful area of investigation than it is for describing an area of research accomplishment. As indicated, there has been very little done to investigate this very available self-aid.

Supportive and Challenging Contexts

An overlooked but important study supports the contention of many professionals whose work centers around older people: "The increasing insecurity and susceptibility to stress of aging individuals become particularly evident when they are placed in an evaluative situation and told that their performance will be compared with that of others" (Ross, 1968, p. 265).

Three types of instructions were given to subjects in a paired-associate learning study. One was a "neutral" instruction, one a "supportive" instruction, and one "challenging." These instructions were given with each of two paired-associate lists, one of easy (high association strength) pairs and one of more difficult (low association strength) pairs. The lists and instructions were given to people in two age groups (18–26 years and 65-75 years) so that one subgroup of each age was given one of the three types of instruction.

The neutral instruction was typical of that used in most paired-associate studies, i.e., "I am going to show to you and read to you a list of words, two at a time. When I finish reading the two words that go together, I am going to say one word of each pair and ask you to tell me the word that went with it." The supportive instruction included, "I need your help with a research project . . . I am interested in finding out something about the characteristics of words. Your performance is *not* my main concern." The challenging instruction included, "The ability to learn this material is a good test of your intelligence. . . . It's to your advantage, then, to do your best . . ." (Ross, 1968, p. 263).

One-half hour following the learning procedure, the task was given again and relearning was measured, but it was the results of the initial learning of the list of difficult associations that were the most impressive. The results, shown in Figure 16.3, demonstrated the importance of the emotional context that the experimenter establishes; this figure shows the effects of the different instructions in relation to age. With the challenging instructions, the older subjects required approximately one-third more trials to learn the paired associates than with the other instructions. The performances of the older people were clearly best in the supportive situation and worst in the challenging one. As with the use of mediators in Canestrari's study (Figure 16.2), the performances of the young were good throughout. They were not at all influenced by whether the context was supportive or challenging.

In view of these results, it is surprising that the effects of instructions were not apparent in the relearning of the lists. Neither was the variation in instruction statistically significant with the easy paired associates, although the trend was the same as with the difficult ones. Perhaps the easy lists were too easy to show the effect, as judged by the very good scores made by both age groups. The implication of this study, then, is

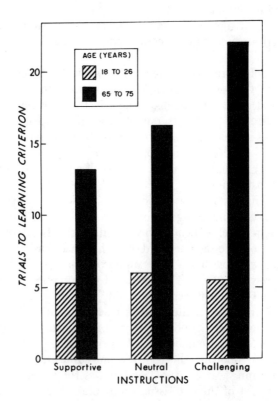

FIGURE 16.3: Mean number of trials taken to learn a paired-associate task in relation to three types of instructions. (Data from Table 1 of Ross, 1968.)

that with difficult materials, at least, supportive contexts can aid, and challenging contexts can harm, the performances of the elderly. However, this effect may be only short-term. The immediate negative response to evaluative situations may indeed be the result of "insecurity and susceptibility to stress of aging individuals."

No other studies of this type of learning in relation to context have been reported; however, two studies of psychomotor learning have been. Psychomotor studies involve speeded response, which typically improves with practice—these two studies sought to see what happens to the rate of improvement when there is support or when there is challenge to the subject.

The results of the study by Lair and Moon (1972) were similar to those of Ross in that elderly adults showed decrement with reproof instructions. They showed gains with praise, but this was not sustained. Bellucci and Hoyer (1975) did not have reproof or challenging conditions but they compared a condition of praise ("non-contingent positive feedback") with a neutral (control) condition. Both old and young benefited from the praise, but the old did so more than the young.

These studies together suggest that the elderly in particular learn poorly with reproof or challenges to their self-worth. They seem to benefit from praise but this may not be long-lasting.

Sensory Mode and Augmentation

Arenberg (1968) sought to determine whether an active role by the respondent when learning simple information would be especially advantageous to older people. He had older men (60-86 years) and younger men (17-22 years) learn four digits, with each of three methods. One method simply involved a viewing of the visual information that was to be learned (visual only). A second method had the subjects view the information, but, in addition, the experimenter read each digit aloud as it appeared (visual with passive auditory augmentation). The third method also included the viewing, but it also had the subjects themselves say each digit aloud as it appeared (visual with active auditory augmentation).

Arenberg found that the age decrement in learning and recalling the four digits was decreased substantially with either of the two conditions of auditory augmentation. While the young subjects were aided by this condition too, the old were aided more. The active auditory role of the respondent was seen as superior to the passive auditory role in the learning of visual information, but not more for one age group than the other.

While it is clear that Arenberg was able to improve performances by passive and active auditory augmentation, it is not clear whether it was the auditory input, irrespective of the visual one, that improved performances: A study by McGhie, Chapman, and Lawson (1965) suggests that auditory stimulation alone would make for better performances of the elderly than would visual information alone. However, it may be incorrectly limiting to suggest that one type of input is better than another type; it seems to depend on the nature of the information learned. Arenberg (1976) demonstrated this in a later study. A distinction is made between primary and secondary memory and this distinction is discussed in some detail in the next chapter. Here, it need be recognized only that these two types of memory are thought to be of different duration and to result from different memory processes. Arenberg used a measure of each of these types of memory to determine whether stimulus mode and augmentation affects them in the same way.

He presented 16 words for learning to men aged 17-19 and 60-70 years. It is well known that the words presented both at the beginning and at the end of the list are remembered better than those presented in the middle. The words presented at the end of the list are thought to be recalled from primary memory and the words from the beginning recalled from secondary. Arenberg had three conditions of learning: (1) The subjects were instructed to say each word aloud as it appeared on a screen (this was called the "Say" condition). (2) In another condition, the experimenter said each word aloud as the subject listened ("Listen" condition). (3) The "Look" condition was where the subjects viewed the words but did so silently. Thus, there was an active auditory condition ("Say"), a passive auditory ("Listen") and a visual-only ("Look").

Arenberg found, as he did before, that the old, as well as the young, benefited in recall from the auditory presentations. But, this was only true of the words at the end of the list (primary memory). Just the opposite was true for the words beginning the list—"Say" was inferior to "Listen," and both were inferior to "Look." Visual only was the best stimulus presentation for recall of secondary memory and, basically, this was found only with the older subjects. Thus, for information that requires organization for longer-term storage, auditory implementation may detract, particularly with older adults.

Results in partial agreement with this were seen in a study by Taub (1975). He presented two types of information to women of three age groups. Women aged 19–31, 41–60, and 61–78 were given passages of meaningful prose to learn and they were also given unrelated digits. Prose requires meaningful organization for secondary memory storage while the digits are not processed in the same way. They are stored largely in primary memory.

Half the subjects of each age group read the prose passages silently to themselves and viewed the digits. The other half listened to the experimenter who read the passages to them and called out the digits. Thus, there was a visual and an auditory presentation of both meaningful prose and unrelated digits.

Taub found that silent reading (visual) made for better recall than did the experimenter reading (auditory). Thus, it was seen that visual input was better for this secondary memory. But, just the reverse was true for digits—the auditory input was better for primary memory. This is in agreement with Arenberg, except that Taub found this so for all age groups, not more for one than for the other.

Taub (1976) followed up this study with another one, inquiring whether reading silently was better for recall then reading aloud (i.e., visual versus visual plus auditory). Women aged 21–36 were compared to women aged 60–80 in both these types of reading. While recall scores were higher for the young than for the old, both types of reading were equally good for both age groups.

Summing up all these studies, it would seem that auditory input, or auditory augmentation of visual stimuli, helps only in the fleeting, short-term recall of primary memory. Moreover, it may help the aged more than the young. On the other hand, auditory inputs can be deleterious to secondary memory, especially to the aged. At best, they do not seem to be helpful. In this summation, it must be recognized that future studies based on more varied learning material may alter these conclusions. Studies in sensory mode and sensory augmentation can prove useful in determining environmental dimensions most appropriate for older people.

Avoidance of Interference

Not so long ago, the most used and favorite explanatory concept psychologists had in the study of learning and memory was that of interference. People do not learn well, or do not retain what they have learned because other information or other response sequences intrude to disorganize the ongoing operations. Typically, in the laboratory, this is investigated as retroactive interference, or simply retroaction. A task is given, then an interfering event is provided, and then the task is given a second time. The decline in performance between the two testings is compared to a similar decline when no interfering event is provided. The greater decline in the former case is attributed to interference.

Much of the age-related performance deficits in laboratories have been attributed to susceptibility to interference effects. The evidence for this, however, has not always been unequivocal. First, many of the studies have not been carried out with appropriate controls. Second, and as important, the age groups have not always been comparable in their learning of the initial tasks. The greater the difference between old and young in the learning of the initial task, the greater may appear the age difference in their susceptibility to interference (e.g., Gladis and Braun, 1958). Third, the fast pacing typically used in laboratory studies, often inappropriately, maximizes interference effects of the elderly (Arenberg, 1967; Traxler and Britton, 1970).

Not only has the evidence been equivocal regarding interference and age, it has been challenged in a most emphatic way. For example, Craik (1977, p. 397) wrote, "However plausible that view may be [interference effects greater for old than young], it has not been supported by empirical studies carried out since 1958 and the view must be rejected." Further, "The general acceptance of the notion is a tribute to the powerful ascendancy of ideas over observations!" (p. 426).

This may be an overstatement; the literature does suggest that interference can explain forgetting and that for this reason, together with other factors, special problems for the elderly may develop. Moreover, some, but not all, of the literature does seem to point to greater interference effects on the part of the elderly. This is true especially if interference is also defined in ways other than by retroaction; for example, interference is inferred when doing two or more things simultaneously, or having two or more thoughts simultaneously, or being stimulated simultaneously by two or more discrepant events. Talland (1965) reported that older people suffer disproportionately when two such operations are involved. Similarly, Taub (1968) concluded that "rehearsing" of one event while recalling another one in "storage" was differentially deleterious to the elderly.

The prescription for the elderly is: Learn one item well before undertaking a second. Avoid, if possible, doing more than one thing at a time. If interfering phenomena must be met, a study by Christensen (1968) suggested that they be delayed as long as possible. She presented to people of a wide age range (18 to 70 years) a learning task and then, either immediately after learning or just prior to recall, she presented a similar task. The interference effect was greater when it was introduced immediately after the learning. It was as if interference immediately after learning partially blocked the consolidation of what had been learned. Christensen found that the recall performances of the older people were poorer than those of the younger people, presumably because they were more susceptible to interference; but the extent to which early interference was greater than later interference was similar for people of all ages. That is, while early interference had a greater effect than later interference, this was no more true for the old than for the young. Despite this latter finding, there is reason to believe that older people may require more time than younger people to consolidate what has been learned. It will be seen in the next chapter that in one animal study, at least, the time at which interfering material was presented had differential effects on young and old. However, whether or not this is the case with human subjects, Christensen's study showed clearly that the performances of the elderly were particularly poor with phenomena interfering soon after learning. Interference should be avoided or, if not possible to do so, delayed as long as possible after learning.

TYPES

Almost all that was discussed in this and in the previous chapter involved verbal learning only. Moreover, the discussion was mainly of the more recent verbal learning literature. There is a large, mainly older, literature bearing on many types of learning tasks. This latter literature has been summarized elsewhere (Botwinick, 1967) in greater detail than need be presented here. Here, only some of these studies will be highlighted, and some newer ones reported briefly, in order to demonstrate the large variety of learning situations in which important characteristics of aging may be inferred.

Conditioning

Conditioning is often considered to be a very simple and rudimentary type of learning. Actually, it is not as simple as it may first appear, although the concept underlying it is simple: through continued pairing of a neutral stimulus (CS) with a noxious or pleasant one (UCS) which by itself elicits a response (UR), the CS soon elicits a very similar response (CR). A very widely studied CR is the eyelid closure response (eyeblink). Braun and Geiselhart (1959) conditioned this CR by pairing an increase in the brightness of a disc (the CS) with a puff of air to the eye (UCS). Among the subjects they examined were men aged 18-25 years and 62-84 years.

Braun and Geiselhart found that it was more difficult to condition the elderly than the young adults, and it was easier to extinguish their responses. From these results Braun and Geiselhart (1959, p. 388) suggested that "in the course of many years of living, the eyelid response as well as probably other responses have been 'adapted out' and thus less susceptible to subsequent conditioning." Kimble and Pennypacker (1963), in a very similar study with similar results, tended to agree with this adaptation hypothesis but with some minor differences.

The data of these eyeblink conditioning studies point to reduced behavioral reactivity in advanced age. The data may also suggest a reduced level of neural arousal as well. A similar conclusion was seen in a study by Botwinick and Kornetsky (1960) in which the galvanic skin response (GSR) was measured. The GSR, like the measure of free fatty acids (FFA) of Powell et al. (1964), and Eisdorfer et al. (1970), discussed in the previous chapter, is believed to be an index of a general level of reactivity or arousal. The GSRs of elderly men (mean age, early 70s) and of young men (mean, 20 years) were conditioned and extinguished, using a tone CS paired with a mild shock UCS. Again, the elderly subjects conditioned less readily and extinguished more readily than the younger subjects. It was concluded that the older subjects were less reactive than the younger ones.*

Another type of conditioning is called operant conditioning. Here, responses are emitted, sometimes spontaneously, and they are made more likely to occur in the future by the reinforcement or reward conditions that the experimenter arranges. Goodrick (1975a) tested both aged and young mice and found that, unlike the classical CR data, the two groups were very similar in their learning rates. Also, unlike the classical conditioning studies, the older animals extinguished more slowly than the younger ones, not more readily.

---

* It is to be noted that these conclusions appear at variance with those based on FFA determinations (see previous chapter). Powell et al. (1964) and Eisdorfer et al. (1970) reported greater reactivity on the part of the elderly, not lesser. It is possible that the difference between the two opposing sets of conclusions is explainable only on the basis of the different measurements involved, i.e., FFA versus GSR. If so, this suggests that the generalization of the concept of arousal or activation is very limited indeed.

There is another explanation, however, and this one suggests a greater generalization of the concept. In the Powell et al. and in the Eisdorfer et al. FFA studies, the subject was jabbed with a needle in the forearm vein, which remained there throughout the experiment. The subject's job required effort and was meaningful—he had to learn a list of words. In the GSR study and in the eyelid closure studies, the subject was in a resting position and simply listened to tones while receiving mild shocks, or watched a light change and received air puffs to the eye. It is quite possible that the different experimental conditions of the two sets of studies made for differential patterns of arousal states in relation to age. The more meaningful stimuli and more noxious procedure of the FFA study differentially raised the arousal levels of the older people, while the less meaningful, less noxious task of the GSR study and the eye blink study differentially lowered the arousal levels of older people.

Verbal Learning

None of the many verbal learning studies have been carried out with greater care or greater attention to problems of sampling than the old studies by Gilbert (1935, 1941), mentioned in the previous chapter. In her 1935 study, Gilbert became impressed with the magnitude of the age deficit in learning paired associates as compared to learning other tasks. She carried out a later study (Gilbert, 1941) in which she compared 174 subjects aged 60-69 years matched exactly for vocabulary level with 174 subjects aged 20-29 years. She used a battery of eleven tests and again found the paired-associate test prominent. Of all the eleven tests, performances on a paired-associate learning test showed the largest percent loss with age.

Ruch (1934) also found an age deficit in paired-associate learning, but he was less impressed with the age decrement in forming this type of new association than in reorganizing those associations already established. His subjects were of three age groups (12-17, 34-59, and 60-82 years). He found greater difficulty with age in learning problems of false equations (e.g., 3 x 5 = 25) than in learning nonsense problems (e.g., E x Z = G), which, in turn, was greater than that of learning meaningful associates (e.g., man-boy). However, in a replication of this study, but with some procedural changes, Korchin and Basowitz (1957) reported somewhat different results. Like Ruch (1934), Korchin and Basowitz found decrement in performance with age in each of these three tasks. Also like Ruch, they found the meaningful paired-associate task least reflective of the age decrement. Unlike Ruch, however, Korchin and Basowitz (1957) did not find a difference in the magnitude of the age decrement between the false equations and the nonsense equations task. They concluded from their data that the primary age deficit was in learning novel material rather than in learning that demands reorganization of previously formed habit patterns.

Rigidity in Learning

There is a recurrent notion that advancing age is associated with a relative inability to learn new things, not so much because of a reduced learning capacity, but because of prior learning which persists even when no longer effective. The more incompatible the new is with the old, the more disadvantaged are the elderly presumed to be relative to the young. The study by Ruch (1934) suggested this, but, as may be surmised by the failure of Korchin and Basowitz (1957) to find larger age decrements in the learning of material which involves reorganization than in the learning of new material, the problem is not nearly as simple nor as clear cut as the recurrent notion might indicate.

An analysis of the experimental problem of rigidity may be seen in great detail in chapters 6 and 7. For the present, it is sufficient to indicate that when older people appear more rigid than younger people, it is necessary to ascertain whether the rigidity is really independent of the ability to learn. It may simply be that older people are less able to learn or to perform well. When people find learning difficult, they run out of alternative ways of acquiring information and tend to try the ineffective alternatives over and over again, rather than do nothing. Thus, what is primary difficulty in learning becomes secondary rigidity.

Opposing Long-Term Habits. One way to investigate aging effects of prior learning is to present the subject with a learning task which is contrary in some manner to a lifelong or at least a long-term habit. Only a few studies have been carried out in this way and some are quite old, as, for example, Snoddy (1926) and Ruch (1934), who opposed lifelong habits of viewing things directly by having subjects reverse right and left relationships by viewing things in a mirror. These studies are discussed briefly in chapter 6. Both Snoddy and Ruch found that the performances of the elderly with mirror viewing were particularly poor and concluded that the ability to modify existing habits becomes impaired with increasing age. There are many other studies investigating this dimension of learning in later life but the results are mixed in that some report a rigidity effect and some do not.

Amending Responses. A second method of investigating the effects of prior experiences on new learning is to observe the manner in which subjects carry out the learning performances. Kay (1951) did this in his analysis of errors in a task involving learning which of the ten response keys extinguished which of the ten lights. Kay concluded that the tendency to "unlearn" and amend the errors diminished with age. Thus the older subjects were seen to repeat their ineffective responses and appear rigid.

This tendency was also reported by Goodrick (1968) in his experiments with rats aged 6 months (young-mature) and 26 months (senescent). The animals learned a 14-unit multiple T-maze and the older ones performed particularly poorly. Those failing to reach criterion made many "perseverative nonrandom" errors. They showed a "behavioral rigidity, defined operationally as the tendency to perseverate in making the same errors on consecutive trials" (Goodrick, 1968, p. 303).

In a later study, Goodrick (1975b) closed the incorrect entrances during learning and thus did not permit the rats to make the perseverative error. He opened the entrances when making his tests of learning and found that the old rats (25 months) made *fewer* errors than the young ones (5 months), that is, the older rats did not enter the incorrect entrances as often. He concluded that while his earlier study had pointed to behavioral ridigity on the part of the older animals, this one pointed to the fact that "The deleterious effect of age on learning and problem solving is not immutable" (Goodrick, 1975b, p. 181).

Transfer of Training. A third method of studying the effects of prior learning involves an analysis of the effect of learning one experimental task on that of learning a second one. The effect is called *transfer of training.* When learning the first task facilitates the learning of the second task, the transfer is positive; when learning the first impedes the learning of the second, the transfer is negative. From the rigidity hypothesis it would be predicted that negative transfer is increased in old age. Negative transfer, it may be seen, is a dimension of interference discussed earlier. Gladis and Braun (1958) tried to test this hypothesis but their results turned out to be of positive transfer instead of negative transfer, i.e., scores on the second task were better than those on the first. Negative transfer in later life requires further investigation.

The concept of negative transfer, i.e., the detrimental effect of learning task 1 on the learning of task 2, is very easily tested with animal subjects. The task can be made so easy with animals that it is a simple matter to have the second task be a near perfect opposite to that of the first task in some crucial dimension. With human subjects, if the task is too easy, learning is immediate and it is difficult to chart its course. Thus, the tasks are made complex, and complete reversal of the major characteristics is not as easily arranged. The general procedure is to train animals to respond to one alternative of a simple dimension such as right vs. left, dark vs. light, etc., and then to train them to respond to the other alternative.

Stone (1929) carried out what was probably the first study of habit reversal of the rat in relation to advancing age. He conceptualized habit reversal as "the readiness with which the old habit of discrimination was broken up and a new one diametrically opposed to it was formed" (Stone, 1929, p. 167). After teaching the rats to choose the bright window, they were then taught to choose the dark one. The difference between old and young animals was not impressive, but Stone considered the problem of ability to modify habits in later life as an important one nevertheless—one deserving further analysis.

Later investigators have agreed with Stone, as judged by the fact that the problem of habit reversal in later life has since then often been researched. Many years after Stone reported these results with the rat, at least five conceptually similar rat studies were carried out. In none of these studies was there evidence which unequivocally argued for an increased rigidity in old age. In many of these studies there was no such evidence at all.

The complexity of this simple-sounding problem of habit reversal in later life was demonstrated in a study which was designed as a follow-up to several studies which ended with equivocal or negative conclusions. It was hypothesized that a task more difficult than the simple, one-dimensional task typically used would show rigidity in later life, even when the simpler ones did not (Botwinick, Brinley, and Robbin, 1963). Instead of a single choice of right or left, rats had to learn and then reverse a pattern of four such choices in serial order.

The hypothesis was not confirmed: The old age group (23-25 months) was the only group of three (3 months and 12-14 months) which *improved* in the first reversal performance over the performance of original learning. This is exactly opposite to that which would be predicted by the rigidity hypothesis of learning in old age.

If the results of these and other diverse human and animal studies of rigidity in learning can be summarized, it is that when an age decrement was found, the decrement tended to be of an overall decline rather than one specific to a rigidity. When there was an indication of an age-related deficit in rigidity in learning, this deficit tended to be marginal and a function of the original learning. In general, then, the evidence of a rigidity learning deficit in later life does not seem impressive.

Perceptual and Psychomotor Learning

Perceptual and psychomotor learning can be characterized as an improvement in a psychomotor skill with the need to acquire new information kept at a minimum. Erber (1976) carried out a psychomotor learning study based on the Digit Symbol subtest of the WAIS, the one which most reflects age decline (see Figure 13.2).

She presented young (18–28 years) and elderly (65–78) women with Digit Symbol tests in 10 different sessions and found that both groups improved almost with each session. While the extent of improvement was not better for one age group than for the other, the fact that the elderly improved as much as they did on a task that is so relatively hard for them showed that they have a plasticity of function not often given a chance to be demonstrated in laboratory experiments.

Improvement over the 10 trials was continuous but it had not yet reached its limit. A follow-up study was carried out with 20 trials to determine whether this would change the picture (Grant, Storandt, and Botwinick, 1978). Essentially the same results were found: The old continued to improve at a rate not very different from that of the young.

More complex tasks were given by Botwinick, Robbin, and Brinley (1960) for the purposes of determining whether the level of difficulty and complexity of the task is important in psychomotor learning in relation to age.

Each subject sorted playing cards by simply matching the number on the sorting card with the number on a stimulus card. Each card was sorted into a slot above which the stimulus card was placed. When a match was not possible, the sorting card was put into a slot designated as "bin." There were five levels of task difficulty, defined by the number of slots that were to be sorted. With each of the five levels of task difficulty, there were four sorting or practice trials of the cards. Although the older people (65-81 years) were slower in sorting than were the younger ones (19-35 years), their rates of improvement with practice were comparable to the younger people, irrespective of the difficulty of the task.

The card sorting task was then made more complex by increasing the number of stimulus aspects that needed to be considered at one time. There were three levels of task complexity. The least complex level involved the simple matching of the numbers on the sort cards with those of the stimulus cards, as just described. In the next level of complexity, the subject was instructed to match the numbers only when "the color is the same." Color here referred to the two suits, red and black. When the color was different, the sort card was place in the "bin." The most complex level required the subjects to sort on the basis of three stimulus aspects: number, color, and whether the numbers were odd or even. The instructions were to match "cards by number and color if the number is even, but if the number is odd, then match number and opposite color" (Botwinick et al., 1960, p. 12). Non-matchable cards were placed in the bin.

The older men were again found slower in their sorting than the younger men, and, although they were disproportionately slow with the combination of the most complex and difficult task, again the two age groups were comparable with respect to the effects of practice. From these results it may be concluded that, while advancing age may be associated with a type of memory deficit (the number of stimulus aspects kept in mind and manipulated), or with an inability to integrate material and be ready for response, once again, the young and aged adults were alike with respect to the rate of learning of these psychomotor tasks.

Practical Learning

The number of studies directed toward practical answers is limited, and often the studies are of poor scientific merit. Typically, the more the study is centered in the factory or in other natural settings (as opposed to the laboratory), the more difficult it is to effect proper controls. According to Shooter, Schonfield, King, and Welford (1956), the results of studies in natural settings tend to fall into four categories: (1) marks in examinations taken during or at the end of training programs; (2) ratings by training staff; (3) length of training to reach a given criterion of performance; and (4) measured progress of the work itself when training is given on the job. Shooter et al. analyzed several sets of data and concluded that the first three categories tended to show decline in the learning with age, and the fourth category tended to show neither decline nor improvement.

In spite of the paucity of good studies of practical learning, their importance is obvious. In a chapter on learning, Birren (1964) devoted almost 40 percent of his discussion to a 1963 report by the U. S. Department of Labor. Workers whose jobs were made either very different or unnecessary due to the technological changes of automation were given retraining. One petroleum company provided courses for two different kinds of employees, production workers and instrument mechanics. The differences between age groups in the learning of the new material were not impressive, and, if anything, the workers over 40 years of age were somewhat superior to those less than 40. It is important to note that here, and in what follows, older age refers to people of about 35 to 50 years.

A different result was seen in the retraining of telephone operators. The perceptual and psychomotor nature of the new tasks required speed and accuracy. Older workers (over 45 years) did not learn the tasks as well as did the younger ones. However, the differences were not large, and there was a suggestion in the data that with further training the older learners would achieve about the same level of performance as the younger trainees.

Not all of the studies carried out for practical purposes were factory or company based; some were carried out in laboratories. A prominent concern has been the assessment of various methods of training, especially as these methods may be advantageous to the older learner.

One study was concerned with programmed instruction and made an effort to determine whether a "discovery" method was superior to a rote-learning method for older workers (Chown, Belbin, and Downs, 1967). In this study the older people were aged 35 to 49 years and the younger controls were aged 20 to 34 years.

All the subjects were required to learn the association between 20 villages and the counties they were in. In the rote method, learning was facilitated by combining in steps new units of information with units already learned. In the "discovery" method the learner had to deduce from the given facts what the correct association must be.

The element of "discovery" helped the older worker-trainees but it neither helped nor hindered the younger trainees. The older trainees learned more and retained more from the discovery program. While they performed less well than their younger peers with the rote-learning method, they were similar to them with the "discovery" method.

It is difficult to summarize these and other studies on practical learning, not only because they are so diverse, but because they cover so many different age periods and because, by their very nature, there is often imprecision and poor scientific control. While performances of older people may be poorer than those of younger people, performance changes are not striking, up to middle age at least. All age groups can learn, and some methods of training are especially helpful to the older worker.

SUMMARY

In typical laboratory studies of learning, elderly people perform less well than do younger people. Among the techniques found to help the older person perform better are: (1) slow the pacing of the experimental events; (2) reduce inappropriate levels of autonomic arousal; and (3) provide more relevant and meaningful tasks than are typically seen in laboratories.

There are other techniques too, and some hold much promise. One of these techniques is that of organizing information. As the units of information within a task can be organized into larger units, the task becomes easier to learn. Elderly people, particularly those of low verbal facility, are not always able to take advantage of this. When taught how to organize the information, however, they benefit immensely, often more than younger people do.

The same is true for mediational techniques. Whereas organizational plans are designed to index and categorize, mediational techniques are designed to highlight and associate elements of information. In studies on aging, mediation techniques have been investigated mainly in paired-associate learning. The subject is told to link the pair, either by a "mental picture" or by a meaningful phrase or sentence; such mediation has been shown very effective. Elderly people, however, unlike younger ones, do not tend to make use of this type of mediation. As with information organizing plans, when instructed on how to use them, older people often improve their performances more than do younger people. Elderly people do not use mediational techniques spontaneously, probably because they tend not to be very able in forming them and in integrating them with the material to be learned.

Another type of help to the aged is a supportive emotional context of work. Often, elderly people are insecure and susceptible to stress, particularly when they are placed in evaluative situations. They often perform best when praised. This effect, however, is not always sustained. They tend to perform poorly when reproved.

Another aid to the elderly in learning was seen in the choice of sensory mode used to convey information. The auditory mode seems better than the visual for fleeting memory such as digits of a phone number used only so long as needed for a single dialing (primary memory). The visual mode seems better for longer-term recall as in the organization required for meaningful prose (semantic elaboration of secondary memory). Proper use of sensory mode and sensory organization helps the elderly in recall as much or more than the young.

A last aid discussed involved interference phenomena. Older adults are at least as susceptible as young adults to interference effects, and their performances tend to be very poor when subjected to them. Two prescriptions seem particularly important: (1) if interference must be encountered, the newly learned information should first be learned as well as possible; and (2) to the extent that it can be arranged, the interference should come as close as possible to the time of response, rather than when the new information is being acquired.

Most all the studies in which these aids have been investigated were of verbal learning. There is a large variety of other types of situations which show important age trends from which important characteristics of the aged may be inferred.

Studies of classical conditioning show that it is more difficult to condition responses of elderly people than those of the young, and that it is easier to extinguish them. It has thus been concluded that older adults tend to be less reactive than younger ones. Operant conditioning and other studies, however, point to different conclusions.

There is a long literature testing the proposition that advancing age is associated with an inability to learn new things, not so much because of a reduced learning capacity, but because of poor learning which persists even when no longer effective. The old are thought to be rigid and this keeps them from overcoming new learning obstacles. While the results of some studies may show some truth to this proposition, the results of many studies are not very impressive in support of it. Rigidity in learning seems to be a general property of learning ability in general.

Another class of studies has been labeled perceptual and psychomotor learning. This type of learning can be characterized by an improvement in a psychomotor skill with the need to acquire new information kept at a minimum. The more complex psychomotor tasks reflect performance deficits of the elderly to the extent that these tasks tap abilities which decline with age. But, given such overall performance deficits, several studies show that often older people improve their skills at about the same rate as do younger people.

Another class of studies was called practical learning. Here, the emphasis is on retraining older workers or developing teaching methods appropriate to them. It is important to note that the older workers in these studies are people as young as 45 years, and sometimes as young as 35 years. Many of these studies are carried out in natural settings and tend to be imprecise. Despite this, they point to a common pattern: up to middle age at least, decline in work performance is not great. All age groups can learn new job patterns, and some methods of training are especially helpful to the older worker.

REFERENCES

Arenberg, D. Age differences in retroaction. *Journal of Gerontology*, 1967, 22, 88–91.

Arenberg, D. Input modality in short-term retention. *Journal of Gerontology*, 1968, 23, 462–465.

Arenberg, D. The effects of input condition on free recall in young and old adults. *Journal of Gerontology*, 1976, 31, 551–555.

Bellucci, G., and Hoyer, W. Feedback effects on the performance and self-reinforcing behavior of elderly and young adult women. *Journal of Gerontology*, 1975, 30, 456–460.

Birren, J.E. *The psychology of aging.* Englewood Cliffs, N.J.: Prentice-Hall, 1964.

Botwinick, J. *Cognitive processes in maturity and old age.* New York: Springer Publishing Co., 1967.

Botwinick, J., Brinley, J.F., and Robbin, J.S. Learning and reversing a four-choice multiple Y-maze by rats of three ages. *Journal of Gerontology*, 1963, 18, 279–282.

Botwinick, J., and Kornetsky, C. Age differences in the acquisition and extinction of GSR. *Journal of Gerontology*, 1960, 15, 83–84.

Botwinick, J., Robbin, J.S., and Brinley, J.F. Age differences in card-sorting performance in relation to talk difficulty, task set, and practice. *Journal of Experimental Psychology*, 1960, 59, 10–18.

Braun, H.W., and Geiselhart, R. Age differences in the acquisition and extinction of the conditioned eyelid response. *Journal of Experimental Psychology*, 1959, 57, 386–388.

Bruning, R.H., Holzbauer, I., and Kimberlin, C. Age, word imagery, and delay interval: effects on short-term and long-term retention. *Journal of Gerontology*, 1975, *30*, 312–318.

Canestrari, R.E., Jr. Age changes in acquisition. In G.A. Talland (Ed.), *Human aging and behavior*. New York: Academic Press, 1968, pp. 169–188.

Chown, S., Belbin, E., and Downs, S. Programmed instruction as a method of teaching paired associates to older learners. *Journal of Gerontology*, 1967, *22*, 212–219.

Christensen, C.R. Interference in memory as a function of age. Unpublished doctoral dissertation, Washington University, St. Louis, 1968. (Also, *Dissertation Abstracts*, 1968, 29, No. 6.)

Craik, F.I.M. Age differences in human memory. In J.E. Birren and K.W. Schaie (Eds.), *Handbook of the psychology of aging*. New York: Van Nostrand Reinhold, 1977.

Craik, F.I.M., and Masani, P.A. Age differences in the temporal integration of language. *British Journal of Psychology*, 1967, *58*, 291–299.

Denney, N.W. Clustering in middle and old age. *Developmental Psychology*, 1974, *10*, 471–475.

Eisdorfer, C., Nowlin, J., and Wilkie, F. Improvement of learning in the aged by modification of autonomic nervous system activity. *Science*, 1970, *170*, 1327–1329.

Elias, M.F., Elias, P.K., and Elias, J.W. *Basic processes in adult developmental psychology*. St. Louis: C. V. Mosby, 1977.

Erber, J.T. Age differences in learning and memory on a digit-symbol substitution task. *Experimental Aging Research*, 1976, 2, 45–53.

Gilbert, J.G. Mental efficiency in senescence. *Archives of Psychology*, 1935, 27, (Whole No. 188).

Gilbert, J.G. Memory loss in senescence. *Journal of Abnormal and Social Psychology*, 1941, *36*, 73–86.

Gladis, M., and Braun, H.W. Age differences in transfer and retroaction as a function of intertask response similarity. *Journal of Experimental Psychology*, 1958, *55*, 25–30.

Goodrick, C.L. Learning, retention, and extinction of a complex maze habit for mature-young and senescent Wistar albino rats. *Journal of Gerontology*, 1968, *23*, 298–304.

Goodrick, C.L. Behavioral differences in young and aged mice: strain differences for activity measures, operant learning, sensory discrimination and alcohol preference. *Experimental Aging Research*, 1975(a), *1*, 191–207.

Goodrick, C.L. Behavioral rigidity as a mechanism for facilitation of problem solving for aged rats. *Journal of Gerontology*, 1975(b), *30*, 181–184.

Gordon, S.K. Organization and recall of related sentences by elderly and young adults. *Experimental Aging Research*, 1975, *1*, 71–80.

Grant, E.A., Storandt, M., and Botwinick, J. Incentive and practice in psychomotor performance of the elderly. *Journal of Gerontology*, 1978, *33*, 413–415.

Heron, A., and Craik, F.I.M. Age differences in cumulative learning of meaningful and meaningless material. *Scandinavian Journal of Psychology*, 1964, *5*, 209–217.

Hulicka, I.M., and Grossman, J.L. Age group comparisons for the use of mediators in paired-associate learning. *Journal of Gerontology*, 1967, *22*, 46–51.

Hultsch, D. Adult age differences in the organization of free recall. *Developmental Psychology*, 1969, *1*, 673–678.

Hultsch, D. Adult age differences in free classification and free recall. *Developmental Psychology*, 1971, *4*, 338–342.

Hultsch, D. Learning to learn in adulthood. *Journal of Gerontology*, 1974, *29*, 302–308.

Hultsch, D. Adult age differences in retrieval: trace development and cue dependent forgetting. *Developmental Psychology*, 1975, *11*, 197–201.

Jerome, E.A. Decay of heuristic processes in the aged. In C. Tibbits and W. Donahue (Eds.), *Social and psychological aspects of aging*. New York: Columbia Univ. Press, 1962, pp. 802–823.

Kay, H. Learning of a serial task by different age groups. *Quarterly Journal of Experimental Psychology*, 1951, *3*, 166–183.

Kimble, G.A., and Pennypacker, H.S. Eyelid conditioning in young and aged subjects. *Journal of Genetic Psychology*, 1963, *103*, 283–289.

Korchin, S.J., and Basowitz, H. Age differences in verbal learning. *Journal of Abnormal and Social Psychology*, 1957, *54*, 64–69.

Lair, C.V., and Moon, W.H. The effects of praise and reproof on performance of middle aged and older subjects. *Aging and Human Development*, 1972, *3*, 279–284.

Laurence, M.W. Age differences in performance and subjective organization in the free recall learning of pictorial material. *Canadian Journal of Psychology*, 1966, *20*, 388–399.

Mason, S.E. and Smith, A.D. Imagery in the aged. *Experimental Aging Research*, 1977, *3*, 17–32.

McGhie, A., Chapman, J., and Lawson, J.S. Changes in immediate memory with age. *British Journal of Psychology*, 1965, *56*, 69–75.

Nebes, R.D., and Andrews-Kulis, M.E. The effect of age on the speed of sentence formation and incidental learning. *Experimental Aging Research*, 1976, *4*, 315–331.

Powell, A.H., Jr., Eisdorfer, C., and Bogdonoff, M.D. Physiologic response patterns observed in a learning task. *Archives of General Psychiatry*, 1964, *10*, 192–195.

Robertson-Tchabo, E.A., Hausman, C.P., and Arenberg, D. A classical mnemonic for old learners: a trip that works. *Educational Gerontology*, 1976, *1*, 215–226.

Ross, E. Effects of challenging and supportive instructions in verbal learning in older persons. *Journal of Educational Psychology*, 1968, *59*, 261–266.

Rowe, E.J., and Schnore, M.M. Item concreteness and reported strategies in paired-associate learning as a function of age. *Journal of Gerontology*, 1971, *26*, 470–475.

Ruch, F.L. The differentiative effects of age upon human learning. *Journal of General Psychology*, 1934, *11*, 261–285.

Shooter, A.M.N., Schonfield, A.E.D., King, H.F., and Welford, A.T. Some field data on the training of older people. *Occupational Psychology*, 1956, *30*, 1–12.

Snoddy, G.S. Learning and stability. *Journal of Applied Psychology*, 1926, *10*, 1–36.

Stone, C.P. The age factor in animal learning: II. Rats on a multiple light discrimination box and a difficult maze. *Genetic Psychology Monographs*, 1929, *6*, 125–202.

Talland, G.A. Three estimates of the word span and their stability over the adult years. *Quarterly Journal of Experimental Psychology*, 1965, 17, 301–307.

Taub, H.A. Age differences in memory as a function of rate of presentation, order of report, and stimulus organization. *Journal of Gerontology*, 1968, 23, 159–164.

Taub, H.A. Mode of presentation, age, and short-term memory. *Journal of Gerontology*, 1975, 30, 56–59.

Taub, H.A. Method of presentation of meaningful prose to young and old adults. *Experimental Aging Research*, 1976, 2, 469–474.

Traxler, A.J., and Britton, J.H. Age differences in retroaction as a function of anticipation interval and transfer paradigm. *Proceedings, 78th Annual Convention, APA*, 1970, 5 (Part 2), 683–684.

Treat, N.J., and Reese, H.W. Age, pacing, and imagery in paired-associate learning. *Developmental Psychology*, 1976, 12, 119–124.

Walsh, D. Age differences in learning and memory. In D.S. Woodruff and J.E. Birren (Eds.), *Aging*. New York: D. Van Nostrand Co., 1975.

Welford, A.T. *Aging and human skill*. London: Oxford Univ. Press, 1958.

Whitbourne, S.K. and Slevin, A.E. Imagery and sentence retention in elderly and young adults. *Journal of Genetic Psychology*, 1978, in press.

Young, M.L. Problem solving performance in two age groups. *Journal of Gerontology*, 1966, 21, 505–509.

17
Memory Theory

Chapter 15 told of aging studies mainly of a stimulus-response type where the subject in the study was a relatively passive responder to environmental or laboratory stimulations. Chapter 16, in discussing aids to learning and memory, indicated that the very process of improving learning, of fixing information in mind for longer term recall, obliged the subject to be more active and change stimulus-response patterns. For longer term memory, one has to actively organize, actively process, actively bring information to more meaningful function. This processing of information has been called semantic memory, about which this present chapter is largely concerned.

CONCEPTIONS OF THE MEMORY PROCESS
One Mechanism

There was controversy at the start of the 1960s emphasis on memory—is there one mechanism of memory or are there more? Melton (1963) was the leading adherent of the one mechanism concept. This concept simply has it that short-term memory operates by the same mechanisms as does longer-term memory. A structural trace is produced in the nervous system and this is produced by a single stimulation. Short- and long-term recall is on a single continuum, with distinctions between them only a matter of convenience. While good evidence can still be mustered in support of this position, with little exception investigators have abandoned it in favor of a more than one mechanism concept.

Two Mechanisms

Waugh and Norman (1965), perhaps more than anyone else, were early identified with a two mechanism position (now more often called

311

"dual process" position). There is a transient, fleeting short-term memory, which they labeled Primary Memory (PM). In addition, there is a more durable, long-term memory, labeled Secondary Memory (SM). Moreover, an item of information may rest in both PM and SM simultaneously. In the main, with varied elaborations, this conception of memory prevails.

Unfortunately, the elaborations are many and there is a profusion and confusion of terms. For example, the term "short-term memory" has been applied to both PM and SM. "Thus," Craik (1977, p. 387) wrote, "to the extent that a 'short-term memory' task reflects PM functioning only . . . no age decrement will be observed; to the extent that short-term retention involves SM . . . old subjects will perform less well." These and other important aspects of memory will be elaborated later. For the present it is important to recognize only that for Craik (p. 400) and others, "SM should not be thought of as 'intermediate memory.'" Further, ". . . characteristics of SM performance after 30 seconds . . . are identical to those observed after months or years." For Craik, then, there is PM and another type of memory—a memory lasting for 30 seconds or for years—it is a type that is characterized by how the information was processed, not by its time duration. "Deep" processing, semantic processing, is what characterizes SM, not time, according to this type of thinking.

More than Two Mechanisms

Thus, given PM, all other memory is of one mechanism, that is, all but a type even more fleeting than PM, a type called by various names, but now mostly called sensory memory. Sensory memory is more akin to perceptual processes and may not be what many investigators call memory at all. For example, Melton (1963) thought that the study of memory involves only information storage and retrieval, not trace formation, which for some would include sensory memory.

The present chapter will consider sensory memory along with PM and SM. And, unlike Craik, at least for the purposes of convenience, SM will be differentiated into short-term memory and long-term memory. While both these may involve the same mechanism, the aging literature suggests different age patterns when the processed recall is of minutes duration than when it is of years. Each of these, sensory memory, PM, and SM, both in its short-term and long-term form, will be discussed in relation to age. But first, more on the tie between learning and memory.

LEARNING AND DELAYED RECALL

The same procedures and behaviors have variously been termed learning and recall. Paired-associates, for example, are presented to the subject for learning and tests are made of what is recalled. The subject's performance has been variously referred to as learning, "immediate memory," and—more often recently—short-term memory. As indicated, many now call it semantic memory if organization or other processing is thought to have taken place.

It is well documented that performances of such short-term or "immediate" memory decline with advancing adult age, and it is equally well known that performances of delayed recall decline also. A question asked by several investigators is whether, in later life, the more primary problem is the decline in "immediate memory" (learning), or the decline in a longer-term, delayed memory.

"Immediate" and Delayed Recall

In the two previous chapters, reference was made to Gilbert's (1941) now classic memory study. In that study, two age groups were compared with respect to their performances on eleven tests, and the older group (60-69 years) was found to perform more poorly than the younger group (20-29 years) on all of them. However, not all the tests showed the same extent of decline. Gilbert concluded that the age decline was somewhat greater for delayed recall of information than for the "immediate" recall of it; performances were poorer later in the test session than they were soon after the information to be learned had been presented.

This conclusion was challenged by Jerome (1959, p. 681):

> . . . though it is true that older subjects showed a 54.6 percent deficit relative to the young . . . on the delayed recall of paired associates, it is important to note that they had a 58.7 percent deficit on immediate recall of this material. They may, therefore, have recalled less on the delayed test simply because they learned less during the acquisition trials, but relative to what they had acquired, their delayed recall was superior to that of the younger subjects.

Jerome concluded that Gilbert's data indicated an age deficit in learning (as measured by "immediate" recall) but not necessarily in retention.

Short-Term and 48-Hour Recall

With a similar concept in mind, Davis and Obrist (1966) carried out a study in which the time of recall was extended. They compared adults of two ages, after matching them almost exactly with respect to scores on the WAIS Vocabulary test, as an estimate of intellectual ability. Davis and Obrist wanted their results to reflect differences between the age groups in learning and memory abilities, not other intellectual abilities. The older adults were aged 65-84 years and the younger ones 19-35 years.

Each subject was seen on two occasions, approximately 48 hours apart. On the first day the subjects were given a paired-associate test, and learning performances were measured. Then, two minutes afterward, a retest was made. Approximately 48 hours later, each subject was retested with the same criterion and same scoring as in the earlier retest. Thus, three scores were available for each subject—a learning score, a short-term (two-minute) retention score, and a 48-hour retention score.

The age groups were significantly different in their learning performances, with the older group performing less well. Accordingly, these learning scores were used to equate the two age groups when comparing their memory test scores. That is, in keeping with Jerome's contention, the memory scores were referred to the baseline of learning scores before age comparisons were made, so that the amount of material learned initially would not bear on the extent of material that could be remembered later. (Covariance analyses were performed on the memory data, with the learning scores as the covariate.)

When the age comparisons were made of the 48-hour retention scores after adjusting for the level of initial learning, the age groups were not found different. This result provided support for Jerome's analysis. However, when this age comparison of the 48-hour retention scores was made after adjusting for the short-term memory scores, not the initial learning scores, the performances of the older group were found poorer. These results suggest that, while the amount of information retained after two days is directly related to how much of it was learned in the first place, it is not related or is much less related to the amount retained much earlier in the memory sequence. This might suggest that there is more than one type of memory process, at least one short-term process and one longer-term process, with a deficiency in later life in the latter. An alternate notion is that older people are more vulnerable to other influences which take place during long periods of delay in recall—interference, for example—and this is responsible for the long-term deficit.

Two methodological details of this study by Davis and Obrist need to be emphasized because they reflect on the conclusions which were drawn. First, in having the subjects learn the list, Davis and Obrist used an old but not a typical method (Method of Adjusted Learning). After a word pair in the list was given correctly twice consecutively, it was removed from the list. Thus the list continually grew shorter and easier to learn. Moreover, tests of recall involved relearning to a criterion of one, rather than two correct responses. Second, perhaps because of this, the relearning scores after 48 hours were better for both age groups than were the scores of initial learning. A repeat of this study with more typical learning procedures, and with recall scores reflecting loss rather than gain, would provide evidence for the broader application of Davis and Obrist's results.

Meaningful Information

Gordon and Clark (1974) tested for memory of meaningful information rather than paired-associate words. A paragraph of prose was given to men and women aged 21–30 and 65–81 years, with instructions to read it and remember as much of it as possible for subsequent testing. Tests of recall and recognition memory were made soon after the reading (immediate recall) and were also made one week later.

The analyses carried out by Gordon and Clark (1974, p. 69) were correlational, such that the effects of the many factors examined in their study could be compared. Their analyses disclosed that "the elderly performed somewhat more poorly than the young on immediate retention, but had much lower scores on delayed recall." Thus, the same possible conclusions apply as in the Davis-Obrist study. That is, either two different memory processes are indicated—one that reflects little age effect, and one reflecting greater effect; or, one process explains both immediate and delayed recall but interference or other factors intervene making for longer-term recall problems for the older subjects.

Extent of Learning

There is a study of special interest because it provides a very clear understanding of the manner in which learning sets the limits of memory. Hulicka and Weiss (1963) gave paired associates to elderly subjects (60–72 years) and to younger ones (30–44 years) after having divided them into subgroups. To one subgroup of each age, the paired-associate lists were presented an equal number of times to all subjects (15 trials). To another subgroup of elderly and young subjects, the lists were presented until a criterion of learning was achieved. All subjects reaching the same criterion were presumed to have reached the same level or extent of learning. A group of elderly subjects was then given training over and beyond the criterion (overlearning).

Five minutes and twenty minutes after this learning, all subjects were tested for their recall of it. Some subjects in the learning-to-criterion condition and in the overlearning condition were tested again one week later.

In the condition of equal experience but not the same extent of learning, i.e., 15 trials to all subjects, the younger adults performed better than the older ones both in the learning and in the memory tests. But the two age groups did not differ significantly in their memory scores when they were equated for what they had learned. The dependence of memory upon learning was made even more evident when Hulicka and Weiss computed a product-moment correlation between the learning and both the five-minute recall and the twenty-minute recall scores. The coefficients of correlation were approximately 0.92.

In learning to criterion, the old people required more trials than did the young. When, however, the two age groups were brought to the common level of learning provided by the criterion, they were seen as very similar in their recall scores measured five minutes, twenty minutes, and one week later. In order to make sure that the age groups were not different in recall because the older subjects had a greater exposure (more trials) with the learning lists, old and young were matched by individuals for trials to criterion. The results again showed that the two age groups were similar on recall.

This study by Hulicka and Weiss (1965) argued clearly that what is remembered is dependent upon what is learned. Memory covering a period of five minutes to one week following the learning of paired associates was seen dependent upon "immediate" recall. Thus, contrary to the results of Davis and Obrist, these results do not provide an argument for more than one process of memory. It would have been interesting, however, had Hulicka and Weiss, with the data based upon an equal 15 trials to all subjects, tested for memory one week later, having adjusted for delayed recall after five or twenty minutes. Had they done this, it is possible that they would have found support for the results of Davis and Obrist.

Recall after Four Weeks

The data of Hulicka and Weiss are clear in showing that, when their subjects were trained to an equal criterion of learning, retention over a period as long as one week was not any the poorer for the older adults than for the younger. Not all studies show this, and one of these was particularly interesting because recall was measured after a delay of 29–30 days. Harwood and Naylor (1969) presented to subjects aged 60–80 and 15–45 years a series of 20 drawings of common objects. As did Hulicka and Weiss, they presented the stimulus materials until a criterion of learning had been achieved, in this case, 80 percent, i.e., 16 or more items of the 20. Without forewarning, the subjects were called for a recall retest about a month later. The test was made without presentation of the stimulus materials and without any prompting whatsoever. In this study, the older subjects, despite having been taught the information to the same criterion as the young, retained it less well. Memory declined in later life even after an experimental adjustment for original learning.

Some support for the position of Hulicka and Weiss was seen in this study by Harwood and Naylor, however. The recall performances, delayed for four weeks following the original learning, were found correlated with the level of this learning achieved in satisfying the criterion, i.e., 16 to 20 items of the 20. Thus, again, learning sets the limits of memory, but in this study, other factors also were seen to influence the extent of recall.

The literature, in relating learning and memory, is not without other contradiction. For example, in a later study by Hulicka (1965), she failed to find an age decline in either learning or recall scores. She attributed the difference between these results and those of her previous study to a difference in the sampling of subjects. Wimer and Wigdor (1958) reported results that were compatible with the earlier study (Hulicka and Weiss, 1965), i.e., age groups were not different in recall when learning was to a criterion; but, in a subsequent one, Wimer (1960) found that age groups were different in recall. In the earlier Wimer-Wigdor study, four paired-associates and a retention interval of 15 minutes were used. In the later Wimer study, seven paired-associates and a 24-hour interval were used. Different test procedures and materials, different learning criteria, different retention periods, and different sample populations may all interact to modify the learning-memory relationship.

Thus, the foregoing discussion on learning and delayed recall can be seen as providing some evidence for more than one mechanism or type of memory, although not everyone would agree with this conclusion. Different types of memory are discussed next, beginning with sensory memory. As indicated, sensory memory is of a type of recall which for some is not really a memory process as much as a perceptual one. For some it may "involve the earliest stages in the processing of information . . ." (Salthouse, 1976).

SENSORY MEMORY
Visual Trace

After a certain kind of event is experienced, there is a kind of after-image that fades away rapidly, within a second or so. It seems to fade as a property of time. The evidence for this comes from a type of experiment introduced by Sperling (1960) where very short-term recall is variously called sensory memory, visual trace, stimulus trace, visual image, or by other names. As Sperling first reported it, the subject is presented with very brief (e.g., 50 msec.) tachistoscopic exposures of letters and numbers displayed in rows. After this stimulus has been presented and is no longer present, the subject is instructed to report only one of the three rows. The particular row is indicated by an auditory signal. Experientially, it is as if the subject is reporting his images. He could continue to "read" information in visual form even after a tachistoscopic exposure is over. It is for this reason that it has also been called the visual image. Sperling (1963, p. 21) wrote, "The visual image of the stimulus persists for a short time after the stimulus has been turned off, and the subjects can utilize this rapidly fading image. In fact, naive subjects typically believe that the physical stimulus fades out slowly."

Judging by the accuracy of the report, much of the trace decays quickly. Immediately after the stimulus is terminated, the report is quite accurate, 76 percent, depending upon the specific procedure. As the presentation of the auditory signal indicating which row to report is delayed, the accuracy of the visual image report declines: After one second, as much as half the information may be lost. The briefness of the stimulus trace has been seen as a handicap to any subject who attempts to report all that he had seen and retained. "More is seen than can be remembered" for reporting (Sperling, 1960, p. 1).

There are only a few age studies of sensory memory and only little and tentative generalization is possible. Together, the few studies suggest diminution with age in sensory memory. In fact, one study (Walsh and Thompson, 1978) reported almost total inability of the aged in sensory memory: 10 older adults (60–68 years) were tested and only two gave evidence of sensory memory. On the other hand, 10 younger adults (18–26) were tested and all demonstrated sensory memory. A second part of Walsh and Thompson's report suggested that visual traces decay more rapidly in the old than in the young. (This, however, was not indicated by several backward masking studies—studies related to sensory memory—discussed in the context of stimulus persistence theory in chapter 11.) If it is so that the elderly tend not to have sensory memory, there is doubt as to whether the visual trace is part of the information processing sequence for recall, because most old adults display primary and secondary memory even if not sensory memory.

While Walsh and Thompson found 8 of their 10 older subjects without evidence of sensory memory, Salthouse (1976) observed otherwise. However, he utilized a longer duration stimulus than Walsh and Thompson and this may raise question as to whether it was sensory memory in the Sperling sense that Salthouse measured. (Salthouse utilized a stimulus duration of 100 msec., while Walsh and Thompson utilized the more typical one of 50 msec. Also, Salthouse may have set higher criteria for subject selection for testing.) In any case, Salthouse observed this type of memory in all his subjects and found that those aged 60–75 were poorer in the partial report, i.e., sensory memory, than those aged 18–30.

This is in keeping with a partial report study by Abel (1972) who also used a modified Sperling technique but whose stimulus exposure durations were so large (half second) as to indicate that it was probably very short-term recall, rather than sensory memory, that was tested.

Abel compared men of three age groups: young (19–22 years), middle (46–52 years), and older (60–77 years). Their recall and decay scores may be seen in Figure 17.1. It will be noted in this figure that two

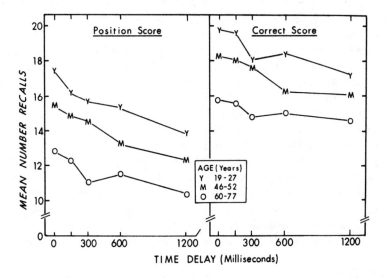

FIGURE 17.1: Very short-term recall as a function of time delay following stimulus termination. Recall was measured both in terms of whether the stimulus items were correct irrespective of their spatial relations (correct score), and whether they were correct in spatial context (position score). Data from Table 1 of Abel (1972).

types of measurements were made. One was simply the number of elements of the tachistoscopic display that were correctly recalled, the other was the number correctly recalled in their actual spatial order in the stimulus row. The former measure was called "correct score" and the latter "position score." The "position score" is the more stringent criterion of the stimulus trace since it reflects a more accurate visualization of the display.

Although Figure 17.1 reflects differences in recall among the age groups, the related statistics bore this out only equivocally. The decay functions, i.e., durations of recall, were similar for the three age groups.

Perceptual (P) System

A study done prior to that of Sperling—and not referring to the term stimulus trace, or any one like it, but referring to a concept which appears similar in some ways—was carried out by Broadbent (1958).* Information such as spoken digits was recorded on tape and delivered to each ear by way of earphones. Although the information was simultaneously delivered to both ears, the information delivered to one ear was different from that delivered to the other one. For example, in the left ear, the digits 4, 8, 3, 7 might be delivered, but in the right ear, the digits would be 6, 9, 5, 1. The digits 4 and 6 would be delivered first and simultaneously, then 8 and 9, 3 and 5, and last 7 and 1.

It may seem surprising, but at certain rates of presentation, the subject first reports all the digits which were presented in one ear, and then reports the digits presented in the other. In so doing, he keeps in storage (short-term) digits heard earlier but reported later. In the example given, the subject might report 6, 9, 5, 1 followed by 4, 8, 3, 7, even though 4 and 6 were the first digits presented. It is as if the subject organizes these inputs by putting half of them in short-term storage while processing the other half immediately.

Broadbent (1958) suggested that those digits reported first are passed through a perceptual (P) system and involve hardly any storage at all. It may be noted how similar were the things said regarding the visual trace. The duration is brief—it passes through or decays quickly, and it is thought to be independent of the central memory system.

A variety of studies were undertaken to investigate the age effects of

---

* It will be recalled that Waugh and Norman (1965) equated their PM with Broadbent's P-system, but not the stimulus trace. Here the stimulus trace and P-system are both included under the same head.

both the P-system and the more stable, short-term memory system. For example, Inglis and Caird (1963) applied Broadbent's technique and dichotic simulation to subjects between the ages of 11 and 70 years and examined recall in relation to age both for the first half sets of digits (P-system) and the second half sets (short-term memory system). They found that recall of the second half set declined with increasing age, but the reports of the first half set did not.

If we equate conceptually the visual trace and the P-system, Salthouse's results and those of Inglis and Caird might be taken to point to different conclusions: Salthouse (1976) demonstrated diminution with age in the strength of the trace; Inglis and Caird did not. Craik (1965), however, carried out a study similar to that of Inglis and Caird but introduced modifications in the procedure. In so doing, Craik observed age decrements in both the first half and the second half sets. He found that functioning of both the perceptual system and the short-term memory system functioning declined with age. This latter result was supported in later studies with still different modifications (Schonfield, Trueman, and Kline, 1972; Clark and Knowles, 1973).

PRIMARY MEMORY

Waugh and Norman (1965) differentiated primary memory (PM) from secondary memory (SM) by referring to PM as a relatively temporary memory of what had just occurred. PM is of the "psychological present," not of the past—it is almost a "read out" of what was just experienced. A person hears a short string of numbers, such as a phone number, and repeats it perfectly. Minutes, even seconds later, it is not available for recall—it is no longer known. As brief a memory as PM is, however, it is longer term than sensory memory. It is a different memory system.

PM, the "read out," is possible only with a short string of numbers or items. If it is a long string, it must be handled differently; it must be processed and become part of SM. A short string of numbers can be part of PM and SM at the same time, but a long string is only of SM. Craik (1977, p. 387) views PM "as a temporary holding and organizing process [more] than as a structured memory store."

How is PM measured? The usual way is by presenting the subject with a string of digits, letters, or even words, and testing for the number of them that can be recalled immediately after. This type of test has been called digit span, letter span, memory span, and by other names.

Memory span has been seen as not changed with age (e.g., Bromley, 1958; Drachman and Leavitt, 1972) or reduced only slightly (e.g., Botwinick and Storandt, 1974; Friedman, 1974).

Craik (1977) argued that memory spans involving even as few as 5 words exceed the limited capacity of PM; thus, even the recall of such a small list "involves the retrieval of one or more items from secondary memory." This reasoning suggests that what differences are found in memory span with age might be attributable to secondary memory. When the span is longer that that handled by PM, it is called supra-span, which almost by definition involves SM. Drachman and Leavitt, among others, demonstrated age differences in digits of supra-span length (15 digits), but not of shorter length (longest sequence recalled correctly).

Another way PM is measured is by free or unordered recall of a long list of items and paying attention only to those items at the end of the list. In the previous chapter, Arenberg's (1976) study of the effects of sensory modality on learning and memory was discussed, indicating that the items at the beginning of the list would be of secondary memory and those at the end of primary memory. The formulation that aging does not affect PM, only SM, would lead to the expectation that the two age groups Arenberg tested (17–19 and 60–70) would be different in recall only with the beginning words, not the end words. Arenberg's data showed small and near equal age declines of the beginning and the end words. Perhaps the notion of PM and SM reflected by end and beginning words, respectively, is not correct; in any case, Arenberg's study was in agreement with much of the literature showing only small decline in what is thought to be PM.

SECONDARY MEMORY: SHORT-TERM RECALL

Primary memory is not the kind of memory people worry about. In the course of a typical day in the lives of most people, it is secondary memory that is important. It is the important process unless one conceptualizes memory or information processing as necessarily flowing from PM to SM (or even sensory memory to PM to SM). Or, as Craik (1977, p. 392) suggested, PM is crucial because "it constitutes the control system for all thinking and remembering. . . ."

Whether or not PM is as important as suggested, the study of SM can stand by itself. The key in SM, as already indicated, is meaningful processing, sometimes called semantic processing or semantic elaboration. The very process of organizing information is thought synonymous with placing it in memory; the greater the processing, the longer term the recall.

Semantic Elaboration

Another way of saying this is that how accurate a memory is, and how long it lasts, depends on how much cognitive work is performed on the information when first experienced. Apparently, cognitive work even without intention to learn makes for relatively good memory. In fact, meaningful cognitive work without intention to learn can make for better learning than intentional efforts that do not involve semantic elaboration.

Three aging studies have been carried out with this thinking in mind. The general pattern of these studies was to contrast several groups in recall performances after they had been instructed differently. One group is called intentional learners in that they are told to study the information and remember it. Other groups are incidental learners in that the instructions do not include the direction to learn and remember, but instead include directions that vary the types of processing. Some groups are instructed to carry out nonmeaningful processing, others to carry out meaningful processing (semantic elaboration). The hypothesis, of course, is that meaningful processing will make for better SM than meaningless processing, better even than intentional learning, perhaps. The latter would be expected if intentional learning involves self-instructed processing that is less adequate than experimenter-directed processing.

Walsh and Jenkins (1973) helped set a pattern for this type of study with results in accord with the hypothesis. Later, three aging studies in this pattern were carried out to see whether levels of processing could account for age differences in recall (Walsh, 1975; White [described by Craik, 1977]; Eysenck, 1974). The three studies were similar both in procedure and results, thus only one of them (Eysenck) will be described; the other two (Walsh and White) were discussed briefly in the previous chapter.

Eysenck tested subjects aged 18–30 years and 55–65. One group of each age was instructed to learn a list of words. A second group of each age counted the letters of each word; a third group found rhymes to each word; a fourth group found suitable adjectives; a fifth group formed images. The level of meaningful processing was thought to increase from group 2 to group 5; the intentional learners were thought of as a type of control group. The expectation was realized: As processing became deeper, as the subjects went from letter counting to imagery, recall of both age groups improved, but more so for the young. Unlike the data of Walsh and Jenkins, intentional learning was best of all in regard to recall, reflecting the greatest age difference. Eysenck interpreted his results as showing disadvantage to the old as opportunities of semantic processing increase. He referred to this as a processing-deficit hypothesis. Again, these results were similar to those of White and Walsh, with the latter concluding, ". . . older adults may be less able than the young to process at deep levels, or alternatively, that the memory traces resulting from processing at deep levels are less durable for the old."

There seems little doubt that SM skills of older people are not as good as those of younger people. What is in doubt is whether the old are less able to benefit from semantic processing opportunities than the young. The studies by Walsh, Eysenck, and to a lesser extent, White, suggest that they are less able, but the series of studies on categorization by Hultsch (1969, 1971, 1975) reviewed in the previous chapter indicated otherwise. Further, the studies on mediation by Hulicka and Grossman (1967) and by Canestrari (1968) also reviewed in the previous chapter suggest otherwise.

These studies suggest that older people do not spontaneously use strategies of semantic elaboration—such strategies as categorization, clustering, and imagery (particularly visual, non-verbal imagery)—but they can be taught to use these, and when they do, they often benefit more than the young. This seems more so for those of low education or low verbal facility because the highly educated elderly seem to use these strategies without aid.

Animal Studies

Consolidation of Traces. Psychologists testing human subjects think in human terms and use concepts appropriate to the subjects, thus, semantic processing. Psychologists testing animals necessarily think in other terms, but some of the underlying concepts may be similar. Clearly, the term "semantic" applied to animals is inappropriate; but such terms as neural organization, or short-term recall, are not inappropriate. The human studies and animal studies may provide some operationally equivalent information.

Information becomes fixed in memory by what is called the consolidation of traces. It is the opposite of trace decay or forgetting. The concept of consolidation is useful to many, as seen in its picturesque description by Pribram (in Melton, 1967, pp. 47-48):

> If one receives a severe blow on the head, the immediately preceding events cannot be retrieved. This . . . is not for all events. It depends on context, it depends on what kind. . . . But if the blow is severe enough, complete amnesia can occur . . . there must be a time during which experience is erasable by such trauma. The converse . . . is called the consolidation hypothesis; that is, an experience takes time to settle in, since the longer it has been set the less easily it is erased.

There is reason to believe that the rate of consolidation of short-term memory traces is slower in later life than during earlier periods—at least as judged by one study. Doty and Doty (1964) showed that older subjects need more time than younger ones to consolidate an event in memory. If this time is not provided to them, retention will be impaired.

Doty and Doty carried out two studies. In the first study, hooded rats of five ages (30, 120, 280, 365, and 600 days) learned to escape a shock by simply entering a compartment when a light cue was presented. Each rat was given only one trial a day for 30 consecutive days to learn this shock avoidance problem. After each daily trial, four subgroups of rats of each age were given a drug thought to disrupt the consolidation process. (The drug was chlorpromazine hydrochloride; intraperitoneal injections, 2 mg./km.) And one subgroup of each age was given an equal volume of a saline placebo as a control.

The rats were injected with the drug at different periods of time, following each trial, in order to determine the time course of the consolidation process. Subgroups of rats of each age were given the drug 10 seconds after each learning trial, one-half hour, one hour, or two hours after each learning trial. The placebo was given to a subgroup of rats 10 seconds after each learning trial.

Doty and Doty found that, with the placebo, the five age groups of rats were similar in their performances of avoiding the shock (dashed line with open circles in Figure 17.2). Also seen in this figure is that performances of the rats of all ages were impaired when the drug was administered 10 seconds after each trial (dashed line with closed circles). This suggests that the consolidation process for this type of material takes longer than 10 seconds. When the drug was administered one-half hour, one hour, and two hours after the learning trials, only the youngest, immature rats (30 days) and the oldest rats (600 days)

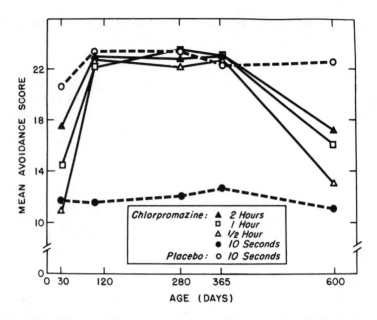

FIGURE 17.2: Mean avoidance score as a function of age of hooded rats. Each rat received one training trial a day for 30 days to avoid shock. After each trial, rats in different subgroups were injected with chlorpromazine hydrochloride or with a placebo, isotonic saline. The time after each trial when the injection was given is indicated in the figure. (Data are from Table 1 of Doty and Doty, 1964. Figure reproduced from Figure 15 of Botwinick, 1967.)

showed impairment in the consolidation of their learning experiences. Thus, it was concluded that, for the oldest rats, the time required for the consolidation of the memory was longer than for younger adult rats.

Massed and Distributed Learning. The second experiment by Doty and Doty (1964) was carried out with the hooded rats learning the same avoidance problem, but this time the consolidation was disrupted, not as in the first study by drugs, but by new learning trials coming soon after the previous ones. Rats aged 30, 120, and 600 days were given 30 learning trials, but only one of five subgroups of each age had one trial per day as in the first study. The other subgroups had trials spaced 10 seconds, one-half hour, one hour, and three hours apart. The massing of trials was meant to have the same effect as the chlorpromazine in the first experiment.

Doty and Doty found that, when trials were spaced 10 seconds apart, performances for all the groups were poor. This lends credence to the idea that the consolidation process for this type of material takes longer than 10 seconds. When the trials were spaced one-half and one hour apart, poor avoidance performance was seen only with the youngest and oldest animals. When the trials were three and 24 hours apart, the age groups were similar with respect to their performances. Thus, these data also suggest that memory disability in advanced age can occur because of poor consolidation resulting from an inadequate period of time allowed for the process to be completed.

To the extent that it is possible to generalize from these data to the broad context of everyday life, it is clear that stimulus pacing is important. This was emphasized in chapter 15. Perception and learning must not be hurried; ample time must be available to the older person to consolidate his experiences. If experiences come one after another at too rapid a rate, the older person will be much disadvantaged.

It would be a mistake, however, to conclude from the study by Doty and Doty that by simply increasing the time between incoming events, the older person would necessarily be helped. The fact is that just the opposite can occur; a distributed presentation of events can be more detrimental to older people than a massed presentation.

Goodrick (1968) compared old Wistar albino rats (26 months of age and older) with younger adult controls (six months) in the learning of a complex maze involving 14 choice points. The old rats learned this maze less well than the young rats, with half of them being particularly slow to learn. Accepting Doty and Doty's massed practice experiment as indicating that an incomplete consolidation may explain these very poor performances, Goodrick continued training his slow old learners by having a spacing of trials of only one per day. This did not help the old slow learners, suggesting that consolidation is not a ready explanation to be employed indiscriminately.

Goodrick then massed the learning trials; originally he gave them four trials a day, the distributed practice was of one trial a day; now he gave the old slow learners twelve trials per day, four consecutively on each of three occasions during the day. Contrary to what might have been anticipated from the results of Doty and Doty, this reduced, not increased, the errors of these old slow learners.

An analogous result was demonstrated with human subjects. Fraser (1958) compared two age groups of teachers (18-29 years and 30-55 years) with respect to the recall of eight-digit numbers. He had two conditions: In one condition the numbers were presented and recalled at a relatively fast rate (120 digits per minute), and in the other condition the rate was slower (40 digits per minute). The faster rate may be thought of as massed presentation and the slower rate as distributed presentation.

The two age groups were similar in their recall of the digits with the more rapid rate, but they differed when the presentation and recall were slower. The older group was poorer in recall than was the younger group when the time between digits was longer. It may be hypothesized that, during the interval, the inputs were not consolidated well—they decayed or were interfered with by extraneous factors. Fraser concluded that the span of immediate memory was the same for the two age groups but the rate of decay of memory was greater in the older group.

It is seen, then, that for the older person, learning and perceiving must not be hurried if memory is to be properly consolidated. On the other hand, there are situations during which, if the pacing is too slow, retention may suffer.

Interference. The concepts of trace consolidation and trace interference are complementary, having much in common; in fact, they are often indistinguishable. Both interference and incomplete consolidation explain poor learning and forgetting, the former on the basis of a blocking of an initial input, and the latter on the basis of decay or inadequate experience. Melton (1967, p. 50) distinguished between these two concepts by indicating that, while with both consolidation and interference a succeeding event can impede the fixation of a previous one, only with the interference concept can there be a blocking of a to-be-recalled event with one occurring *prior* to it. There may be another distinguishing factor, a more important one, perhaps. Interference may be thought to sometimes make for a temporary blockade; failure to consolidate makes for a permanent "erasure."

The data of Doty and Doty could have been described in terms of interference rather than consolidation; the effects of the chlorpromazine hydrochloride and the massing of trials interfered with trace formation. Similarly, the study by Christensen (1968), described in the previous chapter, framed originally in the context of interference, was also discussed in that chapter in the context of consolidation.

Summarizing these data, the studies by Goodrick and by Fraser to the contrary, the generalization that older people are best served by slowing down the rate of inputs and by delaying as much as possible the advent of new inputs seems to hold. This minimizes interference and permits consolidation.

LONG-TERM MEMORY

There are two different conceptions of long-term memory. One is the conception of Craik (1977) quoted earlier: Memories of minutes or even seconds duration if based on meaningful organization of information are formed by the same processes as memories of years duration. The difference is only a matter of depth or extent of the organization. If the information is processed deeply enough it could last a lifetime. Both the memories of minutes or years duration are called secondary memory. The second conception is that short- and long-term recall involve different processes and this would suggest that different principles apply to each. The term "tertiary memory" has sometimes been applied to long-term recall. Thus, the clinical and laboratory observation that old memories are better retained by the aged than are newly learned ones is explained by the first concept as due to old memories having been processed better; it is explained by the second concept as due to different abilities being under examination. The first concept seems to be the one popularly maintained at the present time.

It is difficult to study long-term memory scientifically in the laboratory and for this reason there are very few studies, and none of them are without methodological complications. Two of these studies will be discussed here in some detail, and the others will be described in the next chapter, focusing on different although related issues.

Three Types of Memory

A large scale study was carried out without preconception regarding theories of memory (Botwinick and Storandt, 1974). Adults of wide age range (20–79 years) were given a large variety of memory tests of as many different kinds as seemed feasible, but not including tests of sensory memory. Among the memory tests was a series of information questions—questions having to do with memory of sociohistoric facts, as for example, "In what city was President John F. Kennedy assassinated?"

The questions were chosen to represent information of common knowledge, but clearly, not everyone tested would ever have been able to answer, "Dallas," i.e., not everyone would have known this information in the first place. In such a case the test item was not of memory but of general information. However, the assumption in the study was that all age groups were equal in having acquired the asked-for information at some time in life. Or, stated in a different way, it was assumed that all age groups tested were similar in the percentage of people who at one time learned the asked-for information. With this assumption the series of questions became tests of memory—tests of recalling what at one time was learned. (Alternative ways of testing for long-term recall require other assumptions, often less reasonable to make—see "New and Old Recall" in the next chapter.)

The sociohistoric questions covered four time periods, each 20 years. There were questions of events occurring in the 1950s and 60s, the 1930s and 40s, the 1910s and 20s, and 1890 to 1909. The results of the study showed that age is not associated with decline in this type of long-term memory. The 70-year-olds were about as good as the 20-year-olds, who were no different from those of in-between age. However, Figure 17.3 shows an interesting observation (made about men only since the questions were less appropriate for women, as determined in subsequent unpublished research). While all age groups were similar in overall recall scores, they were different in what they recalled. For example, men in their 30s remembered more sociohistoric facts of the 1950s and 60s than any other age group, while men in their 50s remembered more information of the 1930s and 40s than did the others. This interaction between age and time period was such that memory was best for those events that had occurred at the time the men were between 15 and 25 years of age when experiencing them. The age of the person did not seem important; only the age when the information was acquired seemed important. It may be that the greatest impact or greatest importance of the sociohistoric event (e.g., President Kennedy's death) was felt by those aged 15–25 and that is why it was best recalled.

Perlmutter (1978) used these same long-term memory questions in testing two age groups of men and women, 20–25 and 60–75 years, and reported results which at first may seem at variance with those above by Botwinick and Storandt. First, rather than finding the age groups similar in long-term recall, Perlmutter found her older group superior to the younger one. The age group in the 60s recalled 43 percent of the information asked while those in the 20s recalled only 30 percent. Thus, while different, both studies reported no age decline in this type of

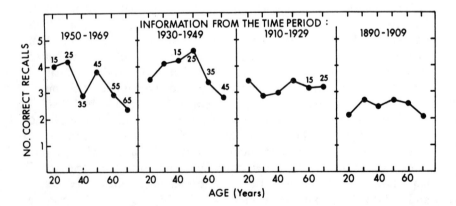

FIGURE 17.3: Long-term memory for sociohistoric events occurring at different time periods. Note the numbers next to the curves; they refer to the mean ages of the men subjects at the time the events took place.

function. Second, Perlmutter did not find the younger subjects recalling more information of one time period and the older recalling more of another period. In other words, she did not find 15 to 25 years a key time to experience sociohistoric facts. However, reference to Figure 17.3 discloses that the age groups Perlmutter tested (20s and 60s) were not very different in their scores, certainly not in three of the time periods. This study and the Botwinick-Storandt study thus point in the same direction.

Accepting the 15-25 year age period as important for learning sociohistoric facts, it can be argued, but only in *post hoc* fashion, that impact and importance make for deep processing and so for long-term recall of secondary memory. However, the results of the Botwinick-Storandt study argue that long-term memory is different from short-term, secondary memory. Since the long-term memory questions made up only a few of the many memory tests given, the scores on all the tests were subjected to the statistical technique of a principal component analysis to determine the relationships among the different performances. Three separate memory factors were determined by the analysis: Not only were factors of primary memory and secondary memory seen, but there was also a long-term memory factor. The statistical analysis disclosed these three memory factors, each independent or unrelated to the other. In this way short-term memory and long-term memory were seen as different memory processes.

In this analysis age was related to primary memory more than the previous discussion on primary memory suggests. Age was clearly related to secondary, short-term memory, but, as indicated, not at all related to long-term memory.

Age of Subject and Age of Memory Confounded

To study age effects it is ideal to keep the age of memories the same among people of different age groups. Thus, the memory of the death of President Kennedy dates from 1963 for people of all ages who noted the event at that time. However, not all studies lend themselves to keeping separate the age of the memory and the age of the person holding this memory. Such studies are sources of interesting information, nevertheless, as can be seen in the study by Bahrick, Bahrick, and Wittlinger (1975).

They tested high school graduates ranging in age from 17 to 74 years. These adults had graduated from high school as recently as 3–4 months prior to the study and as long ago as 47–48 years. They were tested for memory of the names and faces of their classmates from the high school yearbooks.

A variety of tests were made but only two will be discussed here—the other tests will be discussed in the next chapter when the difference between recall and recognition memory is examined. The two tests were the recall of names and the recall of faces. Very simply, the subjects were asked to list all the names of class members that they could. For faces, the subjects were presented with portraits and had to write the appropriate names.

Not unexpectedly, perhaps, recall of both names and names associated with faces declined with time. From 3-4 years after high school graduation to 47-48 years after graduation, recall of names declined 60 percent and recall of names associated with faces declined more than 70 percent. (Later, in chapter 18, it will be seen that this decline in recall was not an index of lost memories because class members were remarkably well recognized even after very long periods as seen by tests of recognition memory.) The point here is simply that recall functions do decline over time; perhaps the information was not well processed in the first place, as evidenced by the fact that even those newly graduated (3-4 months) could recall only 15 percent of the names.

The decline in recall functions over time might suggest a decline with age in long-term memory, contrary to the conclusions of Botwinick and Storandt. It is crucial to emphasize, however, that in the study by Bahrick et al., the age of the memory was confounded with the age of the subject—the older people were out of high school longer and thus the memories were older. One, or both of these together (age of memory and age of person), may have contributed to this decline in recall.

SUMMARY

Learning and memory are measured in comparable ways. In typical laboratory learning studies, be they of paired-associate "learning," serial "learning," or some other learning task, the subjects report what *had* been learned—their *recall* is measured, even if the learning had just taken place. The measurement of this learning sometimes is called "immediate memory."

A question asked by several investigators is whether the more primary problem in later life is "immediate memory" or delayed, longer-term recall. Evidence was seen that when age groups are matched for immediate recall performance, they are similar in delayed recall performance. However, other evidence was also seen, i.e.. differences with age in delayed recall over and beyond differences in immediate memory. This latter evidence might suggest that there is more than one kind of memory process.

Most investigators, probably, would maintain that there is a memory system called primary memory (PM) and another one called secondary memory (SM). The two are different in several ways but the most important is that PM is temporary and limited in capacity, while SM is longer term and of enormous, unlimited capacity. PM is typically measured by presenting the subjects with a short string of digits, letters, or words and measuring recall "immediately." This is the memory span. This recall is almost a "read out"; it is of the psychological present, of what was just now experienced. Old people and young people are not very different in PM, if they are different at all.

PM, being of limited capacity, involves only a very short string of span items. If the string is long, for example 15 digits, it is called supra-span and much or all of it is thought residing in SM, not PM. What characterizes SM is active processing of the information on the part of the memorizer. To improve learning, to fix memories in mind for extended periods of time, it is necessary to organize, to integrate the new information with what is already known. The information must be made meaningful and this is why SM is sometimes called semantic memory.

Age groups are very different in SM—the younger people perform better. Instructions to organize, or providing meaningful processing techniques, help both the old and the young, with some studies showing relatively more benefit to one age group and other studies showing more to another age group.

Beyond PM and SM there is sensory memory. Sensory memory takes the form of a very short-term experience which may be more perceptual than memorial. Sensory memory, in visual form at least, seems less well developed in the old than in the young and one study indicated that few older adults may be able to develop it in the first place.

No studies of sensory memory in its auditory form in relation to age have been carried out, but something that may be close to it has been— dichotic stimulation where one-half of auditory information is processed for recall (SM) and the other half thought "passed through" a perceptual system. The results of studies are mixed in indicating whether this latter type of recall is age-related.

In addition to sensory memory, PM, and SM, there may be a separate very long-term memory system. The evidence suggests that very long-term recall is not affected in an overall way by age, but people of different ages tend to recall different things. One study suggested that socio-historic events experienced during the age period 15 to 25 years seem the best remembered, better than when events are experienced later in life. Perhaps people are more receptive at that age than later and so events have more impact value at that time. This may just be another way of saying that the information is most deeply processed at that time and so remains in storage longest. This interpretation would place long-term recall in SM.

Old memories do seem to decay in time for everyone but, often, this is hard to measure independently of the age of the person. For example, one study measured recall of names and faces of high school class members. This is a one-year memory for most 19-year-olds but a 50-year memory for 68-year-olds. To study age effects, the age of the memory must be the same for all age groups.

REFERENCES

Abel, M. *The visual trace in relation to aging.* Unpublished doctoral dissertation, Washington University, St. Louis, Mo., 1972.

Arenberg, D. The effects of input condition on free recall in young and old adults. *Journal of Gerontology,* 1976, *31,* 551–555.

Bahrick, H.P., Bahrick, P.O., and Wittlinger, R.P. Fifty years of memory for names and faces: a cross-sectional approach. *Journal of Experimental Psychology,* 1975, *104,* 54–75.

Botwinick, J. *Cognitive processes in maturity and old age.* New York: Springer Publishing Co., 1967.

Botwinick, J., and Storandt, M. *Memory, related functions and age.* Springfield, Ill.: Charles C Thomas, 1974.

Broadbent, D.E. *Perception and communication.* New York: Pergamon Press, 1958.

Bromley, D.B. Some effects of age on short-term learning and memory. *Journal of Gerontology,* 1958, *13,* 398–406.

Canestrari, R.E., Jr. Age changes in acquisition. In G.A. Talland (Ed.), *Human aging and behavior.* New York: Academic Press, 1968, pp. 169–188.

Christensen, C.R. *Inferference in memory as a function of age.* Unpublished doctoral dissertation, Washington University, St. Louis, Mo., 1968.

Clark, L., and Knowles, J. Age differences in dichotic listening performance. *Journal of Gerontology,* 1973, *28,* 173–178.

Craik, F.I.M. The nature of the age decrement in performance on dichotic listening tasks. *Quarterly Journal of Experimental Psychology,* 1965, *17,* 227–240.

Craik, F.I.M. Age differences in human memory. In J.E. Birren and K.W. Schaie (Eds.), *Handbook of the psychology of aging.* New York: Van Nostrand Reinhold, 1977.

Davis, S.H., and Obrist, W.D. Age differences in learning and retention of verbal material. *Cornell Journal of Social Relations,* 1966, *1,* 95–103.

Doty, B.A., and Doty, L.A. Effect of age and chlorpromazine on memory consolidation. *Journal of Comparative and Physiological Psychology,* 1964, *57,* 331–334.

Drachman, D., and Leavitt, J. Memory impairment in the aged: storage versus retrieval deficit. *Journal of Experimental Psychology,* 1972, *93,* 302–308.

Eysenck, M.W. Age differences in incidental learning. *Developmental Psychology*, 1974, *10*, 936–941.

Fraser, D.C. Decay of immediate memory with age. *Nature*, 1958, *182*, 1163.

Friedman, H. Interrelation of two types of immediate memory in the aged. *Journal of Psychology*, 1974, *87*, 177–181.

Gilbert, J.G. Memory loss in senescence. *Journal of Abnormal and Social Psychology*, 1941, *36*, 73–86.

Goodrick, C.L. Learning, retention, and extinction of a complex maze habit for mature-young and senescent Wistar albino rats. *Journal of Gerontology*, 1968, *23*, 298–304.

Gordon, S.K., and Clark, W.C. Application of signal detection theory to prose recall and recognition in elderly and young adults. *Journal of Gerontology*, 1974, *29*, 64–72.

Harwood, E., and Naylor, G.F.K. Recall and recognition in elderly and young subjects. *Australian Journal of Psychology*, 1969, *21*, 251–257.

Hulicka, I.M. Age differences for intentional and incidental learning and recall scores. *Journal of American Geriatrics Society*, 1965, *13*, 639–649.

Hulicka, I.M., and Grossman, J.L. Age group comparisons for the use of mediators in paired-associate learning. *Journal of Gerontology*, 1967, *22*, 46–51.

Hulicka, I.M., and Weiss, R.L. Age differences in retention as a function of learning. *Journal of Consulting Psychology*, 1965, *29*, 125–129.

Hultsch, D. Adult age differences in the organization of free recall. *Developmental Psychology*, 1969, *1*, 673–678.

Hultsch, D. Adult age differences in free classification and free recall. *Developmental Psychology*, 1971, *4*, 338–342.

Hultsch, D. Adult age differences in retrieval: trace development and cue dependent forgetting. *Developmental Psychology*, 1975, *11*, 197–201.

Inglis, J., and Caird, W.K. Age differences in successive responses to simultaneous stimulation. *Canadian Journal of Psychology*, 1963, *17*, 98–105.

Jerome, E.A. Age and learning—experimental studies. In J.E. Birren (Ed.), *Handbook of aging and the individual: psychological and biological aspects*. Chicago: Univ. of Chicago Press, 1959, pp. 655–699.

Melton, A.W. Implications of short-term memory for a general theory of memory. *Journal of Verbal Learning and Verbal Behavior*, 1963, *2*, 1–21.

Melton, A.W. Relations between short-term memory, long-term memory and learning. In D.P. Kimble (Ed.), *The organization of recall*. New York: New York Academy of Science Interdisciplinary Communications Program, 1967, pp. 24–62.

Perlmutter, M. What is memory aging the aging of? *Developmental Psychology*, 1978, in press.

Salthouse, T.A. Age and tachistoscopic perception. *Experimental Aging Research*, 1976, *2*, 91–103.

Schonfield, D., Trueman, V., and Kline, D. Recognition tests of dichotic listening and the age variable. *Journal of Gerontology*, 1972, *27*, 487–493.

Sperling, G. The information available in brief visual presentations. *Psychological Monographs: General and Applied*, 1960, *74* (11), 1–28.

Sperling, G. A model for visual memory tasks. *Human Factors*, 1963, *5*, 19–31.

Walsh, D. Age differences in learning and memory. In D.S. Woodruff and J.E. Birren (Eds.), *Aging*. New York: D. Van Nostrand Co., 1975.

Walsh, D.A., and Jenkins, J.J. Effects of orienting tasks on free recall in incidental learning: "difficulty," "effort," and "process" explanations. *Journal of Verbal Learning and Verbal Behavior*, 1973, 12, 481–488.

Walsh, D. and Thompson, L.W. Age differences in visual sensory memory. *Journal of Gerontology*, 1978, 33, 383–387.

Waugh, N.C., and Norman, D.A. Primary memory. *Psychological Review*, 1965, 72, 89–104.

Wimer, R.E. A supplementary report on age differences in retention over a twenty-four hour period. *Journal of Gerontology*, 1960, 15, 417–418.

Wimer, R.E., and Wigdor, B.T. Age differences in retention of learning. *Journal of Gerontology*, 1958, 13, 291–295.

18
Retrieving Memories

This chapter, the last of the four-chapter sequence on learning and memory, focuses on retrieval from memory. Retrieval is thought basic to recall—it is a process whereby items of information are brought up from the memory store so that they can be used. A failure of retrieval is seen with the experience, "I have it at the tip of my tongue, I know his name but I can't come up with it now." Later in conversation the name is recalled. The memory is in storage, but it can't be retrieved at the moment of need.

A major question in aging research is whether it is primarily impairment of retrieval mechanisms or impairment of storage itself that accounts for age decrements in recall. If the problem is storage, the name is forgotten and can never be recalled. The information is no longer available. If the problem is retrieval and not storage, then the information is available but not accessible (Tulving and Pearlstone, 1966). Retrieval is the access mechanism.

Recall memory is said to involve the search and retrieval of information in storage. It is as if there is a large bank of information, and to recall any part of it, a search is necessary; then, the found information must be retrieved. *Recognition memory*, on the other hand, is thought not to involve retrieval. All that is required is a matching of the information in storage with the information in the environment. (There are other views, e.g., Tulving and Thomson [1973], but in the main, this is the prevailing one.) This is an example of a typical question bearing on recall memory: Who was the third President of the United States? The correct answer requires a "search of the data bank" and a "retrieval" of the information, Thomas Jefferson. Here is a question bearing on recognition memory: Among these five names, which one is of the third President of the United States? A "match" is required; retrieval is not thought of as part of the processes.

337

RETRIEVAL FUNCTIONS
Superiority of Recognition over Recall

Utilizing such a model and distinction between recall and recognition, subjects ranging in age from 20 to 75 years were given tests of both types of memory (Schonfield, 1965; Schonfield and Robertson, 1966). On the basis of these tests it was concluded that "the aged show special defects in the remembering of acquired material stored over longer periods of time. These defects seem to be due to a loss in the ability to retrieve memories from storage rather than a deficiency in the storage system itself" (Schonfield, 1965, p. 918).

Schonfield had two lists of 24 words, and he presented the words to the subjects one at a time. Memory of these words was tested by free recall of one list and by recognition of the other. For this recognition test, the subjects were shown the 24 words, each in a group of four other words, and asked to underline those previously seen.

Figure 18.1 shows the results of this study. It shows that there was no decline with age in the recognition scores, but there was a consistent drop in the recall scores. The disparity between the two functions in

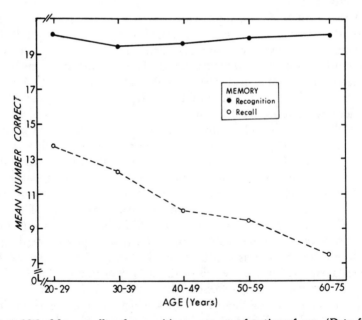

FIGURE 18.1: Mean recall and recognition scores as a function of age. (Data from Table 1 of Schonfield, 1965.)

Figure 18.1 was attributed to retrieval. Older subjects were as successful as the young in their efforts "to match a stimulus with a stored trace." This is not to say that all recognition memory studies show old and young as similar. In fact, one study (Erber, 1974) was modeled after Schonfield's and showed age decline. The point is, however, that most studies, but not all, show greater decline in recall than in recognition.

Erber tested young (19–30) and elderly (65–75) women for recognition and recall memory by giving them a list of 24 words to learn and remember. The test of recognition required the subject to identify each of these words when presented with four others not given before. This procedure was the same one used by Schonfield. In addition a longer list was given for learning—60 words. Unlike what Schonfield found, the old did not recognize as many words correctly as the young with either list length (24 or 60 words). While recognition memory was better with the shorter list than the longer, this was equally true for old and young. Essentially the same results were found with recall of the words learned as in recognition, but the difference between young and old was greater in recall.

Erber's results seem to be typical of many studies, although there are exceptions. Perlmutter (1978), for example, also found recognition performances of newly learned information better than recall, but the extent was similar for people in their 60s and their 20s. Further, an unusual result was reported by Adamowicz (1976). He presented for learning simple and complex geometric patterns, rather than verbal materials, and reported that in one part of the study the older adults' recall memory was the same as that of their younger counterparts, but their recognition memory was somewhat poorer. He concluded that "the data do not provide support for a retrieval deficit hypothesis" (Adamowicz, 1976, p. 45).

Perceptual Matching. Other evidence seen later will also challenge the retrieval deficit hypothesis, but in the main, the results of Schonfield and of Erber, showing that recall performance is more related to age than is recognition performance, seem to be most typical. If Schonfield's data suggest that retrieval processes are a basic problem in the memory of older adults, Erber's suggest so too, but the latter study also suggests that problems in addition to retrieval are involved. Storage may be an issue, as may be the processes of searching and matching within the test field.

Erber presented her subjects with 24 words and found recognition memory decrements with age when testing with five alternatives, one being the correct one learned before. As will be seen shortly, Kapnick

(1971) presented up to 40 words for learning and found no recognition decrement, but he tested with only two alternatives. On the other hand, Botwinick and Storandt (1974, chapter 14) gave their subjects only 8 words to learn but had them identify all 8 within a list of 32 words. In this latter study recognition memory was seen to fall with age. If the job of searching and matching the information in storage with that in the environment is a difficult or complex one, then this perceptual job, rather than retrieval or storage mechanisms, may be a central issue.

Partial Information. While in Schonfield's and Erber's studies, the results were unequivocal in showing that recognition memory held better with age than recall memory, McNulty and Caird (1966) challenged the interpretation that retrieval is all that distinguishes the two types of memory. They argued that, with recognition memory, only a partial learning of the given information is necessary to perform well, while with recall memory, a total learning is necessary. For example, knowledge of only two or three letters of a group may be sufficient for recognizing the whole group, but for correct recall knowledge of all the letters of the group is necessary. If older people acquire and store information less well than young people, and thus have only a partial knowledge of the total, it may be expected that their recall performances would suffer but not necessarily their recognition performances. Partial information, not retrieval, could explain Schonfield's data, seen in Figure 18.1.

Hartley and Marshall (1967) put this thinking to a test; they carried out a study suggested by McNulty and Caird. The assumption of the study was that, as the correct and incorrect alternatives in recognition tests become more similar to each other, more complete information is necessary to distinguish between them. If a very fine discrimination is necessary because the alternatives are very similar, almost a total knowledge of the information is necessary, as it is in recall. Therefore, if there are two lists, one in which finer discriminations between correct and incorrect are necessary, and the other in which less fine discriminations will suffice, older subjects should perform relatively poorly with the former list. If the results of the study were so, the contention of McNulty and Caird would receive support and the one of Schonfield would be put in doubt.

The results of Hartley and Marshall were based upon subjects aged 75-80 years. The mean recognition performances of these elderly subjects were identical for both types of lists. Thus, these data offer no criticism of Schonfield's analysis. Hartley and Marshall suggested, however, that "a more stringent control" of the differences between the lists may be necessary before their hypothesis is discarded.

Delayed Recognition. The recall and recognition performances summarized in Figure 18.1 were made soon after exposure to the stimulus materials. Harwood and Naylor (1969) tested for recall and recognition, not soon after exposure but four weeks after such exposure; their results were quite different.

Part of this study was described in the previous chapter. A series of 20 drawings of familiar objects such as a tennis racket, a ladder, a tree, was presented one at a time to subjects aged 60-80 years and subjects aged 15-45 years. When all 20 drawings were presented, tests of recall were made. If the subject correctly recalled 16 or more items (80 percent), the procedure was regarded as completed. If fewer items were recalled, the procedure was repeated. It was repeated as many times as necessary to achieve at least an 80 percent recall performance.

At this point all the subjects thought the experiment was over, but about a month later they were again tested; this time, with both a recall test and a recognition test. The recognition test followed the recall test and it involved the original 20 drawings plus 40 additional ones as the incorrect alternatives.

The results were comparable to those of Schonfield in that the age decline in recall was greater than in recognition, and it was compatible with Erber's study in that a significant recognition performance decline with age was also found. This decline was not great—the younger group had a mean recognition score of 19.00, while the old had 16.55—but it was statistically significant even after equating for initial learning. The results were also compatible with those of a study by Gordon and Clark (1974). They compared the retention of information read in a paragraph just previously with one read a week earlier. Age differences in both delayed recall and recognition memory were found, with the former being greater. Over one week, the elderly forget more of the information than the young.

The superiority of delayed recognition over delayed recall memory once again argues for a retrieval deficit in later life, but the recognition memory deficit argues for some storage problem as well. The coefficient of correlation between these two types of memories in the study by Harwood and Naylor was effectively zero, suggesting the independence of these two processes. Both processes were related to a small extent ($r = 0.3$) to the number of items correctly recalled after the last stimulus presentation, one month previously. They were not related, however, to the number of presentations required to originally recall the 80 percent correct. Considered altogether, the study by Harwood and Naylor suggests independence of the processes of delayed recall and recognition memory, and some independence of both these processes from short-term recall.

Task Difficulty

Even when the major distinction between recall and recognition is made on the basis of retrieval, and Schonfield's and Erber's conclusions are taken as essentially correct, there are other possible distinctions too. It may be seen in Figure 18.1 that, based upon the measurement of correct response, the recognition task was much the easier of the two tasks. While we may anticipate that the recognition task would be the easier one since recall involves an additional process, retrieval, the fact is that old people perform relatively well on a wide variety of easy tasks, irrespective of whether or not retrieval is involved. For example, in chapter 15, paired-associate learning was discussed, and it was seen that easier associations, that is, the more likely ones (e.g., Table-Chair) make for relatively good performances on the part of the elderly, but the more difficult associations (e.g., Table-Glove) make for a greater disparity between age groups. Perhaps it is not retrieval at all which accounts for the disparity among the age patterns of the two curves in Figure 18.1, but simply the relative difficulty of the two tasks. Difficult tasks require more attention and motivation as well as greater ability than do easier tasks; if, with age, there is greater tendency to distraction, if Schonfield's older subjects were less motivated or cooperative, if they were simply less able overall, then these factors alone could account for the disproportionately poorer performances on the part of the older subjects with the recall task.

Length of Task. Partly with considerations such as these, Kapnick (1971) undertook to examine the role of task difficulty in recognition memory as it is reflected in the length of the task. He presented subjects aged 20 to 62 years with tasks of recognition memory, varied in four difficulty levels. He presented subjects with lists of 10, 20, 30, or 40 words, and then paired each word with one other in asking the subjects to indicate which one they had seen before. If retrieval is not involved in recognition memory, and it is only retrieval among the memory processes which declines with age, and if task difficulty is not to be raised in explanation, then two results should be seen: one, no change in recognition memory performance with age; two, no increased age decrement in recognition performance as the tasks became more difficult (from 10 to 40 words in a list).

Both of these results were observed. Poorer performances were not associated with increased age nor with the combination of increased age and the more difficult tasks. The conclusion of Schonfield that retrieval is not a problem in later life received support.

This study also points to the need for additional ones. First, the age range of subjects that Kapnick tested, while wide, was also limited in the upper ages; no subject was over 62 years. Would people over this age show a recognition memory deficit with his procedure? Second, recognizing a learned word in a complex of only two words remains an easy task, even with 40 words in a list. Would a recognition deficit be found in later life when the stimulus word was embedded in a complex of five or more words? The study by Botwinick and Storandt mentioned in the context of perceptual matching suggested that it would.

Magnitude of Task. Craik (1968a, b) did not ask these questions, but he did ask related ones in the context of free recall situations. First, he reasoned that there are two important task dimensions in retrieval; one is the length of the task and the other is the magnitude of possible responses. The job of retrieval is made more difficult both as more items are to be recalled and as there are more possible items to search for retrieval. He then asked: If older people have less efficient memory retrieval systems than younger people, would this not be reflected more and more as these two dimensions of the retrieval process become greater in magnitude?

Craik set up an experiment to test this by varying the stimulus materials in two ways. First, he varied the length of the list of items that were to be recalled. Then he varied "the total possible vocabulary," i.e., the total possible responses—correct and incorrect, both. His smallest vocabulary was of digits—they could only vary from 0 to 9; therefore the vocabulary was a total of ten items. His next vocabulary list was English county names—clearly more than ten items were possible here; next was animal names; and his largest vocabulary was of unrelated words. In this way, Craik had two simultaneous variations; within each level of vocabulary size he varied the number of items in the list to be recalled. The digits were presented in six lengths, from 5 to 10 digits in a list; the three other vocabularies were presented in these lengths also plus lists of 15 items and lists of 20 items.

The prediction was that recall (retrieval) would become disproportionately poorer for old people as the number of items in a list increased, as the vocabulary size increased, and, even more so, as both of these increased simultaneously. Two age groups of subjects were compared, a young group aged 18-30 years and an older group aged 60-69 years.

In the main, Craik's predictions regarding list length and vocabulary size were confirmed, but the combination of the two was not of special importance. Thus, while not all the facets of Craik's predictions were confirmed, the general notion of retrieval deficits in later life remained valid.

Primary and Secondary Memory. Craik started out with a model of memory similar to the one of Waugh and Norman (1965), discussed in the previous chapter. Craik's model involved two mechanisms: a primary memory (PM) of a limited capacity and a secondary memory (SM), much larger in capacity. "Recall is viewed as occurring in two stages: First a read-out of material still present in PM; and second a search process through the relevant part of SM" (Craik, 1968b, p. 996).

Having this model, Craik made an effort to determine whether it was PM or SM which was most affected by aging. He predicted it would be SM because this involved retrieval, while PM involved only "read-out."

Craik mathematically fit equations to the curves describing recall scores as a function of the length of the lists. He then determined, for each individual, the hypothetical recall score when the task was infinitely easy, i.e., a list of zero length (the intercept of the linear best fit as determined by the least-squares solution). Craik equated conceptually this hypothetical recall score with PM, and compared the two age groups with respect to it. In accordance with his prediction, there were no systematic age differences with this read-out, limited capacity system.

SM, the memory involving search and retrieval processes, was estimated by subtracting the PM estimate from the total recall score. Here, age was seen as important: People aged 60-69 had lower SM scores than people aged 18-30 years. Craik (1968a, p. 164) concluded that "poor registration and less efficient retrieval" characterized the older subjects.

While Craik found supporting evidence in the literature for this conclusion regarding PM—e.g., Bromley (1958) showed that digit span decreases only very slightly with age, and Talland (1965) found this result with word span—one aspect of his results seems to limit the validity of his conclusions. The PM is thought to be independent of the vocabulary size since it is only a "read-out" and does not refer to the total possible variety of responses. Craik did not find this in his analysis; PM was related to vocabulary size. He attempted another, but related, method of estimating PM, and found essentially the same result. Thus, while Craik was clear in his conclusion regarding the aging of PM and SM, he indicated that this conclusion was based on less than optimum estimates of the PM.

A concluding note regarding operational definitions may be in order. In the final analysis, retrieval is defined by recall performances; PM is nothing very different from recall measured with very short lists; and SM is not very different from recall scores measured with longer lists.

Accordingly, we refer back to the earlier discussion of task difficulty and repeat: In a great variety of situations, when the task is very easy, older people are not seen as very different in their performances from younger people; when the task is hard, they differ more.

Rate of Search

A clever procedure was devised to estimate the rate at which people search their memories (Sternberg, 1969), and it was used to compare people of different ages (Anders, Fozard, and Lillyquist, 1972). The procedure has subjects memorize only a few items of information so well that the accuracy of their responses in tests of recognition memory is no longer an issue. That is, storage issues are not in question; only those of rate of search and matching are in question. The recognition task is such that one item is presented at a time to which the subject simply responds "yes" or "no," reflecting whether or not the item was in the earlier memorized list. What is different in this procedure by Anders et al. from the other recognition tasks is that the time to respond is measured rather than correctness of response, since a high level of accuracy is taken for granted.

Anders et al. presented lists of 1, 3, 5, and 7 digits in length to people of three age groups: 19-21 years, 33-43 years, and 58-85 years. The speed with which these subjects made "yes" or "no" recognition responses was analyzed in relation to the length of the list. This was done with the idea that, while the overall response speeds reflected a variety of factors, including motor response times, the differences in response speeds between the longer and the shorter lists reflected the rates with which memory was searched and matches made possible. Figure 18.2 shows the results of this study. The curves of the older groups were steeper in slope than that of the younger group, and were thus thought to indicate that the older groups were slower in their rates of search. The slopes of the two older groups did not differ significantly from each other and were thus thought to reflect similar search speeds.

The rationale behind this analysis is that the more items in store, the more time it takes to search them for any use. Searching seven items, for example, takes longer than searching one item. Given that older people are slower in speed of response than younger people for a variety of reasons, their slowness with seven items relative to one item reflects the increased time they take for searching their memory for the greater number of items.

Anders et al. indicated that this longer time taken to search memory

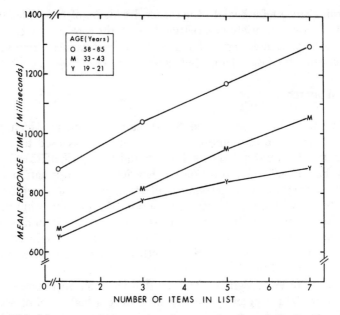

FIGURE 18.2: Mean recognition response time as a function of the number of digits in a list. (Figure developed from Figure 1 of Anders et al., 1972.)

in later life becomes progressively detrimental to recall as there is more information to search. In searching one's memory, there is opportunity for interference and distraction; as the search takes more and more time, these opportunities become greater and greater.

In a subsequent study, Anders and Fozard (1973) sought to estimate rate of search in both primary memory (PM) and secondary memory (SM). For PM, subjects were shown lists of 1, 3, or 5 items only briefly and tested immediately afterwards. For SM, the subjects learned other lists of these same lengths well in advance of testing. The thinking behind this study was that PM is relatively short-term while SM is of much longer duration. The investigators asked whether there were differences with age in the rates of searching both PM and SM.

Men and women aged 20–23 and 49–65 were tested in this fashion. The PM data reflected what Figure 18.2 indicates. Anders and Fozard (1973, p. 413) reported that "Young subjects search through the contents of primary memory at about twice the speed of older subjects." Even though the lists were shown for learning only briefly, few errors were made.

SM search reflected a similar picture, but with the length of list being an even more important factor in estimating age differences in rate of search. The two age groups were not very different in the one-item search, but were very different in the five-item search. Overall, then, these two studies reflected similar results.

Marsh (1975) also carried out this Sternberg procedure while electrophysiologically monitoring brain activity. He wanted to see if rate of search was related to a late positive component of the evoked potential. He did not find such a relationship. Moreover, he did not find elderly and young more different in their search rates of five items than of one item. These results challenge somewhat those of the two studies above in regard to search rates and age, although they are similar in reflecting age differences in response times.

STORAGE FUNCTIONS

Retrieval and storage are the major concepts in memory theory. Retrieval, just discussed, presupposes information already in the memory store. Storage includes two concepts—one, the placement of information in memory (i.e., learning) and two, its being kept there. Chapter 17 told that placing information in storage is accomplished by working on the information, i.e., processing information that is to be retained. Information is processed by organizing it, integrating it with what is already known, and other similar techniques. Once in storage, information is thought to be long lasting if it has been processed well. If not, it is thought to decay or otherwise be lost. Decay of memory is not a satisfactory explanatory concept because it is simply a label describing that memories do not seem to be available for recall. What might appear to be decay at first may be seen as poor retrieval later on. Further, what might appear as decay may be the result of interference—difficulty in differentiating the item in storage from other, similar items experienced before and after learning.

Acquisition, Decay, and Interference

The usual recognition studies, Schonfield's seen in Figure 18.1, for example, have the subject learn a word or other item of information and then identify it among other alternatives. A different technique to study recognition memory that has recently been used involves the presentation of a long list of words, some of them repeating and some not. The subject's job is to identify the words that were seen before and those that were not. Some investigators believe that this is a more realistic way to test for recognition memory since in everyday life people are not typically confronted with a number of alternative choices in recognition. More typically, information continuously appears before us with the need to identify what we know or have seen before.

Wickelgren (1975) carried out such a procedure, testing three age groups, two of adults (18–24 and 60–82 years). The long list of words was continuously presented for two hours, thus, there was good opportunity to chart changes in recognition performance over this length of time. Again, the older adults were poorer than the young ones but, very important, after two hours recognition performance was poorer for both age groups than it was before then; forgetting took place. Also, very important, the rate of forgetting was the same for old and young. Wickelgren (1975, p. 168) concluded, "memory storage dynamics are equivalent over different ages. . . ."

This conclusion accepts the difference between age groups in acquisition and suggests similarity in decay processes. However, it could also suggest similarity in interference effects. From the beginning of the study to the end of it two hours later, many words were viewed and many new ones appeared between old ones. This alone could explain recognition memory decline. In other words, it is not necessarily so that the information is no longer in storage; it may be that it is difficult to differentiate this information from all that intervened. Erber (1978) tested such a notion using a similar procedure, varying the number of new words intervening between ones seen before. Like Wickelgren, she observed that older people (64–77 years) correctly recognized the words less often than younger people (18–29) but she also found that recognition performance decreased with increasing interference. While there was some differential age effect due to interference it was not large or consistent.

Cued and Non-Cued Recall

If information is in storage but not accessible by retrieval mechanisms, memory can be aided by cues or hints. If the cue works, then it is clear that the information was available in storage and that the retrieval mechanisms were not adequate. If the cue does not work, if the information still cannot be recalled, a storage problem *might* be the reason for the failure in recall. Studies comparing cued with non-cued recall, therefore, are thought to compare storage functions with retrieval functions respectively.

Hultsch (1975) compared cued and non-cued recall among men and women aged 18–34, 50–64, and 65–83 years. This study was briefly discussed in chapter 16 in a different context, and it may be recalled that 40 words were presented for learning, four in each of 10 categories. In the non-cued condition, each subject was simply asked to recall the words. In the cued condition, the category name was supplied. Hultsch's results of non-cued recall were typical of those seen throughout this discussion, i.e., the young performed better than the old (but here, not significantly better than the middle-aged). As expected, cued recall was better than non-cued, with the young performing better than both older groups. Thus, Hultsch concluded: Memory difficulties in later life seem attributable to both retrieval and storage mechanisms.

Drachman and Leavitt (1972) also studied cued and non-cued recall. Two lists of 35 words each were given for learning and memory. In the case of cued recall, the first letters were provided to men and women (18–26 and 58–89 years) on answer sheets. In the case of non-cued recall, only the answer sheet (without first letters) was given. The results were compatible with those of Hultsch: The young performed better in both cued and non-cued conditions.

Retrieval of Well-Known Information (Old Storage)

Retrieval by Category. Drachman and Leavitt (1972, p. 308) concluded from their study that ". . . no evidence [was found] for a retrieval deficit as the major cause of the observed memory impairment; a disorder of storage seems more likely at present." This conclusion was based not so much on the cued versus non-cued recall data as on the recall of very familiar information. They had their subjects "retrieve by category," i.e., the subjects had to list as many names of items as they could within certain categories. For example, the category "fruit" was given and the subjects had to itemize all the kinds of fruits they could within a specified time. No differences between age groups were found, leading to the conclusion that retrieval (of fruit names, in this example) was not an issue in memory loss. This finding, together with those of the age difference in both cued and non-cued recall (and in other tasks as well) led to the conclusion that retrieval was not the crucial mechanism in memory loss.

Retrieval and Decision. A somewhat similar study and result was reported by Eysenck (1975). He had subjects aged 18–30 and 55–65 carry out a recall task whereby a category name was given, but also a specified letter. For example, rather than the category "fruit" with the requirement to list different kinds, Eysenck provided a letter that specified the type. Thus, with the presentation of "fruit-a," the subject could correctly respond, "apple." Old and young responded equally quickly on this task, again pointing to intact retrieval.

A recognition task was also given. Here the subject was given the category followed by a word (e.g., fruit-ghost) and had to decide whether the word fit the category (ghost doesn't fit, apple does). In this task, unlike the "recall" task of supplying the word "apple" to the category "fruit," the old were slower. Eysenck thought their slowness was due to cautiousness in decision—a concept perhaps related to perceptual matching in recognition tasks, discussed earlier.

Naming Latency. The studies above, i.e., those of listing well-known items (apple) when presented with the categories (fruit) are almost the easiest and simplest type of recall task possible. There is an even easier one, however. Thomas, Fozard, and Waugh (1977) carried it out with results that could be seen as questioning the conclusion that retrieval mechanisms function perfectly in old age. People aged 25 to 74 were shown pictures of well-known common objects. All they had to do was name these objects (i.e., retrieve the names from memory) as quickly as possible. Older subjects took longer to provide the names than younger subjects, but this was reduced with practice. Thus, while retrieval mechanisms may be seen to function well in later life, they do seem to function more slowly.

In sum, it would seem that all these studies taken together suggest that both retrieval and storage mechanisms may be responsible for memory loss in old age.

OLD MEMORIES

It is universally accepted, it seems, that in old age the search and retrieval of new memories are impaired while those of old memories are not, or that they are impaired to a much lesser extent. Why should old memories be recalled more readily than recent ones? While many reasons have been offered in explanation, rarely has the basic observation itself been questioned and put to a proper test; the observation is based more on clinical impression than on controlled study. For example, rarely, if ever, has effort been made to control for the meaningfulness or relevance of the old stored information. How well remembered is old information that is no more personally relevant than the new information taught by the investigator? Even if this were known, it is extremely difficult to evaluate quantity of information so that it would be possible to say that more of the new is lost than of the old. How similar are the units or chunks of memory that are stored over a period of years to those newly acquired in the laboratory or clinic?

There is another difficulty in studying old memories. It is one thing to say that old memories are retained, but it is quite another thing to say that they are retained independently of the frequency with which they are retrieved. Rarely, if ever, has an effort been made to control the relative amounts of rehearsal and use of the old information as compared to the new. Can a superiority of old recall over new recall be explained simply on the basis that the old has been used often? The belief that new memories are forgotten when old ones are retained may be saying hardly more than that important and frequently rehearsed material is retained better than material which is not as important nor as frequently rehearsed. It was seen, for example, that in the study by Hartley and Marshall (1967), irrelevant information acquired a month previously was largely forgotten by both old and young, but more by the old. The concept that rehearsal of important information makes for good recall is not the same concept as the one that the age of the material in storage makes for good recall.

Unfortunately, the needed experimental controls either cannot be made in the study of old memories, or they cannot be made very well. Most often, all that can be done is to compare some old and more recent recall, and to compare these in old and young people. In effect, this is what constitutes much of the literature involving old memories; sometimes only the age of the memories is compared, not the age of the people.

Four types of studies on old memory as seen in the literature will be characterized here. Not included are the types of old recall studies just reviewed wherein category items are supplied (Drachman and Leavitt, Eysenck) or objects named (Thomas et al.). While carried out in the context of retrieval of old storage, these latter studies deal with hardly more than association or labeling—not with what we generally think of when we talk of old memory.

New and Old Recall

Shakow, Dolkart, and Goldman (1941) tested new and old recall, and did so with subjects covering just about all of adult life-span. As a test of old memories, the subjects were asked to recall such varied information as the place of their birth and age, the name of the President, the name of objects, alphabet reciting, and others. As a test of new memories, subjects were asked to recall digits, sentences, and details of a story just read, and to recognize recently shown pictures.

Part of the data of Shakow et al. may be seen in Figure 18.3. It is clear from this figure that the recall of both new and old memories declined with age, but the forgetting of the new material was greater than that of the old material.

It was already indicated that one difficulty with such a comparison, other than the relative importance to the subject of the two types of information, is the scaling of the units of recall. While it is possible to scale the scores of old and new recall to a common index, their relative meaning would not necessarily be the same. What does it mean when old and young subjects are 15 units apart in remembering old names, but 25 units apart in remembering newly learned digits? There is a lack of a common base with which to compare the difficulty, meaningfulness, and other characteristics of the memories.

Klonoff and Kennedy (1965) also tested for new and old memory, but did so with old subjects only (80-92 years). They also found that the recall of old memories (such as personal information and information of place and time) remained relatively intact, while the recall of new memory (Wechsler Memory Scale) faired less well. Klonoff and Kennedy found a significant relationship between the level of activity of

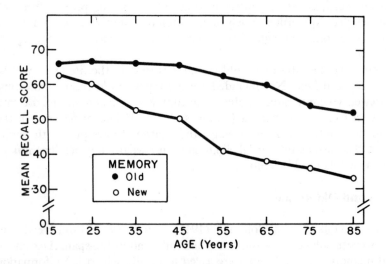

FIGURE 18.3: Mean recall scores of old and newly learned material as a function of age. Data are from the study of Shakow, Dolkart, and Goldman (1941) and reproduced from Figure 13 of Botwinick, 1967.

the subjects and their memory scores. It is not known, of course, whether people who are active retain their memory ability, or whether those who have this ability remain active.

Old Recall and Recognition

Age of Memory and Age of Subject. The old recall in the study by Shakow et al. was of such personal information as age and place of birth, naming objects, alphabet reciting, and other items of this kind. Clearly, while these are items of memory, they are not memory in the sense that we usually think of it. The study by Bahrick, Bahrick, and Wittlinger (1975), discussed in the previous chapter, comes closer to what is commonly meant by memory.

It may be recalled that these investigators tested high school graduates for the recall of names and faces of class members in their yearbooks. As only suggested in the previous chapter, the investigators also studied recognition memory. The recall tasks were simply to: (1) list the names of class members, and (2) indicate the name when presented with the portrait. The recognition tasks were to: (1) identify the portrait of a class member when presented with four other portraits, (2) identify the name of the class member when presented with four other names, (3) match a name with one of several portraits, and (4) match a portrait with one of several names presented with it.

In this study, the age of the memory (number of years since graduation) was confounded with age of the subject. Thus, forgetting could be attributed either to age of memory, age of subject, or both. Forgetting in the sense of recall memory was apparent—the more recent graduates remembered many more names and faces than the old graduates. After about 40 years, recall declined by about 60–70 percent. However, the identification or recognition processes showed remarkable retention. "The viewed information (faces) is retained virtually unimpaired for at least 35 years. Verbal information (names) declines somewhat after 15 years" (Bahrick et al., p. 65). The investigators concluded that retrieval processes are independent of storage processes. This conclusion is implicit in the arguments set forward earlier, as for example, in the study by Schonfield (represented in Figure 18.1).

Age of Memory. The study by Botwinick and Storandt (1974) avoided the confound between age of memory and age of subject. It may be recalled from the previous chapter that men and women of wide age range were asked to recall sociohistoric events that had taken place during different time periods. No overall differences with age in recall were noted. Perlmutter (1978) did note differences in event recall when she compared people in their 20s and 60s, the older adults being superior. Perlmutter also gave a recognition memory test, but the test took a form different from the usual laboratory procedure. The test was of 48 items, each of which had to be responded to as "true" or "false." Again the older subjects were superior, and to about the same extent as she found in the test of recall.

Remote Recall

A distinction has been made between old memories which tend to be practiced often in the course of a lifetime—memories such as names, places, and time—and those which do not. Very old, remote memories which are not practiced are very difficult to systematically examine, and, for the most part, have not been. There are two studies, however, in which such memories have been examined, and these studies are most unusual. In both of these studies, the investigator and subject were one and the same person: At early ages one investigator (Smith) learned verbal material, and another investigator (Hill) learned a psychomotor skill. In both instances, there were retests decades later when there was little or no intentional use or practice of this learning. Although studies of this kind necessarily lack many scientific controls, the data are of such interest and of such extreme difficulty to come by that they warrant special attention. Strictly speaking, these studies are longitudinal studies because the same test is given to the subject at different periods throughout the lifetime. However, the test is of material acquired early in life, and, as such, the measurements confound both age of the subject and age of the memory.

Smith's study was about her ability to recall some well-learned information. During the age period 8-13 years, she memorized the answers to the 107 questions of the Westminster Shorter Catechism and during the next 10 years there was considerable incidental practice of the early portion of the Catechism. More than 20 years after this incidental practice had ceased, Smith (1935) tested herself on her memory of the Catechism. Another 16 years later she had a follow-up test (Smith, 1951), and still 10 years later she tested herself once again (reported in 1963).

Smith was aged approximately 73 years at the last retest, approximately 63 on the one before the last, and approximately 47 years at the first retest. Thus, before the age of 13 years, a perfect score of 107 was achieved and, as may be seen in Figure 18.4, successive retests resulted in scores of 54, 53, and 41. The major loss occurred during the time up to the age of 47 years, and the loss thereafter was small indeed. From age 63 to 73 there was some loss but from age 47 to 63 there was almost none. Was the loss due to decay because of no or little rehearsal? Was it due to interference from a wide variety of subsequent experiences? Was storage or retrieval mainly accountable for the forgetting? Smith's data, of course, do not answer these questions, but do indicate that from age 47 to 73 she forgot very little of what was originally very well stored.

In Figure 18.4, the curve of open circles and dashed lines shows that at the first retest, 44 answers were remembered with little prompting (a cue of no more than two words was given). At the second retest, 39 answers were so remembered, and at the last retest, 32 were so remembered. With more prompting (closed triangles) 9, 15, and 34 were recalled in the successive retests. At every retest, the total of items recalled with and without prompting totaled the 107. It is clear then that, although memory fell off in time with age, none of the items of information was ever totally forgotten. This would suggest a retrieval difficulty, not storage, but Smith (1963) concluded that the answers which tended to be most forgotten were the more difficult ones and those less rehearsed in childhood. This may suggest storage.

Hill (1957) reported data which were similar to those of Smith in that he was his own subject, and he tested himself during different periods of his life. Instead of verbal material, Hill reported results on typewriting skills. At age 80, Hill tested himself in typewriting, having done this 25 and 50 years earlier as a follow-up retest of his original learning.

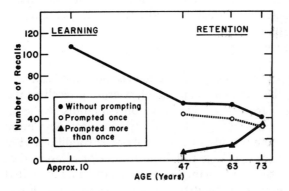

FIGURE 18.4: At the age of approximately 10 years, Smith (1963) learned 107 answers to the questions of the Westminster Shorter Catechism. With little intervening practice she tested her memory of this learning when aged 47, 63, and 73 years. The total number of recalls was 107 at each testing but the number of promptings necessary for these recalls increased with age. (Figure reproduced from Figure 14 of Botwinick, 1967.)

Thus at age 30 years, Hill learned to typewrite and at ages 55 and 80 years, he tested himself. It is of importance that the original learning took place when he was a student-subject for an experiment and the conditions of learning were carefully recorded. He was able to retest himself with very similar conditions and, apparently, with very little practice between testings.

Hill's data are interesting, not only because of the nature of these measurements, but because at each testing he had practice curves extended to at least 35 days. There were two sets of data. One set involved typing the same 100-word paragraph thoughout the experiment. The other set of data involved typing a page of approximately 300 words which were different at each test period. The typing of both the 100- and 300-word tasks took place nearly every day for five months during the initial learning (Hill, Rejall, and Thorndike, 1913).

The 100-word typing during the first day of the first retest was carried out at a level which took Hill 27 days to achieve 25 years previously. Fifty years after the original learning, the first typing was at a level which took eight days to achieve initially. In 25-30 days in both the two recall periods, Hill had performed at a level equivalent to that which had taken him 126 days to accomplish originally. In general, the data of the 300-word typing were similar, although the rate of relearning during the retestings was not as high as it was with the 100-word typings.

The conclusion based upon these observations is that, while there was forgetting of this very old unrehearsed information, there was considerable retention over the period of 50 years. The retention took the form of both an apparently residual skill and a savings in relearning.

Laboratory Learning

All three types of studies described above under the heading "Old Memories" have the common character of measuring recall or recognition of information learned years ago in personal life outside the laboratory. If the experimenter attempts to teach the subject new information for later recall, there is gain in the control of the conditions of learning and storage but he might have to wait a lifetime to measure the old memories. Clearly, the experimenter in this type of study is limited as to how old the memories can be at the time of measurement. Fozard, Waugh, and Thomas (1975) were limited to about two and a half years.

These investigators presented subjects with 100 picture postcards, representing many different kinds of scenes and environments—oceans, airports, persons, and other. The postcards were presented one at a time by slide projection. Immediately after viewing the 100 slides, a test of recognition was given: Each of 20 (of the 100) pictures was paired with one not in the original series. The subject's job was to identify the one seen before.

Three groups—median ages 35, 50, and 67 years—were compared in this immediate test of recognition memory and also in a later test given either 4, 8, 16, 32, 65, or 130 weeks afterward. Fozard et al. found that recognition memory was 95 percent correct immediately after viewing the pictures and fell to 55 percent after 130 weeks. Most of the decline in memory occurred over the first 4 weeks and it was at that time only that the three age groups differed. A small number of the oldest subjects performed poorly, but otherwise, age was not seen as very important in forgetting.

In the main, these four types of studies together do confirm the observations of clinicians. Old memory does seem well maintained. Retrieval does not seem a problem. New information, in not being placed in storage well enough, in not being processed deeply or adequately enough, is less well retained. This conclusion is not the same as that made at the end of the discussion of "Storage Functions." There, retrieval was also seen as a problem.

CLINICAL RESEARCH

Studies of memory in later life often suffer from poor descriptions of subject populations and from uncertain information regarding mental and physical health. This was seen clearly in a series of studies by Kral (1958a, b; 1959). He examined 162 men and women aged 60-96 years who were residents of an old people's home. Roughly two-thirds of this population showed memory deficits both on psychiatric examination and on psychological tests of memory. The deficits were of specific old memories and progressive impairment of newer ones. Kral's (1958a) data highlight the important problem of subject description because many of the subjects were diagnosed psychiatrically. Only about 40 percent of the people diagnosed were considered free from psychosis. Since psychoses are in part defined by memory function, the problem becomes tautological.

Irrespective of conditions of mental and physical health, however, it seems that most people do not avoid some memory impairment in later life. Thus, it is not surprising that research has been directed to the goal of ameliorating or minimizing such impairments. It is surprising only that so relatively few clinical research efforts have been directed to this goal.

Since RNA (ribonucleic acid) is thought to be the store of learned information in the nerve cells, there was a hope that the administration of RNA and DNA (deoxyribonucleic acid) would prove useful in restoring memory ability (Cameron, 1958; Solyom, Enesco, and Beaulieu, 1967, for example); there was hope that pharmaceutical agents related to RNA levels would be helpful. TRIAP was tested by Talland, Mendelson, Koz, and Aaron (1965), RNA-d was tried by Britton et al. (1972), and magnesium pemoline (Cylert) was tested by Eisdorfer, Conner, and Wilkie (1968); sex hormones were tried (e.g., Kral and Wigdor, 1961); and even negative ionization of the air was tried to see if memory in later life can be improved (e.g., Duffee and Koonitz, 1965). Each of these efforts, for a time at least, looked promising, but in the end, none remained useful to the point where clinical recommendations based upon them were possible. Most of these directions, in fact, have been discarded.

A newer procedure that seemed promising was thought so useful that some hospitals began using it. It is a process called hyperoxygenation—in a special chamber, a hyperbaric chamber, 100 percent oxygen is inspired at high atmospheric pressures. It is well known that oxygen deprivation (hypoxia) negatively affects learning and memory; it is thought that hyperoxia might affect these processes positively.

In a most promising attempt, Jacobs, Winter, Alvis, and Small (1969) provided deteriorated elderly patients with such hyperoxygenation. They also had a control group who, instead of breathing 100 percent oxygen, breathed 10 percent oxygen in nitrogen. All subjects were given tests both before and after the treatments, and the results were remarkable. On the Wechsler Memory Scale, for example, the deteriorated senescent subjects made a mean score of 76 before the treatment with 100 percent oxygen, and 103 afterward. The controls, breathing 10 percent oxygen, made a score of 80 before and only 78 afterward. The improvement with 100 percent oxygen was statistically significant, while the effect of the 10 percent oxygen of the control group was not.

Jacobs et al. then provided the control group with 100 percent oxygen also. Their levels rose to a mean score of 100, essentially the same performance level as that of the experimental group after treatment.

The improvement with hyperoxygenation was thought to result from improved function of brain tissue that might be marginally oxygen-deficient. Unfortunately, however, other research efforts to corroborate these results ended in failure (Goldfarb, Hochstadt, Jacobson, and Weinstein, 1972; Thompson, 1975). Hyperoxygenation therapy still has its adherents, but its promise of a few short years ago is clearly on the wane.

Perhaps the most promising development now is still in the hands of neurochemists—it has not yet reached the point of behavioral tests of clinical improvement. Learning and memory may be seen as involving information that is encoded or transferred into electrical qualities to get from one brain cell to another. To get from one cell to another, to cross the synapse, substances referred to as neurotransmitters (for example, acetylcholine) must be released to diffuse across the synapse to excite the post-synaptic brain cell.

Thus, chemicals called neurotransmitters are thought important in learning and memory. Several recent studies have focused on an enzyme called choline acetyltransferase (C.A.T.) which is important in the synthesis of neurotransmitters. It has been found in autopsy that the brains of dementia patients are deficient in C.A.T. (e.g., Spillane et al., 1977). Even normal aging may be associated with decline in the activity of C.A.T. and other such enzymes in the cerebral cortex (McGeer and McGeer, 1976). Perhaps pharmaceuticals based on cholinergic activity will be a key to aiding those with problems of memory.

SUMMARY

Recall is thought to involve the search and retrieval of information in the memory store; recognition is thought not to involve retrieval. Utilizing this distinction, adult subjects of wide age range were given tests of both recall and recognition memory, and differences with age were found to be greater in recall than in recognition. Thus, the aged were said to suffer loss of retrieval functioning. Such results and conclusions, however, are seen mainly in studies of new learning. When required to retrieve very old, basic information, such as the names of objects or of selected category items, little or no retrieval difficulties are seen at any age.

There are other interpretations as well. For example, with recognition memory, only a partial learning of the given information seems to be required to perform well; with recall memory, a total learning is necessary. If older people acquire and store information less well than young people, and thus have only a partial knowledge of the total, this could explain the recall-recognition disparity. In this case storage is seen as a problem. Storage involves both the placing of information in memory and keeping it there. In regard to the latter, the length of time a memory is in storage may be a factor in the age decline. Studies show that when recall and recognition tests were made soon after learning and one week or one month afterward, both recall and recognition memories were seen to fall off with age. Thus problems of retrieval and storage both appear to be present in later life.

Search and retrieval go together. A clever study was devised to estimate the rate that people of different ages search their memory stores. The procedure of this study involved speed of recognition in relation to the number of items in the memory store. The speed with which several items are searched relative to the speed with which only a few are searched provides estimates of search rate over and beyond limitations in speed of response attributable to motor functions. Older adults were found slower in their rates of search than younger adults, and it was thought that this becomes more and more a handicap to them as there are more items of information to search.

It is generally accepted that, in old age, the search and retrieval of new memories is impaired while those of old memories either are not impaired or are impaired to a much lesser extent. An often overlooked but obvious fact is that the observation is based more on clinical impression than on controlled study. For example, rarely, if ever, has an effort been made to control for the meaningfulness or relevance of the old stored information; little effort has been directed to the quantification of information such that it would be possible to say that more of the new is lost than of the old. Little concern has been seen in the frequency with which old information is retrieved. The belief that new memories are forgotten when old ones are retained may be saying hardly more than that important and frequently rehearsed material is retained better than material which is not as important nor as frequently rehearsed. The idea that rehearsal makes for good recall is not the same as the idea that the age of the material in storage makes for good recall. Four different types of long-term memory studies are seen in the literature. Each type has a different shortcoming in experimental design, but each points to a remarkable stability with age of old memories.

Many, if not most, people suffer memory impairments in later life. It is surprising, therefore, that more research has not been directed to the goal of minimizing such impairments. Those efforts that have been made seemed to hold promise for brief periods, only to end with disappointment. There is a current procedure that seems very promising but, unfortunately, it is still at the level of neurochemistry rather than clinical behavioral research. The procedure involves enzyme substances in the brain that synthesize other substances called neurotransmitters. These latter substances permit impulses to pass from one brain cell to another, which is thought to underlie the course of learning and memory. Let us hope that this research will lead to the help so many of the less fortunate among us need.

REFERENCES

Adamowicz, J.K. Visual short-term memory and aging. *Journal of Gerontology*, 1976, *31*, 39–46.

Anders, T.R., and Fozard, J.L. Effects of age upon retrieval from primary and secondary memory. *Developmental Psychology*, 1973, *9*, 411–415.

Anders, T.R., Fozard, J.L., and Lillyquist, T.D. The effects of age upon retrieval from short-term memory. *Developmental Psychology*, 1972, *6*, 214–217.

Bahrick, H.P., Bahrick, P.O., and Wittlinger, R.P. Fifty years of memory for names and faces: a cross-sectional approach. *Journal of Experimental Psychology*, 1975, *104*, 54–75.

Botwinick, J. *Cognitive processes in maturity and old age.* New York: Springer Publishing Co., 1967.

Botwinick, J., and Storandt, M. *Memory, related functions and age.* Springfield, Ill.: Charles C Thomas, 1974.

Britton, A., Bernstein, U., Brunse, A.J., Buttigheri, M.W., Cherkin, A., McCormack, J.H., and Lewis, D.J. Failure of ingestion of RNA to enhance human learning. *Journal of Gerontology*, 1972, *27*, 478–481.

Bromley, D.B. Some effects of age on short-term learning and remembering. *Journal of Gerontology*, 1958, *13*, 398–406.

Cameron, D.E. The use of nucleic acid in aged patients with memory impairment. *American Journal of Psychiatry*, 1958, *114*, 943.

Craik, F.I.M. Short-term memory and the aging process. In G.A. Talland (Ed.), *Human aging and behavior.* New York: Academic Press, 1968(a), pp. 131–168.

Craik, F.I.M. Two components in free recall. *Journal of Verbal Learning and Verbal Behavior*, 1968(b), *7*, 996–1004.

Drachman, D., and Leavitt, J. Memory impairment in the aged: storage versus retrieval deficit. *Journal of Experimental Psychology*, 1972, *93*, 302–308.

Duffee, R.A., and Koonitz, R.H. Behavioral effect of ionized air on rats. *Psychophysiology*, 1965, *1*, 347–359.

Eisdorfer, C., Conner, J.F., and Wilkie, F.L. The effect of magnesium pemoline on cognition and behavior. *Journal of Gerontology*, 1968, *23*, 283–288.

Erber, J.T. Age differences in recognition memory. *Journal of Gerontology*, 1974, *29*, 177–181.

Erber, J.T. Age differences in a controlled-lag recognition memory task. 1978, in preparation.

Eysenck, M.W. Retrieval from semantic memory as a function of age. *Journal of Gerontology*, 1975, *30*, 174–180.

Fozard, J.L., Waugh, N.C., and Thomas, J.C. Effects of age on long term retention of pictures. *Proceedings of the Tenth International Congress of Gerontology*, Jerusalem, Israel, 1975, *2*, 137. As reported by Fozard, J.L., and Poon, L.W. in Research and training activities of the mental performance and aging laboratories (1973–1976). Technical Report 76-02, GRECC, Vet. Adm., Boston, 1976.

Goldfarb, A.I., Hochstadt, N.J., Jacobson, J.H., and Weinstein, E.A. Hyperbaric oxygen treatment of organic mental syndrome in aged persons. *Journal of Gerontology*, 1972, *27*, 212–217.

Gordon, S.K., and Clark, W.C. Application of signal detection theory to prose recall and recognition in elderly and young adults. *Journal of Gerontology*, 1974, *29*, 64–72.

Hartley, J., and Marshall, I.A. Ageing, recognition and partial learning. *Psychonomic Science*, 1967, 9, 215–216.

Harwood, E., and Naylor, G.F.K. Recall and recognition in elderly and young subjects. *Australian Journal of Psychology*, 1969, 21, 251–257.

Hill, L.B. A second quarter century of delayed recall or relearning at 80. *Journal of Educational Psychology*, 1957, 48, 65–68.

Hill, L.B., Rejall, A.E., and Thorndike, E.L. Practice in the case of typewriting. *Pedagogical Seminary Journal of Genetic Psychology*, 1913, 20, 516–529.

Hultsch, D. Adult age differences in retrieval: trace development and cue dependent forgetting. *Developmental Psychology*, 1975, 11, 197–201.

Jacobs, E., Winter, P.M., Alvis, H.J., and Small, S.M. Hyperoxygenation effect on cognitive functioning in the aged. *New England Journal of Medicine*, 1969, 281, 753–757.

Kapnick, P.L. *Recognition memory of verbal material of varying lengths as a function of age*. Unpublished doctoral dissertation, Washington University, St. Louis, Mo., 1971.

Klonoff, H., and Kennedy, M. Memory and perceptual functioning in octogenarians and nonagenarians in the community. *Journal of Gerontology*, 1965, 20, 328–333.

Kral, V.A. Neuro-psychiatric observations in an old people's home; studies of memory dysfunction in senescence. *Journal of Gerontology*, 1958(a), 13, 169–176.

Kral, V.A. Senescent memory decline and senile amnestic syndrome. *American Journal of Psychiatry*, 1958(b), 115, 361–362.

Kral, V.A. Types of memory dysfunction in senescence. *Psychiatric Research Reports*, 1959, 11, 30–40.

Kral, V.A., and Wigdor, B.T. Further studies on the androgen effect on senescent memory function. *Canadian Psychiatric Association Journal*, 1961, 6, 345–352.

Marsh, G.R. Age differences in evoked potential correlates of a memory scanning process. *Experimental Aging Research*, 1975, 1, 3–16.

McGeer, E., and McGeer, P.L. Neurotransmitter metabolism in the aging brain. In R.D. Terry and S. Gershon (Eds.), *Aging Vol. 3: Neurobiology of aging*. New York: Raven Press, 1976.

McNulty, J.A., and Caird, W. Memory loss with age: retrieval or storage? *Psychological Reports*, 1966, 19, 229–230.

Perlmutter, M. What is memory aging the aging of? *Developmental Psychology*, 1978, in press.

Schonfield, D. Memory changes with age. *Nature*, 1965, 28, 918.

Schonfield, D., and Robertson, E.A. Memory storage and aging. *Canadian Journal of Psychology*, 1966, 20, 228–236.

Shakow, D., Dolkart, M.B., and Goldman, R. The memory function in psychoses of the aged. *Diseases of the Nervous System*, 1941, 2, 43–48.

Smith, M.E. Delayed recall of previously memorized material after twenty years. *Journal of Genetic Psychology*, 1935, 47, 477–481.

Smith, M.E. Delayed recall of previously memorized material after forty years. *Journal of Genetic Psychology*, 1951, 79, 337–338.

Smith, M.E. Delayed recall of previously memorized material after fifty years. *Journal of Genetic Psychology*, 1963, 102, 3–4.

Solyom, L., Enesco, H.E., and Beaulieu, C. The effect of RNA on learning and activity in old and young rats. *Journal of Gerontology,* 1967, *22,* 1–7.

Spillane, J.A., White, P., Goodhardt, M.J., Flack, R.H.A., Bowen, D.M., and Davison, A.N. Selective vulnerability of neurones in organic dementia. *Nature,* 1977, *266,* 558–559.

Steinberg, S. Memory scanning: mental processes revealed by reaction-time experiments. *American Scientist,* 1969, *57,* 421–457.

Talland, G.A. Three estimates of the word span and their stability over the adult years. *Quarterly Journal of Experimental Psychology,* 1965, *17,* 301–307.

Talland, G.A., Mendelson, L.H., Koz, G., and Aaron, R. Experimental studies of the effects of tricyanoaminopropene on the memory and learning capacities of geriatric patients. *Journal of Psychiatric Research,* 1965, *3,* 171–179.

Thomas, J.C., Fozard, J.L., and Waugh, N.C. Age-related differences in naming-latency. *American Journal of Psychology,* 1977, *90,* 499–509.

Thompson, L. Effects of hyperbaric oxygen on behavioral functioning in elderly persons with intellectual impairment. In S. Gershon and A. Raskin (Eds.), *Aging Vol. 2: Genesis and treatment of psychologic disorders in the elderly.* New York: Raven Press, 1975.

Tulving, E., and Pearlstone, Z. Availability versus accessibility of information in memory for words. *Journal of Verbal Learning and Verbal Behavior,* 1966, *5,* 381–391.

Tulving, E., and Thomson, D.M. Encoding specificity and retrieval processes in episodic memory. *Psychological Review,* 1973, *80,* 352–373.

Waugh, N.C., and Norman, D.A. Primary memory. *Psychological Review,* 1965, *72,* 89–104.

Wickelgren, W.A. Age and storage dynamics in continuous recognition memory. *Developmental Psychology,* 1975, *11,* 165–169.

19
Research Methods

Most all that has been discussed in this book was based upon comparisons among people of different adult age groups. This practice, while useful, can lead to faulty conclusions. Observe the following:

> Occasionally I have the opportunity to chat with elderly people who live in the communities near by Cushing Hospital. I cannot help but observe that many of these people speak with an Italian accent. I also chat with young adults who live in these same communities. They do *not* speak with an Italian accent. As a student of human behavior and development I am interested in this discrepancy. I indulge in some deep thinking and come up with the following conclusion: as people grow older they develop Italian accents. This must surely be one of the prime manifestations of aging on the psychological level.   (From an address by Robert Kastenbaum)

Quite obviously this was said with tongue in cheek. The central point, however, is quite serious—so many of the studies in aging are based upon descriptive statements of differences between young and old, yet they tell us little, or nothing, of the basis of these differences.

AGE AND CULTURE CONFOUNDED

It is very reasonable to infer that the elderly people with Italian accents were immigrants, or at least grew up in a *culture* where English was not the primary or sole language spoken. The elderly people were of a different *generation*, born in a different era than the young people, and it is these cultural-generational influences, not *maturational-age* influences, which made for Italian accents.

In actual practice it is not at all easy to separate out those behaviors which are attributable to cultural-generational (*cohort*) influences and those attributable to maturational-age influences. For example, when intelligence test performances are lower in the elderly than in the young, the relative contributions of cohort versus age are not nearly as clear as they were in the case of the age differences in spoken accents.

Cross-Sectional Studies

The confounding of cohort and age is most apparent in cross-sectional studies, i.e., studies in which two or more age (cohort) groups are compared during the single period of the examination. The age groups are compared in intelligence and other test performances, with the knowledge that the quality and quantity of formal education has been different for old and young. Age groups are compared although researchers know that so many of today's sources of cognitive stimulation were unknown generations ago. Social patterns, values, and attitudes were different when grandmother was a girl—how can people of different ages be compared?

There is no problem in making comparisons when the comparisons are kept on a descriptive level; the problem arises when explanations underlying the descriptions are attempted. Here, utmost caution must be maintained always. If education, good health, experience in taking tests, and many other factors are involved in making good test scores, than we can anticipate that an observed age difference today may not be seen tomorrow. To the extent that such culturally determined factors underlie the observed age differences and to the extent that future cohorts improve with respect to such factors, we may expect that "the larger will be the difference between present and future random samples of elderly subjects, and the more will the differences between age groups diminish in time" (Botwinick, 1959, p. 758).

The point, very simply, is, what so often is attributed in cross-sectional studies to age may not be due to age at all but to cohort effects. This is the major shortcoming of cross-sectional studies.

Longitudinal Studies

Among investigators of aging processes, it is generally understood and accepted that cross-sectional studies confound the influences of age and culture. It is less understood, and not generally accepted or emphasized, that longitudinal studies can also confound age and culture. While it is possible that the confounding is less frequent in longitudinal studies than in cross-sectional ones and, when present, not as great, the confounding must be recognized, nevertheless. In longitudinal studies the same people are examined during several periods of time, usually with a number of years between examinations.

Let us examine a longitudinal study analogue of the cross-sectional study in which the discovery was made that as people grow older they develop Italian accents. A recent longitudinal study showed that as people age, if they also become psychotic, they begin to speak Yiddish! Two colleagues described this discovery to me.* They were carrying out investigations of deteriorated psychotic elderly who resided in a nursing home and who required custodial care. Actually, the investigators did not carry out longitudinal studies, but they did learn much about the past life of the nursing home residents from retrospective accounts. They learned that the native tongue of these Jewish residents was Yiddish, but that they had resided in this country for many, many years and, during this time had spoken English as their usual language. In late life and in senile deterioration, however, they reverted to their mother tongue. Had these two investigators made periodic longitudinal observations of their subjects from the time of young adulthood when English was spoken to the time of old age and senile deterioration, it would have been seen that as they grew older they began to speak Yiddish.

In this example, the confounding influences of culture and age took place within the lifetime of the individual. The confounding was apparent and not a problem in the interpretation. But there are many longitudinal studies where the confounding is much less apparent. Kuhlen (1963) may have been the first to recognize this problem in the context of aging research; he provided some examples. Nelson (1954) tested college students and then, 14 years later, tested them again. He noted a marked trend in liberalism. Fortunately, Nelson tested a new sample of college students at the time he retested the initial sample. He found that the scores of the new college students and those retest scores of the older subjects were about the same. The cultural influences had their impact, confounding the maturational effects, all in the course of a single lifetime.

In another study (Bender, 1958), college students were given a test of values and then retested fifteen years later. A trend in greater religious interest was seen. Again, however, a sample of new college students tested for the first time when the older sample was tested the second time, showed similarity of values. Kuhlen (1963) indicated that per-

---

* Dr. Rodney Coe of St. Louis University and Dr. Eva Kahana, then of Washington University, now of Wayne State University, in discussing their research, described this incidental observation; needless to say, their interpretation of it was along different lines.

formances on attitude scales (Nelson, 1954) and scales on values (Bender, 1958) are not the only types that reflect the confounding of cultural and age effects within one lifetime. Intelligence test performances can reflect this also. Tilton (1949) found that *gains* were made in intelligence test scores during the period covering the last two World Wars.

It might be well to mention again that few, if any, researchers in the study of aging fail to recognize the intrinsic confounding between cohort and age effects in cross-sectional research. Fewer researchers seem to recognize this problem in longitudinal research. Perhaps a reason for this is that the confounding effects of culture in longitudinal studies may be less apparent than they are in cross-sectional studies. Perhaps, too, when they do occur in longitudinal studies, they are not so extensive. Whatever the explanation, it is necessary to recognize that cultural influences are not avoided necessarily by recourse to longitudinal investigation. As the tempo or rate of cultural change increases, the potential for cultural confounding within a lifetime increases. It is reasonable to expect, therefore, that this problem will grow in importance with future longitudinal studies.

AGE AND TIME OF MEASUREMENT CONFOUNDED

Cultural effects that confound age effects in longitudinal research are typically not referred to as such. The concept of cultural effects is typically applied only to cohort differences, i.e., people born in different eras exposed and molded by different sociocultural conditions. Exposure and molding by events or conditions within the lifetime of the experiment is referred to as time of measurement effects. This is not necessarily to say that the root "cause" or basis of cohort and time of measurement effects are always different. For example, the change in liberalism described before in Nelson's study may have the same character in cohort differences as in time of measurement differences. But, the concepts of culture and time of measurement are distinguishable even in this example, and, moreover, in most studies their characters are different. For these reasons, the confound with age in longitudinal studies is referred to as time of measurement effects. Schaie (1965, 1967), perhaps more than others, emphasized the problem of time of measurement and made its importance a common concern among researchers in aging.

Time of measurement "denotes that state of the environment within which a given set of data were obtained . . . changes in the state of the environment may contribute to the effects noted in an aging study"

(Schaie, 1967, p. 129). While it is possible that Schaie would not emphasize or even agree with all the aspects of explanation given here, there is no doubt or disagreement about the importance of the concept, "state of the environment." It is a concept with which all developmental researchers must cope.

Subject Effects

It is the opinion here that time of measurement should be defined broadly to include not only states of the physical and social environment but also states of the subject and experimenter as part of the environment. If conditions of measurement are not identical at time 2 and time 1 with respect to the states of subject and experimenter, then longitudinal comparisons involve ambiguity of interpretation.

Practice. Among the more obvious considerations regarding the state of the subject, the one most often emphasized is the effect of practice. The experience of taking a test is expected to have an effect on taking it a second time. The subject knows the test better, he may even look up the answers he missed, and, as important, perhaps, the unknown, anxiety-producing aspects of the test environment may be diminished. In short, the state of the subject is altered by his environmental experiences, independent of his age. Is improvement in test 2 a reflection of true age gains, or of the practice? Would an observed age decrement be even greater had there been no practice?

The role of practice, intrinsic to a *repeated measures* design, which, in turn, is intrinsic to the longitudinal method, may be overcome experimentally by examining only part of a sample of subjects during the first test period. For the second testing, rather than examine the same subjects again, the other part of the sample, the part not yet tested, is examined. This design is of unrepeated or *independent measures.* The independent measures design is difficult to execute because it is necessary to start with a well-defined subject pool, to test only half the subjects at time 1, and to be able to locate and test the other half at time 2. If both repeated and independent measures are made concurrently, the practice effect can be estimated. However, even the estimated practice effect will be confounded with other time-of-measurement factors.

Motivation and Interest. In 1919 male freshmen students at Iowa State College were tested in a group with the Army Alpha Intelligence Test. Approximately 30 years later, Owens (1953) was able to locate and retest nearly a third of the ex-students. There were eight subtests and on four of them increases were found. It is not necessary here to consider all the factors, apart from age, which may have made for these results—many of these were considered by Jones (1959) and by Botwinick (1967, p. 32)—but one factor is relevant here. As Kuhlen (1963, p. 115) pointed out:

> Tests administered to *groups* at freshman week in college . . . are seldom administered under conditions of high motivation. When these same subjects are retested individually under vastly different conditions of motivation at a later time, important questions can be raised as to the meaning of the obtained differences.

Motivation and interest on the part of the subjects seem to be a special aspect of the sampling problem. Miles (1934) reported age decrements in a two-year follow-up study of a general population, but increments, except for the oldest subjects, with a subsample of subjects who voluntarily chose to be retested because of their interest in the study.

Motivation and interest are but two subject effects which are part of the time-of-measurement problem. There are many others, e.g., fatigue, ill health, personal concern, etc. If these effects are appreciable in a study, the observed changes will be more a reflection of the measurement variable than the maturational variable.

Experimenter Effects

The experimenter effect has become of great interest to psychologists doing behavioral research (e.g., Rosenthal, 1966). It is known, for example, that investigators who are white may obtain different data in black communities than investigators who are black. Sex of the experimenter has been known to influence the nature of the research data. An investigator who likes animals and fondles them may bring out different learning performances in rats than an experimenter who is afraid or dislikes animals. A clinical tester who is experienced may find different test scores than one who is a novice. It seems not unreasonable to expect that the age of the experimenter would also be an important variable in the determination of research findings. Donahue (1965) emphasized the need to examine and control the experimenter age effect. It is possible that this effect is different in the administration of tests to people of different ages.

If longitudinal research involves years between testings, the same experimenter surely is a different person at time 2 than at time 1. If different experimenters are involved, then this factor may be crucial. The interaction between subject effects and experimenter effects may also be important. This area of potential methodological importance has yet to be explored.

Environmental Effects

So far we have discussed subject and experimenter influences as aspects of time-of-measurement problems. There are laboratory and social factors which also are important, but, unfortunately, their impacts often are not even known to exist. Examples of laboratory and social effects will elucidate this.

Laboratory. A reaction time experiment was carried out which involved comparisons between young adult and old adult subjects. The study was a cross-sectional study, not a longitudinal one, but, since the data were being collected over a relatively long period of time, the experience can very easily be applied to both types of studies. In the actual experiment, most of the subjects of one age group were examined at the beginning of data collection, and most of the other age group were examined months later. (Interdigitation of subjects of both age groups is the correct procedure, but the desired type of subject is not always available and often this less correct procedure is followed.)

The experiment was proceeding smoothly until it was noticed, almost by accident, that the response key used in the reaction time measurement was bent—only a few millimeters, but bent enough to cause doubt about the similarity of the measurement made at the beginning of the experiment and later stages of it. All the associated electronic gear was working perfectly; from all indications, so was the investigator, but the simple component of the total environment, the little metal lever of a micro-switch, used as the response key, was bent. How reliable is a measured change in reaction time if the times of measurement involve years and the laboratory equipment is either very old or replaced by different equipment?

Social. It was already seen that cultural influences are involved in longitudinal investigation. Cultural influences in developmental research are considered those associated with earlier life history, i.e., those general to a specific cohort. But more personal and immediate environmental factors play important roles also. If between time 1 and 2 of testing, there is an appreciable drop or increase of income, opportunity for social and cognitive stimulation, death in the family, marriage, new friends, or others, the measured performances could reflect this as a factor confounding the maturational changes.

COHORT AND TIME OF MEASUREMENT CONFOUNDED

It was seen that cross-sectional studies confound age and cohort effects and that longitudinal studies confound these effects too, but mostly it is the confusion between age and time of measurement to which Schaie

(1965, 1967) attended. To clarify these complex functions, Schaie indicated the need to investigate yet a third type of study, one which also involves confounded sources of variation, in this case between cohort and time of measurement. Schaie called this type of study *time lag*, possibly because there is a lag in the time of measurement during which people of different cohorts are examined. In the usual longitudinal study, a single cohort is measured at different periods of time. In time lag studies, several cohorts are examined, each at a different period of time.

This may be seen more clearly, perhaps, in Table 19.1. Cells G, E, C constitute a time lag group comparison. Subjects born in 1910 and tested in 1960 (aged 50 years) are compared to subjects of the same age but born in 1920 and tested in 1970, and subjects born in 1930 and tested in 1980. It may be seen in Table 19.1 that cells D and B represent a time lag group comparison too, as do cells H and F. In Table 19.1, vertically grouped cells (e.g., A, D, G) represent cross-sectional studies, and horizontal cells (e.g., A, B, C) represent longitudinal studies.

Three-component Model

For Schaie (1965, 1967) the analysis of developmental change must take into account the three sources of variation: maturation or age, cohort, and time of measurement. Schaie's is a three-component model and ideally the three types of studies must be planned and carried out: cross-sectional, longitudinal, and time lag. Each of these studies is confounded by two sources of variation.

TABLE 19.1
Three Cohorts Examined at Three Separate Time Periods

		Time of Measurement	
Time of Birth, Cohort		1960	1970	1980
1930	30 A	40 B	50 C
1920	40 D	50 E	60 F
1910	50 G	60 H	70 I

Time Lag →

Age in years are in cells

Two-component Model

Baltes (1968) criticized the three-component model on the basis that the three components are not truly independent. This may be derived algebraically, but it is at least as easy to demonstrate this empirically. Table 19.2, utilizing some of the values of Table 19.1, shows that, in doing cross-sectional and longitudinal studies simultaneously, the time lag comparison (arrow) is automatic. There is no need to arrange for a new time lag study; it is there for the asking just as long as the cross-sectional and longitudinal studies are carried out. This is true whether or not the subjects in 1980 were the same ones tested in 1970 (repeated measures) or were different subjects (independent measures). In similar fashion, cross-sectional or longitudinal comparisons can be obtained if the alternate two types of group comparisons are arranged. Schaie (1970) responded to this criticism by acknowledging the intrinsic tie indicated in Table 19.2, but he insisted that it makes a difference which two of the three components are chosen for study.

The simplest but not complete method of differentiating age and cohort involves two cohorts, two ages, and three times of measurement. Table 19.3 elucidates this: 1) A + C versus B + D is an age comparison (50-year-olds versus 60-year-olds), holding cohort constant and varying times of measurement; 2) A + B versus C + D is a cohort comparison (1910 versus 1920), holding age constant and varying the same times of measurement. With this design it is possible to compare the relative contribution of age and cohort effects, each in interaction with two times of measurement, which are, however, different times of measurement.

THREE SEQUENTIAL DESIGNS

Over the years a pattern has developed in aging and developmental research that incorporates much of this type of thinking. The pattern is of experimental designs called sequential designs or sequential strategies.

TABLE 19.2
After Age and Cohort Variables Are Defined,
the Time Lag Function Is Fixed

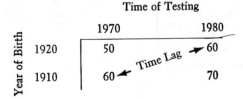

TABLE 19.3
The Simplest Situation Permitting Differentiation
Between Age and Cohort

		Time of Measurement		
		1960	1970	1980
Year of Birth	1920		50 C	60 D
	1910	50 A	60 B	

There are three of them: cross-sequential, time-sequential, and cohort-sequential (sometimes called bifactorial model). These designs and the underlying assumptions that have been made in carrying them out will be described in the following section.

Cross-Sequential Strategy

Experimental Design. The cross-sequential design can best be described as a combination of cross-sectional and longitudinal studies. Here is a shortened and approximate version of how Schaie and Labouvie-Vief (1974) carried it out in their study on intelligence (see chapter 13).

In 1956 people of seven age-cohort groups were tested. This is represented at the top of Table 19.4 by "Cohort" and "Mean Age" under the heading "1956, Test 1." Then, seven years later, they retested these people, and this is represented as "1963, Test 2." The upper part of Table 19.4 shows that Test 1 scores are listed by capital letters (A, B, C . . .) with the average of them being I. Test 2 scores are listed by lower case letters (a, b, c . . .) and their average is II. (There was still a third testing in 1970, but for purposes of an easier understanding of the cross-sequential design, only the first two test periods will be considered, although the principles of analysis are the same with two as with more than two testings.)

It will be recalled that the cross-sectional studies confound age and cohort, and the longitudinal studies confound age and time of testing. Table 19.4 shows a cross-sectional study and a longitudinal study with these confounds. Cross-sectionally, there are seven age-cohort groups, and longitudinally, there are two age-time of testing groups (1956 versus 1963). The statistical technique called analysis of variance is now applied: In essence, this technique asks three questions of the data in Table 19.4. The first is, are the seven age-cohort groups different in

TABLE 19.4
Sequential Analysis

Cohort	1956, TEST 1 Mean Age	Test Score	1963, TEST 2 Mean Age	Test Score
1	25	A	32	a
2	32	B	39	b
3	39	C	46	c
4	46	D	53	d
5	53	E	60	e
6	60	F	67	f
7	67	G	74	g
Mean	46	I	52	II

Design	Confound	Test Scores	Assumption of No Effect	Measured Effect
Cross-Sequential	Age and C^1	A + a vs B + b . . .	Age	C
	Age and TM^2	I vs II	Age	TM
Time-Sequential	Age and C	B + a vs C + b . . .	C	Age
	C and TM	I vs II^3	C	TM

^1C = Cohort.
^2TM = Time of Measurement.
^{3}Subjects making scores A are not included, but subjects aged 74 making scores H (not shown) are included.

regard to their test scores? This is answered by comparing scores A + a with B + b, C + c . . . and G + g. The second question is, are the scores of Test Time 2 different from those of Test Time 1? This is answered by comparing I and II, the averages of the two times of testing. The third question is the most interesting and, typically, the most important. Do scores change from Time 1 to Time 2 in a greater way for one age-cohort group than for another? This is answered by comparing A − a with B − b, C − c . . . G − g.

Note that while the above was described in terms of the same people taking the tests at Time 1 and Time 2 (called repeated measures), the design applies also to different, but comparable, people taking the test at Time 1 and Time 2 (independent measures). In fact, Schaie, Labouvie, and Buech (1973) used this latter design.

Interpretation. Recall again that this design, along with the others, was developed to disentangle three interacting effects: age, cohort, and time of measurement. It is not often recognized that these designs developed to do just this have been used with the paradoxical assumption that the effects are not confounded. When so used, each design becomes limited in its intended purpose. When the designs are used together and no such assumptions are made, however, they are valuable.

As described, the two main effects, portrayed in Table 19.4, are age-cohort (A + a compared to B + b . . . G + g) and age-time of measurement (I compared to II). There is much to learn from these two effects, as, for example, the change in test scores over time seen among the different age-cohort groups. This tells us much more than does a simple change in score over time for one group (longitudinal comparison), or simple differences in score among several groups (cross-sectional comparison). However, when disentanglement of confounded effects has been attempted, controversy has resulted.

Here are assumptions that have been made in one of several cross-sequential studies (e.g., Schaie and Labouvie): First, the age and cohort confound (A + a versus B + b, C + c . . .) is a cohort effect only; age is not a factor. If this assumption was necessarily true, then all cross-sectional studies could be carried out without further issue since only cohort or cultural effects would be measured, not age. The second assumption is that the age and time of measurement confound (I versus II) is a time of measurement effect only; again age is not a factor. The fact that the people of Test Time 2 are older than Test Time 1 is assumed not important. Thus, by these assumptions, the cross-sequential design is made to reflect only cohort and time of measurement effects. How relevant is this design to research in aging when the assumptions place age itself into a category of nonconsideration? Cross-sequential designs are valuable, but only without the above assumptions; they permit descriptions of the changes of the different age-cohort groups.

Time-Sequential Strategy

Experimental Design. This design includes the time lag analysis. The time-sequential experiment asks the same three questions as does the cross-sequential experiment, but the questions refer to different effects. (1) Are the age-cohort groups different? Here, scores B + a are compared to C + b, D + c . . . G + f (and, if possible, to the scores of an eighth group tested at Time 1 added to g). (2) Are the scores of Time 2 different from those of Time 1? The operations are similar to those of the cross-sequential design: I is compared to II (except that score A is not in the average while the score of the eighth group at Time 1 is). (3) Do scores change more from Time 1 to Time 2 for some groups than others? B — a is compared to C — b, D — c and so on.

Interpretation. Again, taking the study by Schaie and Labouvie as a prototype, it had been assumed in this design that the group difference

(B + a versus C + b, etc.) is an age difference, not cohort. (See bottom of Table 19.4.) Also, it had been assumed that the Time 1 versus Time 2 scores (or I versus II) is a time of measurement effect, not that of the confounded cohort effect. Thus, with these assumptions, only age and time of measurement are factors—cohort is not regarded as a factor.

Note that here, as in the cross-sequential design, the opposite assumptions could have been made, viz., age (and not cohort) is the relevant variable in cross-sequential comparisons, and cohort (and not age) is relevant in the time-sequential comparisons. Similarly, age (and not time of measurement) is involved in Time 1 versus Time 2 comparisons in cross-sequential designs, and cohort (and not time of measurement effects) in time-sequential designs. As seen at the bottom of Table 19.4, a justification for the Schaie and Labouvie assumptions is that only one assumption is necessary in each strategy—age is assumed not a factor in the cross-sequential design and cohort is assumed not a factor in the time-sequential design. Otherwise, more than one assumption in each design would be required and this is less parsimonious. Accepting this justification, it remains true nevertheless that analyzing and comparing the results of cross-sequential and time-sequential analyses tells us nothing more than is implicit in the assumptions that are made. The above assumptions preclude teasing apart age and cohort effects, a main reason for the designs in the first place.

Cohort-Sequential Strategy

Experimental Design. This design is probably the best of the three in terms of disentangling age and cohort effects. This is so because in each of the designs assumptions must be made, and here only assumptions relating to time of testing are made. Unfortunately, the cohort-sequential design takes so much time to carry out that it becomes impractical to compare age groups other than very similar ones, or cohort groups other than those not very different in year of birth. Observe in Table 19.5 the length of time it takes to carry out a cohort-sequential study if three age groups and three cohort groups are compared—three of the same compared before in the other designs (ages 53, 60, and 67, and cohorts 7 years apart, 1917, 1910, and 1903).

In the cells of Table 19.5 are indicated the years during which testing must be done to do this study. As seen in the table, the first testing is to have begun in 1956 and the last in 1984, a research commitment of 28 years. Further, as more age groups per cohort are tested, more years are needed to do the research. And, as the differences between age and

TABLE 19.5
Cohort Sequential Design

Time of Birth, Cohort	Age in Years		
	53	60	67
1917	1970	1977	1984
1910	1963	1970	1977
1903	1956	1963	1970
	Years of testing are in cells		

cohort groups are increased for comparison purposes, even more years are needed. For example, to compare people aged 50, 60, and 70 from cohort birthdates 1920, 1940, and 1960, as much as 60 years are required to carry out the cohort-sequential strategy.

The very simplest cohort-sequential study possible involves two age and two cohort groups; this requires three times of measurements. For example, in Table 19.5, if cohorts 1903 and 1910 are compared in relation to age groups 53 and 60 years, tests must be made during the years 1956, 1968, and 1970, a research commitment taking 14 years.

Interpretation. Scrutiny of Table 19.5 discloses that the different cohorts are of the same age but comparisons of them involve different times of measurement (i.e., different years at testing). Similarly, the different age groups involve the same cohorts, but again, the time of testing is confounded. If it is assumed that time of testing is not important, then we can compare age and cohort effects meaningfully, and evaluate their interaction. Of all the assumptions, this may be the most tenable one to make in aging research (although this is not to say that it is necessarily a correct assumption. Moreover, as the times of measurement increase, i.e., as the total time span of the study increases, the assumption of no effect of time of measurement becomes less tenable.) In the abstract, the cohort-sequential design is the one of choice, but as indicated it is not the one of choice for practical reasons. This experimental design can take a major part of a lifetime to carry out.

A Practical View-Point

If cross-sectional comparisons are oversimplified and considered as age effects only, or cohort effects only, if longitudinal comparisons are considered as either environmental or age effects but not both, then there is a problem with interpretation. But, if the intrinsic confounding is recognized and kept in mind always, then meaningful interpretations are possible.

Cross-sectional studies are very adequate for ascertaining age differences. Descriptive statements can be clear and meaningful. When explanation is desired, however, the relative contributions of the maturational and cultural determination must remain uncertain. The interpretation must involve a logical judgment as to which types of functions are more bound to the culture than others. Religious beliefs, for example, would be more likely a function of culture than would reaction time. There is no reason to maintain, however, that reaction time, or any other behavior, for that matter, is totally free from cultural impact.

Longitudinal studies are preferable, but the cost is high, and it is important to weigh whether the cost is worth the potential results. (Advantages and disadvantages of longitudinal research will be discussed in the next chapter.) Longitudinal studies tell us much about how people change over time. Whether the change is due more to age than to the time-of-measurement factors is also a matter of what the measured behavior change is. Visual acuity is more likely to be related to age apart from time of measurement than is measured liberalism. Again, however, both may reflect the impact of time of testing.

The three sequential designs above are the best strategies yet devised. They are difficult to arrange, costly to carry out, and imperfect, but they provide for the best approximations we can make at this time in tearing apart the confounded factors. However, because of the difficulty and expense, because they are relatively new, because of the inadequate interpretations that have been made, most of what is found in the aging literature is not the best. Although it seems likely that the number of studies using sequential strategies will increase, it also seems likely that cross-sectional studies will remain the bulwark of the data that are available. What was read in this book, therefore, and what probably will be read in future books, reflect this state of affairs. The bulk of the data in the study of aging involves the confounding of age and cohort—this should be kept in mind always.

SUMMARY

The most typical study in aging involves the cross-sectional method, a method by which two or more age groups are compared during the single time period of the examination. This method is appropriate for describing differences among groups born during different eras, but it does not permit unequivocal explanation regarding maturational processes. The reason for this is that the age of the person is synonymous with the cultural context of his time of birth and upbringing. It is said, therefore, that cross-sectional studies confound age and cohort.

The longitudinal method, a method by which the same people are examined during several periods of time, usually with a number of years between examinations, also involves confounding between age and culture. This is not often recognized; it certainly is not often emphasized. It is referred to in longitudinal research as the confounding between age and time of measurement. Time of measurement involves three types of factors, each related to immediate or recent environmental impacts. There are subject factors such as motivation, interest, fatigue, practice, health, personal problems, and others, each affecting performances. If these are different at one time of measurement than another, they cloud what effect aging processes may have on the measurement.

There are experimenter effects too. These have not been investigated in aging studies, but it is not unreasonable to expect that since the experimenter is not the same person, i.e., does not function the same way, throughout the years of testing, this would have a bearing on the subject's performance. The interaction between subject and experimenter effects may negate any clear interpretation of aging effects.

The laboratory environment may change in its physical characteristics, and this also introduces artifacts of time of measurement. The laboratory change may be imperceptible, but large enough, nevertheless, to affect the measurements. It is not uncommon that a move from one city to another, or even from one room in a building to another, will make for slightly different measurements.

The immediate social environment is important in affecting measurements. Positive impacts such as new opportunities and new sources of cognitive stimulation, and negative influences such as death of spouses and loss of income, can affect the longitudinal results. The subjects, the experimenter, the physical and social environmental influences together constitute the time-of-measurement confusion with age.

To unravel the confounding, three research designs have been proposed: they are called cross-sequential, time-sequential, and cohort-sequential. These designs appear the best available for developmental research but their value in the published literature has been negated by the underlying assumptions that have been made. Despite this, the designs, with careful interpretation, have the potential of providing better understanding of the three important confounded variables: age, cohort, and time of measurement.

REFERENCES

Baltes, P.B. Longitudinal and cross-sectional sequences in the study of age and generation effects. *Human Development*, 1968, *11*, 145–171.

Bender, I.E. Changes in religious interest: a retest after 15 years. *Journal of Abnormal Social Psychology*, 1958, *57*, 41–46.

Botwinick, J. Drives, expectancies, and emotions. In J.E. Birren (Ed.) *Handbook of aging and the individual: psychological and biological aspects*. Chicago: Univ. of Chicago Press, 1959, pp. 739–768.

Botwinick, J. *Cognitive processes in maturity and old age*. New York: Springer Publishing Co., 1967.

Donahue, W. Relationship of age of perceivers to their social perceptions. *Gerontologist*, 1965, *5*, 241–245, 276–277.

Jones, H.E. Intelligence and problem-solving. In J.E. Birren (Ed.) *Handbook of aging and the individual: psychological and biological aspects*. Chicago: Univ. of Chicago Press, 1959, pp. 700–738.

Kuhlen, R.G. Age and intelligence: the significance of cultural change in longitudinal vs. cross-sectional findings. *Vita Humana*, 1963, *6*, 113–124.

Miles, C.C. The influence of speed and age on intelligence scores of adults. *Journal of General Psychology*, 1934, *10*, 208–210.

Nelson, E.N.P. Persistence of attitudes of college students fourteen years later. *Psychological Monographs*, 1954, *68*, 1–13.

Owens, W.A., Jr. Age and mental abilities: a longitudinal study. *Genetic Psychology Monographs*, 1953, *48*, 3–54.

Rosenthal, R. *Experimenter effects in behavioral research*. New York: Appleton-Century-Crofts, 1966.

Schaie, K.W. A general model for the study of developmental problems. *Psychological Bulletin*, 1965, *64*, 92–107.

Schaie, K.W. Age changes and age differences. *Gerontologist*, 1967, *7*, 128–132.

Schaie, K.W. A reinterpretation of age related changes in cognitive structure and functioning. In L.R. Goulet and P.B. Baltes (Eds.) *Life span developmental psychology: research and theory*. New York: Academic Press, 1970, pp. 485–507.

Schaie, K.W., and Labouvie-Vief, G. Generational versus ontogenetic components of change in adult cognitive behavior: a fourteen-year cross-sequential study. *Developmental Psychology*, 1974, *10*, 305–320.

Schaie, K.W., Labouvie, G.V., and Buech, B.U. Generational and cohort-specific differences in adult cognitive functioning: a fourteen-year study of independent samples. *Developmental Psychology*, 1973, *9*, 151–166.

Tilton, J.W. A measure of improvement in American education over a twenty-five year period. *School Sociology*, 1949, *69*, 25–26.

20

Operational and Conceptual Issues in Research

Experimental designs important in developmental research were discussed in the previous chapter. The designs bear on three types of group comparisons: cross-sectional, longitudinal, and time lag. This chapter continues with a discussion of the longitudinal method, focusing upon operational considerations. Sampling problems and the associated difficulties in interpreting the age effects are discussed along with the meaning of age in developmental research. Special research procedures and strategies are indicated.

LONGITUDINAL STUDIES

It is clear that if it is not possible to carry out simultaneously both cross-sectional and longitudinal studies, then, all things being equal, the longitudinal study is the method of choice. All things are not equal, however; the longitudinal method is much more difficult to carry out. Fortunately, not all questions require research with this more difficult method. The cross-sectional method is appropriate for answering many questions. Let us examine why the longitudinal method is the more advantageous, and then, what some of its special problems are.

Advantages

The longitudinal method is the only possible method for charting changes over time for the individual person. Not only does this method permit measurement of average changes for the individual, it also permits analysis of intra-individual (within the individual) variations. Such analysis often has value, not only for theoretical purposes but for practical applications as well. For example, if during the period of testing at time 1, a subject's performance scores *vary* by 10 units, but during the same testing period at time 2 they *vary* by 100 units, the experimenter might develop hypotheses important to the subject. There may be a loss of interest or motivation to maintain sustained attention, there may be a transient personal problem, but the experimenter might look also for signs of arteriosclerosis, or other states making for inconsistency. Cardiovascular problems could keep the amount of blood reaching the brain very variable; since the brain needs the nourishment carried by the blood, performance may be expected to be variable. The experimenter may suspect nervous system pathology, especially if cardiovascular disease is not apparent. It is only in longitudinal research that the individual may be so examined.

Longitudinal research has other advantages too. It is becoming almost routine in long-term longitudinal projects to examine retrospectively differences between survivors and those who have died. A later section, "Sampling," discusses this from a different aspect, but here the relevant questions are: Which of the measurements made earlier in the longitudinal study, and in what combinations, differentiate the later survivors from those who have died? Which functions, and what combination of them, appear to be predictive of impending disease? A most meaningful strategy, one very costly to carry out, is to make such retrospective analyses and then, following this, make prospective analyses in a subsequent longitudinal study. The first longitudinal, retrospective study should be the basis for the hypotheses tested in the second longitudinal, prospective study.

Disadvantages

There are a variety of problems in longitudinal research which may be classed as logistical or functional.

> Longitudinal investigations . . . are costly, require much patience, and oblige the investigator to retain outmoded procedures when newer and better ones become available. Longitudinal studies also enforce the need to carry through many years some of the mistakes and poor decisions made during an earlier period (Botwinick, 1967, p. 32).

The costliness is synonymous with the fact that longitudinal research requires long-term attention. The long-term character of the research makes for a problem of continuity of personnel. Much patience is required because there are long periods of time spent waiting for the results to come in; there is no "pay-off" in ready publications. Waiting for results is not a very rewarding pastime, and most investigators find it necessary to carry out other, more short-term pursuits in the interim.

The logistics of data storage and data analysis are burdensome, especially when large quantities of data are collected over many years of work. They are so burdensome that many years of work have been negated in some instances. Fortunately, recent advances in computer technology have made the continuous recording and storage of data more manageable. Moreover, many directors of long-term longitudinal research projects, especially inter-disciplinary projects involving many measurements, have learned to consult with statistical experts from the very beginning. This avoids the confusion, disappointment, and waste which can result when data are collected and stored in forms that are unusable or misleading. The trend of computer storage and statistical consultation holds much promise for longitudinal research.

The very nature of longitudinal research makes for problems, and it is the prudent investigator who thinks twice before he engages in it. He should ask again and again before he starts whether his question requires longitudinal investigation and, if so, whether the question is worth answering.

SAMPLING PROBLEMS

It was seen in the previous chapter that in one study (Miles, 1934), subjects who voluntarily chose to be retested two years after an initial test showed increments in their performances, while subjects of a more general population showed decrements over the same period of time. This result demonstrated that aging patterns will be different for different types of populations. They will also be different for people of different ability levels and, probably, for people of different health and life expectancies. Several studies demonstrate this.

Riegel, Riegel, and Meyer (1967) tested a group of 380 men and women aged 55 and over during the years 1956-57. Five years later, during 1961-62, they made an effort to locate and retest these same men and women, but only 202 of them were available. Death, illness, and lack of cooperation reduced the sample size by nearly a half. A reduction in sample size is a typical and to-be-expected result in all long-term longitudinal studies. It may be recalled that in the study by Owens (1953), discussed in the previous chapter, only one-third the number of subjects aged approximately 19 were available for retest 30 years later.

Riegel et al. (1967) compared the original performances of those 202 subjects who were retested with those 178 who were not. The scores of the two groups were different from each other, with those of the retested subjects being superior. Special analyses involving states of health and whether or not the subject was living during the second testing showed the original superiority of the healthy and living subjects. Riegel et al. concluded that aging research involves increasingly biased samples of subjects as their ages increase. Riegel et al. maintained that studies previous to theirs have underestimated the amount of attrition; the "biologically weak subjects will die earlier or will become increasingly unable to participate in the testings" (Riegel et al., 1967, p. 347).*

The study by Riegel et al. is not an isolated example of the problem; more and more studies are showing it. For example, Baltes, Schaie, and Nardi (1971) tested 500 men and women aged 21-70 years in 1956. Seven years later, in 1963, all they could retest were 302, an attrition of nearly 40 percent. The original performances of the retested subjects were compared with those unavailable for retest, with results similar to those of Riegel et al. (1967). The retested subjects were the initially superior. The data on senescent twins, studied by Jarvik and Falek (1963), also demonstrate the initial superiority of those testable at later periods of time.

Figure 20.1 shows this clearly. The figure is a graphic representation of selective subject dropout, i.e., the fact that those who fail to return for retest perform less well in tests than those who do return.

Eisdorfer and Wilkie (1973) gave a test of intelligence (WAIS) to two groups of older adults, only one of them shown in Figure 20.1. They were of approximate mean age 64 years when first tested, approximately 68 when tested a second time, 72 a third time, and 74 the fourth time. The results of this 10-year longitudinal study are shown by the solid circles in the figure. Note that the WAIS scores declined over the 10-year period.

This study was continued another five years with three more test sessions during this time (Wilkie and Eisdorfer, 1973). Thus, there were seven test sessions in the course of 15 years, shown by the open circles in the figure. An important fact regarding the data of Figure 20.1 is that *only* those subjects who appeared for *all* four tests during the first 10 years were considered in the function of solid circles, and *only* those who appeared for *all* seven tests during the 15 years of the study were considered with the open circles. This study was discussed briefly in chapter 13.

Note the different results seen during the first 10-year period in both curves of Figure 20.1. With relatively little dropout over 10 years, WAIS

---

* Subsequent to this study, Riegel et al. reported data of a second follow-up, five years after the first and ten years after the original testing. The selective bias in sampling was not only maintained, it was increased. In fact, elderly people still alive and testable during the second follow-up demonstrated performances comparable to those of young adults in their peak years.

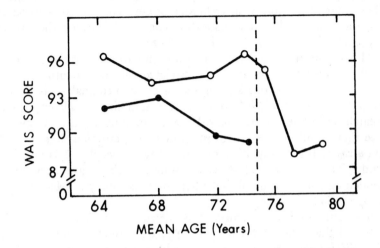

FIGURE 20.1: A comparison of subjects tested four times in the course of 10 years (solid circles) with the same subjects tested seven times in the course of 15 years (open circles). Fewer subjects were available for all seven testings than were available for only the first four testings. Data culled from the presentations of Eisdorfer and Wilkie (1973) and Wilkie and Eisdorfer (1973).

scores were seen to decline with age. With more dropout over 15 years, the WAIS scores were not seen to decline with age during the first 10-year period. The sampling problem of selective subject attrition obfuscated the decremental age patterns.

COMMON ERRORS

Three problems, even errors, are often seen in the published literature and these will be briefly highlighted. The first two are of data analysis, one bearing on issues of sampling, the other on sequential designs (see chapter 19). The third problem bears on the need for control groups.

Covariance Analysis

Let us say that we want to compare two age groups on intelligence test scores. Random sampling of subjects from an elderly group and a young adult group will result in two groups with different levels of formal education because, years ago, people tended not to go to school for as long as they do now. Since we know that intelligence test scores are affected by levels of education, the age comparison might be unfair. Investigators often resort to the statistical technique of covariance analysis to handle this; they statistically "hold education constant" between the two age groups and then compare them for intelligence.

This is considered incorrect—it is an error to use covariance analysis when the covariate (education) is correlated with the "treatment condition" (age). In fact, one assumption of covariance analysis is that the two are independent. Unfortunately, the sampling problems in aging research are often of this kind. We want to compare age groups, and have them similar in regard to some matching criterion, but the criterion measure is typically different with age when people are sampled randomly. There are several statistical solutions that have been recommended and seen as useful, but none so far is totally satisfactory (e.g., George and Okun, 1976).

A recent opinion challenged this. Overall and Woodward (1977) indicated that when the covariate (e.g., education) is both a reliable and valid measure, then covariance analysis is correct. Their position is new and controversial. Not all expert opinion has yet been heard in response to it.

Comparing Cross-Sectional and Longitudinal Sequences

Table 19.4 presents one design of a type of study called cross-sequential and time-sequential; in this table, seven age-cohort groups are compared cross-sectionally over two longitudinal test periods. Thus, Table 19.4 shows cross-sectional comparisons of groups aged 25 at Test 1 and 32 at Test 2 with older groups ranging in age to 67 at Test 1 and 74 at Test 2. Cohort 7 is 42 years older than Cohort 1. The longitudinal comparison covers a period of 7 years, 1956 to 1963.

If we are to make interpretations regarding the relation between cross-sectional and longitudinal results, comparing a 7-year difference with a 42-year difference is not logical. In fact, it was pointed out algebraically that when the cross-sectional and longitudinal time spans are disparate, errors of interpretation are likely. If little or no difference in scores over the 7-year longitudinal period is found, and sizeable difference in scores over the 42-year cross-sectional comparison is found, "the conclusion that age differences are 'generational' (cohort or cultural) and not due to age changes within individuals may be wrong" (Botwinick and Arenberg, 1976, p. 55).

A meaningful cross-sectional and longitudinal comparison in Table 19.4 is of equal time spans. For example, Cohort 1 and 2 may be compared cross-sectionally (A versus B), as may the respective longitudinal comparison (A versus a). Here, a 7-year cross-sectional comparison is related to a 7-year longitudinal one (25 versus 32 years). Other age groups may be similarly compared, e.g., score F versus G and F versus f (age 60 versus age 67 years). Cross-sequential and time-sequential studies should be carried out with equal time spans in comparing the group differences.

Control Groups

Most students now seem aware of the need for a control group in assessing the effects of drugs, therapy, and other modification or intervention techniques. Not everyone, however, seems aware of the need for a control group when inferences are made as to the mechanism or basis of the modification. This was discussed in chapter 14 under the heading "Modification Studies," so only brief reference to the issue will be made here.

In several studies efforts were made to train older people to perform well in tasks that are typically hard for them. The purpose of these studies was to demonstrate a plasticity with age—an ability to change and to improve. Another purpose was to infer the reasons why the tasks were hard for old people in the first place. The thinking was that if appreciable improvement were seen with behavioral intervention procedures—teaching and guidance, for example—it would be unlikely that the original problem was of biological origin; rather, it was likely to be of experiential or psychological origin.

This thinking is incomplete at best. If improvement of elderly people's performances is observed after modification training, no inference can be made regarding the basis of original difficulty, i.e., biological or experiential. Similar training might help young groups as much or more even though they had little of the original difficulty that the older people had. Such a finding could make for a very different conclusion regarding the basis of elderly people's original difficulty from the findings of studies in which only elderly subjects were tested. The young group is a control group—a control not for testing the effectiveness of the intervention, but for ascertaining the basis of difficulty. If improvement on the part of the elderly were found greater than that of the young, a biological basis of original difficulty could not be ruled out, but an experiential basis as an explanation might have a better foundation.

GRADIENTS

There is no reason to believe that the sampling problem is unique to longitudinal research. In fact, the problem may very likely be more serious in cross-sectional research, but, unfortunately, there seems to be no way of determining its extent. There seems to be little possibility in developing quantitative estimates of the relative magnitudes of the sampling problem in cross-sectional and longitudinal research. It is difficult enough to compare the results of cross-sectional and longitudinal investigations, irrespective of the sampling biases.

It is frequently maintained that, when age curves obtained in cross-sectional studies are compared to those in longitudinal studies, the latter curves are less steep. Even when cross-sectional investigations disclose large decrements in performance with age, it is often held, longitudinal investigations disclose no decrements with age, or lesser ones. More often than not, however, such declarations do not take into consideration initial ability levels of the subjects, the age range of the subjects, and, most important perhaps, the nature of the performance itself. It is true that able young adults, performing functions which do not decline greatly with age in cross-sectional studies, will show little or no decrement in these functions when aged 50 years in longitudinal studies. On the other hand, it is very likely that less able adults, performing functions which decline greatly with age in cross-sectional studies, will show longitudinal decrements at age 70 years. Only now are data becoming available which bear on such matters, permitting comparisons of cross-sectional and longitudinal aging studies.

Schaie (1970) insists that it is not correct to compare the results of cross-sectional and longitudinal age studies. In cross-sectional studies, data are collected during a single period of time, while in longitudinal studies, data are collected at two or more periods of time. Comparability demands that the same number of time periods be involved in both types of studies. Schaie (1970) evolved a method of analysis which solves this problem, but it does so at the expense of making for artificial, highly abstract age functions.

Longitudinal

Schaie's goal was to construct longitudinal and cross-sectional gradients so that each is anchored in the same points of time. To demonstrate his solution, let us construct a longitudinal gradient based upon some of the information in Table 19.1. Cell A in Table 19.1 represents a group of subjects aged 30 years; let the average score for this group be 100. Let the longitudinal follow-up show scores of 70 and 40 for cells B and C, respectively. Similarly, let the cohort born in 1920 have scores of 40 and 35 for the ages 40 and 50, respectively. These data are shown in Figure 20.2 (A), by the heavy solid lines, ABC and DE.

The longitudinal gradient is constructed in Figure 20.2 (B). The longitudinal segment AB goes from 100 to 70, a drop of 30 points; this is connected to longitudinal segment DE, which, in going from 40 to 35, drops 5 points. Thus, the longitudinal gradient in Figure 20.2 (B) is based upon two longitudinal sequences, one involving two observations of the 1930 cohort, and one sequence involving two observations of the 1920 cohort.

It may be seen that the level of the constructed function in Figure 20.2 (B) is irrelevant—only the shape is meaningful. Instead of a function with the scores 100, 70, and 65 for ages 30, 40, and 50, respectively, the scores could just as easily have been shown as 35, 40, and 70 for ages 50, 40, and 30, respectively.

Cross-Sectional

Table 19.1 shows that cohorts born in 1930, 1920, and 1910 were tested in 1960. The scores of 100, 40, and 20, respectively, of this cross-sectional age comparison may be seen by the dashed line ADG in Figure 20.2 (A). Similarly, dashed line BE is a cross-sectional comparison, with scores of 70 and 35.

The cross-sectional gradient in Figure 20.2 (B), like the longitudinal gradient, is based upon connecting disparate comparisons. And, as with the longitudinal gradient, the observations are based upon two measurements of the 1930 cohort and two of the 1920 cohort.

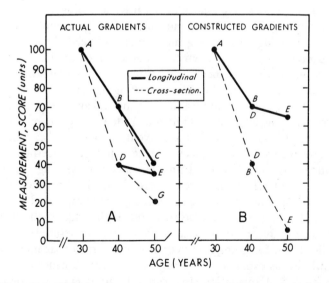

FIGURE 20.2: Hypothetical measurements or scores of people categorized into three age groups. Section A of the figure refers to cells A, B, C, D, E, and G of Table 19.1; Section B connects disparate age comparisons (see text).

The effect of constructing the longitudinal and cross-sectional gradients, therefore, is to provide opportunities for comparing the two gradients at what Schaie (1970) calls "the same points of environmental impact." The points of origin being coincident for both gradients further makes comparisons meaningful. But, as already indicated, this gain in opportunity to make the comparison is at the expense of making for highly artificial age functions.

AGE, AN INDEPENDENT VARIABLE

Dissatisfaction with the use of age as an independent variable in developmental research is widespread. The dissatisfaction is so widespread that Baltes and Goulet (1971) found it necessary to review the different reasons for it and to suggest special strategies in coping with it. The dissatisfaction takes extreme form in the comments of Bijou and Baer (1963) and Baer (1970), that age *per se* is not germane to the purpose of studying developmental patterns.

Causality

It is not difficult to argue for this extreme position. Age, as a concept, is synonymous with time, and time in itself cannot affect living function, behavior or otherwise. Time does not "cause" anything; it does not have physical dimensionality to impinge upon the sensorium, and it does not have psychological meaning independent of related social and biological parameters. (It is this which underlies much of the philosophers' age-old concern with the meaning of time, and, it seems, the scientists' more recent concern with the definition of aging. From a research point of view, only the operational meaning of time and aging is possible.)

To continue the argument: Time is a crude index of many events and experiences, and it is these indexed events which are "causal." If we study these events and experiences, we need not be concerned with the crude index of time. We need not be concerned with age in order to understand that which has been "caused" by the time-indexed variables. These variables, unlike age itself, can be manipulated experimentally while holding related factors constant. Unlike age, the independent variable can be regarded as explanatory as well as descriptive.

While all the foregoing is correct, it is also correct that much of what we regard now as explanatory, or causal, is so only because our information is limited. Explanation and causality in science are matters of improving approximations, of determining better empirical associations. Age may be used as an explanation or predictor until better ones become available. For example, knowing the age of a person, we can predict his blood pressure levels within broad limits. Knowing about his state of arteriosclerosis, our prediction would be more accurate. Neither age nor arteriosclerosis would be as useful as information regarding the efficiency of the cardiac muscle. Knowing all these together, our predictions are best. Predictability, i.e., explanation based upon the degree of association, constitutes one definition of causality in science.

There is an important social reason, even if not a scientific one, for maintaining that age *per se* is germane to the purpose of studying developmental patterns. If age is regarded as irrelevant in studying developmental patterns, then focus will be only on function, not the person. If focus is not upon the person as well as the function, then we end up with a cadre of cardiovascular specialists, for example, but few geriatricians. The problems of childhood require special focus and receive it in pediatrics; the problems of old age are too extensive and too important to negate a geriatric specialty. Our present knowledge of aging processes is too meager, and our social needs too great, to insist upon study of only what appears to be the more immediate, causative variables. A working hypothesis here is that a specific focus upon age *per se* will not only be relevant to our social goals, but will lead to a more precise delineation of the variables more immediately "causal."

Two Research Stages

Just as the extreme position of classifying age as irrelevant is not satisfactory, so is the insistence that the more precise, more immediate stimulus conditions be left uninvestigated. Both need to be examined, perhaps in a two-stage process: first by studying age functions, and then by subsequent research for the purpose of further elucidating and modifying the age functions (Baltes and Goulet, 1971). While not all problems may lend themselves to these two research stages, many do.

An example involving three studies may elucidate this research strategy; each of the three studies is what Baltes and Goulet (1971) would call part of the second stage. The first stage involves an extensive literature demonstrating that in a wide variety of situations, elderly people become slower in executing their behaviors. Reaction time (RT) increases as adult age increases.

One study of the second stage posed the question as to whether sensory loss in later life is responsible for the slowdown. For example, elderly people have hearing losses—does this account for their slowness in an auditory RT study? The loudness of the stimulus was adjusted on an individual basis for the purpose of determining a more immediate, precise "cause" of the RT slowing with increasing age (Botwinick, 1971).

The second study investigated a state-of-the-organism variable as a "cause" of the slowdown. Several stage-one studies suggested that older people tend to be more depressed than younger people. Since depression is often defined in terms of psychomotor slowing, it was thought that this state may be a "cause" of RT slowing. A depression scale was administered, and the scores were correlated with RT measures (Botwinick and Thompson, 1967).

The third study also examined a state-of-the-organism variable, but did so on the basis of its variation as a function of an experimenter manipulated stimulus condition. The question underlying this study involved the assertion that EEG activation makes for quick RTs. Since EEG activation may be expected to be different in young and old adulthood, the response slowing with age might be explained by age changes in levels of EEG activation. Thompson and Botwinick (1968) varied the EEG response by manipulating the foreperiod or preparatory interval in an RT experiment.

Each of these three stage-two studies was negative in the sense that more refined explanations regarding the slowdown with age did not result. The point here is that, while stage-two types of studies must follow the stage-one study for a fuller understanding, stage-one studies provide a type of understanding in their own right; some stage-one studies constitute the basis of the only understanding we have at the present.

TEST USEFULNESS

The usefulness of a test is determined by its reliability and by its validity. More often than not, adult tests and questionnaires are standardized on the basis of the performances of young adults only, thus making the reliability and validity uncertain for older people. More often than not, therefore, the usefulness of standardized tests and questionnaires for elderly people is left uncertain or doubtful.

Reliability

The reliability of a test is synonymous with its accuracy. There are two aspects to this accuracy. One involves the extent to which a test score of a particular person varies from the "true" score, and the other involves the extent to which scores of one group of subjects will be consistent with the scores of another group. The first aspect involves the *error of measurement* and the second aspect the *error of sampling*. These "errors" relate to the confidence we have in repeating our findings and in generalizing from them.

Error of Measurement. The reliability of tests is determined by coefficients of correlation of three types. One type is based upon the relatedness of scores of a test given on two occasions. A second type is similar, except that the second testing is with a parallel form of the test, rather than with the same test. The third type of reliability coefficient involves the correlation of the odd-numbered items with the even-numbered ones, all of a single test.

Since the computed reliability of the test or questionnaire is nothing more than a coefficient of correlation, its magnitude is dependent upon the variability of test scores, both within and among the individual subjects. The elderly person tends to be more variable in his performance than the younger person, and individual differences tend to be greater among elderly people than among young adults. Thus, in the absence of other information, there is reason to expect that a particular test or questionnaire may not be equally reliable for old and young adults.

The large intra-individual variance associated with advanced age might tend to decrease the repeatability of test score. The large inter-individual variance would tend to increase the size of the reliability coefficient, but not necessarily. Perhaps the statistic, standard error of measurement, rather than coefficient of reliability, is more appropriate for comparing this aspect of test usefulness in old and young adults (Botwinick, 1953).

Error of Sampling. It is often difficult to determine whether the results of a study are a reflection of the low reliability of the test, or of real differences among the people studied. It was seen earlier in this chapter that people change over the years such that the less able become less available for longitudinal retest. Clearly, the consistency of results is a reflection of the consistency or representativeness of the sample selected. Similarly, as seen in the previous chapter, both cross-sectional and longitudinal age group comparisons reflect changing cultural and environmental influences. A low correlation between testings might be a reflection of changes some individuals undergo, even during brief intervals, rather than of test unreliability.

Validity

The validity of a test or questionnaire is a matter of whether it measures what we want it to measure. There are various ways of determining this, all of them dependent upon a clear understanding and assessment of the criterion, i.e., upon what we want to measure.

The problem of validity in aging research may be more apparent in the measurement of I.Q. than in other types of measurements, but it is general to all functions. I.Q. tests, for example, were devised originally to predict school performance. The test would be judged valid if predictability was high. Adult tests of I.Q. tend to be used for other purposes —purposes more related to the social and cognitive needs of the everyday life of adults. Clearly, if the cognitive worlds of the young and the aged are different, a single test will be differentially valid for the two age groups. For example, knowing where and how to claim medicare credit may or may not involve the same functions as claiming credit via school attendance. Indeed, Demming and Pressey (1957) demonstrated an information test comprising items of a very practical nature which reflected rises in scores with age among the very people who showed declines with the more traditional tests.

A test is useless if it is invalid. It may be worse than useless if its validity is mistaken and misrepresented. It is most desirable, if not crucial, that the criterion, the purpose to which the test is directed, is understood and defined publicly.

DESCRIBING AGE GROUP DIFFERENCES

Biologists often describe changes or differences between age groups in terms of percentages. For example, if at age 20 the mean score on a test is 80, and at age 70 the mean score is 40, the age difference or change is described as 50 percent (40 divided by 80, or, 80 — 40 divided by 80).

This description is inadequate because it tells nothing about individual differences. Is the 50 percent change something on which we can rely? Traditional statistical tests help to answer this question by comparing a measure of difference between or among age groups, and a measure of difference within the age groups. An age difference is statistically significant when its magnitude is large relative to the magnitude of individual differences.

Units of Standard Deviation

Age group differences are typically described in terms of differences in their means or medians. This leaves a lot to be desired because it tells little directly of the overlap between the groups. A more helpful index is mean difference in units of standard deviation. Thus, if the mean difference in the age groups above is 40, and the standard deviation of, say, the young group is 8, then the difference between the groups may be described as 5, i.e., the mean difference divided by the standard deviation.

Describing group differences in this way can represent information in ways not otherwise discernible. It was seen earlier, in the chapter on intelligence, that some functions measured by tests hold up well with age and some decline. The extent of the decline of those functions will sometimes be seen differently if the index is simply mean age difference rather than if it is mean age difference in units of standard deviation. An example of this was seen with the Wechsler-Bellevue Test in comparing two elderly groups, one normal and one psychotic (Botwinick and Birren, 1951). In Figure 13.3 the Picture Completion subtest, for example, showed a large mean difference, but a small mean difference in units of standard deviation. Rather than an interpretation that the subtest is an effective measure for differentiating the groups, the measure involving standard deviation suggests that the subtest is ineffective. A test to be maximally effective must not only distinguish between groups in a statistically significant way, but it must describe sizable differences both independent of, and related to, individual differences.

Percentage of People as a Score

A more direct index of the groups' overlap is the simplest measure of all —the percentages of people in the different groups who overlap. It was inadvertently discovered in one study that diverse habits of exercise among subjects in a young control group may have been an importrant contributing factor in the results (Botwinick and Thompson, 1968). Accordingly, an age analysis was made on the basis of whether or not the young adult subjects were athletes. There were 17 young non-athletes in the study and 13 elderly subjects who similarly did little exercise. With a score of 18 as a criterion, five of the young non-athletes made poorer scores than nine of the elderly subjects; that is, seventy percent of the elderly subjects were superior in their responses to thirty percent of the non-athletic younger subjects. Percentages change with the different criterion scores; thus, with a criterion of 13 in the study, the scores of only six young non-athletes were superior to and did not overlap with the scores of the elderly subjects.

> We wager that, if all age comparisons were made on the basis of some such a combination of percentage and . . . [criterion score] . . . much of the age difference which may seem impressive at first would lose its interest (Botwinick and Thompson, 1968, p. 27).

SUMMARY

This chapter dealt with operational aspects of research in aging. Sampling problems, errors commonly made, difficulties in interpreting age effects, the meaning of age—all these, and other issues were discussed, focusing on the method of longitudinal research more than other methods.

The longitudinal method is difficult to carry out. It is costly, requires much patience and time, often necessitates the use of outmoded procedures, enforces continuance of practices based upon poor decisions made at earlier periods of study, and is burdensome logistically. It is the prudent investigator, therefore, who thinks twice before embarking on a longitudinal course of study. Fortunately, not all questions require research with this difficult method.

There are some questions, however, which can only be answered longitudinally. It is the only method permitting analyses of changes in the individual person over time. It is the only method by which variations in performance of the individual person may be examined. It is the only method by which measurements and their combinations can be used to learn about impending disease and death.

One problem of sampling intrinsic to long-term longitudinal research is that the initially less able and less healthy subjects tend to be relatively unavailable for later-life retest. As the age of the subjects in a study increases, the attrition of the subject pool increases, with the less adequate subjects being progressively less represented in the sample.

This type of attrition would seem to be at least as great in cross-sectional studies, but this is difficult to ascertain. It is difficult enough to compare the results of cross-sectional studies with those of longitudinal studies, let alone their respective sampling biases. It is difficult to compare the two types of studies because cross-sectional data are collected during a single period of time and longitudinal data are collected at two or more periods of time.

The previous chapter (19) discussed sequential designs that aid in the comparison of cross-sectional and longitudinal measures. However, these designs are often used incorrectly—a common error is in making comparisons between a relatively brief longitudinal sequence and a relatively long cross-sectional sequence. An example from the literature was given where a 42-year cross-sectional (age-cohort) difference was compared with a 7-year longitudinal difference. Other common errors involve the misuse of covariance analysis and the lack of properly used control groups.

Schaie (1970) devised a method of constructing cross-sectional and longitudinal gradients which permits a comparison during the same periods of testing. These gradients are not the same as those normally described; the gradients are constructed on the basis of connecting disparate group comparisons. The construction, described in detail, refers to Figure 20.2. While cross-sectional and longitudinal gradients permit comparisons based upon the same periods of time, they do so at the expense of forming abstract and artificial functions.

Age comparisons, be they constructed gradients or traditional age curves, constitute a source of uneasiness or dissatisfaction among many investigators. Simply put, age in itself cannot affect or cause events, and is not a true independent variable. Age cannot be manipulated experimentally, and the related biological and social factors cannot be held constant. Despite this, aging studies were seen as important both scientifically and socially. While age cannot cause behavior, it is associated with it and describes it. It may also be used as predictor of it.

A meaningful research strategy involves two stages. The first examines the association between age and the behavior, and the second stage examines more precise explanatory variables. For example, a stage-one study describes the slowing of behavior in relation to age; a stage-two study attempts to explain the slowing with age on the basis of environmental and organismic variables.

The usefulness of a test is defined, in part, by indices of reliability and validity. The reliability of a test is a function of the variability of the people tested. Since the variability of old people is greater than that of young people, the reliability of a test may be different for old and young. The validity of a test is related to the purpose for which the test was originally designed. Since the purpose for which tests are used with old people is often different from that for which they are used with young people, the validity of the test may be different for old and young. Thus, the usefulness of a test established on the basis of young adults may be of questionable usefulness when appled to older adults.

When a test is given to both old and young, there is most always overlap between age groups, even when mean differences are statistically significant. The overlap may be made more apparent if the index used to describe the differences between age groups is expressed in units of standard deviation. The overlap may be emphasized further by a description in terms of the percentage of subjects overlapping in relation to a measure of central tendency.

REFERENCES

Baer, D.M. An age-irrelevant concept of development. *Merrill-Palmer Quarterly,* 1970, *16,* 238–245.

Baltes, P.B., and Goulet, L.R. Exploration of developmental parameters by manipulation and simulation of age differences in behavior. *Human Development,* 1971, *14,* 149–170.

Baltes, P.B., Schaie, K.W., and Nardi, A.H. Age and experimental mortality in a seven-year longitudinal study of cognitive behavior. *Developmental Psychology*, 1971, *5*, 18–26.

Bijou, S.W., and Baer, D.M. Some methodological contributions from a functional analysis of child development. In L.P. Lipsitt and C.C. Spiker (Eds.), *Advances in child development and behavior*. New York: Academic Press, 1963, vol. 1, pp. 197–231.

Botwinick, J. Wechsler-Bellevue split-half subtest reliabilities: differences in age and mental status. *Journal of Consulting Psychology*, 1953, *17*, 225–228.

Botwinick, J. *Cognitive processes in maturity and old age*. New York: Springer Publishing Co., 1967.

Botwinick, J. Sensory-set factors in age differences in reaction time. *Journal of Genetic Psychology*, 1971, *119*, 241–249.

Botwinick, J., and Arenberg, D. Disparate time spans in sequential studies of aging. *Experimental Aging Research*, 1976, *2*, 55–61.

Botwinick, J., and Birren, J.E. Differential decline in the Wechsler-Bellevue subtests in the senile psychoses. *Journal of Gerontology*, 1951, *6*, 365–368.

Botwinick, J., and Thompson, L.W. Depressive affect, speed of response, and age. *Journal of Consulting Pscyhology*, 1967, *31*, 106.

Botwinick, J., and Thompson, L.W. Age difference in reaction time: an artifact? *Gerontologist*, 1968, *8*, 25–28.

Demming, J.A., and Pressey, S.L. Tests "indigenous" to the adult and older years. *Journal of Consulting Psychology*, 1957, *2*, 144–148.

Eisdorfer, C., and Wilkie, F. Intellectual changes with advancing age. In L.F. Jarvik, C. Eisdorfer, and J.E. Blum (Eds.), *Intellectual functioning in adults*. New York: Springer Publishing Co., 1973.

George, L.K., and Okun, M.A. Misuse of analysis of covariance in aging research revisited. *Experimental Aging Research*, 1976, *2*, 449–459.

Jarvik, L.F., and Falck, A. Intellectual stability and survival in the aged. *Journal of Gerontology*, 1963, *18*, 173–176.

Miles, C.C. The influence of speed and age on intelligence scores of adults. *Journal of General Psychology*, 1934, *10*, 208–210.

Overall, J.E., and Woodward, J.A. Nonrandom assignment and the analysis of covariance. *Psychological Bulletin*, 1977, *84*, 588–594.

Owens, W.A., Jr. Age and mental abilities: a longitudinal study. *Genetic Psychology Monographs*, 1953, *48*, 3–54.

Riegel, K.F., Riegel, R.M., and Meyer, G. A study of the dropout rates in longitudinal research on aging and the prediction of death. *Journal of Personality and Social Psychology*, 1967, *5*, 342–348.

Schaie, K.W. A reinterpretation of age related changes in cognitive structure and functioning. In L.R. Goulet and P.B. Baltes (Eds.), *Life span developmental psychology: research and theory*. New York: Academic Press, 1970, pp. 485–507.

Thompson, L.W., and Botwinick, J. Age differences in the relationship between EEG arousal and reaction time. *Journal of Psychology*, 1968, *68*, 167–172.

Wilkie, F., and Eisdorfer, C. Intellectual changes: a 15-year followup of the Duke sample. Unpublished manuscript read at the 26th Annual Meeting of the Gerontological Society, Miami, Florida, 1973.

Index

Abstraction, 239–242, 273–274, 278
Accommodation, 143–144
Achievement tests, 26, 209, 215–216, 230
Activity, 35–36, 39, 63–64, 81
Adjustment
  compensatory, 179–180, 181
  hostility and, 31–33
  illness and, 35
  life review and, 60
  to relocation, 28–35, 39
  to retirement, 77–80
Aggression, 31–33
Aging
  cellular, 9–13
  defined, 1–8
  dependence model for, 6
  medical model for, 6
  social norms and constraints in, 74–76
Alcohol and health, 19, 52
Animal studies
  fruitfly, 11, 22
  housefly, 11, 14, 18, 22
  mealworm, 11, 14
  mice, 17, 22
  rabbit, 14
  rat, 11, 17–18, 22, 53, 91–94, 191, 301, 302, 325–327
  rotifer, 13, 16, 18, 22
  spider, 11, 22
Anoxia, 178–179
Anxiety, 60, 124, 134, 270
Army Alpha Intelligence Test, 222, 368
Arousal activation, 268–271, 278
Arteriosclerosis, 19, 23, 216, 229, 382, 391
Attention, 165–168, 180–181, 342–343, 382
Attitudes, 1, 7, 29–35, 57, 74–75, 82, 90, 150, 336–367

Audition
  cautiousness and, 136–137, 140
  click fusion, 159
  compensatory adjustment in, 179, 180–181
  continuous sound, 165–166
  intelligence and loss of, 229–230
  pitch discrimination, 148–149, 152
  pitch threshold, 147–148, 152
  sensory augmentation in, 293–295, 306
  speech perception, 165
  speed of response and, 186–188, 391
Autonomic nervous system, 268–271, 278. *See also* Central nervous system

Bender-Gestalt Test, 29
Biological clocks, 9–10
Blood pressure. *See* Cardiovascular function
Brain function, 34–35, 227, 231
Brain syndrome, 34–35
Brightness discrimination, 146
Bronchitis, 15, 23

Cancer, 5, 19–21, 23
Cardiovascular function, 6, 15, 19–21, 34–36, 55, 194–195, 227–229, 382, 391
Career. *See* Life satisfaction; Work
Carefulness, 114–115
Cataracts, 144
Categorization, 283–286
Causality, 390–391
Cautiousness
  cognition and, 114–126
  compensatory adjustment and, 179
  decision making and, 128–140
  in learning, 270–271
  personality and, 114–126
Central nervous system, 154, 158, 167,

Central nervous system—*cont.*
185, 189–195, 197–199, 203–205, 214, 227, 268–270, 302–303
Cerebrovascular diseases, 5–6
Certainty, 116–126
Choline acetyltransferase (C.A.T.), 359
Click fusion, 159
Cognition, 1, 25–29, 39, 72, 122, 128, 198–205, 234–239, 257
Cohort considerations, 364–367, 370–372, 376–377, 379
Cohort-sequential design, 376–377, 379
Color afterimage, 170–171
Color vision, 145–146
Commission error, 115–116, 125, 134, 137, 289
Comrey Personality Inventory, 123
Concentration. *See* Attention
Conditioning, 297–298, 306
Confidence, 116–122
Consequence hypothesis, 115
Conservatism, 113
Consolidation, 324–328
Continuous sound, 165–167
Coping ability, 29, 39
Covariance analysis, 385–386
Creativity, 254–256
Critical flicker fusion (CFF), 157–159
Critical loss, 28–29
Cross-sectional studies, 66–72, 100–108, 208–209, 222–226, 364–365, 373–375, 378–379, 387–390, 396–397
cohort-age, 364–365
gradients in, 387–390, 396–397
of intelligence, 208–209, 222–226
vs. longitudinal, 386–387, 396
personality change, 66–72
rigidity, 100–108
sampling problems in, 387–388, 396
Cross-sequential design, 373–375, 376, 379

Dark adaptation, 145
Death. *See* Disease; Life expectancy
Decay, 347–348. *See also* Memory; Storage
Decision making, 128–140, 204
Delayed recall, 313–317
Deoxyribonucleic acid (DNA), 358
Depression, 30–31, 39, 60, 69–71, 81–82. *See also* Anxiety
Desurgency, 69
Developmental change models
three-component, 371
two-component, 372
Diabetes, 15
Diet, 17–19, 22–23. *See also* Health

Disease, 4, 6, 15, 19–21, 34–35. *See also* Health
Disengagement, 37, 61–74, 81–83, 123–124, 134–135
activity and, 63–64
cautiousness and, 123–124
deprivation and, 62–63
personality changes and, 66–74
risk avoidance and, 134–135
Dogmatism, 94–97
Draw-A-Person Test, 29

Economic status. *See* Income
Education
cautiousness and, 138–139
intelligence and, 221–222, 230
life expectancy and, 37
problem solving and, 241–242, 258
Edwards Personal Preference Schedule, 68
Ego development, 59–61
Einstellung effect, 242–243, 244
Electroencephalogram (EEG), 193–194, 227
Electromyogram (EMG), 191
Environment effect, 370, 379
Episodic memory. *See* Memory
Exercise, 19, 22, 35–36, 40, 200–201, 205, 395. *See also* Activity
Experimenter effect, 369, 379
Extinction. *See* Interference
Extroversion, 68–69

Failure. *See* Cautiousness
Family relations, 37–38
Figural aftereffect, 167–168
Flexibility. *See* Rigidity
Free fatty acids (FFA), 268–270, 273, 298
Friendships (social integration), 76–77

Galvanic skin response (GSR), 273, 298
Generational differences, 59, 118–119, 122, 129–132, 275–276, 364–367
Genetic factors, 10–14
Gestalt Completion Test, 116
Glare, 144
Gradients, 387–390, 396–397
Guilford-Zimmerman Temperament Survey (GZTS), 73
Gustation, 149–150

Habit. *See* Rigidity
Happiness. *See* Life satisfaction
Health
activity and, 35–36, 63–64
diet and, 17–19, 22–23

in general, 4–5
intelligence and, 226–230
memory and, 357–359
morale and, 63, 64, 80
sexual waning and, 54–55
See also Disease
Heart. *See* Cardiovascular function
Heredity. *See* Genetic factors
Hooper Visual Organization Test, 174
Hostility, 31–33
Hyperoxygenation, 358–359
Hypochondriasis, 71

Illumination, 144–145
Illusion, 172–173
Immediate memory. *See* Memory
Impotence, 52–53
Inadequacy. *See* Cautiousness; Confidence; Sexual waning
Income, 4, 8, 37, 39, 77–80, 82, 370
Independent measures, 368
Individual differences, 7, 201, 256, 381, 393, 394
Inflexibility. *See* Rigidity
Institutionalization. *See* Relocation
Instruction. *See* Learning
Integrating information, 39, 116, 156–177, 180–182, 215–216, 230, 247, 276–279, 282–297, 305
sequential, 156–168, 180–181
spatial, 173–177, 181
temporal, 168–173, 180–181
See also Learning
Intelligence, 100–109, 208–231, 234–238, 393–394
age decline in, 211–214
cross-sectional studies of, 208–209, 222–226
differential decline in, 213–214, 216–219
fluid vs. crystallized, 222
health and, 226–230
longitudinal studies of, 222–226
problem solving and, 234–238
rigidity and, 100–109
survival and, 219–220
tests of, 209–213, 393–394
See also WAIS
Interference, 295–297, 328, 347
Introversion, 68–69
I.Q. *See* Intelligence; WAIS
Isolation, 76–80

Learning
aids to, 282–297, 305–306
cautiousness and, 270–271
clinical, 357–359

conditioning as, 297–298, 306
delayed recall and, 313–317
distributed, 326–328
integration and, 283–286, 305, 347
laboratory, 356–357
massed, 326–328
mediational techniques and, 286–290
motivation and, 268–272, 278–279
note writing in, 290–291
paired-associate, 263–267, 271, 274–275, 279, 287–291, 313, 315–317, 342
perceptual, 302–303, 307
performance and, 261–279
practical, 304–305, 307
psychomotor, 293, 302–303, 307
response bias in, 271–272
rigidity and, 90–94, 299–302, 306
sensory augmentation in, 293–295
serial, 264–265, 270
supportive and challenging contexts in, 291–293, 306
total time principle, 265–266
types of, 297–307
verbal, 299, 306
Life expectancy, 2, 9–23, 25–40, 219–220
attitudinal factors in, 34–35
biological factors in, 9–15, 21–23
environmental factors in, 16–23
intelligence and, 219–220
medical factors in, 34–35
psychological factors in, 25–35, 38–40
social factors in, 35–40
Life review, 60, 73
Life satisfaction, 60–65, 76–80
Loneliness, 76–80, 82
Longevity. *See* Life expectancy
Longitudinal studies, 72–74, 109–111, 222–226, 365–397
advantages of, 381–382
cohort-age, 365–367
cross-sectional and, 386–387, 396
cross-sequential design and, 372–375
disadvantages of, 382–383
errors in, 385–387
of intelligence, 222–226
personality change, 72–74
rigidity, 109–111
sampling problems in, 383–385
time of measurement in, 367–370
Long-term memory. *See* Memory

Masturbation, 44, 47, 48, 51
Maturational age
in cross-sectional studies, 364–365

Maturational age—*cont.*
 in longitudinal studies, 365–367
 and time |of measurement, 367–370
Maudsley Personality Inventory, 68
Memory
 age of, 331–332, 353–354
 episodic, 261–279
 immediate, 313, 316, 332
 intelligence and, 221
 long-term, 312–314, 328–333
 neurochemistry of, 357–360
 old, 350–357
 primary (PM), 294–295, 306, 312,
  321–322, 331, 333, 344–347
 problem solving and, 239
 recall, 337–345, 348–349, 351–356,
  359–360
 recognition, 337–345, 348, 350, 356–
  357, 359–360
 retrieval from, 337–360
 secondary (SM), 294–295, 306, 312,
  321–328, 331, 333, 344–347
 semantic, 262, 276–277, 306, 311–
  334
 sensory, 312, 317, 318–321, 333
 short-term, 312, 313, 314, 320-321,
  322–328, 333
 storage in, 347–350, 360
 very short term, 318, 333
Menopause, 53–54
Metabolic rate, 16–17
Method of loci, 289–290
Mill Hill Vocabulary Test, 218–219,
 223
Minnesota Multiphasic Personality Inventory (MMPI), 69–71, 118
Models. *See* Aging; Developmental
 change models
Motivation, 202–203, 205, 268–272,
 278–279, 368–369, 379, 382
Motivation hypothesis, 115
Motor time (MT), 191–192

Necker cubes, 172–173
Negative instance, 244–245
Neural conduction-transmission, 156–
 157, 163, 186, 189–192, 203–205.
 See also Central nervous system
Nobel Prize, 255

Obesity, 18–19
Olfaction, 149–150
Omission error, 115–116, 124–125, 134,
 136, 137, 271, 289
Opinionation, 137–138
Organization. *See* Integration
Orgasm, 44–45, 46, 47, 48, 50, 53

Otis Intelligence Test, 223

Pacing, 263–267, 270, 278, 296, 305,
 327, 333
Pain threshold, 150–151
Paired-associate learning. *See* Learning
Parental age, 10–14, 22
Perceptual ability
 and reaction time, 185–205
 See also Cognition; Sensation
Perceptual changes, 156–182
 anoxia, 178–179
 compensatory adjustments, 179–180
 sequential integration, 156–168
 spatial integration, 173–177
 temporal integration, 168–173
Perceptual modification, 175–177
Perceptual (P) system, 320–321
Personality
 cognitive and sensory factors in, 72
 conformist and passive patterns in,
  66–68
 cross-sectional studies of, 66–72
 depression, 69–71
 desurgency, 69
 disengagement and, 66–74
 hypochondriasis, 70
 introversion, 68–69
 longitudinal studies of, 72–74
 rigidity and, 71–72
 social forces in, 74–80
 tests of, 68–73
Pitch discrimination, 147–149
Population statistics for the aged, 2–4,
 50–51
Post-mortem studies, 18, 25
Premotor time (PMT), 191–192
Preparatory interval (PI), 192–194, 202–
 204
Presbycusis, 147–148
Presbyopia, 143–144
Primary memory. *See* Memory
Primary Mental Abilities Test, 225
Principal-component analysis, 61, 100–
 105, 109, 198–199, 204, 215, 220,
 230
Problem solving, 234–258
 abstract thought in, 239–242
 concept attainment in, 243–244, 252–
  254
 concrete thought in, 239–242, 251–
  252
 creativity and, 254–256
 intelligence and, 234–238
 memory and, 238
 modification studies in, 252–254
 negative instance in, 244–245

orderly search in, 248–249
redundancy in, 245–247
rigidity and, 242–245
sex differences in, 249–251
training, effect of, on, 251–254
Progressive matrices, 198, 219, 223, 234–235, 244
Prospective analyses, 29, 39, 382
Psychomotor abilities, tests of, 215–216
Psychosis, 216–219, 230, 357

Raven Progressive Matrices, 123, 198
Reaction time (RT), 187–205, 391–392
cardiac rhythm and, 194–195
choice, 195–197
cognitive ability and, 197–200
EEG to measure, 193–194
exercise and, 200–201
individual differences in, 201
motivation and, 202–203
motor time (MT), 191–192
perceptual ability and, 197–200
practice and, 201–202
premotor (PMT), 191–192
preparatory interval (PI), 192–194
response preparation, 192–193
stimulus duration and, 196–197
stimulus expectation and, 192–193
Recall memory. See Memory
Recognition memory. See Memory
Redundancy, 245–247
Relocation, 29–34
Repeated measures, 368
Research
operational aspects of, 381–397
strategies for, 391–392, 394–395, 397
Response, slowing of. See Speed of response
Retinal rivalry, 173
Retirement, 77–80, 82
Retrieval, 337–350, 359–360
rate of search, 345–347
storage and, 347–350
task difficulty, 342–344
Retrospective analyses, 29, 39, 382
Ribonucleic acid (RNA), 358
Rigidity, 71–72, 87–98, 100–112, 242–245, 299–302, 306–307
age and, 104–105, 109
animal studies of, 91–94
cross-sectional studies of, 100–108
dogmatism and, 94–97
intelligence and, 100–109
learning and, 90–94, 299–302, 306–307
longitudinal studies of, 109–111
motor-cognitive, 101, 110

multidimensional, 100–112
personal and general, 95
personality-perceptual, 101, 110
problem solving and, 242–245
psychomotor speed and, 101, 110–111
shift and, 106–108
simple, 87–98
speed of response and, 102–106
Rorschach Test, 72

Sampling, error of, 392–393, 396
Secondary memory. See Memory
Self-appraisal, 74–75
Semantic elaboration, 322–323
Semantic memory. See Memory
Sensation, 72, 142–153, 156–182, 186–188, 293–295, 306, 320–321. See also Cognition
Sensory augmentation, 293–295, 306
Sensory changes, 143–152
audition, 146–149
gustation, 149–150
olfaction, 149–150
pain, 150–151
touch, 151–152
vision, 143–146
Sensory memory. See Memory
Sequential designs, 372–378
Sequential integration, 156–168
Serial learning. See Learning
Set. See Reaction time
Sex differences, 2, 4–5, 8, 10–11, 17–18, 22, 30–32, 44–56, 66–68, 71, 78–82, 148, 192–193, 204, 249–250
Sexuality
changing role relationships, 80–81, 82–83
relative pattern of both sexes, 48–50
research studies on, 42–56
Sexual waning
female, 46–51, 53–55
male, 44–46, 48–50, 51–53
psychological factors in, 51–54
sexual fulfillment and, 50–55
significance of, 55–56
Shift
rigidity and, 106–108
Short-term memory. See Memory
16 Personality Factor (16 PF) Test, 68–69, 73
Slowing of response. See Speed of response
Smoking, 19–21
Social constraints, 74–75
Sound perception, 165–167
Spatial integration, 173–177
Speech perception, 165

Speed of response
    cautiousness and, 116–117
    cognitive ability and, 197–200
    exercise and, 200–201
    intelligence and, 105, 214
    neural conduction and, 156–157, 163, 186, 189–191, 203–205
    pacing and, 263–267, 270
    perception and, 185, 197–200
    problem difficulty and, 105–106
    reaction time and, 187–204
    rigidity and, 105–106
    sensation and, 185–188, 197–200
    sequential integration and, 156–157
    slowing of, 185–205
    stimulus intensity and, 186–188
    synaptic delay and, 191
Spiral aftereffect, 169–170
SRA Primary Mental Ability (PMA) Test, 101
Stanford Binet Test, 28
Stimulus
    ambiguous, 176–177
    dissociated, 174
    enhancement of, 160–162
    expectation of, 192–193
    fusion of, 157–160
    masking of, 160–162
    meaningful, 239–240, 272–277, 279, 315, 323–324
    persistence of, 156–182
Storage, 347–350, 360. See also Memory
Street Test, 174
Stress, 30, 37, 270, 291
Stroke, 5
Successful aging, 62–66
Suicide, 30–32, 39
Surgency, 69
Survival. See Life expectancy
Synaptic delay, 191

Temporal integration, 168–173
Terminal drop, 26
Tests
    intelligence, 209–213, 393–394
    psychomotor ability, 215–216
    reliability of, 392–393, 397
    standard deviation in, 394–395
    validity of, 393–394, 397
    verbal ability, 213–219

See also Cross-sectional studies; Longitudinal studies
Thematic Apperception Test (TAT), 68
Thermal regulation, 16–17
Time lag, 371, 372, 375–376, 379
Time of measurement
    age and, 367–370, 379
    cohort and, 370–372, 379
    environmental effects on, 370, 379
    experimenter effects on, 369–379
    subject effects on, 368–369, 379
Time-sequential design, 375–376, 379, 387, 396
Touch, 151–152
Trace, 156–158, 163–168, 175, 180–181, 189, 312, 318–320, 324–328
Transfer of training, 301–302
Twins, studies of, 12–13, 21, 22, 26–28

Verbal abilities, 213–219
Verbal imagery, 287–289
Vigilance performance, 166–167
Vision, 143–146, 152
Visual acuity, 143, 152
Visual imagery, 287–289
Visual perception, 163–165
Vocabulary, 123, 299

Wechsler Adult Intelligence Scale (WAIS), 28, 30, 198–199, 200–218, 219, 221–223, 228–230, 384–385
    Digit Symbol subtest, 28, 30, 213, 216–217, 219
    Performance subtests, 213–214, 222, 228
    Verbal subtests, 213–219, 222, 228–229
    Vocabulary subtest, 215, 216, 217, 219
Wechsler-Bellevue Test, 26–27, 28, 214, 395
Wechsler Memory Scale, 358
Weight judgment, 162–163
Widowerhood, 50–51
Widowhood, 50–51
Withdrawal. See Disengagement
Work, 4–5, 36–37, 51–52, 63, 77–80. See also Life Satisfaction; Retirement